Body and Organization

Body and Organization

edited by
John Hassard, Ruth Holliday and Hugh Willmott

SAGE Publications
London • Thousand Oaks • New Delhi

First published 2000

SAGE Publications Ltd
6 Bonhill Street
London EC2A 4PU

SAGE Publications Inc.
2455 Teller Road
Thousand Oaks, California 91320

SAGE Publications India Pvt Ltd
32, M-Block Market
Greater Kailash – I
New Delhi 110 048

British Library Cataloguing in Publication data

A catalogue record for this book is available
from the British Library

ISBN 0 7619 5917 3
ISBN 0 7619 5918 1 (pbk)

Library of Congress catalog card number 99–85719

Typeset by Mayhew Typesetting, Rhayader, Powys
Printed and bound in Great Britain by Athenaeum Press, Gateshead

Contents

PART FOUR: SELF AND IDENTITY

Notes on Contributors

Joanna Brewis is Lecturer in Management at the University of Essex, UK. Her current research centres on the experience of having a female body in and outside of work, prostitution, and sexuality and organization more broadly. She has published recently in the journals *Human Relations* and *Time and Society* and is currently working on a book with Stephen Linstead.

Gibson Burrell is Professor of Organizational Behaviour at the University of Warwick, UK. Previously he taught at the University of Lancaster. He is currently attempting to write a book on the 'Histories of the Concept of Organization' but the consanguineous notion of Chaos is proving more interesting.

Catherine Casey is a Senior Lecturer in the School of Business and Economics at the University of Auckland, New Zealand. She holds a PhD from the University of Rochester, New York, and is the author of *Work, Self and Society: After Industrialism* (Routledge, 1995). Her current research interests are in critical organization studies and social and cultural theory.

Karen Dale is a Lecturer in the Industrial Relations and Organizational Behaviour Group at the University of Warwick, UK. She previously worked in the National Health Service and local government. She has published on gender, race and equal opportunities and is currently writing a book on the body and organization theory.

Philip Hancock is a Lecturer in Sociology at Glasgow Caledonian University, UK. His research and publication interests are in critical organization and management studies, aesthetics and something he's called the 'management of everyday life'. He has recently published in *Organization* and *Journal of Management Studies*.

John Hassard is Professor of Organizational Analysis at the University of Manchester Institute of Science and Technology, UK. His current research concerns actor network theories of organization and enterprise reform experiments in China. Recent publications include *Organization/Representation* (Sage, 1999, with Ruth Holliday) and *Actor Network Theory: And After* (Blackwell, 1999, with John Law).

Johanna Hofbauer teaches and researches at the Institute of Sociology at the University of Economics, Vienna. She has published on the history of work discipline and on conceptual issues in organization studies and industrial sociology, especially regarding the formation of subjectivity in modern organization. Her current research interests also include gender studies and workplace relations.

Ruth Holliday is Senior Lecturer in Cultural Studies at Staffordshire University, UK. Her research interests lie in the areas of sexuality and popular culture. She is currently completing a video-based project for the Economic and Social Research Council. Recent publications include *Organization/Representation* (Sage, 1999, with John Hassard) and *Contested Bodies* (Routledge, 2000, with John Hassard).

Deborah Kerfoot is Lecturer in Organizational Behaviour at the University of Leeds, UK. Her research interests are in the sociology and critical study of management, empirical research on employment, poststructuralism, and gender and sexuality in organizations. She is Book Review Editor for the *Journal of Management Studies* and an Associate Editor of *Gender, Work and Organization*.

Ian Lennie is the Quality Improvement Manager for FPA Health, a large non-government agency in Sydney, Australia. He has a PhD in Sociology and an MA in English Literature, and has taught previously at the universities of New South Wales and Wollongong. He has a background in management and health research.

Hugo Letiche is the *Emergence* Professor of 'Meaning in Organizations'. He is the Director of the Advice, Organization & Policy programme at the University for Humanist Studies, Utretcht, NL and teaches at the Rotterdam School of Management as well as Keele University, UK. His current research focuses on theorizing coherence and emergence (book with Michael Lissack, MIT Press) and the theoretical roots of complexity (special number of *Emergence* on Artaud with Heather Hopfl and Stephen Brown).

Stephen Linstead is Associate Director (Research) and Research Professor of Management at the University of Sunderland, UK. His current research interests include sexuality and sexual identity related to organization theory and change, with special reference to postmodern thought. He is currently working with Joanna Brewis on a book to be titled *Sex, Work and Sex Work* (Routledge).

Martin Parker is a Senior Lecturer in Social and Organizational Theory at the University of Keele. His most recent books are *Ethics and Organization* (Sage, 1988), *The New Higher Education* (with David Jary, Staffordshire University Press, 1988) and *Organizational Culture and Identity* (Sage, 1999). His body does other things too.

Craig Prichard is a network of historically embodied practices, knowledges and artefacts. 'Craig Prichard' appears on a list of babies born in Waverley, New Zealand, in 1962 and reappears on a list of PhD graduates of the University of Nottingham, UK, in 1998. A passport shows he 'came ashore' in the UK in 1990 and his Inland Revenue records show he left in 1998 for Massey University, New Zealand.

Janice Richardson is a Senior Lecturer in Law at the University of Staffordshire, UK. She was previously a trade union solicitor. Her research interests lie in the areas of feminist metaphysics and feminist legal theory. She has recently published in the journals *Law and Critique* and *Feminist Legal Studies* and is currently editing a book on feminist perspectives on law and theory with Ralph Sandland of Nottingham University.

John Sinclair is Senior Lecturer in the Human Resource Management Group at Napier University, Edinburgh, UK. He lectures and researches in the areas of organizational change and ethics. He is a board member of the Standing Conference on Organizational Symbolism (SCOS) and a past Editor of the SCOS Newsletter.

Melissa Tyler is a Lecturer in Sociology at Glasgow Caledonian University, UK. She has published on issues of gender, aesthetics, organization and the body. Her current research interests lie in queer theory, embodiment and the management of sexuality.

Hugh Willmott is Professor of Organizational Analysis at the University of Manchester Institute of Science and Technology. He is currently working on a number of projects whose common theme is the changing organization and management of work. Hugh has served on the editorial boards of a number of journals, including *Administrative Science Quarterly, Organization, Organization Studies* and *Accounting Organizations and Society*.

INTRODUCTION

The Body and Organization

'Are you sitting comfortably? Then I will begin.' This phrase, used to settle young children before reading a story to them, was used daily to introduce the BBC radio programme 'Listen with Mother', the intention being that children would sit with their mothers after lunch each weekday to hear a radio story. The rhetorical question has subsequently become a cliché used to humorous, ironic effect when attempting to get the attention of others, such as a student audience at the beginning of a lecture. None the less, it provides a relevant point of departure for this book.

First, the question makes a key connection between activities and the body. It assumes, or understands, that the activity of listening to a story, of concentrating upon it, will be accomplished more easily and more pleasurably if the child adopts a comfortable, sitting posture. Listening is implicitly recognized to be an embodied activity; and it is understood that some forms of embodiment, such as sitting, are more congruent with being attentive to a story, and deriving pleasure from it. Yet the question 'Are you sitting comfortably?' is not entirely benign. It also implicitly seeks to engender a self-disciplined willingness to become comfortable as a condition of the story being read (or the radio being left on), and thereafter not to fidget or show signs of allowing the mind to wander. Unless the child requests that the radio is switched off, there is a tacit expectation that attention will be sustained, and that some form of punishment will ensue if the psychological contract between parent/guardian and child is perceived to be broken. Mothers, no less than their listening children, are disciplined by the (disembodied) voice. It is expected that they will ensure that children sit still and listen. The question is also gendered – not only because the question is associated with the female voice of the Mother substitute or virtual Mother of BBC radio but also because it exemplifies a nurturing, matriarchal relationship with the child. The child is not told to 'Sit still and listen up, kid!' but instead is invited to make him/herself comfortable.

A number of dimensions to the relationship between the body and organization are illustrated by this example. Bodies are recognized to be sensual and gendered. Bodies experience feelings that may be more or less pleasurable. Bodies are identified as male or female. In this example, the person with the child is expected to be female. This person is positioned by the ascription of historical and cultural attributes of femininity: she is expected to care for the child by ensuring that the child is sitting comfortably. In all this, there is a politics of the body. The qualities attributed to the bodies – including what is characterized as sensual, sexual and gendered – are not given, but are socially organized (Mumby and Putnam, 1992).

It is perhaps tempting to regard the body as something that is 'natural', a brute material fact that is beyond 'the social' and exempt from postmodern epistemological doubts. But, on reflection, it is evident that 'the body' is a construct, differentiated from its other by a series of conventions that occasion a forgetfulness of how the zone of the body is arbitrarily demarcated and therefore vulnerable to deconstruction and reconstruction. More fundamentally, it may be questioned whether bodies exist independently of the interactions with the world that are productive of a conventional sense of the body existing as an independent entity that comprises diverse organs. As Parker (this volume) puts it, instead of thinking of cyborgs as bionic people comprising natural and synthetic elements, it makes more sense to say that 'we are already cyborgs . . . The hand only becomes a hand when it holds a tool. The eye becomes an eye when it sees an icon.'

This book is motivated by two, related concerns. First, it seeks to redress a tendency for analyses of organization to be disembodied in ways that marginalize the body as a medium of organizing practices. It explores a number of avenues for re-membering or making connections between the body and organization, notably gender (Acker, 1990; Roper, 1992) and sexuality (Burrell, 1984; Hearn and Parkin, 1987). Others might also be included, such as age and disability. Second, it is intended to counteract a marginalization of the realm of employment and work organization within contemporary analyses of the body (Scott and Morgan, 1993; Shilling, 1993; Turner, 1996). The study of the body has tended to become estranged from the study of work just as analysis of work organization has been abstracted from the body.

Most of the papers selected for this volume were originally presented at a conference organized by the editors at Keele University. A companion volume, edited by Ruth Holliday and John Hassard, titled *Contested Bodies*, is in preparation. This volume concerns issues of embodiment largely from the perspective of cultural studies and explores the significance of realms of corporeal regulation and resistance. *Body and Organization* signals an understanding that organizing is an embodied practice whilst simultaneously recalling that conceptions of the body, including the importance ascribed to its presence in practices of organization and the effects that this ascription produces, are a product of organizing practices. The book is intended to contribute to an emergent interest in the embodied quality of organizing and to encourage the development of a greater appreciation of the mutual constitution of bodies and organizing practices.

In this introductory chapter, we begin by exploring the relationship between organizing practices and embodiment. We problematize the common sense separation between mind and body and we note how the theory and practice of organization has tended to privilege rationality, which it is now seeking to counteract by paying attention to sentiment and bodily pleasures. We then focus upon gender and sexuality as two central aspects of the social organization of bodies within work organizations. Throughout we indicate where the issues that we raise are taken up by contributors to this volume.

Organizing practices and embodiment

In the study of the social world, attention to the body has been characterized as 'an absent presence' (Shilling, 1993: 19). In other words, the existence of human bodies tends to be taken for granted in analyses of social life. Studies of 'society' or 'institutions' assume but rarely examine how social practices are embodied and, in this sense, rely upon human embodiment for their enactment. The analysis of social practices has been abstracted from the embodied media through which these practices are accomplished, even when agency is understood to play a creative part in their negotiation or enactment. Given the everyday connections that are made between bodily posture and sensation and mental and spiritual attitudes, this disjuncture is quite remarkable. As the wife of one of the authors claims when commenting on an analysis of her drawings: 'I make the best drawings when I'm relaxed and sloppily dressed. If I have to try to be "pretty", it's disastrous. If I feel in harmony with life, then I have the nerve to set lines powerfully on paper' (in Letiche, this volume).

The desire to consider the body in relation to practices of organization forms part of a wider, postmodernist and feminist movement in social and cultural analysis where issues of agency, reflexivity and identity formation are becoming increasingly central. Attention to issues of gender and sexuality have been at the heart of this analysis. With a few partial exceptions (e.g. Collinson and Hearn, 1996; Hochschild, 1983; Pringle, 1989), however, the significance of the body in the context of work organizations is rarely, or very selectively addressed (e.g. Davis, 1997; Ryan and Gordon, 1994; Scott and Morgan, 1993). An attentiveness to agency and identity, notably by feminists (e.g. Butler, 1990) but also by mainstream theorists (e.g. Giddens, 1991) and a few management researchers (e.g. Boje and Hettrick, 1992; Knights and Willmott, 1985), has unsettled the common sense dualism between actors and structures, leading to a growing interest in forms of (poststructuralist) theory. Poststructuralist theory challenges the established (humanist) view of people as unified, rational agents and has challenged its associated conceptions of authenticity, choice and responsibility (Lorraine, 1990). Feminism and queer theory (Fuss, 1991), in particular, have problematized taken-for-granted dualisms between observer and observed, theory and practice, body and mind, heterosexuality and homosexuality, people and machines and, more generally, between subjects and objects.

Undoing dualisms

This volume opens up an exploration of how the body is organized as an (identifiable) topic for examination and invites further consideration of how bodies are engaged in, and engaged by, the shifting complexes of organizing practices that are routinely described as organizations (see Dale and Burrell, this volume). Parker (this volume) commends the conceptualization of human beings as cyborgs as a way of recalling that 'bodies are only ever given realization through their connection with non-human materials'. *Body and Organization* seeks to advance and explore the understanding that organizing practices are embodied; and that bodies are organized through practices that ascribe meanings and expectations to the body on the basis, for example, of its perceived age and gender (see Hancock and Tyler, this volume).

The status of the body as 'an absent presence' is nowhere more 'apparent' than in the study of organizations, and especially work organizations (Barry and Hazen, 1996). Ergonomics or human factors comprises the field of knowledge that has paid most direct attention to the embodied nature of work. Here people are treated as extensions of tools and machines, the objective being to develop their most productive integration (see Hofbauer, this volume). Ergonomics is prototypically modernist (and masculinist) as it strives to achieve total control over the design of productive processes. Modernism, as Letiche (this volume) comments, 'has analysed and assembled, conquered and rearranged, in order to prioritize success and innovation'. In ergonomics, the human body is analysed as a complex, machine-like object comprising a multitude of capabilities and limitations that must be fully exploited and accommodated when designing the tools, machines and environment in which the human body works (Sanders and McCormick, 1992). Alternatively, where work is characterized as 'mental', the study of organizational behaviour tends to represent human beings as cognitive processors comprising perceptions and motivations who, if they are executives, design structures and manage meanings.

Such understandings pay scant attention to how thoughts and feelings, body and mind, sentiment and calculation are bound together even as they are dissociated from each other. Consider the account of the manager interviewed by Lennie (this volume), who recalls how she came to the decision to dismiss a member of staff. Instead of simply justifying or rationalizing the decision in terms of organizationally competent reasons, she explains how her awareness of a problem developed through an intuitive feeling of 'tension in the air' and the (visual) sense of elements in 'the environment beginning to react negatively to the other parts of the environment' (see also Prichard, this volume). This illustrates the embodied sense of the practices of organizing and organization, a point made force-fully by Albrow (1994: 108) when he observes that conceptions of work and organizations

> which seek to minimize the emotional aspects of performance are inadequate and misleading . . . Rigid, inflexible, cold behaviour is just as emotional as warm and loving responses. But for some actors it is easier to call upon the rejection of emotions in the name of rationality than to acknowledge that the requirement is the training of anger, disdain and contempt.

There is an emotional tone associated with behaviour that is 'rigid' and unyielding no less than there is with behaviour that is more flexible or accommodating, caring or compassionate. The socially organized training of emotions promotes the expression of some feelings as it represses the expression of others (Fineman, 1993). Cold behaviour is no less emotional but it requires the development of feelings of contempt or disdain for the other in addition to the control of anger which might otherwise erupt to thaw the ice. Yet, perhaps because masculinity is associated with ration-ality that is counterposed to emotionality, emotionality tends to be attributed exclusively to 'warm and loving' expressions of feeling that are more routinely connected with images of femininity (see Linstead, this volume).

Disembodied organizational analysis

Even if the dream of an ergonomically perfect matching of human bodies and machines ever materialized, these bodies are conditioned by, and connected to, each other, through social relations of production. These relations can influence employees' willingness to exercise the capabilities and minimize the limitations identified by ergonomists. This suggests that work is rarely, if ever, brutishly manual. At the very least, physically arduous and repetitive work requires the wilful determination to do it. Equally, mental work is not disembodied. It may not be bodily taxing, although sufferers from obesity, piles and repetitive strain disorder associ-ated with sedentary occupations might beg to differ. But it is not devoid of emotion. There may be an inclination to exclude from modern work organizations feelings which are deemed to be unproductive – such as love, hatred and other emotions (Weber, 1978: 975) when they are considered to cloud judgement, generate resentments (for example, over favouritism) and disrupt rationally established procedures. But, equally, there has been a recurrent concern amongst designers of work and organization to improve motivation and morale by endeavouring to make it more meaningful and pleasurable. Even Taylor, the champion of scientific management, sought, however naively and technocratically, to develop industrial relations in which the dark, painful emotions associated with 'antagonism and strife'

would be progressively supplanted by a warm culture of 'friendly cooperation and mutual helpfulness' (Taylor, 1947: 60).

That said, neither Frederick Taylor nor Max Weber, as founders of
modern analysis of work organization, directly considered the embodied
quality of organizational work. Taylor concentrated upon the design of the
tasks to be undertaken by workers. This design included careful measurement of the bodily movements performed by the most efficient operatives so
that, in contemporary management-speak, the 'technology' of systematic
management could be 'transferred' by training others to follow this 'best
practice'. In common with contemporary human factors design, however,
Taylor's 'scientific management' included minimal consideration of the
social relations of production, including the feelings of managers as well as
those of workers. In contrast to Taylor, who uncritically embraced the
promise of technical reason to construct a utopia of 'cooperation and
mutual helpfulness', Weber anticipated a dystopia where 'the performance
of each worker is mathematically measured, each man becomes a little cog
in the machine' (Weber cited in Meyer, 1956: 127). Weber set his discussion
of work organization in the context of a rationalizing drive to replace
traditional methods of organizing productive activity. In traditional
methods, feelings about, and attachments to, established practices were
valued, honoured and respected. With modern methods, in contrast, practices are in principle assessed according to rational, impersonal measures of
performance. Instead of being vested in 'blood' or personal connections,
authority in modern work organizations is ostensibly founded upon an
impersonal system of credentialism and technical competence where, in
principle, 'everyone is subject to formal equality of treatment' (Weber,
1978: 225).

In order to draw the body into organizational analysis, it is necessary to
recognize modernist pressures to comply with the ideals of rationality,
including the recruitment, training and promotion of employees using
standardized, impersonal techniques but without denying their design by
and implementation to embodied organizational employees. The ritualized
effort to emulate a spirit of formalistic impersonality should not be con-
fused with the exclusion of bodily passions and emotions from the workplace. On the contrary, this spirit is kept alive only so long as there is
passionate dedication to it and determination to defend it.

Managing hearts as well as minds

Far from denying or excluding emotions, their rational management is
most consistent with (Weber's conception of) the modernist project of
rationalization. This understanding resonates with the contemporary focus
upon 'changing the culture' by management consultants, business leaders
and politicians who equate processes of modernization with managing
values and other elements of culture, including emotional factors, that

are considered to facilitate or obstruct the process of rationalization. Consider the following passages from Weber and from Peters and Waterman, respectively:

> . . . everything is rationally calculated, especially those seemingly imponderable and irrational, emotional factors. (Weber, 1978: 1150)

> All that stuff you have been dismissing for so long as the intractable, irrational, intuitive, informal organization *can* be managed . . . the real role of the chief executive is to manage the values of the organization. (Peters and Waterman, 1982: 11, 26)

The continuing interest in culture in the field of organization and management is not so much a tardy acknowledgement of the 'irrational', embodied qualities of organizations as it is an extension of the modernist project. The earlier, rationalist vision of modernism tended to regard employee values as its Other, which were beyond its reach for ethical as well as technical reasons. At best, managers were advised to tread carefully, and especially to avoid taking actions that, by violating 'functional' employee values and understandings (for example, the ascription of expertise to managers), might undermine an unthinking acceptance of managerial authority (Barnard, 1936). In contrast, the new postmodern rationalism dedifferentiates 'economy' and 'culture' (Willmott, 1992) and has few qualms about striving to colonize the area of 'affective and sensual sensibilities' (Casey, this volume) that had previously eluded managerial control (Peters and Austin, 1986). This move is proclaimed to be liberating as it encourages employees to be excited by their work and to have fun (Peters and Waterman, 1982: 291), so long as this is consistent with the framework of values established by management over which employees have no direct influence.

Being able to manage the domain of culture, including its desexualized bodily pleasures of excitement and fun, is understood to provide the key to raising performance by removing the remaining (emotional) obstacles to managerial rule (Van Maanen and Kunda, 1989). Taylor had sought to discipline the physical bodies of workers by measuring and training their motions. Human Relations had sought to improve workers' self-image by providing psychological compensations for the performance of uncreative, repetitive tasks. Corporate Culturism seeks to control the hearts as well as the minds of employees by establishing control, through 'hoopla, celebration and verve' (Peters and Waterman, 1982: 263) over what had previously been regarded as an intractable other (see Casey, this volume). Further, it may seek to manage whatever aesthetics of the body (for example, poise, quality of eye contact) are deemed to communicate the hearts of employees, and thereby enhance the exchange value of the product or service (see Brewis and Sinclair, this volume) as, for example, in recruiting and training caring as well as competent personnel (see Hancock and Tyler, this volume).

Casey (this volume) reports the use of 'aura' readings when interviewing job applicants, decision-making based upon interpretations of tarot cards, and 'the widely welcome employment of the language of "the gut", intuition, of the spirit, and of "meditation"', all of which are invoked 'in the service of enduring rational and high-tech production and organizational profitability'.

Instead of tightly specifying and supervising the actions of employees (Taylorism) or providing a managerial substitute for the emotional support of fellow workers (Human Relations), the advocates of 'strong cultures' claim to return their autonomy to employees by engineering the replacement of distinctive and potentially transgressive employee values and sources of pleasure (for example, enjoyment derived from subverting managerial control or engaging in horseplay) with a corporate 'set of shared values', including those concerned with the aesthetics of bodily appearance (Gagliardi, 1990, 1996). Establishing this set of values, it is asserted, can 'provide the framework in which practical autonomy takes place routinely' (Peters and Waterman, 1982: 322). In other words, the management of values is intended to foster a sense of autonomy whose terms are freely accepted by employees entering into contracts of employment, yet whose contents are defined and policed, in technocratic and totalitarian style, by their employers. As Dale and Burrell (this volume) observe, postmodern conceptualizations of organizing practices, which tend to stress their fluidity rather than their structure, 'do not entirely constitute a rupture in the modernist rationalist modes of organization, self and body, even if they go some way to problematizing the concepts of structures, boundaries and wholes . . .'. While programmes of training and performance monitoring may be designed to fuse employee autonomy with corporate heteronomy, or to 'feminize' management by becoming less hierarchical and more fluid, there is invariably the possibility of slippage and resistance whenever employees experience corporate demands to transgress their embodied sense of self-identity or established investments of bodily desire (see Prichard, this volume). As Casey (this volume) contemplates, 'a new recognition and listening to the body' may promote resistance to instrumental and com-modified forms of being as a non-dualistic experience of embodied being is dis-covered and restored (see Willmott, 1994).

Gender and sexuality in organization studies

It is possible to accept that Weber was broadly correct in identifying key features of the 'pure' type of modern organization, as exemplified by the techniques of Taylor's scientific management, without believing that the drive to remove inefficiencies, including those arising from forms of corruption and nepotism, necessarily eliminates or even displaces the affective dimensions of organizational work. Equally, it is possible to accept that this affective dimension can become an explicit target of managerial control without assuming that employees will identify closely with these values rather than complying selectively with them. In arguing that strong cultures 'give their employees a mission as well as a sense of feeling great' (Peters and Waterman, 1982: 323), their advocates underestimate the embodied attachment of employees to a sense of self-identity derived from other diverse affiliations, including gender, ethnicity and sexual orientation as well as family, class, community and religion. Employees are unlikely to abandon or even wholly suspend affiliations from which they already derive a sense of 'mission' or valued feelings (see Prichard, this volume). Instead, they are likely to exemplify modernist rationalism as their cooperation is calculated rather than unconditionally given, with an accompanying mix of emotions including resentment, relief and guilt. On occasion, however, this controlled response may boil over in expressions of rage or what one of Prichard's interviewees terms 'a "seething mass" of tensions and conflicts' (Prichard, this volume). But even when boiling point is not reached, 'Can anyone doubt that organizations are emotional cauldrons?' (Albrow, 1992: 323).

The gendering of work

It may be asked whether the harnessing and selective expression of emotions within work organizations reflects a distinctively gendered process that privileges a patriarchal and 'masculinist' mode of organizing (see Kerfoot, this volume) and presentation of self (see Brewis and Sinclair, this volume). Some feminists have argued that modern work organizations, exemplified in bureaucratic practices and discourse, are expressive of what, culturally rather than biologically, is considered to exemplify the modern conception of masculinity (Ferguson, 1984). In other words, dominant notions of rationality, and the modernist project of rationalization more generally, are understood to articulate a particular, socially constructed conception of masculinity which men display to demonstrate their (patriarchal) credentials; or which, in the context of masculinist institutions, such as work organizations, women may seek to emulate in order to demonstrate their competence (McDowell and Court, 1994). In striving to compete with men, women may anticipate or discover that their bodies are obstacles to full participation where few allowances are made for dealing with such body processes as 'menstruation, lactation and the pre-menstrual tension that many women experience' (Halford et al., 1997: 27).

Even when established forms of patriarchal organization are challenged by those who associate new, less hierarchical and team-based forms of organizing with the skills ascribed to women, there is the suspicion that this change of heart is motivated by the self-interest of corporations and consultants that identify women as more amenable to the casualized and fragmented ways of working that are described by elites as more progressive, flexible and responsive to changing market conditions (see Calas and Smircich, 1993). That said, there may also be scope for transgressing the apparent impersonality of work organizations – for example, by flirting or otherwise playing upon physical attractiveness to highlight femininity – in ways that reduce levels of stress as well as gaining attention in 'a man's world' (see Brewis and Sinclair, this volume) (or vice-versa). Rather than viewing these activities simply as pandering to vanity or reinforcing and legitimizing predatory inclinations, it is possible to understand them as an active and pleasurable, postfeminist alternative to approaches that uncritically assume that women are best served by being treated as potential victims who must be protected from the inevitability of female vulnerability to male domination in their relations (see Richardson, this volume). Instead of collaborating in the fantasy of excluding sexuality from the workplace through the use of bureaucratic codes and punishments, there is the possibility of eroticizing the workplace by actively celebrating sexuality in ways that are not colonized by masculinist desires to conquer and control. Such male fantasies are oppressive, postfeminists have argued, insofar as they represent women as victims and continue to be 'silent on female sexuality and on women's capacity to be the subject of pleasure' (Gherardi, 1990). To this it may be added that feminist analysis and scholarship has tended to deny, or at least displace, consideration of issues, including the incidence of industrial accidents, diseases and stress, where the bodies and lives of men are generally at greater risk (Alvesson and Due Billing, 1997).

The intertwining of gender and sexuality

It is by creating and developing modern (bureaucratic) organizations that men, in the main, have been able to confirm and secure a common sense image of themselves as the rational, dominant and authoritative dispensers of disembodied reason who are detached, task-oriented, combative and controlled. And, indeed, this image has been equated with management itself, so it continues to be widely represented as a branch of engineering comprising a tool box of 'hard' and 'soft' techniques (see Lennie, this volume). It is difficult to deny the connection between notions of rationality ascribed to modern ways of organizing and the values most closely associated with masculinity. This is hardly surprising, as it is principally men who have commended and developed modern ways of organizing. In turn, men have placed a positive value upon 'masculinist' kinds of activities which place those who are unfamiliar with, or antithetical to, such gendered activities at a disadvantage. For example, Brewis and Sinclair (this volume) report the example of a vacancy for a senior maintenance job for which their female respondents had not applied because, as they put it, they lacked a vital qualification for performing the job:

> we haven't got a todger . . . it was a technical, plant maintenance job, you know, very much todger oriented. So we wrote 'Todger' on the advert, you see, 'Todger required' . . .

In this example, there is an artful reversal of the more routine use of sexual language by men that exposes and ridicules subordination in the workplace (see also Gherardi, 1990). It is not difficult to think of other jobs, often located at the lower end of the gendered status hierarchy, which might invite the graffiti 'Fanny needed' or 'Cunt required'. Instead, however, there are frequently unadvertised requirements, such as visual (sexual) attractiveness. As Adkins and Lury (1996: 214) note, 'the gendered structuring of the relations of production actively produces "sexuality" in the labour market'.

There is clearly much work to be done in appreciating the presence of sexuality in organizations, especially as it shapes and influences relationships between people of the same sexual orientation as well as different, dual or changing orientations. In these interactions, each person is simultaneously enmeshed in images of gender so that sexuality can be understood as a key element in the accomplishment of gendered identity. The 'absent presence' of sexuality is probably the most glaring of the silences about the body in organization studies (Burrell, 1984; Hearn and Parkin, 1987). Pointed reference to the male organ, the 'todger', serves to highlight the common sense gendering of certain jobs that reduces applications from women and diminishes the likelihood of a successful outcome by those with the temerity to apply.

In another instructive example, Halford et al. (1997: 232) report the observations of an 'out' lesbian who noted how her male colleagues, especially those more senior to her, found themselves at a loss about how to relate to a woman who had openly declared her lack of sexual interest in men. This highlights the way in which interactions, whether at work or elsewhere, are implicitly structured by sexual preferences routinely ascribed to gender identities. It is further illustrated by this respondent's account of how a heterosexual female colleague had addressed the incongruity by flirting with her 'as if I were a man, and I found that bizarre'. The central point is that interactions with others are tacitly and routinely sexual in the sense that a sensibility about another person's known or presumed sexual orientation conditions how we relate to them – a point that is brought home in encounters with people whose sexuality is ambiguous or is found to be the reverse of what has been assumed (see Ekins and King, 1998).

There are at least three possible ways of addressing this issue. First, a discourse can be constructed in which it is assumed that people are assigned to a predefined and fixed category of sexuality (for example, male or female) and gender (for example, masculine or feminine) with associated behavioural patterns (predatory and dominant or victimized and submissive). This discourse resonates with the institutions of patriarchy. Within this discourse, the 'todger' graffiti (see Brewis and Sinclair, this volume) could conceivably be interpreted as a submissive confirmation of plant maintenance as a masculine preserve. Second, it is possible to construct a discourse in which all differences are erased or at least suspended for the practical purposes of allocating people to jobs within work organizations.

Here there is a pretence that practices of sexuality and gender can be excluded or suppressed. This is associated with a modernist emphasis upon legal rationality, equal opportunity and contemporary conceptions of political correctness. The 'todger' graffiti directly challenges and disrupts this discourse by drawing attention to its limits and hypocrisy. Equal opportunities are simply not possible without a radical restructuring of institutions through which jobs are gendered and women are positioned as 'carers', not maintenance workers. Third, there is the possibility of a discourse that allows for a plurality of dynamic sexual orientations and images of gender where 'the guarantee of freedom is freedom' (Foucault, 1984: 8, cited by Richardson, this volume). In what might be described as a postmodern turn, fluidity, diversity and playfulness are encouraged and celebrated within a discourse of queerness. In this context, the 'todger' graffiti expresses a playful reversal and assault upon the male organ, the totemic nature of which is laid bare as an object of desire and derision.

It is our intention that this volume will advance discussion of the embodied quality of organizing in a way that counteracts the mainstream tendency to represent employees, managers and workers as bloodless designers or executors of organizational functions. In this respect, it forms part of the 'embodied turn' in social science where an appreciation of the body, as a topic, is a distinguishing feature of contemporary analysis. At the same time, contributions to this volume help rectify the remarkable neglect of the domain of work and organizations within studies that have been attentive to the body. It is our hope that the chapters will be of much interest to those – students as well as teachers and researchers – who have a general sociological or psychological interest in the embodied quality of human activity, as it is to those with a more specialized interest in the study of work and organization. To the extent that this hope is fulfilled, we look forward to the development of a closer and mutually beneficial dialogue between them.

References

Acker, Joan (1990) 'Hierarchies, jobs, bodies: a theory of gendered organizations', *Gender and Society*, 5: 390–407.

Adkins, Lisa and Lury, Celia (1996) 'The cultural, the sexual and the gendering of the labour market', in Lisa Adkins and Vicki Merchant (eds), *Sexuality and the Social: Power and Organization*. London: Macmillan.

Albrow, Martin (1992) 'Sine ira et studio – or do organizations have feelings?', *Organization Studies*, 13 (3): 313–29.

Albrow, Martin (1994) 'Accounting for organizational feeling', in Larry J. Ray and Michael Reed (eds), *Organizing Modernity: New Weberian Perspectives on Work, Organization and Society*. London: Routledge.

Alvesson, Mats and Due Billing, Yvonne (1997) *Understanding Gender and Organizations*. London: Sage.

Barnard, Chester (1936) *The Functions of the Executive*. Cambridge, MA: Harvard University Press.

Barry, David and Hazen, Mary Ann (1996) 'Do you take your body to work?', in D. Boje, R. Gephart and T. Joseph (eds), *Postmodern Management and Organization Theory*. London: Sage.

Boje, David and Hettrick, William (1992) 'Organization and the body: post-Fordist dimensions', *Journal of Organizational Change Management*, 5 (1): 48–57.

Burrell, Gibson (1984) 'Sex and organizational analysis', *Organization Studies*, 5 (2): 97–118.

Butler, Judith (1990) *Gender Trouble: Feminism and the Subversion of Identity*. London: Routledge.

Calas, Martha and Smircich, Linda (1993) 'Dangerous liaisons: the "feminine in management" meets "globalization"', *Business Horizons*, March–April: 71–81.

Collinson, David and Collinson, Margaret (1997) '"Delayering managers": time–space surveillance and its gendered effects', *Organization*, 4 (3): 375–407.

Collinson, David and Hearn, Jeff (eds) (1996) *Men as Managers, Managers as Men*. London: Sage.

Davis, Kathy (ed.) (1997) *Embodied Practices: Feminist Perspectives on the Body*. London: Sage.

Ekins, Richard and King, David (1998) 'Towards a sociology of transgendered bodies'. Paper presented at the British Sociological Association Annual Conference, Edinburgh.

Ferguson, Kathy (1984) *The Feminist Case Against Bureaucracy*. Philadelphia: Temple University Press.

Fineman, Steven (1993) *Emotion in Organizations*. London: Sage.

Foucault, Michel (1984) 'Space, knowledge and power', in P. Rabinow (ed.), *The Foucault Reader*. New York: Pantheon.

Fuss, Diana (1991) *Inside/Out*. New York: Routledge.

Gagliardi, Pasquale (ed.) (1990) *Symbols and Artefacts: Views of the Corporate Landscape*. Berlin: de Gruyter.

Gagliardi, Pasquale (1996) 'Exploring the aesthetic side of organizational life', in S.R. Clegg, C. Hardy and W. Nord (eds), *Handbook of Organization Studies*. London: Sage. pp. 565–80.

Gherardi, Sylvia (1990) *Gender, Symbolism and Organizational Culture*. London: Sage.

Giddens, Anthony (1991) *Modernity and Self-Identity*. Cambridge: Polity Press.

Halford, Susan, Savage, Mike and Witz, Anne (1997) *Gender, Careers and Organizations*. London: Macmillan.

Hearn, Jeff and Parkin, Wendy (1987) *'Sex' at 'Work'*. Brighton: Wheatsheaf.

Hochschild, Arlie (1983) *The Managed Heart: Commercialization of Human Feeling*. Berkeley, CA: University of California Press.

Knights, David and Willmott, Hugh (1985) 'Power and identity in theory and practice', *Sociological Review*, 33 (1): 22–46.

Lorraine, Tasmine E. (1990) *Gender, Identity and the Production of Meaning*. Boulder, CO: Westview Press.

McDowell, Linda and Court, Gillian (1994) 'Missing subjects: gender, power and sexuality in merchant banking', *Economic Geography*, 70 (3): 229–51.

Merton, Robert K. (1952) 'Bureaucratic structure and personality', in R.K. Merton et al. (eds), *Reader in Bureaucracy*. Glencoe, IL: Free Press. pp. 361–71.

Meyer, J.P. (1956) *Max Weber and German Politics*. London: Faber & Faber.

Mumby, Dennis and Putnam, Linda (1992) 'The politics of emotion: a feminist reading of bounded rationality', *Academy of Management Review*, 17 (3): 465–86.

Peters, Tom and Austin, Nancy (1986) *A Passion for Excellence*. London: Collins.

Peters, Tom and Waterman, Robert (1982) *In Search of Excellence: Lessons From America's Best-Run Companies*. New York: Harper & Row.

Pringle, Rosemary (1989) *Secretaries Talk: Sexuality, Power and Work*. London: Verso.

Roper, Michael (1992) *Masculinity and the British Organization Man since 1945*. Oxford: Oxford University Press.

Ryan, Michael and Gordon, Avery (eds) (1994) *Body Politics: Disease, Desire and the Family*. Boulder, CO: Westview Press.

Sanders, Mark S. and McCormick, Ernest J. (1992) *Human Factors in Engineering Design*, 7th edn. New York: McGraw Hill.

Scott, Sue and Morgan, David (eds) (1993) *Body Matters: Essays on the Sociology of the Body*. London: Falmer Press.

Shilling, Chris (1993) *The Body and Social Theory*. London: Sage.

Taylor, Frederick W. (1947) 'Shop management' (first published in F. Taylor [1911]), in *Scientific Management*, New York: Harper and Brothers.

Turner, Bryan (1996) *The Body and Society*. London: Sage.

Van Maanen, John and Kunda, Gideon (1989) '"Real feelings": emotional expression and organizational culture', in L.L. Cummings and B.M. Staw (eds), *Research in Organizational Behaviour*, 11. Greenwich, CT: JAI Press. pp. 43–104.

Weber, Max (1978) *Economy and Society*, 2 vols (trans. G. Roth and C. Wittich). Berkeley, CA: University of California Press.

Willmott, Hugh (1992) 'Postmodernism and excellence: the de-differentiation of economy and culture', *Journal of Organizational Change Management*, 5 (1): 58–68.

Willmott, Hugh (1994) 'Theorising agency: power and subjectivity in organization studies', in J. Hassard and M. Parker (eds), *Towards a New Theory of Organizations*. London: Routledge.

PART ONE

FUNCTIONS AND FLOWS

---

1   What Shape Are We In? Organization Theory and the Organized Body

Karen Dale and Gibson Burrell

> For us, it is the structure of our bodies and of their organs that is the essential, a structure whose stability is for us the image of the stability of our psychic identity. The fluids in our bodies but circulate refurbishment throughout the structure; their seepings into it and evaporations or discharges from it are neither regulated by our public codes nor valued in our politico-economic discourse. For the Sambia of Papua-New Guinea, it is the fluids that are the essential. The body is perceived essentially as a conduit for fluids – for blood, milk, semen. Body fluids are drawn from without, from couplings with other bodies, from couplings with other organism-conduits in outside nature. Among the Sambia, the transmissions of fluid from one body-conduit to another are metered out as social transactions.
>
> (Lingis, 1994: xi)

This comparison between how the body is culturally and socially constructed by modern Western societies and the Sambia of Papua-New Guinea is the leitmotif of this chapter. It indicates that, despite 'scientific' theories of the body which claim to be universal and objective, our understanding of the body is yet contingent. As Lingis puts it: 'The human body is a product of natural evolution, but also of our own history' (1994: vii). The body of Western history is predominantly, as Lingis describes, an 'organized body' (Carter, 1983): it is made up of structures, boundaries and organs. The crucial link between this conception of the body and an organization theory based upon the pillars of Cartesian modernism, namely rationalism and scientism, is the urge to organize, delineate and define. In this chapter we explore some aspects of the development of the organized body and its relationship to the development of large-scale institutions for the collective achievement of objectives such as production, scientific knowledge, education and health. We go on to examine how the emphasis on structures, functions and boundaries has shaped organization theory and its relationship to ideas drawn from biology (as the structured body of knowledge about the body). However, recent developments, such as virtual reality technologies, genetic engineering and the new reproductive technologies, create a body which is more fluid and disorganized. These challenge the bounded nature of the typical body image and the stability of our identities. Similarly, recent work in organization theory looks at fluidity, flexibility and the transgression of boundaries. We look at this 'postmodern' trend (Turner, 1996: 17) and suggest that, despite the hype, Cartesian 'judges of normality' (Foucault, 1977) are still at play, maintaining our rigid boundaries.

The organized body

The idea of 'organization' stems from that of 'organ'. It derives directly from the structured view of the body to which Lingis refers. The *Oxford Dictionary* defines 'organ' as 'a distinct part of an animal or plant body, adapted for a particular function'. Common textbook definitions of 'organization' also emphasize a definite structure and function. For example, 'organizations are social entities that are goal-directed, deliberately structured activity systems with an identifiable boundary' (Daft, 1989: 9–10).

In what follows we focus on three of the main ingredients that might be argued to make up the recipe of the organized body. First, there is the splitting of the body into parts; second, the machine metaphor guides the perception of the relationship of these parts; and third, there is an interweaving of these conceptual schemes with actual institutional arrangements.

We start with the mind/body split, central to Descartes's 'sceptical rationalism'. It is this separation of the mind as the source of Reason from the merely material body which allows the 'objective' mind to cut up and examine the structures and functions of the body. This anatomizing of the body through biology constructs the body as a set of organs with related systems of response (see Dale and Burrell, 1995; Dale, 1997 for a fuller discussion of the 'anatomizing urge'). In a letter of 1645 to Mesland, Descartes makes it clear that he believes the reason for the life of a body is because it possesses organs, which are made up of 'particules' of matter. It is the interrelationship of these parts which gives the living body its disposition to receive a soul – like a machine which only works when its parts are connected together in a particular way (Carter, 1983: 99–100). To him, each person has the capacity to control their bodily impulses through 'spiritual mechanics' (Carter, 1983: 111). Thus emotions and passions are separated off from the mind, by which they are to be controlled through Reason. Here we see the development of the concept of rationality and the rational person, which are also central to Weber's theory of bureaucracy and much of organization studies (Bologh, 1990; Fineman,

1993). To Descartes, the greater the degree of organization or ordering – the more complex is the machine – the further down the path of evolution or progress is the entity (Carter, 1983: 193). It is interesting, in relation to the quotation from Lingis with which we began, that Descartes is only concerned with bodily fluids from the perspective that they 'permit coagulating and rarification, so that the finer parts can form masses of relatively heavier matter . . .' (Carter, 1983: 198). For him, structures of the mind are much more significant than fluids of the body.

For another major figure in the scientific revolution, Francis Bacon (1561–1626), the purpose of science is 'an understanding of the patterns in which matter is organized in accordance with mechanical laws' (Lloyd, 1984: 10), and furthermore, the significance of these laws is that they permit Man [*sic*] to control nature. The machine has been seen as a defining metaphor of modernism (for example, Gergen, 1992). The object under study becomes a bounded whole, a unitary entity. Parts are defined in relation to the overall purpose of the whole, emphasizing function and structure and obscuring difference and contradiction. The better the parts are specified and understood, the more complete the knowledge of the whole object, and therefore the more complete the power over it. The machine is the instrument of control over the world.

It is significant that it is 'the dominion of *man* over the universe' (Francis Bacon, quoted in Easlea, 1983: 19, emphasis added) because rationality, reason and science become associated with masculinity whilst femininity is separated off and linked with nature and the body. Thus the Cartesian boundaries become gendered and the resulting structures take on a naturalistic gloss: the constructed dualism comes to seem inevitable. And since the (feminine) body has been anatomized and classified by the (male) mind, the categories appear objective due to their association with rationality. This is written into scientific assumptions throughout much of the scientific revolution. Bacon, for example, writes of scientific discovery: 'I am come in very truth leading to you Nature with all her children to bind her to your service and make her your slave' (quoted in Jordanova, 1989: 25). There is also the nineteenth century statue of a woman undressing in the Paris medical faculty: 'Nature Unveiling Herself Before Science'. Jordanova argues that 'It implies that science is a masculine viewer, who is anticipating full knowledge of nature, which is represented as the naked female body' (1989: 87). And women have long been excluded from the science laboratory, except where there is a legitimating male 'guardian', husband or father (Rose, 1994). Marie Curie, the first person ever to win two Nobel prizes, was denied membership of the prestigious Académie des Sciences in 1911 because she was a woman. No woman was elected to full membership until 1979 – over 300 years after it had been founded (Schiebinger, 1989). Thus science and rationality are not only about man's control over nature, but also man's control over women and over the body.

Although Bacon is seen as a pioneer in scientific methodology, particularly in empiricism, in many ways he was more of a politician than a 'pure' scientist (Martin, 1993; Woolhouse, 1988). He was equally interested in institutions, both in political terms and their part in the production of 'objective' knowledge. He worked his way up from barrister, through attorney-general to the position of Lord Chancellor. One of his greatest concerns was authority and control in knowledge production. (He essentially wished to maintain the status quo of the monarch's power, in accordance with his own role within the state!) His vision for the 'systematic and collaborative' (Woolhouse, 1988: 14) production of scientific knowledge, as set out in his posthumously published *New Atlantis*, was 'an institutional one, with hierarchically organized structures for information-gathering, assessment, and command' (Martin, 1993: 77). This was to take the form of 'Solomon's House' – a royal institution with a hierarchical division of labour among the 'Brethren' who were to be state officials. They were to obtain scientific information from books, travel and experiments, and collect this together so it could be assessed by committees. Bacon characterized his method as 'mechanical' (Woolhouse, 1988: 23), the byword of the times, and took his organizational inspiration for how this was to be achieved from the bureaucratic state institutions – the body politic – of England.

Indeed, science *is* a product, not only of ideas and experimental results, but of powerful institutional arrangements. In the early ferment of the scientific revolution these were not always in the highly structured form which Bacon idealized. For example, the Parisian salons, chiefly organized by women, could be very influential in the careers of male scientists in the early years of the Académie Français (Schiebinger, 1989), and in England there was an interesting cluster of relations between the Royal Society, the Freemasons and itinerant lecturers. Both these developments took place towards the end of the seventeenth century (Jacob, 1987). They were fluid arrangements, more akin to 'network' ideas which are currently in vogue, than to Bacon's bureaucracy.

But gradually, 'organs' and 'organization' took on a central importance as structuring concepts and as structured institutions. Hoskin argues (as do Figlio, 1976; Foucault, 1970, 1973; Pickstone, 1981) that 'around 1800, the term "organization" discovered its modern power as [a] key explanatory metaphor, both in biology and the sciences of man' (1995: 145). In France there was vehement dissent in biology around the physiological apparatus and processes for sensitivity and irritability within an organism. Figlio argues that divergent views in these debates were eventually reconciled by the use of the term 'organization'. The work of men such as Cuvier (1769–1832) and Bichat (1771–1802), which emphasized the importance of 'organization', triumphed in the development of a dominant paradigm in biology. Cuvier brought together the areas of anatomy and classification of species. Unlike earlier classificationists, and directly because of his practice of anatomy, Cuvier systematically compared the internal organization of organisms rather than their external features. It is this distinction which leads Foucault to regard him as central in the making of modern biology (Foucault, 1970;

Heilbron, 1995: 139). Pickstone (1981) suggests that Bichat's work was formulated in such a way as to 'fit' with the socio-political language of the time and the bureaucratic institutions being developed in the Directorate. His particular way of looking at the body was as a 'set of parallel sub-systems, variously subordinated' (1981: 118). His focus was on classifying the tissues which make up the organs, and on membranes, since these delineate the edges of similar parts – that is, they form boundaries within the organism. Bichat's organization of the body finds resonance within the

> highly structured, bureaucratic medical school, itself part of the new executive apparatus of the Directory. In this sunset of the Enlightenment, scientific rationalism finally attained political influence, and was embodied in a series of parallel administrative, educational and military systems, extending and rationalizing the bureaucracy of the ancien regime. (Pickstone, 1981: 127)

In post-Revolutionary France, universities, hospitals and state bureaucracy grew rapidly (Foucault, 1973; Pickstone, 1981). Heilbron argues that the Revolution had a radical effect in opening up the possibility of new institutions being formed, once the monopolistic position of the guilds had been broken (1995: 119). At around the same time in England there was also a period of institutional consolidation through the Industrial Revolution, which was to produce the more usual subject matter of organization studies: that of business corporations (Harrison, 1984).

Returning to Directorate France, Foucault, in *The Birth of the Clinic* (1973), argues that the connection between the organizing of the body into regular, reproducible and visible features was essentially worked out through the institutionalization of the hospital in this period. Initially, the hospital was developed as a place where the poor could be treated, those who could afford it still being treated individually and privately in their own homes. But the progress of 'scientific' medicine required consistent and large scale experimentation and observation: 'There is boundary, form, and meaning only if interrogation and examination are connected with each other, defining at the level of fundamental structures the "meeting place" of doctor and patient' (1973: 111). This clinical gaze sought to 'see, to isolate features, to recognize those that are identical and those that are different, to regroup them, to classify them by species or families' (1973: 89). The institutional achievement of these objectives was brought about slowly and hedged around by arguments about the greater good of society, since it disrupted the moral relationships between doctor and patient, society and the poor.

Bichat's physiology of the body was also to find a parallel in the political thought of Saint-Simon (1760–1825), described as 'the prophet of organization' (Pickstone, 1981: 123). Both 'tended to see the operations of wholes as bundles of separate functions carried out by constituents; at each level of organization the analysis could be repeated' (Pickstone, 1981: 123). Saint-Simon stressed stability, albeit one achieved through the functions of science and industrialism, rather than religion and traditional authority (Clegg and Dunkerley, 1980: 16). It is interesting that in presenting Saint-Simon as one of the forerunners of organization theory, Clegg and Dunkerley describe his as 'a basically *organic* view of society' (1980: 17, emphasis added), thus underlining the assumption of the organism as an organized, structured and hierarchical one. (And it is important to note that whilst texts such as Clegg and Dunkerley's *Organization: Class and Control* explicitly seek to analyse the field of organization studies they also construct it.)

These ideas of structure, function and boundary, then, are common to both biology's examination of the body and the idea of 'organization' itself. The bounded nature of the body comes to be constructed through biological theory. What it contains in the way of 'structures' becomes conceptualized as patterned and ordered and 'natural'. And we already see the germs of this organized body in the theories of organization held by such influential figures as Saint-Simon, Weber and Taylor. The twentieth century has witnessed the greatest development of the principle of separation, through rigid structures and functions within the organization. The 'mind' controls the 'body' in the rise of large-scale capitalist organization, which uses workers' bodies as though they were mindless and controls the body and the organization through the principle of rationality. But management practices such as Taylorism and Fordism have only put into practice the existing ingredients of Cartesian rationalism and the organized body.

In some senses, at least then, we can say that biology and organization theory draw on a common pool of corporeality and both attempt to create a theoretical object which is their own. In the next section we look at how organization theory has attempted to draw boundaries around the organization, trying to control both the intractable worker's body and its own subject matter.

Organization theory and the organ(ism) under modernity

In *Images of Organizations*, Gareth Morgan suggests a link between biology and organization studies, in that 'think[ing] about organizations as if they were organisms' has led to 'many of the most important developments in organization theory over the last fifty years' (1986: 39). Biology, as the science of living organisms, is one key to the images, metaphors and 'knowledge' that we have of the body. Therefore it does seem important to consider the basis of the multiplicity and changing biological and biomedical views on the body which have been adopted as key ideas in understanding organizations. The biological metaphors which organization theory draws on are consistently those of the 'organized body' of Cartesian rationalism. In what follows, we take just a couple of examples to illustrate the pervasiveness of biological metaphor and the predominance of structure across a range of different approaches.

One consistent theme across organization studies is the construction of organizations as bounded and structured entities which have therefore a sense of internal cohesion which is differentiated and separated from the external 'environment'. This can be illustrated by quotations from a best-selling textbook in the Marxist tradition of labour process theory, *Work Organizations* by Thompson and McHugh (1995). They say 'let us define organizations as consciously created arrangements to achieve goals by collective means' (1995:3) where 'the essence of organization is the creation of regular, standardized behaviour and orderly structure' (1995: 4). They go on to note that 'despite the self-activity of their members, organizations as corporate bodies do have economic and political powers above and beyond those of the particular individuals that comprise them' (1995: 5).

Thus organizations are theorized as structures which self-determine – are goal-seeking – in their own right. They are seen as organisms – biological entities – which behave in particular ways in order to carry out certain functions in order to survive. There are, of course, many difficulties with this anthropomorphism and reification which have been articulated by many other writers (for example, Mouzelis, 1975; Silverman, 1970). The anthropomorphism of the goal-seeking entity of the organization can be seen across work as diverse as social systems theory, population ecology and institutional theory.

Burrell and Morgan (1979) argue that the work of Chester Barnard (1886–1961) is one of the first attempts to develop a comprehensive academic theory of the organization. Along with the work of Herbert Simon, they characterize this approach as an 'equilibrium model' of organization. Barnard was a member of the Pareto Circle at Harvard, which was strongly influenced by the ideas of the biochemist L.J. Henderson, who sought to bring biology into the curriculum and research agenda of business and social theory. For Barnard, the organization's goal is to achieve internal equilibrium through three necessary and sufficient conditions: communication, willingness to serve and common purpose. Biological arguments are put forward to defend this proposition. It is a 'unitary' perspective on organization (Burrell and Morgan, 1979: 149), based on the elision between organization and organism. Barnard saw as pathological those people who are 'unfitted for co-operation' (1938: 13). Thus we see how individual people are conceptualized as members of the organization, fitting into the overall function as cogs in a machine, with no room for superfluity or different motives. We can see how this notion of equilibrium, the balance of properties within the organism/organization which keep it functioning properly, is also prevalent in key work in biology of the same period. At the time Barnard (1938) was writing, Cannon, also at Harvard, utilized the notion of homeostasis to describe equilibrium in the blood and this was seen as further justification for the conceptualizations being employed by the Circle. It was an idea also used by Beadle at Stanford in the development of the principle of 'one gene, one enzyme', through the process of ascertaining what metabolic products were absent when a gene was mutated and how balance was recreated when these were added back in through diet.

The way in which Herbert Simon uses Weber's concept of rationality in organization theory also draws on the notion of the organized body, particularly the Cartesian separation of body from mind. Simon states that '*the central concern of administrative theory is with the boundary between the rational and non-rational aspects of human social behaviour*' (1947: xxiv, emphasis in original). In the development of his use of Weber's notion of rationality, Simon first separates off the rationality of the individual as limited – 'bounded rationality' – and then allows it to be occluded by the more encompassing organizational rationality through a process of 'identification'. Thus the mind of the individual is effectively taken over by the mind of the organization: 'through his [*sic*] subjection to organizationally determined goals, and through the gradual absorption of these goals into his own attitudes, the participant in organization acquires an "organization personality" rather distinct from his personality as an individual' (1976: 198). Rational organization requires that people become predictable parts of the whole. There is an assumption that members of the organization will act as 'members' – in the sense of hands, limbs, appendices, tools. A biological member is not a brain. It is controlled by the brain at a distance through some means of communication. Since it is deeply problematic to control in this way, Simon's solution is 'identification' whereby organizational members are made to be 'of one mind'.

It is interesting that in these approaches, the organization is seen as the primary unit of analysis and the environment plays a very secondary role. The corporate entity is a bounded entity. The function of the executive is to keep it that way. Whereas boundary-maintenance is here an active and significant process, other fields within organization studies take the boundary as a given: the organization as an entity has become an unquestioned concept. As Rowlinson says of organizational economics, questions about why and how organizations are there in the first place become rhetorical (1997: 3). However, this is most clearly seen in the case of population ecology. This approach has become popular in the US since it gives a naturalistic gloss to sociology and draws in a quite specific way upon currently high status biological and mathematical conceptualizations. Here the level of focus is not the individual organization and its attempt to maintain its own boundary, but within a whole population of organizations who are struggling to survive in a particular environment. The elision between organization and organism is taken for granted as analysis examines the life cycle of organizations from birth to death.

In a similar vein, institutional theory (Scott, 1995: xiv) continues the tradition of open systems theory. However, unlike the vast majority of the population ecologists, institutional theorists see the organization as capable of responding to the environment in positive ways. In a mixed metaphor of unusual proportions, Scott says: 'Organizations are creatures of their institutional environments, but most modern organizations are constituted as active players, not passive pawns' (1995:132). It is interesting to note that developments in institutional theory also pave the way for a symbolic-interactionist understanding of the boundaries between organization and environment, where it is the active construction and interpretation of the organization as a bounded entity which, symbolic in itself, produces material effects (Hatch, 1997: 64). It is from approaches such as this that the organization/organism can begin to be deconstructed.

A further point of interest is that these organization/organisms are 'organs without bodies' – they have the functions of a living organism, but are not enfleshed. The structures that they have are the cognitive structures of the Western intellectual tradition still dominated by Cartesianism. The managerial literature on 'knowledge work' (for example, Badaracco, 1991; Cohen and Levinthal, 1990; Hedlund, 1994) can be used to illustrate this lack of enfleshedness. The language used to describe processes of transfer of knowledge and learning within an organization takes the organization/organism as the level of learning – it holds knowledge together which cannot be held by its individual parts. The words to describe the process of learning are highly mechanical – drawing on the still prevalent view of the human body/brain as a mechanical object which, as we have seen, stems from Descartes and the tradition of anatomy. The dominant objectivist assumption about the nature of knowledge is reflected in a tendency for an image of the knowledge worker as an 'empty vessel', a 'receptor' for information, as an 'interface' between the organization and the environment (for example, Cohen and Levinthal, 1990). The knowledge worker would appear to be reduced to the status of electronic gadgetry.

The failure of the organization/organism concept in these approaches to enflesh its theoretical object is also possibly a function of a specifically male cognition. Weber, central to the theorizing of rationality and influential in the development of organization theory, attempted to suppress emotion, separating off the private person from the public function (Bologh, 1990). This may well be associated with masculine Reason: the cutting out of emotions as well as the unpredictable body from which they emanate (see Lloyd, 1984). As we have discussed above, the body has been associated with the subjugated feminine principle, whereas the mind is more valued. It is also linked to the domination of (masculine) reason over (feminine) nature (see Easlea, 1983; Lloyd, 1984).

As we have also noted, the theoretical object across organization studies is, of course, the organization. Because organization studies needs to actively maintain its own disciplinary boundaries from the encroachment of other fields of study, this particular concept is privileged and given ontological status. In so doing the notion of boundary is accepted as part of the baggage: as a fixed object with ontological status it has to be bounded from the non-organization. And, of course, this bounding is often given ontological status because it has huge political implications. The 'organization' gives the writer meaning, a structured place of theorizing, and by addressing client concerns also mobilizes resources.

The organization, when the legitimacy of its ontological status is questioned, is treated as if it were an individual, and the individuals within it in turn become parts or members. Weber himself said 'the corporation, a fictive person, has replaced the company of equals as the legal scaffolding of work' (Abbott, 1989: 273). In this simplified version of the structures and functions of biology, individual members of the organization become merely its organs. They have functions which are linked, usually through the managerial function, into the overall goal of the organization. Although the individuals in an organization are bounded entities themselves, they are still only parts of the whole, which function through their interrelationship. As in the prevailing modernist view of the body, these interrelationships are seen in a predominantly mechanical way, ironically even though the organization itself may be conceptualized as an organism. Thus structure is important, because attaining the right structure is the way to achieving the overall balance (equilibrium) of functions to gain the desired outcome. Those elements which do not function correctly or disrupt the structure must be excised or treated, like cancers in the body.

The idea of organizations/organisms simply as larger bodies, corporate entities with their own bounded shapes, anatomies and morphologies, which have powers over and above their members, obscures the real operation of power, its pervasiveness and its links to the creation of knowledge and meaning (Foucault's views of power may be useful in dismantling this approach). However, even specifically power orientated books in the Radical Weberian tradition rely upon the concept of the bounded organization. By way of exemplar let us consider Graeme Salaman's (1979) *Work Organizations: Resistance and Control*. Here

> a sociological approach to organizations centres on the concept of organizational structure. This concept is used to describe the regular, patterned nature of organizational activities and processes. Obviously, organizations are composed of people, but the regularities displayed by members of an organization are not the result of their personal preferences or psychologies, but of their exposure to various organizational controls, which more or less successfully limit, influence or determine their behaviour. (1979: 5)

And we have already indicated how this approach is also consonant with Marxist labour process and radical analyses such as those by Clegg and Dunkerley (1980) and Thompson and McHugh (1995). Over and over again, the structured, bounded image of the organization/organism would seem to underlie modernist organization theory.

Leaky boundaries

Turner (1996: 17) suggests that we can see postmodern theory as a critique of the Cartesian view of reality. In postmodern theory boundaries become blurred: between mind and body; body and technology; self and other. The body is no longer a clear bounded entity but can be restructured and the image of the self, projected via the body, can be recreated.

The changing conditions of modern life seem in many ways to challenge the boundaries of the body (and hence both the coherence of the self and the object/subject split on which Western rationality is based). The body can be changed and re-shaped by diets, exercise and cosmetic surgery. Technology can allow the separation of biological and parental roles in reproduction. Body parts can be exchanged – sometimes through the economic system – in transplants and prostheses. Genetic engineering holds out the spectre of altering the very foundation of human life – scientists might argue about the difficulty of changing the actual germ-line, but the fantasy has taken a stronghold in the popular imagination (fuelled by such events as the cloning of Dolly the sheep). Technologies, too, can offer the prospect of a disembodied existence – computer and virtual reality technologies suggest a disruption of somatic knowledge of place, space and time (that is, a change in the lived experience of being-in-the-world, rather than the scientific versions of location with their 'objective' measurements).

These disruptions to the body structure are often portrayed as liberating choices, particularly in terms of the consumer culture where they enable the (still sovereign) individual to change their self-image and be whoever they want to be, to overcome biological constraints and explore right over the margins of what is physically possible. It has also been portrayed as politically liberating in Haraway's cyborg image (1990). Here, however, the sovereign individual with rights and free choice is to be transgressed, for it has been exposed by the politics of race and gender to be hiding a white, male, able-bodied norm.

But these changing possibilities for the body are not always seen as opportunities. Often there is fear and threat involved in the potential breach of body boundaries. For example, AIDS is a particularly cogent symbol of the 'panic' about the breakdown of the body's boundaries – it links together images of invasion of the body by the virus, together with the fear of death through the contamination of 'unclean' body fluids (Kroker and Kroker, 1988). The predominant image of the protection against this 'leakage' is the containment of the (male) body (symbolically the whole male through its most important organ?!) in impermeable rubber. This maintains the most potent symbol of Western phallocentrism as a 'safe' entity. It also links to the continuing fear of Nature, in the form of woman, which rational science since Bacon has explicitly attempted to control (Easlea, 1983; Jordanova, 1989). Both the fear of AIDS, which is perceived as a predominantly homosexual threat, and the fear of women's 'leaky bodies' (Grosz, 1994: 203; Shildrick, 1994), enact the fear of the transgression of how 'normal' male gendering and the norm of the male body is formed. As has already been noted, the organized body is first and foremost the ideal of the male body. Thus postmodern challenges to the boundaries of the body are of particular threat to male Cartesian rationalism. In fearing leakages, it is the disruption of *organ*-ization, of the *structure* of the body which is a problem.

The boundaries of the organization are also under question, particularly in relation to debates around the 'postmodern' issue in organization studies. 'The postmodern organization has no centrally organized rational system of authority on which such spatial metaphors as "hierarchy" can be placed. It becomes a shapeless and flowing matrix of shifting and flexible exchanges, a federation of organizational styles and practices each surviving on its capacity to respond to demand' (Crook et al., 1992: 187). The organization seems to be moving away from the emphasis on structure and boundaries which Lingis argues is so central to us in the West.

We will consider two texts that deal with the 'postmodern' organization. In Clegg's *Modern Organizations* (1990) the stance is taken that we live in a postmodern age and in terms of the significance of this shift for organizations we must look towards boundaryless organizations and networking. The Third Italy of Emilia Romagna and the 1980s phenomena of Silicon Valley have both been used by organization theorists to show that some successful organizations do not resemble the bounded large bureaucracies of the Fordist era. New organizational 'forms' are developing. These developing concepts of a supposed postmodern age often relate to the trichotomy which is made between the three basic forms of organizing – namely, market, hierarchy and network – and the political systems attendant upon them – capitalism, socialism and corporatism. There is a need to look at 'previously untranslated organizational forms' (Clegg, 1990: 23) which do not originate in what many call the world of 'organizations' as usually understood within the boundaries of organization studies as a discipline. This can be seen as a tremendous threat by organization theorists.

But the threat posed by the concept of the boundaryless organization to organization theory should be more accurately seen as a threat to *bureaucratic* hierarchy. The boundaryless organization does not threaten organization theory if one sees our concern as being with organi*zing* rather than with *the* organization. The object of our conceptualization can be organization, but not the bounded entity. The organization is an anatomized object; organizing is not necessarily so!

This point is picked up in work by Gephart, Boje and Thatchenkery. They say that: 'For us, the meaning of organization is problematic. Rather than conceiving of organizations as concrete facticities embedded in artifacts such as policies and buildings, we regard organizations relationally . . . as a concept of social actors that is produced in contextually embedded social discourse and used to interpret the social world . . .' (1996: 2). Thus their focus is upon organizations and organizing (1996: 3) in a search for the enhancement of a field in which many possible theories of organization exist. They still use the term 'organization theory' in the singular but this is not necessarily constructed in a way which would be comfortable for all.

As we have already pointed out, the notion of the boundaryless organization can be justifiably perceived of as a threat to our area. In order to protect our territory – our theoretical object – we protect our conceptualizations. In like manner to the notion of the bounded body we develop defence mechanisms against the invading organism as it seeks to come into our home territory. For example, Pfeffer (1993) defends the boundaries of organization theory against the predations of the economists. Within organizational theory itself, his vision – the 'Pfefferdigm' (Van Maanen, 1995) – is of control of the discipline by an elite (analogous with the brain?) who decide what is right and proper for organization theorists to do. In the same frame of mind, Donaldson states that his own aim is to reassert organization studies as 'purposeful, coherent and with its own criteria' (1985: xii). In his more recent book, *For Positivist Organization Theory* (1996), he continues to develop this position, dismissing any theoretical approach to the study of organizations other than contingency theory. This views organizations as having structures which are determined by contingencies such as size, leaving no scope for strategic choice or the conflicting interests of members. It is also correctly proclaimed to be functionalist, with particular structures seen as producing certain outcomes such as efficiency, innovation and so on. It is clear, then, that the structured, bounded organization/organism is alive and well in some quarters where the seepage of postmodern theory will never reach.

On the other hand, the openness of the organization and its boundaries are sometimes welcomed as post-bureaucratic. The language of welcome is often one based on the liberation of the individual from a forced and needless identity with the organization itself. Since much of the new rhetoric is much more individualistic, it *appears* to open up new opportunities for the individual, and encourage entrepreneurialism, self-expression and an end to alienation. The leaky boundaries of the theoretical object known as 'the organization' are often welcomed by managerially oriented 'post-bureaucratic' consultants. However, a particular twist to the notion that these ideas might be 'liberating' becomes clearer when seen in the context of a statement such as: 'Organizations are now viewed as organic, holistic, value-driven, information processing networks with permeable internal and external boundaries. They are lean and mean, smart, and motivated by enlightened self-interest that puts profits in their proper perspective' (Mead and Mead, 1992: 121). Individualistic language may even become another example of reification of the organization as an entity itself. If the organization is a self-interested individual, we are back to the problem of its members being merely its mechanism or organs.

In some ways it may be that the 'boundaryless' organization is not so much one without boundaries or structures, but is an attempt to redraw the boundaries to try to achieve that confluence of knowledge and power which has so long been the purpose of rational science. The industrial revolution recognized the control benefits of bringing large groups of workers under one roof, and controlling them through the disciplining of their bodies in space and time through machine control and the pacing of the line. Today the by-word may be flexibility, but often this disguises a widening of the boundaries of the organization, again in space and time, through homework or the expectations of professionals and managers to deal with 'work' issues, whenever and wherever. Technologies such as the mobile phone, the modem link and portable PCs all contribute to this (for example, Massey, 1993). The surveillance of the organization into more and more areas of employees' lives (the technological extension of Ford's 'sociology department'?) may also represent less the blurring of boundaries than their extension in a one-directional way. Although this is not necessarily through the structure of the bureaucratic organization, it is facilitated by the same rationalist logic. The same may also be true of the 'new' forms of relationships with suppliers and customers. Thus, in 1996 Ford made efforts at Valencia and Dagenham to reproduce Highland Park by bringing a concentration of suppliers onto one site. It was Ford himself who recognized that 'The 5 Dollar Day' was necessary so that the workforce could afford to buy his products. This recognition that the boundary between 'employee' and 'customer' is often a false one, is also behind such initiatives as arguing 'the business case for equal opportunities' or 'managing diversity'. Here a rich diversity of employees is advocated so that the company may better understand a diverse section of customers and therefore the coverage of market for service or products will be better. However, it is likely that 'tolerance' of diversity will still be defined and controlled by dominant groups and concepts (such as 'organizational efficiency' and 'the bottom line') (Cockburn, 1989; Essed, 1991). In all of these examples, it may be that senior managers are trying to bring consumption *inside* organizations to control this process as well as that of production. If modernity is still with us, perhaps management is still about creating the inside and the outside of the bounded organization (cf. Barnard, 1938).

In conclusion, then, we would suggest that the 'postmodern' ideas presented above of the disruption of the organ/organization do not entirely constitute a rupture in the modernist rationalist modes of organization, self and body, even if they do go some way to problematizing the concepts of structures, boundaries and wholes as we have considered them as part of the 'modernist project'. It is less easy to accept either a naturalized body or standardized definition of 'organization' any longer without a willing suspension of disbelief.

Perhaps, then, one of the fears that we have is that the (postmodern) rhetoric of fluidity over structures is a legitimatory discourse for the consumption of the other (Bauman, 1995: 122–5). Zygmunt Bauman argues that there has been a move from touching the 'other' to tasting them. In the social world which we inhabit today the other is no longer known through mutual physical contact, body to body, in a shared way of communication but is consumed. We taste the other rather than embrace them. This may disrupt the boundaries of the other, but confirms the entity which consumes anything different from itself (Dale, 1997).

Thus, we return to Lingis's quote, and suggest that the boundaries of body, self and organization are on the whole being defended against fluidity, however fashionable, and that the key to this is the 'stable psychic identity' which has been created as the rational, self-examining self of modernity. Even if leaking, we are still imprisoned in relatively fixed bodies and relatively fixed bodies of knowledge. The task, perhaps, is to wallow in the fluidity and to imagine the consequences of that for organization theory.

References

Abbott, A. (1989) 'The new occupational structure: what are the questions?', *Work and Occupations*, 16 (3): 273–91.

Badaracco, J. (1991) *The Knowledge Link*. Boston, MA: Harvard Business School Press.

Barnard, C. (1938) *The Functions of the Executive*. Cambridge, MA: Harvard University Press.

Bauman, Z. (1995) *Life in Fragments*. Oxford: Blackwell.

Bologh, R. (1990) *Love or Greatness*. London: Unwin Hyman.

Burrell, G. and Morgan, G. (1979) *Sociological Paradigms and Organizational Analysis*. London: Heinemann.

Carter, R. (1983) *Descartes' Medical Philosophy*. Baltimore, MD: Johns Hopkins University Press.

Clegg, S. (1990) *Modern Organizations*. London: Sage.

Clegg, S. and Dunkerley, D. (1980) *Organization, Class and Control*. London: Routledge and Kegan Paul.

Cockburn, C. (1989) 'Equal opportunities: the long and short agenda', *Industrial Relations Journal*, 20 (4): 213–25.

Cohen, W. and Levinthal, D. (1990) 'Absorptive capacity: a new perspective on learning and innovation', *Administrative Science Quarterly*, 35: 128–52.

Crook, S., Pakulski, J. and Waters, M. (1992) *Postmodernization*. London: Sage.

Daft, R. (1989) *Organization Theory and Design*, 3rd edn. St Paul, MN: West Publishing Company.

Dale, K. (1997) 'Identity in a culture of dissection: body, self and knowledge', in K. Hetherington and R. Munro (eds), *Ideas of Difference*. Oxford: Sociological Review Monographs, Blackwell. pp. 94–113.

Dale, K. and Burrell, G. (1995) 'Under the knife: labours of division in organization theory'. Paper presented to the first annual CSTT Workshop 'The Labour of Division', Keele University, November 1995.

Donaldson, L. (1985) *In Defence of Organization Theory*. Cambridge: Cambridge University Press.

Donaldson, L. (1996) *For Positivist Organization Theory*. London: Sage.

Easlea, B. (1983) *Fathering the Unthinkable*. London: Pluto.

Essed, P. (1991) *Understanding Everyday Racism*. Newbury Park, CA: Sage.

Figlio, K. (1976) 'The metaphor of organization: an historiographical perspective on the bio-medical sciences of the early nineteenth century', *History of Science*, xiv: 17–53.

Fineman, S. (ed.) (1993) *Emotion in Organizations*. London: Sage.

Foucault, M. (1970) *The Order of Things*. London: Tavistock.

Foucault, M. (1973) *The Birth of the Clinic*. London: Routledge.

Foucault, M. (1977) *Discipline and Punish*. London: Allen Lane.

Gephart, R., Boje, D. and Thatchenkery, T. (1996) 'Introduction', in D. Boje, R. Gephart and T. Thatchenkery (eds), *Postmodernism and Postmodern Organization Theory*. Thousand Oaks, CA: Sage.

Gergen, K. (1992) 'Organization theory in the postmodern era', in M. Reed and M. Hughes (eds), *Rethinking Organization*. London: Sage.

Grosz, E. (1994) *Volatile Bodies*. Bloomington, IN: Indiana University Press.

Haraway, D. (1990) 'A manifesto for cyborgs', in L. Nicholson (ed.), *Feminism/ Postmodernism*. London: Routledge.

Harrison, J.E.C. (1984) *The Common People*. London: Fontana.

Hatch, M.J. (1997) *Organization Theory*. Oxford: Oxford University Press.

Hedlund, G. (1994) 'A model of knowledge management and the N-form corporation', *Strategic Management Journal*, Summer.

Heilbron, J. (1995) *The Rise of Social Theory*. Cambridge: Polity Press.

Hoskin, K. (1995) 'The viewing self and the world we view: beyond the perspectival illusion', *Organization*, 2 (1): 141–62.

Jacob, M. (1987) 'Scientific culture in the early English enlightenment: mechanisms, industry and gentlemanly facts', in A. Kors and P. Korshin (eds), *Anticipations of the Enlightenment in England, France and Germany*. Philadelphia, PA: University of Pennsylvania Press.

Jordanova, L. (1989) *Sexual Visions: Images of Gender in Science and Medicine between the Eighteenth and Twentieth Centuries*. London: Harvester Wheatsheaf.

Kroker, A. and Kroker, M. (eds) (1988) *Body Invaders*. Basingstoke: Macmillan.

Lingis, A. (1994) *Foreign Bodies*. London: Routledge.

Lloyd, G. (1984) *The Man of Reason*. London: Methuen.

Martin, J. (1993) 'Francis Bacon: Authority and the Moderns', in T. Sorrell (ed.), *The Rise of Modern Philosophy*. Oxford: Clarendon Press.

Massey, D. (1993) 'Scientists, transcendence and the work/home boundary', in J. Wacjman (ed.), *Organizations, Gender and Power*. Warwick Papers in Industrial Relations, 48. Warwick: University of Warwick.

Mead, W. and Mead, J. (1992) *Management for a Small Planet*. London: Sage.

Morgan, G. (1986) *Images of Organization*. London: Sage.

Mouzelis, N. (1975) *Organization and Bureaucracy* (2nd edn). London: Routledge and Kegan Paul.

Pfeffer, J. (1993) 'Barriers to the advance of organizational science: paradigm development as a dependent variable', *Academy of Management Review*, 18 (4): 599–620.

Pickstone, J. (1981) 'Bureaucracy, liberalism and the body in post-revolutionary France', *History of Science*, xix: 115–43.

Rose, H. (1994) *Love, Power and Knowledge*. Cambridge: Polity Press.

Rowlinson, M. (1997) *Organisations and Institutions*. Basingstoke: Macmillan.

Salaman, G. (1979) *Work Organizations: Resistance and Control*. London: Longman.

Schiebinger, L. (1989) *The Mind has no Sex?* Cambridge, MA: Harvard University Press.

Scott, R. (1995) *Institutions and Organizations*. Thousand Oaks, CA: Sage.

Shildrick, M. (1994) 'Leaky bodies and boundaries: feminism, deconstruction and bioethics'. Unpublished PhD thesis, University of Warwick.

Silverman, D. (1970) *The Theory of Organizations*. London: Heinemann.

Simon, H. (1947) *Administrative Behavior* (3rd edn, 1976). Cambridge, MA: Harvard University Press.

Thompson, P. and McHugh, D. (1995) *Work Organizations*. Basingstoke: Macmillan.

Turner, B. (1996) *Body and Society* (2nd edn). London: Sage.

Van Maanen, J. (1995) 'Style as theory', *Organization Science*, 6 (1): 133–43.

Woolhouse, R.S. (1988) *The Empiricists*. Oxford: Oxford University Press.

2   Dangerous Fluids and the Organization-without-Organs

Stephen Linstead

The body is, of course, one of the dominant metaphors underlying the various 'systems' approaches to organizations which have developed to contest the supremacy of the 'machine' metaphor. As such, the body image which is deployed beneath the surface of corp-orate thinking is, where it is acknowledged (Morgan, 1986), the body of no one in particular, and is genderless. Despite the fact that the embodied organization can be strong, weak, lean, in need of trimming the fat, sick or healthy, it is never said to have prostate trouble or PMS. But organizational body images – those embodied in structures, systems, power relations, decision-making, reasoning processes, artefacts and architecture – are not gender-neutral. They are inescapably male.

The historical connections between rationality and masculinity have been well identified by Bordo (1986), Eason (1981) and Lloyd (1984/1993). From the time of the Greeks, men have been associated with dryness, solidity, firmness and containment – the male body was a body of parts, of organs that were self-contained and connected in a machinic way, a body to be mastered and controlled (Foucault, 1990) and sealed-up against penetration or invasion. The social body with its specific forms of order, its hierarchies, its taboos and licences, its sacred places, its striated values and its disciplines, was literally written on the body. Different cultures view the body in different ways, which both reflect and determine approaches to social structure, such that a change in either can affect the other.

Women's bodies were historically associated with wetness and fluidity, with flux and change, with fecundity and uncontrollable cycles of nature, with mood swings and passion. Women, through their changeability and association with fluidity, were a threat to the order and stability which men struggled to achieve and maintain. Physically fluid, women were also socially mobile, and their movements had to be socially regulated by marriage rules and kinship systems – the Ancient Greeks in particular had a welter of regulations of this nature. Women also crossed disciplinary and moral boundaries – in fact, their capacity to render established boundaries permeable what was gave them such a powerful social significance – and in moving across boundaries they could introduce pollution of behaviours and ideas which could threaten the health of the social system just as physical disease threatened the body.

In what follows I will look at the connections between fluidity and pollution, and the connections with male and female sexuality. Looking particularly at the significance of sexual fluids, and the symbolic importance of male ejaculation, I will then examine the curious case of the female ejaculation and its suppression or dismissal, particularly over the past 200 years, in the face of some 2000 years of evidence and debate. Finally I will connect the female ejaculation to Deleuze and Guattari's (1984, 1987) construction of desire and their concept of the Body-without-Organs, which as Grosz (1994) argues, has more in common with female bodily experience than that of the fully socialized Western male. I conclude with an invitation to read this new bodily understanding into organizing processes, reconstructing desire, replacing the overshadowing symbol of the phallus with that of the ejaculating woman, and perhaps moving towards the idea of an Organization-without-Organs?

Pollution and fluidity

Dirt, Mary Douglas (1980) argues, is matter which is out of place. Nothing in itself is dirty, until it disrupts order. Nothing can possess the property of disruption unless in relation to a system, in a specific context, and order is imposed in the system at the cost of excluding 'dirt'. The presence of dirt then signals a threat to the system of order, whether individual or social, and remains a mark of the vulnerability of the system. Anywhere dirt is found is therefore dangerous to the system – margins and boundaries are perilous sites, and entrances and exits, where unincorporable pollutants might gain access, need to be policed and purified with care. Anything which moves, or flows, across such boundaries, is a potentially dangerous substance.

Douglas argues that certain pollutants are used as analogies for the social order. In particular she uses the example of sexual fluids, about which there are beliefs that each sex is a danger to the other through fluid contact. In other cultures, the belief may be that only one sex is a danger to the other, and which one again may vary. These symbolic patterns of sexual danger, she argues, relate to the patterns of hierarchy or symmetry found in the wider social system (and may pose problems for the understanding of physiological problems, like the mechanics of sexually transmitted diseases, for example). Bodily orifices can come to represent points of entry or exit to social units, and the places where eating and defecation takes place assume a wider than functional significance (Linstead, 1985). As Grosz (1994: 193) argues,

> the body can and does function to represent, to symbolize, social and collective fantasies and obsessions: its orifices and surfaces can represent the sites of cultural marginality, places of social entry and exit, regions of confrontation or

compromise. Rituals and practices designed to cleanse or purify the body may serve as metaphors for processes of cultural homogeneity.

Cultural symbolic investment then selects and privileges some parts of the body whilst neglecting others, valorizes certain organs whilst proscribing their neighbours, marking some out for emphasis and attention whilst erasing others. Kristeva (1982) adds a psychological dimension to Douglas's work, focusing on the ways in which individual bodies are sorted and demarcated to become social bodies, separated from the outside yet dependent upon it. Bodily fluids are reminders of the permeability of the body and the presence of the unspecifiable within, which occasionally leaks out. As Grosz (1994: 194) observes, 'Body fluids flow, they seep, they infiltrate; their control is a matter of vigilance, never guaranteed . . . they are necessary but embarrassing.'

As she goes on to note, Douglas (1980), Sartre (1958) and Irigaray (1985) have drawn attention to the significance of the *viscous*, which is customarily viewed with horror because of its stickiness, its clinging quality, its indeterminacy, its refusal to be unequivocally either solid or liquid. For Grosz and Irigaray, the viscous and fluid is implicitly associated with femininity because it is subordinated to the unified, the solid and the self-identical, in a social order which renders female sexuality similarly fluid, indeterminate and marginal. The fluid is a marginal state between liquid and solid, passing between them, borderline and dangerous. Douglas, however, parts company with Grosz here, as she takes a rather traditional view of the role of fluids in sexual relations, arguing that both male and female bodies can be understood as a 'precious vessel' which must not pour away or dilute its vital fluids. Females are the container and must not allow anything polluting to enter them; males must not allow themselves to be enfeebled by carelessly 'spending' their fluids.[1] Grosz contests this view, in that it reduces the circulation of pleasure and desire within a relationship to the transmission of seminal fluid from the testes to its appropriate resting place in the female body. Female fluids then are merely preparatory for the arrival of male fluid in Douglas's view, which as Grosz notes, is still fairly close to the dominant contemporary biological models of sexual relations.

The money shot

Seminal fluid, following from this view, is metonymically constructed in terms of what it makes, does and causes. The fact that it is a fluid and essentially uncontrollable, that it seeps, leaks, spreads, oozes and lacks form is, as Grosz argues, 'displaced onto its properties, its capacity to fertilize, to father, to produce an object'. The semen is solidified and phallicized as in its fluid state it is 'an obstacle to the generalization of an economy restricted to solids' (Irigaray, 1985: 112–13). The male function here is to create *at a distance*, to extend power and proprietorial interests beyond the body to mother and child, as if by *remote control*. This in my view applies equally in the typical climax of the pornographic film, where the male ejaculates on the body or face of the female. Leaving aside the aesthetics of the spectacle, the act has two main features – the withdrawal of the male, and the acting *upon* the female. The significant dynamics of covering the female with semen are frequently followed or perhaps accompanied by ingestion by the female, reproducing penetration and impregnation. This seems to be supportive of Irigaray's position. However, Williams (1989: 94) argues that the visible presentation of ejaculation is a means of metaphorization of the female interior, and the mirrored externalization of the *female's* presumed inner sense of fulfilment and pleasure, as it presents the male's *actual* climax. Of course, this can *only* be metaphorical as the withdrawal of the male indicates that the female climax has been deferred (although in the limited lexicon of the pornographic film it has probably already been dramatically represented at least once). Despite the fact of the clitoral orgasm being widely and gleefully embraced by the genre, the final moment makes a triumphant metaphorical return to the Freudian vagina, as the penis as the source of pleasures is reunited with the phallus as the seat of power.[2] However, the power represented is usually ambiguous – the fecund power to actively create (the pleasure of another, another life) and the power to control (delay and deferral of one's own pleasure, the pleasure of another) being simultaneously implied.[3] Both of these qualities are semiotically represented by the quantity of semen and by some combination of its quality (thickness, coloration) and the distance to which it is projected.

The fact that females frequently take an active role within pornographic films reinforces this point insofar as they primarily become active to initiate their own pleasure. This is usually represented not as the female being in *control* of her pleasure but rather of *abandonment* to it, possessed by and in the grip of it – the male body becomes a mere instrument for this, sucked up in its wake, which generates in the male (viewer and viewed) a condition of terror and erotic excitation which was familiar to the Greeks.[4] Nevertheless, even as passive instrument, the male remains bounded and solid.

Grosz argues, following Irigaray, that men have reduced the understanding of flows within the body to those by-products of pleasure and reproduction which emerge as occasioned by circumstance. This, she argues, could be seen to be part of men's overall attempt to distance themselves from the sort of qualities that have been historically attributed to women – irrationality, uncontrollability, excess, disruption, expansiveness, hysteria, lack of self-control. She goes on to suggest that the ways in which men live and experience their own bodily fluids, as Douglas might have argued, mirror the demands of a society which establishes and regulates heterosexual opposition – where women are attributed, through the process which Kristeva (1982) identifies as abjection, with the qualities that men most fear in themselves. For Irigaray (1985: 113) the object of *desire* (as understood within Freudian and Lacanian psychoanalysis) is to transform the fluid into the solid – to turn the uncontrollable into the controlled, the nebulous into the defined, the unclear into the lucid, the flaccid penis into the turgid phallus, the fuzzy and floppy into something we can get hold of – *the triumph of rationality itself.*[5] For Grosz, this emerges in the ways in which men attempt to deny what they see as elements of femininity in themselves, holding women in contempt or reverence; their capacity to distance themselves from their passions, to be different persons in work life, social life, domestic life and sexual encounters; to regard their sex organs as autonomous; to distance themselves from intimacy whether through anonymity, promiscuity, voyeurism, or the reification of bodily organs. As the male body is phallicized, with the panoply of senses subordinated to the sensations of the penis and pleasure focused on penetration and ejaculation, it becomes sealed up and impermeable.

> Perhaps it is not after all flow in itself that a certain phallicized masculinity abhors but the idea that flow moves or can move in a two-way or indeterminable direction that elicits horror, the possibility of being not only an active agent in the transmission of flow but a passive receptacle. (Grosz, 1994: 201)

Grosz then argues for a body that is permeable, that opens itself up, that transmits in a circuit, that responds as well as initiates, that is unsealed, that neither virilizes nor reviles its masculinity. This requires a rethinking not only of male sexual morphology, but a *transformation in the structure of desire* which would enable men sexually to take on passive positions, to explore different parts of their and others' bodies, to explore different forms of pleasure, to 'reclaim, reuse, reintensify, body parts, zones and functions that have been phallically disinvested'. As Dollimore (1991) writes, this is a transgressive reinscription involving a recoding of significances which disrupts the prevailing order. Annie Sprinkle, the multi-faceted performance artist (Straayer, 1993: 163), deliberately mixes the genres of pornography and sex education in order to widen the sexual and semiotic repertoires of her audiences – introducing males to anal penetration, erotic urination, and other non-standard but also non-fetishized sexual practices, combining the roles of nurturing mother and sexual animal which for Freud had to be hierarchically separated in order to avoid the Oedipal nightmare.[6] As Hite (1976: 547–8, quoted in Segal, 1994: 110) observes (though somewhat against the general thrust of her other work), 'a passionate desire to be "taken" or "possessed" by someone during sex is not automatically a sign of victimization, as long as it is not the only feeling you ever have'; but as Segal adds, even if it *is* the only feeling you ever have does not automatically mean that you are victimized, as recent work on sado-masochism demonstrates (Brewis and Sinclair, 1996). The anus could, for example, be regarded as a universal erotogenetic zone, or even sexual organ, shared by both sexes and multi-functional as are most of our other organs. When Hite (1993: 166 in Segal, 1994: 110) turns her attention to male desires for penetration she is able to report

Most men, of either heterosexual or homosexual experience, who have tried being penetrated said that they enjoyed it; it brought feelings of deep pleasure and fulfilment. The main characteristic of being penetrated described by men was an extreme feeling of emotional passion – followed by a feeling of peace and satisfaction.

Segal conjoins that feminist argumentation tends to construct feelings of fulfilment, completion and satisfaction as acquiescence to male domination, victimization by male power through phallic sex. But she asks, if men can have these feelings in response to penetration, whether by a finger, a vibrator, tongue, penis, or other object, why should females too not legitimately feel the same way? Feminism has too often mirrored masculinist sexuality by focusing on both orgasm (at the expense of wider contextual considerations of circuit and flow) and control.[7] As she argues and as Hite reports (but again tends to disregard), desire is as much about letting go, about *losing* control (Segal, 1994: 41). The 'wanton woman' so despised by the ancient Greeks and De Sade then, may be no more than 'seeking the autonomy to be in control of the time [she] can be out of control'. Conversely, the male may be seeking *permission* to be out of control, to be no longer responsible for how pleasure takes its course.

Most men did not want to be penetrated, either physically or emotionally – and yet *did* want it . . . they want to penetrate the other, to be in charge, in control . . . and yet they long for the opposite, to be out of control, also dominated by the other . . . most men *do* want to be in deeper contact – to feel more – to not only take, but also be penetrated and taken . . . Passion is one of the most beautiful parts of all sensuality – the desire to possess, to take, to ravish and be ravished, penetrate and be penetrated . . . What is love? Love is talking and understanding and counting on and being counted on, but love is also the deepest intermingling of bodies. In a way, the body memory of a loved one is stronger and lasts longer than all other memories. (Hite, 1993: 166–7 in Segal, 1994: 111)

The female ejaculation

The enduring significance of male dryness, continence, rigidity and the characteristic focus of male sexuality on organs and fluid rather than bodily flows and fluidity, can hardly be underestimated – as de Beauvoir (1972: 79) comments, for the traditional male 'the length of the penis, the force of the urinary jet, the strength of erection and ejaculation become for him the measure of his worth'. It is therefore instructive by way of contrast to look at the phenomenon of female ejaculation, which has been discussed and contested for centuries and in recent years denied, suppressed and rejected by pornographers, sexologists and feminists alike. Potentially, however, it offers a way of reinscribing ejaculation itself, becoming a contra-phallic symbol under whose sign, as Grosz indicated, we might begin to challenge and change the structures of desire. Shannon Bell (1991) argues that female ejaculation has been understood as fecundity, sexual pleasure, social deviance, medical pathology and as a scientific problem in the past and I will broadly follow her argument to this point. However, I will develop her own further argument on the phenomenon as a symbol of liberation/ resistance, and also consider it as a performance which deconstructs and transgressively reinscribes assumptions about sexuality and sexual practice. In the concluding section of the paper I will return to consider how a linking of our knowledge of female ejaculation to Deleuze and Guattari's (1984) construction of desire without a cathected object can open the way for the deflation of the phallus and a more fluid social practice – a rhizomatics of the *body without organs*.

The emission of fluids during sexual activity was regarded by many Greek and Roman physicians and philosophers to be normal. Debate centred around whether the female fluids contained seed or not which was the essence of the *fecundity* argument. Hippocrates (460–377 BC) and later Galen contended that the fluid was fertile, and that the two forms of semen were necessary to the production of offspring (Hippocrates, 1978; Laqueur, 1987: 4–9; Maclean, 1980: 30ff; Rousselle, 1988: 24–32). Heat was important for gestation and the colder woman had to reach the right temperature for the female semen to literally boil off the blood (all bodily fluids including mother's milk were fungible products). Orgasm then was essential for procreation (Laqueur, 1987: 8; 1990: 43–52). Aristotle argued against the two-semen theory, noting that the discharge was not seminal and was connected with *pleasure* not the reproductive function, being 'on a different scale from the emission of semen and far exceeds it' (Aristotle, 1912, quoted in Bell, 1991: 156).

Galen supported the pleasurable theory but maintained that there were two fluids – one pleasurable, the other fertile. The pleasurable fluid came from the female prostate and 'manifestly flows from women as they experience the greatest pleasure in coitus' (Galen in Bell, 1991: 156). The theory of the female seed survived long after the Middle Ages, according to Jacquart and Thomasset (1988), but De Graaf (1672/1972) re-presented the controversy and denied the existence of female semen. However, he did identify what he called the female prostate or parastate, which produced a fluid to be emitted through the ducts around the neck of the vagina and the urinary passage, and which gave as much pleasure to the female as did the corresponding male phenomenon. He also noted that the fluid came out in one gush, rushing out. Sevely and Bennett (1978) summarize the historical literature on the female prostate and argue that:

1 both male and female have prostates;
2 in females, size and distribution of this gland varies widely;
3 the male prostate produces most of the fluid ejaculated (the testes contribute only a small amount containing sperm);
4 in some women the female prostate (or para- and peri-urethral glands) allows ejaculation of a fluid, which is not identical with urine, through the urethral meatus.

They go on to argue, that, following De Graaf, the Aristotelian argument tended to be resolved in favour of the Aristotelians, and the two-semen theory gradually disappeared. Consequently, the term semen came to be reserved for the male semen, and no corresponding term was coined for the female variety. At the same time, medical writers used terms such as 'vestigial' and 'atrophied' to describe the different varieties of organ found in both sexes, and as a consequence not only was sexual bipolarity emphasized but the concept of female ejaculation was delegitimized. It duly disappeared from view along with the concept of female semen.

Thomas Laqueur (1987; see also 1990: 1–3) argues that towards the end of the eighteenth century orgasm was dissociated from reproduction. Orgasm, previously at the centre of the generative process, was now regulated to the world of mere sensation, like the warm glow after a good meal. Whilst there was no contestation that orgasm accompanied ejaculation in males, despite its overall contingency, for females this was not the case and it opened the way for a new conceptualization of the 'passionless' female which dominated the nineteenth century (Cott, 1978). This model proved difficult to overturn, despite the efforts of sexual reformers such as Havelock Ellis (1905) and Van de Velde ([1928]/1980), who recognized the possibility and importance of female pleasure. Both Ellis and Van de Velde nevertheless saw the sexes as different, and desirous of male dominance.[8] The previous model of the sexes in which men were relationally but platonically oriented and women were the slaves of their own sexual passions, posing a threat to men, was overturned as the idea that women were not troubled with sexual feelings became more widespread and the great concern with sexual technique shown by the Greeks was discarded by the Victorians.

Laqueur also argues that this inversion occurred alongside a more extensive one which reconfigured the place of the female body. At least since Galen, the view commonly held was that women had the same genitals as men, only theirs were inside the body and the men's were outside. Despite the obvious differences, the ovaries and testicles were known by the same word; there was no technical term for the vagina 'as the tube or sheath into which its opposite, the penis, fits' in Europe until around 1700 (Laqueur, 1990: 5). Yet around 1800, men and women became contrasts, the *opposite* sex, and began to be described accordingly in medical texts without the presence of any scientific discovery or breakthrough. The disconnection of orgasm from conception was not supported by any scientific discovery until 1840, and that only in dogs – in fact our contemporary understanding of the hormonal control of ovulation was not achieved until the 1930s (Laqueur, 1990). Indeed the idea of homologues in genital anatomy, which could have supported either a one-sex or two-sex model, persisted in the nineteenth century as the understanding of the nature of the human embryo developed. As Laqueur argues, with Foucault, it was a shifting social context that made it both possible and necessary to construct the identity of women in a particular way. To simplify a whole nest of complex arguments, the Enlightenment ushered in a widespread concern for the rights of 'Man'. Morally, there could be no distinction between men and women as sentient beings and capable of reason, which meant that women should have the same socio-political and personal rights as men. The liberal body was gender-neutral in this sense. In order to justify the fact that men and women did not by any means enjoy the same rights and privileges, it was therefore necessary to ground theories of political and social difference in biological arguments, which came to underpin the sexual division of labour, the restriction of suffrage to males, the sexual double standard, and a range of otherwise indefensible social and cultural practices. Laqueur (1987: 21–4) notes the problems that both the early feminist writer Wollstonecraft (1787, 1789), in such works as *The Female Reader*, and a domestic ideologist such as Ellis (1842), in *The Wives of England*[9] and *The Daughters of England*, have in constructing an acceptable place for the active and intelligent woman in late eighteenth and early nineteenth century England (see also Poovey, 1990).

This social redefinition of the body informed the *social deviance* argument as female sexual fluids were later linked with disease. The discovery of the Skene glands in 1880 was linked to the problem of draining them and avoiding infection. The ejaculating female body became a grotesque body: ejaculating females were abnormal and dirty. Krafft-Ebing (1886/1965) from a psychological point of view identified female ejaculation as a *pathological* condition of 'sexually neurasthenic females' – subject to seizure-like disturbances caused by weakness in the nervous system. Ejaculating females were sick. More recently, the feminist Jeffreys (1985, 1990) is scathing in her rejection of this view, without accepting the existence of the phenomenon. Krafft-Ebing she says *invented* female ejaculation as part of his fantasies about lesbianism. In this she is not alone – Marcus (1966) notes a common 'fantasy' that females ejaculate. Nevertheless, by the twentieth century anthropological reports of female ejaculation were commonplace (Bell, 1991: 158).

More recently, scientific reports have identified the existence of the female ejaculation. Gräfenberg (1950) described the physiological process involved in some detail, yet as Bell notes, Kinsey et al. (1953) deny its existence, Masters and Johnson (1966) regard it as erroneous, and repeat that opinion in Masters et al. (1982). Sevely and Bennett (1978) produced a paper which originated the contemporary debate, which was followed by a rash of papers over the next decade which de-eroticized the phenomenon and turned it into a scientific problem. Tests were conducted on the composition of female ejaculate, different response patterns to 'local digital stimulation', muscle strength of female ejaculators, and connections with urinary stress incontinence. Bell (1991: 161) discusses some of the continuing research, including the evidence for the fluid being non-urinary, and also two books – Ladas et al. (1982) and Sevely (1987) – which have rich accounts of the process, and she concludes her piece by offering her own experience of becoming ejaculatory, including a how-to-do-it guide.[10]

Bell (1991: 160–1) argues in her review of the scientific studies that male investigators with a psychic investment in the sexually privileged position of the 'spending male' have distorted or simply failed to acknowledge the evidence in front of them. She also argues that feminists who have an equally significant investment in preserving a different and oppositional view of female sexuality have also denied the existence of female ejaculation.

> The ejaculating female body has not acquired much of a feminist voice, nor has it been appropriated by feminist discourse – the questions posed and the basic assumptions about female sexuality are overwhelmingly premised on the difference between male and female bodies . . . women have the ability to give birth and men to ejaculate . . . feminists, in their efforts to revalorize the female body usually devalued in phallocentric discourse, have privileged some form of the mother-body as the source of *Écriture-féminine*: writing that evokes women's power as women's bodily experience . . . The fluids, reappropriated in feminine sexual discourse . . . have been the fluids of the mother-body: fluids of the womb, birth fluids, menstrual blood, milk: fluids that flow. Ejaculate – fluid that shoots, fluid that sprays – has been given over to the male body. To accept female ejaculate and female ejaculation one has to accept the sameness of male and female bodies. (Bell, 1991: 162–3)

Straayer (1993) takes issue with Bell's somewhat monolithic description of feminism, and argues that there is no either/or about either the motherhood or the ejaculating approaches to feminine sex-positivity. As Straayer points out, the binary system of sexual division is leaky – men can have multiple orgasms too, even if they are non-ejaculatory, just as they can ejaculate without orgasm (Robbins and Jensen, 1978). Similarly, Heath (1984) argues that the vagina and clitoris are not helpfully considered as separate organs in considering female ejaculation, but anterior vagina, clitoris, glands and vulva function as one linked, single organ – which is an image more usually associated with male genital functioning. For Straayer (and Sprinkle) the sort of contradictions seen, for example, by Hochschild (1983) in the organizational demands of Delta Airlines on their flight attendants to be 'proto-mother sex queens' would not be abnormal, necessarily unusual or insurmountable despite their context. Bell concludes by indicating some possible positive images for female ejaculation, including some taken from pornographic film-making (both simulated and real). Her basic argument is that a recognition that female ejaculation exists and can be learned can help to appropriate and reclaim the female body, to give women greater control over their body. Not only can ejaculation be achieved, it can be repeated indefinitely, as the supply of fluid is not, as in the male, 'spent' and exhaustible, and can be spectacularly copious when delivered, especially if the newly discovered A-spot – the *anterior fornex erogenous* (Sussman, 1996) – is stimulated. Images of female ejaculation can be a powerful educatory tool in deconstructing patriarchal sexuality.

Annie Sprinkle, as discussed by Straayer (1993) and Williams (1993), has worked a demonstration of female ejaculation into stage performances, autobiography (Sprinkle, 1991) and videos which inhabit the boundary between pornography, sex education, and art[11] – and we might add New Age mysticism and kitsch. Sprinkle, though considering herself a feminist, refuses to be drawn into any kind of oppositional stance, preferring to resist being drawn into positions and treating a variety of activities, techniques, relationships and experiences as options, part of an ever-widening repertoire which she shares with others of either sex. Sprinkle is somewhat slippery in her discussion of female ejaculation in public, due to censorship laws in some US states, but typically she does not see a clear distinction between urine and ejaculate, nor the need for one. She argues that there are four kinds of erotic female fluids:

> vaginal secretions, 'golden showers', the squirting or dribbling of non-urine fluid through the urethral opening (which can occur with or independently of orgasm), and erotically induced urination. (Straayer, 1993: 173)

The latter roughly corresponds to being so titillated that you need to pee.[12] Sprinkle currently demonstrates Tantric sex and 'energy' orgasms in her stage performances and workshops, as well as the female ejaculation. In one of her classic works, *The Sluts and Goddesses Video Workshop* (Beatty and Sprinkle, 1992), she demonstrates an ejaculation with the help of two assistants whilst holding a form of galvanometer to her vulva which monitors the level of her orgasmic excitation. The technique of a two camera shoot allows her to present the ejaculation with a lower body shot, then demonstrate what purports to be a five minute and ten second orgasm with an upper body shot, although they occur simultaneously in performance. Throughout the performance, Sprinkle draws attention to the artifice involved in being one or other type of sexual persona – slut or goddess – and as elsewhere in her work she crosses boundaries between spirituality and sexuality, mother and whore, art and the everyday, pornography and art, normality and sodomy, golden showers and ejaculation, heterosexuality and homosexuality.[13] She literally *enacts* fluidity. Whether her orgasms and ejaculations are genuine at any one performance or not we cannot definitively say, even with the evidence available and even accepting the fact of female ejaculation. Nevertheless, the fact that they are only now becoming *represented* raises the question as to why they became part of a realm of unknowing for so long, and why both male pornography (with its apparent quest to represent the unpresentable) and feminism (with its quest for the return of control of women's sexuality to women) suppressed or denied this knowledge.

The answer lies in the reliance of both of them on forms of sexuality which essentially originated in the eighteenth century, though drawing on symbolic and semantic resources of great antiquity, and developed in the nineteenth century in conjunction with contemporary social demands. The body of which Annie Sprinkle provides an image is not the divided, organicized, solidifying body propelled by its desire to be a *unit* – but a body of flows and intensities, a body of surfaces and intersections, where sensations are not demarcated but blend together. Just as the social maps the body, so a reconfiguration of the physical body can occasion a deconstruction of the social body – a restructuring of *desire*, and a new understanding of the corporeal dynamics of social power.

Intensities, flows and the Body-without-Organs

> The universal, in fact, explains nothing; it is the universal which needs to be explained. All the lines of variation which do not even have constant co-ordinates. The One, the All, the True, the object, the subject are not universals, but singular processes – of unification, totalization, verification, objectivation, subjectification. (Deleuze, 1992: 162, quoted in Doel, 1995: 235)

In Freudian psychoanalytic approaches to the understanding of subjectivity, but more widely if implicitly in other epistemologies, the idea of the 'other' has two forms – sometimes referred to as Big Other and little other. Little other is the other person constituted as difference, a target which shifts according to the subjective frame in focus. Women are the other of men, femininity of masculinity, which in much of the work we have so far discussed has been explicitly constructed as an object of the discourse. As we have implied, where masculinization of thought (and writing – see Calás and Smircich, 1991; Derrida, 1978) occurs this feminine other may be silently constituted. The Big Other is the ordering principle which contains and controls the universe – a rational principle, a sense of completeness, balance, finality and unity – to which human activity tends and to which we defer, the *logos*. The very existence of the little other, other human beings embodying difference, reminds us of the incompleteness of our own knowledge, feelings and experience – our existential *lack*. Desire for completeness then flows toward the other, the different, but as a symptom of the deeper ontological lack of totality, of power, of completeness, which is a desire for the Big Other. Desire originates in lack and acts to attempt to transcend difference.

This transcendence, as Derrida (1978) has demonstrated, works in practice only through the deferral of difference by the subordination of one of the paired objects – the supplication of subjectivity to the cathected object or the symbolic incorporation of the desired other. Women traditionally being reconstituted as an extension of their husband's will on marriage would be an example of this. This process depends upon an acceptance of subjects as being demarcated units, as having a fixed self-identity, and of hierarchy as being a principle capable of containing this difference, whether it be consciousness or biological evolution. If these principles are closely examined, as Gilles Deleuze (1992) argues, our sense of the universal, the absolute, the totalizing and the fixed – of the *logos* – can be seen to be an outcome and result of the processes which we set in motion to achieve it, and therefore a wholly contingent construction. Our sense of rationality, for example, is inescapably gendered, although specific historical moves have made significant qualitative differences in the socially constructed (but psychically *lived*) relationship between masculinity and rationality from *episteme* to *episteme*, as Foucault (1979) has argued extensively. Bodies are understood in terms of universalities, binaries, individuations: they are centred, organized in terms of an overarching consciousness, cohesive through intentionality and reflexivity, capable of combination in purposeful ways as part of a teleology which restores a greater oneness. Desire works through a recognition of incompleteness and drives towards this restoration.

Deleuze and Guattari (1984) contest this understanding of the body. They begin with the position of the infant as commonly represented in psychoanalysis – a subject not yet formed, without identity, but yet with organs that work as mouth, anus, lips, ears, eyes – with no developed identity to bring them into subordination to consciousness. This they call Organs-without-a-Body (OwB). The development of a unitary subjectivity brings consciousness into primacy, holding together these essentially fragmented units into an ordered whole, the body-with-organs, the organism. Psychoanalysis accordingly regards the body as

> a developmental union of partial objects, organs, drives, orifices each with their own significance, their own modalities of pleasure which through the processes of Oedipal reorganization, bring these partial objects and erotogenic bodily zones into alignment in the service of a higher goal than their immediate, local gratification. (Grosz, 1994: 169)

These significances can be discerned, purposes derived and pathologies identified and remedied, and the body as a metaphor for other forms of organization allows order, system development and higher consciousness to be imputed to social structures, workplaces and seats of learning. This body is also in the grip of desire, and Deleuze and Guattari (1984: 5–7) identify what they call 'desiring-machines', of which the body is composed and which combine in different ways – the body is an eating machine, an anal machine, a talking machine, a breathing machine, organ machines and energy machines coupled, flowing and interrupted constantly, rather like the Freudian id (Lash, 1991: 268–70). As they say,

> Desiring machines make us an organism; but at the very heart of this production, within the very production of this production, the body suffers from being organized in this way, from not having some other sort of organization or from having no organization at all. (Deleuze and Guattari, 1984: 8)

Simultaneously, social apparatuses catch the body and make it signify, create lack and channel its desire, mark it, make it situated, embodied, white, black, male, female, fat, thin, cool, ripped, pumped, grotesque, working class and so on. Yet this work is always in process and the body is always a site of internal recombination and external contestation – it is always a body *to come*, a body *in process*. It 'endures through continually breaking down' (Doel, 1995: 231) as becoming is itself a desire to escape particular body limitations.

> Deleuze and Guattari see desire and the body as positive, in motion to make creative linkages, driven not by lack and the need to overcome it but by the constant instability, the ceaseless motion of parts, the recombinative effects which produce – the body is seen in terms of what it can do, the things it can perform, the linkages it establishes, the transformations and becomings it undergoes, the machinic connections it forms with other bodies, what it can link with, how it can proliferate its capacities . . . Desire does not take for itself a particular object whose attainment it requires; rather it aims at nothing but its own proliferation or self-expansion. (Grosz, 1994: 165)

The Body-without-Organs is a body which lies underneath the desiring machines. It is the *field of immanence* of desire, the *plane of consistency* specific to desire (with desire defined as a process of production without reference to any exterior agency, whether it be a lack that hollows it out or a pleasure that fills it) (Deleuze and Guattari, 1987: 154).

It resists being structured, channelled and formed, it refuses hierarchization, sedimentation, striation, layerings and overcodings – it is a changing pattern of intensities and flows; it seeks to empty itself of significances, to break away, not from the organs, but from the organization of the organs which is called the *organism*. It seeks to disassemble 'the union constituting the organization, the unification that constitutes the subject, and the structure of significance' (Grosz, 1994: 170).

Deleuze and Guattari identify specific forms of 'becomings' on the way to the full Body-without-Organs, which are specific forms of movement, speed, slowness, directions and flows of intensity. *Becoming-animal* is a way of becoming intense, *becoming-woman* is a way of 'putting into question the coagulations, rigidifications and impositions required by patriarchal . . . power relations' – a way of dismantling the fantasmatic forms of femininity, which is just as much a process for women as men to undergo, just as each needs to *become-man*. These becomings are particular ways of experiencing the *flows* that produce, moving away from the idea that *subjects* produce – a means of demassifying binaries and both re-experiencing and re-theorizing them in terms of microprocesses, intensities and flows which refuse to be bounded, refuse to conform and refuse to align to the requirements of formal organization. It entails the recognition and experience of the unpresentable, the unboundable. Organization, of bodies, selves and societies, is always becoming, always in play.

The work of Deleuze and Guattari has had relatively little impact in organization theory. Given the fact that the body metaphor and its associated functionalist epistemology are still widespread throughout the field, this is perhaps unsurprising, but it also offers an exciting prospect. Thinking through the Body-without-Organs as a metaphor for the Organization-without-Organs would give some greater texture to the silenced areas of organizational processes which, where they are studied, are often deprived of their energy, frozen in time and solidified, with the sense of their flow, interruption and recombination lost. It could also provide a means of rethinking hierarchy and many of the structural features of organizations that we frequently take for granted and treat as reality rather than fantasm. It could also release, through its emphasis on flow as *productive*, new understandings of innovation and the improvised organization. This rethinking would necessarily entail some reversals in the relationships between rationality and passion, fluidity and power, deflating the organizational phallus in the process.

Finally, then, the image of the female ejaculation could usefully replace this detumescent phallus as a sign under which organizational deconstruction might proceed. As a case of repression, denied yet silenced for so long, it offers a rich metaphorical resource. Yet because of some of its other properties – being joyous, generous and inexhaustible – it could be regarded as a symbol of flows that flow from the body without organs. As such it becomes transgressive, subversive of patriarchy, dissolving boundaries between binaries, refiguring our understandings of bodily control, and rewriting femininity out of its polarized opposition to masculinity. In Deleuzian terms, it represents a step of *becoming*, perhaps towards the Organization-without-Organs.

Notes

1 Dollimore (1991: 251) cites Clement of Alexandria's *Christ the Educator*: 172–3, where he notes the view of the seed as homunculus (little man): 'Does not lassitude succeed intercourse because of the quantity of seed lost? "For a man is formed and torn out of a man." See how much harm is done. A whole man is torn out when the seed is lost in intercourse.' This homuncular view is sometimes taken towards the penis itself (cf. D.H. Lawrence's 'John Thomas').

2 I would not wish to imply that all films in the genre are covered by this description. A huge number of films are in existence and directorial styles are diverse, and frequently display ironic and self-reflexive tendencies as well as the more traditional features. The *Femme* group of female (some of them regard themselves as feminist) pornographers led by Candida Royale makes films that deliberately seek to meet the erotic demands of the genre whilst emphasizing more feminine dimensions of sexual pleasure – specifically, their products represent orgasm/ejaculation as bringing the participants together, the man remaining inside the woman.

3 That the cross-cultural definition of sexuality, to the existence of third and even fourth sexes, has considerable variation is well documented in anthropological literature (Geertz, 1983: 80–4). However, the significance of fertility is perhaps nowhere more marked than in the case of the Sambia tribe of New Guinea (Herdt, 1994: 432–41). For the Sambia, males are superior to females in every way except reproduction. Females mature quickly because of their possession of a menstrual blood organ (*tingu*) and females are initiated in a women's hut forbidden to males at

the onset on menstruation. Males however, cannot mature properly without semen, which they cannot themselves produce – the semen organ (*kerekukereku*) is small, hard and empty at birth. Semen is the spark of human life but it must be externally introduced, and ritual homosexual fellatio is performed throughout puberty in order to provide the engine for growth and store excess semen in the body for adult use. Repeated inseminations produce manhood, marked by a ritual six-stage process culminating in the birth of the father's first child. However, it is only at the birth of the second child that he can be considered to be fully adult, fully a man. That the self, physically as well as psychologically, is not only a relational product but a community achievement, with power coming through the ability to absorb the strength of others, makes an interesting contrast to Western constructions of masculine impenetrability to the point of the illegality of homosexual fellatio in some states.

4 For a discussion of the submissive dimension involved in viewing pornography, see Kaite (1988, 1995) and for an organizational application of these ideas, Linstead (1995).

5 The connection between masculinity and rationality developed beyond the early Greek identification of femaleness with matter and maleness with form which informed Plato's early distinction between reason as a quality of the soul and the non-rational as a bodily intrusion. Plato's later work saw the soul as itself *divided* into reason and both noble and ignoble passions – love as emotional turmoil and jealousy but also as 'a divine frenzy which impels the soul through the pursuit of knowledge to an immortal joy' (Lloyd, 1984/1993: 20). Passionate love is itself a point of entry to the intellectual life – the love of wisdom – but later it came also to be seen as a gateway to the spiritual life (as for example in the poetry of Donne). Lloyd also notes that Philo, Augustine and Aquinas attempt to blend Greek thought with Judaeo-Christian theology through a retelling of the Genesis myth. For Philo, Sense-perception must be subordinated to Mind, lest it engulf reason. He produces a table of oppositions, but identifies a male and female element in each soul – the male 'assigns itself to God alone', the universal creator, whilst the female clings to 'all that is born and perishes'. For Augustine, woman is spiritually equal, in terms of rational capacity, but bodily subordinate. This breaks with the Greek conception that woman is rationally a lesser form of man, an earlier form of teleological development, but nevertheless woman remains associated with bodily perturbation which distracts reason from its proper functioning. Aquinas constructs man as the principle (and principal) of humanity, that from which all its operations flow, with woman as his helper and supporter but not made in God's image. For complementary discussions of these early notions of feminine/masculine, see also Laqueur (1990) and Maclean (1980), who trace the growth of the teleological approach from Aristotle to the Renaissance; and Rouselle (1988) in relation to Greek notions of the body. Lloyd also discusses the idea of Reason as attainment, particularly through Descartes (see also Bordo, 1986) and Hume in the context of the passions, Kant and Hegel in regard to progress and transcendence. Connell (1995) in a rich and nuanced discussion of masculinity points out the contemporary problematics and paradoxes associated with being a 'man of reason' (Connell, 1995: 164–81) and the contestations of the contemporary men's movement of the identification of masculinity with power. In a complementary vein, Lloyd argues that to identify the historical processes by which maleness and reason have become linked and reason masculinized, and by implication to challenge the social and cultural consequences of these processes, is not necessarily to repudiate either reason or philosophy, despite the fact that philosophy has 'defined ideals of Reason through exclusions of the feminine' (Lloyd, 1984/1993: 109). It is, however, important to critically reflect upon deeper assumptions which have gendered social thought in both folkways and philosophy.

6 Straayer (1993: 157) cites Freud's description of the psychology of male love binarizing women:

> In only a very few people of culture are the two strains of tenderness and sexuality duly fused into one; the man almost always feels his sexual activity hampered by his respect for the woman and only develops full sexual potency when he finds himself in the presence of a lower type of sexual object; and this again is partly conditioned by the circumstance that his sexual aims include those of perverse sexual components, which he does not like to gratify with a woman he respects. Full sexual satisfaction only comes when he can give himself up wholeheartedly to enjoyment, which with his well brought-up wife, for instance, he does not venture to do. Hence comes his need for a less exalted sexual object, a woman ethically inferior, to whom he may ascribe no aesthetic misgivings, and who does not know the rest of his life and cannot criticize him. It is to such a woman that he prefers to devote his sexual potency, even when all the tenderness in him belongs to one of a higher type. (Freud, 1912/1963: 64)

As Straayer notes, this dichotomous psychoanaesthesia incurs that where these men love they have no desire, and consequently where they desire they cannot love. For Freud, the qualities of the wife are also those of the mother, and the avoidance of passionate involvement with the wife is the psychical avoidance of incest. Other women, or cultural objects of sublimation selected to avoid incest, are not only artificially degraded themselves but enable the equally artificial elevation of the incestuous object. That this situation has its contemporary forms of demand and supply is indicated by the following advert which appeared in the 'Adult Services' section of the Sydney *Daily Telegraph*, Tuesday 10 September 1996:

> CORRINE: Greek/American Who Loves to do what your Partner Won't . . . (telephone xxxxx)

7 The phenomenon of phallic feminism and the 'lesbian phallus' are discussed by Butler in 'The lesbian phallus and the morphological imaginary' (in Butler, 1993: 57–97, esp. 88–91) and Waldby (1995: 273–5).

8 Segal (1994: 86) notes that despite his recognition of the importance of female pleasure in the sexual act, this was still subordinate to the male will for Van de Velde, who asserted that 'The wife *must* be taught, not only how to behave in coitus, but, above all, how and what to feel in this unique act' (Van de Velde, 1928: 232). She also (Segal, 1994: 87) points out that Maxine Davis in *The Sexual Responsibility of Women*, feels it necessary to remind them that 'A man's sexual nature is so dissimilar from her own that a wife has to give it full attention for a long time in order to understand it with her reflexes as well as her brains' although the male is not likely to make reciprocal efforts on her behalf (quoted in Haste, 1992: 157).

9 *The Wives of England* has no publication date, but was printed in London around 1840 (see Laqueur, 1987: 39 n.46). Laqueur acknowledges Myers (1982) for this argument.

10 Whilst not wishing to burden the reader with sources on this topic, most of which are medically orientated, the interested will find a full bibliography prepared by Dr Gary Schubach on his website, *The G-Zone* (http://www.doctorg.com/), where over 80 scholarly sources and debates on the existence or otherwise of the Grafenberg Spot, the female prostate and the female ejaculation are to be found. Of particular interest are Winton (1989), Zaviacic (1987), Zaviacic et al. (1988), Zaviacic and Whipple (1993) and four papers only available from the author via the site, Schubach (1997a, b, c; 1998).

11 Sprinkle worked with and was heavily influenced by Carolee Schneeman in the 1970s, as Straayer notes. Schneeman's work is also discussed by Frank (1991).

12 As a response to stimulation, this is not confined to the sexual alone. Live performances by Billy Connolly have been known to produce the 'Sprinkle effect' in robust Glaswegian constitutions.

13 The video's own blurb describes it as 'a humorous, absurd, heartfelt and worshipful look at SEX . . . You will encounter flagellation with oak leaves, Chinese sword dancing, striptease, body contortions, tattoing, piercing and shaving, feminine masquerade and gender-play. You will learn about Tantric breathing, primal screaming, the joys of group masturbation while meditating, and not least of all, you will witness a profound five minute-long orgasm! . . . Challenging the boundaries of femininity, the 'good girl'/'bad girl' myths as well as the sexual norms, it is controversial and thought provoking and thus best viewed in a group. This insightful work of art will remind you that your sexuality is precious and sacred.' Sprinkle's ideas are taken further in another performance piece, *Metamorphosex* (1996). Two other related video pieces are Sprinkle and Harlot (1999) and Sundahl (1998). For a more scholarly visual take on this subject the collaboration by Beverly Whipple (consultant) and Mark Schoen (film-maker), *Orgasmic Expulsions of Fluid in the Sexually Stimulated Female*, is available from Focus International Inc., 1776 Broadway, New York, NY 10019.

References

Aristotle (1912) 'De Generation Animalium' (trans. Arthur Platt), in J.A. Smith and W.D. Ross (eds), *The Complete Works of Aristotle*. Oxford: Clarendon Press.

Beatty, Maria and Sprinkle, Annie (1992) *The Sluts and Goddesses Video Workshop, or How to be a Sex Goddess in 101 Easy Steps*. New York: Leslie Barany Communications.

Bell, Shannon (1991) 'Feminist ejaculations', in Arthur Kroker and Marilouise Kroker, *The Hysterical Male: New Feminist Theory*. London: Macmillan. pp. 155–69.

Bordo, Susan (1986) 'The Cartesian masculinisation of thought', *Signs*, 11 (3): 439–56.

Brewis, Joanna and Sinclair, John (1996) 'The intimacy of symbolic oppression: sadism/masochism, imagination and fashion'. Paper presented to a Conference on the Symbols of Oppression, Bolton Institute, March.

Butler, Judith (1993) *Bodies that Matter: On the Discursive Limits of 'Sex'*. London: Routledge.

Calás, Marta B. and Smircich, Linda M. (1991) 'Voicing seduction to silence leadership', *Organization Studies*, 12 (4): 567–607.

Carson, Anne (1990) 'Putting her in her place: woman, dirt and desire', in David M. Halperin, John J. Winkler and Froma I. Zeitlin (eds), *Before Sexuality: The Construction of Erotic Experience in the Ancient Greek World*. Princeton, NJ: Princeton University Press. pp. 135–70.

Connell, Robert W. (1995) *Masculinities*. Sydney: Allen & Unwin.

Cott, Nancy (1978) 'Passionlessness: an interpretation of Victorian sexual ideology, 1790–1850', *Signs*, 4 (21): 219–36.

de Beauvoir, Simone (1972) *The Second Sex*. Harmondsworth: Penguin.

De Graaf, Rainer (1672/1972) 'New treatise concerning the generative organs of women' (annot. trans. H.B. Jocelyn and B.P. Setchell), *Journal of Reproduction and Fertility*, Supplement 17, Oxford: Blackwell.

Deleuze, Gilles (1992) 'What is a *Dispositif*?', in T.J. Armstrong (ed.), *Michel Foucault: Philosopher*. Hemel Hempstead: Harvester Wheatsheaf.

Deleuze, Gilles and Guattari, Felix (1984) *Anti-Oedipus: Capitalism and Schizophrenia*. London: Athlone Press.

Deleuze, Gilles and Guattari, Felix (1987) *A Thousand Plateaus: Capitalism and Schizophrenia*. Minneapolis: University of Minnesota Press.

Derrida, Jacques (1978) *Writing and Difference*, trans. Alan Bass. London: Routledge and Kegan Paul.

Doel, Marcus (1995) 'Bodies without Organs: schizoanalysis and deconstruction', in Steve Pile and Nigel Thrift, *Mapping the Subject: Geographies of Cultural Transformation*. London: Routledge. pp. 226–40.

Dollimore, Jonathan (1991) *Sexual Dissidence: Augustine to Wilde, Freud to Foucault*. Oxford: Clarendon Press.

Douglas, Mary (1980) *Purity and Danger*. London: Routledge.

Eason, Brian (1981) *Science and Sexual Oppression: Patriarchy's Confrontation with Women and Nature*. London: Weidenfeld & Nicolson.

Ellis, Henry Havelock (1905) *Studies in the Psychology of Sex*, 2 vols. New York: Random House.

Ellis, Sarah (n.d) *The Wives of England*. London.

Ellis, Sarah (1842) *The Daughters of England: Their Position in Society, Character and Responsibilities*. London.

Foucault, Michel (1979) *The History of Sexuality, Volume I: An Introduction*. Harmondsworth: Allen Lane.

Foucault, Michel (1990) *The History of Sexuality, Volume 3: The Care of the Self*. Harmondsworth: Penguin.

Frank, Arthur W. (1991) 'For a sociology of the body: an analytical review', in Mike Featherstone, Mike Hepworth and Bryan S. Turner (eds), *The Body: Social Process and Cultural Theory*. London: Sage. pp. 36–102.

Freud, Sigmund (1912/1963) 'The most prevalent form of degradation in erotic life', in *Sexuality and the Psychology of Love*. New York: Collier Books.

Geertz, Clifford (1983) 'Common sense as a cultural system', in *Local Knowledge*. New York: Basic Books. pp. 73–93.

Gräfenberg, Ernest (1950) 'The role of urethra in female orgasm', *International Journal of Sexology*, 3: 145–8 (full text available at http://www.doctorg.com/grafenb.htm).

Grosz, Elizabeth (1994) *Volatile Bodies: Towards a Corporeal Feminism*. Sydney: Allen & Unwin.

Haste, Cate (1992) *Rules of Desire: Sex in Britain – World War I to the Present*. London: Chatto & Windus.

Heath, Desmond (1984) 'An investigation into the origins of a copious vaginal discharge during intercourse: "Enough to Wet the Bed" – "That" is not urine', *Journal of Sex Research*, 20 (2): 194–215.

Herdt, Gilbert (1994) 'Mistaken sex: culture, biology and the third sex in New Guinea', in Gilbert Herdt (ed.), *Third Sex, Third Gender: Beyond Sexual Dimorphism in Culture and History*. New York: Zone Books. pp. 419–45.

Hippocrates (1978) *De Geniture* (ed. and trans. W.C. Lyons and J.N. Hattock). Cambridge: Pembroke Press.

Hite, Shere (1976) *The Hite Report: A Nationwide Study of Female Sexuality*. New York: Dell.

Hite, Shere (1993) *Women as Revolutionary Agents of Change: The Hite Reports, 1972–1993*. London: Bloomsbury.

Hochschild, Arlie R. (1983) *The Managed Heart*. Berkeley, CA: University of California Press.

Irigaray, Luce (1985) *This Sex Which is Not One*. New York: Cornell University Press.

Jacquart, Danielle and Thomasset, Claude (1988) *Sexuality and Medicine in the Middle Ages* (trans. Matthew Adamson). Cambridge: Polity Press.

Jeffreys, Sheila (1985) *The Spinster and her Enemies: Feminism and Sexuality, 1880–1930*. London: Routledge and Kegan Paul.

Jeffreys, Sheila (1990) *Anticlimax: A Feminist Perspective on the Sexual Revolution*. London: The Women's Press.

Kaite, Berkeley (1988) 'The pornographer's body double: transgression is the law', in Arthur Kroker and Marilouise Kroker, *Body Invaders: Sexuality and the Postmodern Condition*. London: Macmillan. pp. 150–68.

Kaite, Berkeley (1995) *Pornography and Difference*. Bloomington and Indianapolis: Indiana University Press.

Kinsey, Alfred J., Pomeroy, Wardell B. and Martin, Clyde E. (1953) *Sexual Behaviour in the Human Female*. Philadelphia: Saunders and Co.

Krafft-Ebing, Richard von (1886/1965) *Psychopathia Sexualis*. New York: Paperback Library.

Kristeva, Julia (1982) *Powers of Horror: An Essay on Abjection* (trans. Leon S. Roudiez). New York: Columbia University Press.

Kroker, Arthur and Kroker, Marilouise (1991) *The Hysterical Male: New Feminist Theory*. London: Macmillan.

Ladas, Alice, Whipple, Beverly and Perry, John (1982) *The G-Spot and Other Recent Discoveries About Human Sexuality*. New York: Dell.

Laqueur, Thomas (1987) 'Orgasm, generation, and the politics of reproductive biology', in Catherine Gallagher and Thomas Laqueur (eds), *The Making of the Modern Body: Sexuality and Society in the Nineteenth Century*. Berkeley, CA: University of California Press. pp. 1–41.

Laqueur, Thomas (1990) *Making Sex: Body and Gender from the Greeks to Freud*. Cambridge, MA: Harvard University Press.

Lash, Scott (1991) 'Genealogy and the body: Foucault/Deleuze/Nietzsche', in Mike Featherstone, Mike Hepworth and Bryan S. Turner (eds), *The Body: Social Process and Cultural Theory*. London: Sage. pp. 256–80.

Linstead, Stephen (1985) 'Breaking the purity rule: industrial sabotage and the symbolic process', *Personal Review*, 14 (3): 12–19.

Linstead, S.A. (1995) 'Averting the gaze: power and gender on the perfumed picket line', *Gender, Work and Organizations*, 2 (4): 192–206.

Lloyd, Genevieve (1993) *The Man of Reason: 'Male' and 'Female' in Western Philosophy*. London: Routledge (first published 1984).

Maclean, Ian (1980) *The Renaissance Notion of Woman: a Study in the Fortunes of European Scholasticism and Medical Science in European Life*. Cambridge: Cambridge University Press.

Marcus, Steven (1966) *The Other Victorians: A Study of Sexuality and Pornography in Nineteenth Century England*. New York: Basic Books.

Masters, William and Johnson, Virginia (1966) *Human Sexual Response*. Boston: Little, Brown.

Masters, William, Johnson, Virginia and Kolodny, R.C. (1982) *Masters and Johnson on Sex and Human Loving*. Boston, MA: Little, Brown.

Morgan, Gareth (1986) *Images of Organization*. London: Sage.

Myers, Mitzi (1982) 'Reform or ruin: a revolution in female manners', *Studies in the Eighteenth Century*, 11: 199–217.

Poovey, Mary (1990) 'Speaking the body: mid-Victorian constructions of female desire', in Mary Jacobus, Evelyn Fox Keller and Sally Shuttlewo (eds), *Body/Politics: Women and the Discourses of Science*. New York: Routledge. pp. 29–46.

Robbins, Mina B. and Jensen, Gordon D. (1978) 'Multiple orgasms in males', *Journal of Sex Research*, 14 (1): 21–6.

Rousselle, Aline (1988) *Porneia: On Desire and the Body in Antiquity*. Oxford: Basil Blackwell.

Sartre, Jean-Paul (1958) *Being and Nothingness*. London: Routledge.

Schubach, Gary (1997a) 'The G "Crest" and female ejaculation'. http://www.doctorg.com

Schubach, Gary (1997b) 'The G-spot controversy'. http://www.doctorg.com

Schubach, Gary (1997c) 'Did Gräfenberg really mean spot?' http://www.doctorg.com

Schubach, Gary (1998) Urethral expulsions during sensual arousal and bladder catheterization in seven human females: the G-Zone. Novato, CA. Research paper available from the author only at http://www.doctorg.com

Segal, Lynne (1994) *Straight Sex: The Politics of Pleasure*. London: Virago.

Sevely, Josephine (1987) *Eve's Secrets: A New Theory of Female Sexuality*. New York: Random House.

Sevely, Josephine Lowndes and Bennett, J.W. (1978) 'Concerning female ejaculation and the female prostate', *Journal of Sex Research*, 14 (1): 1–20.

Sprinkle, Annie (1991) *Annie Sprinkle: Post-Porn Modernist*. Amsterdam: Torch Books.

Sprinkle, Annie and Harlot, Scarlet (1999) *Herstory of porn*. Oakland, CA: Save the Mermaid Productions. Video available from http://www.doctorg.com

Straayer, Chris (1993) 'The seduction of boundaries: feminist fluidity in Annie Sprinkle's art/education/sex', in Pamela Church Gibson and Roma Gibson (eds), *Dirty Looks: Women, Pornography, Power*. London: British Film Institute. pp. 156–75.

Sundahl, Deborah (1998) 'Tantric journey to the female orgasm: unveiling the G-spot and female ejaculation'. Santa Fe: Dasero Isis Media. Video available from http://www.doctorg.com

Sussman, Lisa (1996) 'Hit the A-Spot!', *Cosmopolitan*, Australasian Edition, June: 90–5.

Tysh, Chris (1991) 'Parading the masculine: figures, decoys and other canards', in Arthur Kroker and Marilouise Kroker, *The Hysterical Male: New Feminist Theory*. London: Macmillan. pp. 149–54.

Van de Velde, T.H. ([1928]/1980) *Ideal Marriage, Its Physiology and Technique*. Westport, CT: Greenwood Publishing Group.

Waldby, Catherine (1995) 'Destruction: boundary erotics and refigurations of the male body', in Elizabeth Grosz and Elspeth Probyn, *Sexy Bodies: The Strange Carnalities of Feminism*. London: Routledge. pp. 266–77.

Williams, Linda (1989) *Hard Core: Power, Pleasure and the 'Frenzy of the Visible'*. Berkeley: University of California Press.

Williams, Linda (1993) 'A provoking agent: the pornography and performance art of Annie Sprinkle', in Pamela Church Gibson and Roma Gibson (eds), *Dirty Looks: Women, Pornography, Power*. London: British Film Institute. pp. 176–206.

Winton, Mark A. (1989) 'The social construction of the G-spot and female ejaculation', *Journal of Sex Education and Therapy*, 15 (3): 151–62.

Wollstonecraft, Mary (1787) *Thoughts on the Proper Education of Daughters; with reflections on female conduct in the more important duties of life*. London: Printed for J. Johnson. (Also in J. Todd and M. Butler (1989) *The Works of Mary Wollstonecraft, Volume 4*. London: Pickering.)

Wollstonecraft, Mary (1789) *The Female Reader*. London: Printed for J. Johnson. (Also in J. Todd and M. Butler (1989) *The Works of Mary Wollstonecraft, Volume 4*. London: Pickering.)

Zaviacic, M. (1987) 'The female prostate: nonvestigial organ of the female, a reappraisal', *Journal of Sex and Marital Therapy*, 13 (2): 148–52.

Zaviacic, M., Zaviacicova, A., Holoman, I.K. and Molcan, J. (1988) 'Female urethral expulsions evoked by local digital stimulation of the G-spot: differences in the response patterns', *Journal of Sex Research*, 24 (3): 311–18.

Zaviacic, M. and Whipple, B. (1993) 'Update on the female prostate and the phenomenon of female ejaculation', *Journal of Sex Research*, 30 (2): 148–51.

PART TWO

DISCOURSE AND REPRESENTATION

3   Sociology Sensing the Body:
     Revitalizing a Dissociative Discourse

Catherine Casey

The dominant sociological tradition, along with that of the rest of the social sciences, and its practitioners, have increasingly abstracted enquiry and analysis from lived, embodied, self-reflective experience. There is a long history to the modern trajectory of rationalization and differentiation that is not simply reducible to Cartesian dualism and Kantian transcendent-alism. By the twentieth century modern philosophical biases against the corporeal were prevalent. Yet while social and cultural interest in the nature of bodily being in the world – of embodiment – were marginalized, modern thought and practice did not deny the body, nor dismiss its importance as a 'problem' and as an object of mind. The body, along with emotions, was regarded as the domain of 'nature', of private inner sensations, instincts, and desires driven by 'unreasoned' forces. The subjugation and control of instinctual man (and woman most especially), the domination of nature by culture, was a necessary condition of Western civilization. Yet classical theorists, following Descartes's postulated autonomy of soul/mind and body, upheld a nature/culture dualism that neither denied the body nor resolved their ambivalence about it. The classical theorists' privileging of reason and culture did not elide the material origins of human subjectivity, rather they believed in its rational transcendence as accomplishment of self. The modern humanist subject-self was the reasoning agent acting in a world that was scientifically knowable, and rationalizable (see Taylor, 1989).

Importantly, though, in the sociological tradition both Durkheim and Weber emphasized the importance of domains of human life that are not rational nor rationalizable. Weber, although more concerned with dispirited disenchantment than disembodiment, profoundly criticized the trajectory of unmitigated instrumental rationalization and technicization that character-ized modernity and its diverse practices, including that of sociology. While

Weber most significantly pointed to the cultural and spiritual distortions of human life resulting from unintended consequences of the cultural institutionalization of Protestantism and its secularized asceticism, mid- and late twentieth century criticism has most emphasized alienation and truncation, and now dissolution, of self through domination by modern rationalization.

A secularized asceticism as the dominant cultural form, notwithstanding its incorporated counter-moment in material consumption, in Western industrial capitalist society legitimated the spread of modern rationality and eventually normalized its technologized, dispirited, disembodied, desensitized, form of social organization, and human being. That sociology, in the institutionalized service of this project, did not, indeed could not, encompass an embodied, immanent, theory of the body bespeaks the modern discipline's cultural delimitation (cf. Mellor and Shilling, 1997; Turner, 1984). Ironically, contemporary social and cultural conditions provide sociology with rich opportunities for redress and revitalization.

A new attention to the body, and to the soul, gaining prominence in social and cultural studies, as in popular culture, has most notably emerged in anthropology and increasingly in sociology, social theory and psychology (see, for example, Csordas, 1994a; Featherstone et al., 1991; Frank, 1991; Shilling, 1993; Synnott, 1993). The current sociological interest in the body may indicate a significant movement within the sociological project that seeks a broadening of enquiry, an excavation of subjugated discourses, and an opening of categories that may allow a sensing of embodied, non-linguistic, sensory, affective knowledge. Or it may protract the disembodied objectification and petrification characteristic of the dominant traditions of modern industrial thought that have not yet given way in post-industrial conditions.

This chapter explores the body's material, sensual, emotional absence from the dominant tradition of sociology, and its continuing objectification in most contemporary social and cultural theorizing, even that which newly emphasizes the body. It proposes that sociology's delimitation by the instrumental rationalities of the modern project that produced it has rendered its discourse, like that of most of the social sciences more generally, acutely abstracted and dissociated from lived embodied experience. An unfeeling, avoidant awareness of the matter and sense of the body, notwithstanding a resurgence of sociological and cultural interest in it as discursive product and textual object, is the normalized positioning of sociological enquiry. In apparent neglect of the emphasis of many early theorists and a few others over the decades – importantly Durkheim, Simmel, Nietzsche, Freud, and later Merleau-Ponty and Mary Douglas – the gaze of the well-trained sociologist is now typically sharpened to an acute rationality that is unable to glimpse, hold and wonder at the sensual, the spiritual and the counter-rational as creative dimensions by which we constitute human being and human society.

Although there are important exceptions (for example, Bendelow and Williams, 1998; Crossley, 1997; Csordas, 1994a; Harre, 1991; Mellor and

Shilling, 1997), much recent theorizing and commentary on the body displaces a so-called modernist view of transcendental individual selves and natured bodies with an even more dissociative and disembodied view in the discursive de-naturing, dissolution and diffusion of body-self. Against this condition I join the discussion that seeks a return to the body as source of subjectivity, and of intersubjectivity.

Absenting the body – dissociation as normalized science

Notwithstanding the recent and rapidly growing interest in the body in social and cultural studies, the discourse on the body both now, and in modern history, displays a profound ambivalence. Modern industrial society generated and often celebrated, a denaturalization of nature and, eventually, in the social sciences a culturalization of the human world. The Italian cultural theorist Alberto Melucci points out that modern and contemporary thought now regards 'nature and the body as entirely defined within culture' (Melucci, 1996: 150). We have moved from a view that there is a nature 'out there', or 'in here' in the case of our own bodies, and rejected traditional and premodern views that held embodiment as the grounds of being and culture. 'Today', Melucci says (reluctantly), 'there is no nature left . . .' (p. 150).

Yet despite this now dominant modern (and postmodern) view, there have long been competing and conflictual discourses, and practices of the body – and paradoxically a resurgence in popular attention to our bodies. Sociology's distancing itself and the gaze of its practitioners from recognition, and sensing of bodily lived experience, of embodiment of mind and doing, limits its capacity to understand and analyse contemporary and imminent social, and psychic, conditions. Many postmodern contributions through poststructuralism and constructionism to sociology and social theory have tended to exacerbate this failure. The proclamations of much contemporary cultural theory of the 'death of the subject' and the 'obsolescence of the body' intensify, rather than eliminate, modern alienation and its attendant conditions.

The current attention in social and cultural studies now placed on the body has come about largely because of the postmodern critique of the modern project of rationalization. Postmodern critics have raised new debates that reject Cartesian dualisms, essentialisms and logocentricism. Importantly, they have drawn attention to the body and reopened apparently fixed notions of subjectivity and of the relationship between reason and desire, control and freedom. Many in the current generation of theorists widely hold or acknowledge the critique of reason as emancipation and many now turn to the body seeking a site, if not of emancipation, at least of 'resistance' (the only one left for Foucault). The body is regarded paradoxically as both the site of discourses and operations of power, and of resistance to power. A now fragmented, and re-configured, self-agency may be practised by the body through multiple identity representations and resistances of discursive power. For many feminists (implicitly retaining a remnant of nature) the body as site of resistance still refuses total colonization of the everyday life world by instrumental masculinist reason.

To speak of a dissociated, disembodied social science does not suggest that the body has been entirely ignored in social and cultural studies before the current interest emerged. The body, especially other people's (and other culture's), has been thoroughly gazed upon, described, inscribed, operated upon, probed, dismembered, interrogated and interpreted by modern social and biological sciences. Even as recent attention has turned to the examination and problematization of our own bodies (especially evident in feminist sociological interest in diet, reproduction, cosmetic implant technologies etc.) interest, as Shilling (1993) has pointed out, is not so much *from* the body but *about* it. A scientific distance toward the body as a knowable object of mind and increasingly a denaturalized object of science as a crowning accomplishment of Enlightenment reason, is the established mode of enquiry. The trajectory of disembodiment resulted from the Western cultural privileging of the self-conscious individual self that valued, historically, the subjugation of the flesh for the achievement of religious goals, and post-Enlightenment, for the achievement of reasoned, dispassionate, appraising selves.[1] Now, postmodern body practices encourage a manipulation and technologization of the body to ensure its viability as an object of visual desire. Of course, alongside these culturally privileged values and goals, competing body-self practices among the 'masses' continued. But the processes of institutionalization, and modern industrial production, ensured that these counter-practices were subjugated and delegitimated.

Sociology is a discursive product of the culmination of the Enlightenment's vision and modernity's technologies. Our modes of knowledge and enquiry are exemplars of a modern condition typified by rationalization and secularization, by production and consumption. Practitioners in the field are full participants in that same project, actively reproducing it in their constructions of knowledge. By the mid-twentieth century the professionalization of sociologists into the professional managerial classes (Eyerman, 1990; Gouldner, 1985; Turner, 1994) relegated competing and counter-narratives within the dominant modern trajectory to further marginalization.

The necessity of distance from the body for the achievement of the dispassionate rational self and scientific enquirer rendered the body – one's own and others' – an abstracted object. Dissociation from conscious feeling of one's own body, other than within a culturally prescribed and delimited arena that included selective recognition of pain and disease, assisted the objectification of all bodies, and the disembodiment of the enquirer. Importantly, within the psychoanalytic tradition a recognition of bodily knowledge, bodily memories and somatic expression of affective pain and desire was maintained. Similarly, the symbolic interactionist work of Goffman in particular (1959, 1967) described and interpreted the engagement of the body in social interactions and meaning-making systems. But these interests rarely challenged the prevalence of the scientifically abstracted gaze upon such bodily experiences.

The typical professionalization and institutionalization of sociology ensured that sociology and sociologists assumed the functions of dispassionately analysing and serving the processes and problems of societal modernization. The differentiation of sociology within the social sciences also ensured that attention to grand scale social processes, structures and systems increasingly prevailed over micro-social phenomena, including the body and psyche. Such interests were deferred to other disciplines such as anthropology and psychology, in turn discretely differentiated and disciplined. Differentiation and consolidation of sociology as a profession incorporated into economic and bureaucratic systems institutionalized the gaze and mode of enquiry of modern rationalized science.

Predominantly, the critical voices raised against modern instrumental delimitation of human beings and of social enquiry were those of theorists closely echoing the criticisms of the classical thinkers, most especially Marx, Durkheim, Weber and Freud. The Frankfurt School theorists especially pointed to the losses and distortions of human potentialities generated by the dominance of modern rationalization. Their later descendants added criticism of an incorporated, functionalist sociology to the critical agenda. For the Frankfurt School (notably Horkheimer and Adorno, 1972 and Reich, 1972), for Merleau-Ponty and the emergent feminist commentary, social and cultural critique included a concern with bodiliness and subjective experience. The feminists particularly criticized an embedded masculinist distortion that normalized detached, objective, technocratic rationalities, and their social and affective outcomes (Bordo and Jaggar, 1989; Chodorow, 1974; Griffin, 1978; Martin, 1987).

Alienation, anomie, disenchantment, surplus repression, sexual domination – the persistent criticisms of the classical and critical theorists – all bespoke a recognition of the costs of a dispirited, disembodied, modern rationalization on human beings and human bodies. Of course, sociology did to some extent retain this critical dimension but it did not seriously theorize a critique that reintegrated sensory (let alone spiritual) dimensions of human being. Sociology did not encompass an embodied, immanent, theory of the body. Its attention was directed toward grand and mezzo scale social structures and processes in modern industrial societies ironically devoid of a body.

The social contexts in which these developments in theory and society took place include not just those of modern institutionalization but the material and discursive practices of production. Modern industrialism required subjugated, disciplined, producer bodies. Bodies accommodating to and shaped by the rhythms of industrial machine technology and minds reasoned to serve the attainment of 'higher' goals and needs facilitated (and required) a gradual dissociation from physical feeling states and emotional feelings. Physically, and culturally, distanced from the rhythms of the natural world – season, weather, daylight and darkness – industrialized human beings manifested a drive to rationalize, and control, all spheres of life. The efforts of ruling elites to control and discipline the vagaries of human beings in the service of production were directed through the immediacy of the materiality of their bodies. The subjugation of nature, all nature, required a disparagement of sensuality and feeling, of pain and affect and a valuing of intellectual labour over physical labour, of 'cultural' pursuits over sexuality. Of course, human beings did not stop feeling their bodies nor medically attending to them. But these attentions were mediated with enduring ambivalence and contradiction.

The social scientific objectification of the body produced extensive literature describing and analysing the ways in which bodies are presented and displayed, used as significations of social strata and power, and socially and culturally reproduced. The multiple functions of bodies, like those of other social processes and relations, were extensively interrogated and mapped. Inner bodily events, such as emotion and psychosomatic affect, were largely ignored or interpreted as functions of social interactions (Goffman, 1959; Mead, 1934), or marginalized with psychoanalysis throughout the mid-twentieth century.

Importantly influencing the anthropological tradition somewhat more than that of sociology, is the work of the phenomenologist Merleau-Ponty. Merleau-Ponty challenged the Cartesian view of the body, and the body/culture dualism retained by the modern critics. Influenced by Freud and psychoanalysis, Merleau-Ponty argued for the body as the agent of experience, and the basis for all knowledge (Merleau-Ponty, [1946] 1962). It is primarily through the body that persons perceive the world and gain access to the world. For Merleau-Ponty the 'body-subject' is the basis of human subjectivity and intersubjectivity.

Feminist theorists of the 1970s shared, variously, Merleau-Ponty's view of the body-subject (for example, Eisenstein, 1984; Griffin, 1978; O'Brien, 1981). They argued for recognition of the materiality of the body in social practices of domination, violence and marginalization, as well as in constructions of gender and identity. Their arguments for a natural, embodied basis of human being and human society have more recently been criticized by contemporary feminist theorists for their modern 'naturalist essentialism' and dualism.

Although many of the modern critics have been forgotten in the current postmodern discourse on bodies and selves, modern (and premodern, see Synnott, 1993) ambivalence toward the body continues to be evident in the postmodern discourse of the body. The resurgence of popular cultural interest in the body in recent decades, from the 1960s efforts to emancipate the body through sexual liberation to the various bodily practices of the 1990s, including exercise and fitness regimes, alternative health and medical practices, yoga, and the like, are raised within a dominant Western discourse that privileges the intellectual over the physical, the rational over the emotional. For Melucci, the discourse on the body is 'simultaneously a continuation of and a challenge to the rationalization processes going on in the West' (1996: 151).

In similar vein, the recent growth in a sociology of emotions endeavours to describe and analyse the connections between body and feeling, and the social (for example, Bendelow and Williams, 1998; Harre, 1986; Hochschild, 1983; Kemper, 1990; Scherer and Ekman, 1984; Williams and Bendelow, 1996). Yet this development, too, is considerably influenced by postmodern and poststructural theories in cultural sociology that has lead many to dispute and reject a bodily role in emotions. Gergen's influential constructionist psychology (1994), an exemplar of this development, argues for 'emotion as relationship', that emotions are 'cultural constructions' without any a priori biological propensity. Biology is admitted, for Gergen, to the degree that, 'to *perform the emotions properly* . . . may require a substantial biological contribution (heart rate, blood pressure, and so on)' (Gergen, 1994: 221, emphasis added).

Generally, then, the considerable growth in sociological and cultural interest in the body reflects the new prominence of the body in social practice. Yet, paradoxically, for all the promise of this new scholarly interest in the body there is not much bodiliness in it. To date, sociologies of the body have largely continued modern science's dissociated detachment from the body. There is much interest in body fashioning, from cosmetic surgery, body piercing, diet, shape, colour, sexual identities, and varieties of identity-expression and display, and so forth. Yet the body continues to be treated in theory, either materially or discursively, as an empirical object. And in popular practice the body is treated as the object, or surface, of a now fragmented and dispersed self-project. The objectification and disembodiment of the body is retained and an embodied experiential interest continues to be rare.

Many contemporary efforts to gaze upon the body have brought with them modern positivism's dispassionate, abstracted, dissociated methods and instruments. The feminists of a few decades ago, who insisted that violence upon the body of a woman was unalterably, profoundly, both personally bodily and social, and who tried to sensitize, as well as politicize, sociology have been surpassed by poststructuralist feminisms. By the 1990s most feminist and other cultural theorists within sociology have relinquished those earlier political projects and see in the poststructural dissolution of the subject-body-self opportunities of freedom from structural fixities and biological delimitation and for multiple reconstructions of malleable identities.[2]

No body, no self

The now well-documented crisis in Western social thought over the past few decades has fuelled the search for other 'sites' of political and intellectual activity other than, as I have noted elsewhere, those of economy, pro- duction and class (Casey, 1995). The turn to culture (for many post- structurally abstracted from economy) influenced by the 'new' French philosophy and social theory of recent decades has profoundly and irrevoc- ably challenged modern thought and generated a thorough calling into question of most of Western philosophical assumptions and social institu- tions. The vitality in this movement has, though, in many instances been circumvented in an incorporated, commodified version of poststructuralism (and constructionism) that sees, in the academy at least, a now ready acceptance of the collapse of all Western meta-narratives and an incredulity toward many pivotal modern categories. Among them is a problematizing of the modern concept of self. A seemingly popular contemporary theor- etical reconstitution of modern industrialism's individual self substitutes the narrative and practice of the individual as consumer and identity-maker, ostensibly free of any fixed signification by class, gender, traditional insti- tutional locus, or biology, as the successor of the modern, allegedly tran- scendental, individual self. Discursively constructed de-differentiated relational selves (Gergen, 1994) are freer than ever before to construct variable self-identities from a marketplace of commodities, ideas, cultural bric-à-brac and sexualities. The domain for this accomplishment is the surface (and surfaced inner) of the body.

The body has assumed a new prominence in both cultural theory and popular practice at the very time in which the role of subject-self has been decentred and denigrated, and reconstituted as identity-making consumer. Ironically, in the political and economic arena, the body assumes a heightened role in identity politics, human rights and contestations over technological interventions and health rights as the modern subject-self is fractured and dispersed. In sociology, the influence of French theory, particularly that of Foucault, Derrida, Lacan, has brought a view on the subject-self that deconstructs sociology's modern category. At a time of theoretical hesitation and circumspection within modern sociology the poststructural contestation and formulation has been variously adopted.

In rejecting an Enlightenment humanist, transcendental subject self, Foucault's (1980) widely influential theorization proposes a discursive construction of subjective identity and the body as products of power/ discourse – power that is always already there. Yet Foucault displayed a persistent ambivalence toward the body. On the one hand, the body is a historically contingent discursively determined product without an agentic self, and on the other the body is an entity, a site of desire, pleasure and resistances that may be practised through variable constructions and expressions of identities. Resistance and construction assume some form of agentic subject reminiscent of the humanist self. As Foucault's body disappears in power/knowledge schema, he ironically tries to retain, as Turner points out (Turner, 1994: 38), a sort of 'natural', pre-social and apolitical emanation of the body. It is this site, however desocialized and depoliticized, upon which new forms of subjectivity may arise. While there is no escaping of discourse and power, for the Foucauldians, the use of the body as a site of identity and resistance, even though ultimately incorporated, substitutes for the modern 'transcendent' agentic subject.

The discursive invasion of the body that renders all experience constituted through language – for the Lacanians even unconscious experience is linguistic – eliminates admission of pre-cultural substrates or non-cultural and co-constituent dimensions, including the biological. The materiality of the body, insisted upon by Foucault (1980), is not so much a fleshy, organic materiality, but an abstract object of power and semiotics. For the Foucauldians, discursive practices, which are at once products and conduits of (external) power/knowledge, construct and position subjectivities which are inscribed upon the body. The natal materiality of the body is immediately, and already, discursively inscribed leaving no spaces for sensual experiences uncolonized, and unrepresented, by discourse. The body is knowable only as a discursive product, and linguistic representation. Although ostensibly insisting on a bodily materiality – against ideological structural materialism – poststructuralism engenders a dematerialization and denaturalization of the body and completes the discursive dissolution of the modern agentic self. Culture is thereby entirely privileged over nature, to the extent, as Melucci (1996) points out, of a dismissive eradication of nature.

None the less, many commentators point out that poststructural theories of decentred subjectivities and dissolved body-selves open up intellectual and political possibilities through recognizing the cultural variability and arbitrariness of social and political practices. Modern (and pre-modern) political subjugation and structural fixation of natural, gendered, subaltern subject-selves and social roles give way to postmodern freeplay and multiplicities of meaning and being. Pluralities of identity display and deployment of the body are illustrative of poststructural freeplay of signification and postmodern subjectivity. Yet, these possibilities of identity are composed, and delimited, within discursive practice. A non-discursive, language-refusing phenomenon of bodily being is excluded by the hegemony of discursive cultural practice over all human experience. As subject-selves fragment into nodes of power relations from which even counter-practice is reduced to bodily-inscribed identity play, bodies and bodily being are elided and rendered obsolete. Poststructural freeplay celebrates a routinized, normalized, dissociation from the materiality and organic sense of the body through its substitution as image – a disembodied product of discursive practice. Representation as disembodied image displaces non-linguistic experience.

Psychologists along with sociologists and cultural theorists have now joined the debates on social constructionism and postmodern contestations to modern forms of knowledge. For some the debate is a continuation of the 'nature/nurture' debate long contested with their colleagues in the biological sciences. For others, the constructionist derivation of European cultural theory embraces not only the dissolution of the modern individual subject-self but its biological constituents as well. Gergen (1994), as an exemplary proponent of this argument, points to the discovery of considerable cultural variation in emotional expression and in emotional meaning constructs. Variation and contingency prompts the rejection not only of modern scientific constructions of universal and objective facts, but the rejection of biology as constitutive of human being as well. In this view, biology, as a modern narrative, has no irrefutable grounds upon which to claim 'natural' biological elements and propensities universal to human beings and distinct from cultural creation. For constructionist psychologists, emotions, like bodies, are culturally discursive constructs that use biological faculties in their presentation.

Constructionist psychology extends the discursive construction of human being beyond self-identity constructs to all biological rudiments as well. Biological features and differences are themselves discursively constructed. In this view, there are multiple natures variously constructed by historically variant cultural processes. Biology's contribution to human being is simply the raw material upon which cultural discursive practices construct subjectivity, motivation and meaning. There is no nature, no biology, outside of that which is culturally produced, selected and discursively meaningful and legitimated.

The body is thus rendered another text (a product of discursive practices) that may be variously represented in images, symbols and words. Textual bodies are highly malleable and open to considerable variation in identity constructions and representations. Disembodied and abstracted textual bodies are dissociated from feeling and sensing domains of human being that are not constituted by language – indeed such domains are precluded by insistent textual rendition. The enduring physicality of violence, pain and normalized political-economic oppression exercised upon the bodies of human beings by others may be denied through discursive dissociation. The discursive constitution and textual representation of all experience is upheld as the means by which human beings are produced and reproduced, and by which they are knowable. Knowledge of the body is mediated through the abstraction of representations of the body. All other knowledges – non-linguistic, sensory, spiritual – are subjugated and dissociated (but not silenced).[3]

The dissolution of the self as subject and the denaturing of the body that have assumed an ascendant position in postmodern criticism and cultural and social theory, have rendered the obsolescence of the body, and the assertion of denaturalization as the successor to Cartesian dualism. Domination gives way to dissolution.

The growing literature on postmodern bodies and identities predominantly focuses on aspects of image, style and various technologies of body and identity configuration. There is much endorsement of the apparent freedom from naturalistic and gendered fixities and delimitations. Constructed only by cultural processes, it is argued, persons are 'free' to use and appropriate diverse cultural elements in the service of configuring and reinventing their identities and bodies. Diffuse selves may variably constitute themselves abstracted from broader social and political processes and relations. Despite criticism from some sociologists of the body (for example, Mellor and Shilling, 1997; Turner, 1984), much of the new cultural and social theorizing tends towards an acceptance, more or less, of the subjective identity schema proposed by Foucault. Resistance (curiously retained from an older modern politics) may now be practised through localized identity presentations that avoid altogether broader social and political conditions, and through insurgent pluralities of meaning and knowledge as counter-practice.

These developments obscure and deepen the conditions and experience of the quintessentially modern problematic: alienation. Alienation, as the denudation of self and the loss of human agency, vigorously contested under modern conditions, is now normalized in postmodern conditions. As Wexler has pointed out, 'both the disease and the cure are now more extreme' (Wexler, 1996: 159). The conditions for a more serious, and not regressively playful, counter-practice and for self-creation are forged, in the first instance, through recognition that the apparent palliative offered to chronically anxious modern selves by postmodern dissociation and disembodiment of body-self is an exacerbation of modern alienation, not a solution to it.

Renewing sociology: from the body

The postmodern dissolution of self, and body, is incomplete. While the subject self is displaced into identity and surface representation of discursive playfulness, the body, and bodiliness, has not disappeared. Dissociated and disembodied, the subject is none the less effortful. Attention is fixed on the image of the subject, as its substance erodes. Cultural critic Christopher Lasch argued that modern capitalist America had produced a culture of narcissism in which self, though ostensibly gratified in vast opportunities for consumption and assertion, was weakened and eroded by attachments to its image, and by over-reliance on external technological experts. Lasch's criticisms, often misunderstood as egocentrism that required a reinstatement of traditional repressions and authorities, described the dissolution of a character-self that Lasch argued is achieved through agentic processes of maturation through engagement in communities of recognition, enablement and delimitation (Lasch, 1978, 1984).

Lasch's criticisms of modern theoretical degradation and the narcissistic loss of self in a technologized consumer, survivalist culture seem even more pertinent in contemporary conditions. The postmodern dissolution of self, and dissociated disembodiment generates a normalization of alienation, and the abandonment of a project of self-creation. Although the initial movement of liberating the overly repressed, rigidly controlled modern industrial self signified an emancipatory break, this effort too has foundered in excess.

Dissolution and disembodiment offer only momentary release and not a creative, generative, emancipation.

The image of the now hyperalienated modern self is the object of post-modern narcissistic attachment. Postmodern cultural theory that postulates the dissolution of the modern agentic self offers in its place a subject identity that is pursued and constructed through consumption and display of the products – especially discourse, image and sign – of post-industrial production and alienated labour. Postmodern narcissism that denies both self and body forecloses the space in which subjective-embodied-self may be created, and in which intersubjective relatedness with other may be discovered.

The narcissistic dissolution of the self (the Greek myth describes Narcissus's loss of self through his attachment to his image) may, however, enable, after the postmodern cultural loss of the modern over-individuated repressed self, the creation of a new self – an embodied, relational, agentic and flexible yet delimited self. Narcissistic loss may be mobilized into growth and re-creation (ironically) by relinquishing the fixation on image and discourse and the eliding of the body. The regressive linguistic play-fulness celebrated in poststructural cultural theory may give rise to growth, or decay slowly with the beautiful Narcissus.

Recent popular efforts in sociological work to liberate the structuration of Cartesian dualism have thus far resulted in a tendency to dissolve the nature/culture dualism through a privileging of culture and the foreclosure of a non-cultural domain. Various iterations of Derrida's 'there is nothing outside the text' have generated, in particular, a current normalization in social and cultural theory of an over-socialized account of the body. The denigration of biological constituents of human being in a relegation of these elements and of biology itself to cultural discursivity only furthers the polarization and entrenchments typical of the science and culture debate. It is as fruitless to reject biological constituents and biological arguments outright as it is to assert their determinancy. Notwithstanding considerable cultural variation in the manifestation and value of body expression, extensive research in the neurosciences and human development indicates that there is (at least) a degree of pre-cultural – and non-cultural – sub-strate in human beings. It is pre-eminently anthropocentric to claim that culture determines humans and genetics determines all other life forms. For cultural theory to ignore recent extensive research in human development as culturally constructed empiricism and therefore dismissible outright is to assert a discursive determinancy that is as untenable as a conventional modern scientific positivism.

The recent popularity of discussions on essentialism, universalities, reductionism and indeterminacy, and so forth, thus far still displays attachments to points of view representing old polarities between cultural and social theories and science. Current social and cultural theory tends to reinvoke those polarities in its very efforts to privilege culture and dis-cursivity over phenomenology. An examination of the scientific literature, particularly biology and psychology, indicates that the theoretical impasse between culture and nature may have deepened. Yet social and cultural theory may move beyond the current apparent impasse through a self-reflexive examination of newly current orthodoxies, a reconsideration of nature and a new attention to non-cultural dimensions of human being. We may look to the neurosciences and human development research (for example, Greenfield, 1997; Oswald, 1989; Pinel, 1993; Van der Kolk, 1994), in which recent work argues for relationships between body and culture that are continuously interactive and malleable, and which already offers new formulations of these categories.

We may, in the first instance, consider the empirical embodiment of the human infant at birth, immediately entering cultural and discursive practices, yet in possession of strata that are pre-cultural, and non-cultural – prepared to be shaped by culture from and near birth. This 'natural' state of the neonate occurs notwithstanding the actuality that reproduction may be culturally chosen and technologically assisted. A pre-cultural and non-linguistic 'substrate' includes a range of propensities and attributes of human babies that are biologically hardwired, and universally found in human beings across culture, geography and history. At the very least these elements include propensities for bonding with caregivers, for the acquisition of language, for physiological masteries (perception, muscular coordination, mobility etc.) and for an affective repertoire that are all subsequently culturally selected and experientially learned and inscribed.

The extensive recent empirical research in human development and neurological science challenges those cultural essentialists now prevailing in sociology and social theory to reconsider biological imperatives in disposing the neonate to cultural development. At the same time, the new research challenges overly biological theories of human development. Particularly important is the high malleability of the infant brain, in which social and physiological developmental experience organize the structures of the brain and shape its ongoing development (Greenfield, 1997). High malleability continues through early childhood and varying degrees of malleability continue thereafter. Structural organization is consequent of the infant's learned social experiences in those early years which then pattern the responses and effects of later experiences. In establishing that the human brain is a malleable organ, it is throughout the life course interactive with social experience and co-constitutive of it, the importance of both cultural and biological processes in the construction of body-selves is recognized.

There are complex social and political reasons for the rise in popularity of poststructuralism and constructionism in social and cultural theory, and the rejection of biological, and other, empiricisms. The current rise of constructionist theories in the social sciences – in particular in those with the most scientific heritage, for example, cognitive and behavioural psychologies – may be in part a reaction to the dominance of the modern biological sciences and their assumptions of universality and determinancy for more aspects of human being than was warranted. But for the constructionist psychology as enunciated by Gergen (1994) to privilege itself over all knowledges and materialities, to dissolve bodies into figments of discourse is just as universalizing and essentialist as the paternal science that begot them and which they have endeavoured to kill off.

The readmission of biology and 'nature' to cultural theory in sociology, although important, may, however, simply retain a nature/culture dualist continuum that is theoretically 'managed' by drawing more flexible borderlines and domain boundaries. We need to go further than that.

Embodied subjectivity

While there is now a popular emphasis on the body and the use of the term body, these efforts lack a sense of bodiliness, invoking instead an idea of the body as a synonym, or substitute, for self or person. The objectification of bodies as 'things' without subjectivity, intentionality or agency, precludes the possibility of intersubjectivity rendering relations between persons relations between objects. This eliding of subjectivity facilitates the treatment of other humans as objects of utility and of violent subjugation. Social theorists cannot ignore the climate of violence in Western societies as the context in which theories of a dissolved subject and denatured body abound. Against hegemonic, disembodied cultural essentialism we may endeavour to develop theoretical and practical formulations that encompass, or return, the body as *source of subjectivity*, not just as the natural ground of cultural formation. Recent anthropological theory, such as Csordas (1994a, 1994b), drawing on Merleau-Ponty and Ricoeur, offers a creative turn.

Csordas (1994a, 1994b) argues for being-in-the-world, a term from the phenomenological tradition, to evoke a sense of existential immediacy. For Csordas, this immediacy is 'temporally/historically informed sensory presence and engagement' (Csordas, 1994a: 10). Csordas seeks to place the body as a central analytic theme, 'the existential ground of culture and self'. Csordas stresses the distinction between representation and being-in-the-world: 'Representation is fundamentally nominal, and hence we can speak of "a representation." Being-in-the-world is fundamentally conditional, and hence we must speak of "existence" and "lived experience"' (p. 10).

Against the culturalist view that language wholly constitutes experience, Csordas, following Ricoeur, argues that language gives access to the world of experience in so far as experience is brought to language. Ricoeur refers to the 'derivative character of linguistic meaning . . . It is necessary to say first what comes to language' (cited in Csordas, 1994a: 11). Language, we might say, *evokes* rather than represents bodily experience as the source of subjectivity. In this sense, then, it becomes possible not simply to speak *of* the body but *from* the body.

Recognizing not just the elements of biological distinctiveness and propensities in shaping bodies as shaped by cultures, but recognizing our bodily being in the world can allow for new listenings and new awareness to occur. These new awarenesses are not only those of the individual body-self – yet that is where we must begin – they are awarenesses of bodily selves that can reawaken relations between others that are embodied. The dissociated normalization of violence against others, the denial of the subject, and the denial therefore of intersubjectivity, prevalent in contemporary society, may be altered by a new theory of, and lived practice of, an embodied intersubjectivity.

Returning the body as a material, language-refusing, co-constituent of socially produced body-selves may refine constructionism's new hegemony and reopen questions and possibilities for the self project in conditions that are at once institutionally constructed and defied. As Melucci says: 'not everything has been said . . .' (Melucci, 1996: 143) – nor, I would add, can be, nor should be.

Returning to the body, even if initially regressive, may enable an embodied new self-project to be creatively, relationally, embarked upon. Sensing (knowing through sensory and affective processes) our bodies regenerates the rudiments of self through which, and by which, relational 'mutually recognizing' (Benjamin, 1988, 1995) selves may be created. Mutually recognizing selves are not the over-individuated monadic self of Cartesian modern thought, nor the subjectively dissolved figments of discourse for Foucault and Lacan and their followers, nor also similarly the over-culturalized, de-differentiated nodes of constructionism as depicted by Gergen's (1994) psychology of relationships.

What might we sense and know if we listen to the body? We may feel sensations as non-linguistic myriad expressions of pain and pleasure, need and sorrow, contentment and joy. We may sense fear and anxiety, hope and excitement, long silenced by language and speech acts that evoke not simply regressive longings but progressive and ingressive energies of being. We may sense knowledges of experiences long forgotten by the mind but always known by the body before language was privileged as the sole representer of knowledge and experience. And we may sense present experience and bodily knowledge that refuses and surpasses language. We may sense a knowledge of mortality and fragility that belongs uniquely to the body, and we may sense a new or restored sensory recognition of the other's body. While these feelings can never be entirely communicable to others they can awaken a recognition and honouring of the bodiliness, and embodied being, of others.

If such senses are indeed rediscovered and restored, we may awaken a dimension of human being that undoes the dissociation from oneself and from embodied otherness that could not only expand and enhance experience of being human but herald new forms of social theory and practice. A new ethic – an ethic of being-*with*-in-the-world – may be discovered and practised. Such a project, already emergent in social theory after postmodernism, would, as Smart, following Levinas (and Weber), suggests, restore discussion of 'ultimate and sublime' values, and moral, ethical and political concerns to a central focus of analytic attention (Smart, 1996: 76).

Conclusion

The rising interest in the body may encourage sociology to return from dissociative absence – and absence initially resultant from an over-zealous subjugation of the body in pursuit of rational science and social order and more recently through an eliding of the body through adoption of cultural theories that dissolve materiality into discourse and sign. The dominance of semiotics over phenomenology in cultural theory, the constitution and reading of the body as text, exacerbate postmodern alienation and dissociative refusal.

The post-Marxist numbing of feeling and its displacement in vigorous sensual treatments – diet, exercise, piercing, medications, and visual, textual division – may well be historically and politically understandable, but as popular practice is already indicating, a more growthful renewal of engaged theory is required, and indeed, is emerging. In popular practice the growing interest in various body practices that bring the body to the foreground may indicate the path social and cultural theory may follow, even if it is no longer able to lead discussion of cultural ideas. The struggle against alienation is now more complex as the condition has become more obscure, and as professional interests in the academy are distracted from the historical intellectual task of leading critical debate. A revitalized sociology would allow space for non-discursive silence, for a sensing attentiveness, and for a groundedness in the body as a powerful potential for change. It would involve, too, a recognition of the generative contribution enabled by postmodernism's breaking up of modern rationalities, logocentricism and rigid congealment. Such a move would avert the implosion precipitant in a postmodern acceptance of cultural essentialism and domination through dissolution of body-selves. A much more creative path is before us.

Melucci again:

> (T)aking cognizance of the body in our everyday life fosters awareness of ongoing change; it brings to light neglected or unknown levels of experience. Paying attention to the body is therefore essential, but it also constitutes a provisional stage along the road to awareness, one point of view that may reveal another and bring hidden questions to the surface. The body is a message to be listened to, to be deciphered, to be answered. (Melucci, 1996: 74)

And further: 'Once the process of an experiential approach to the body is triggered through new forms of awareness, it can never be entirely controlled again' (p. 151).

Such a listening and responding may lead to a revitalization and transformation of social theory and of social practice to open up. It may delimit modern hypertrophy, technocratic rationalities and instrumental materiality and open new agendas of discussion. Sensing the body again in sociology is a first step toward discussing those questions of ultimate value that earlier sociologists made central to their task.

Notes

1 Foucault (1988) described the pre-history of self-reflection and the encouragement of 'technologies of self' that religious (Greco, Judaeo, Christian) discourses produced.

2 Of course, some feminists have criticized this tendency and have argued against the abandonment of modern feminism pointing out that the deconstruction of the category 'woman' has come about at the very moment at which women have gained greater recognition of subjective agency (see, e.g. Bordo, 1990; Fraser and Nicholson, 1990).

3 The subjugation and de-legitimation of such bodily knowledges that may none the less find expression in the body have typically being labelled, for instance, as paraesthesia, somatism, hallucinatory sensation, religious hysteria.

References

Bendelow, Gillian and Williams, Simon (eds) (1988) *Emotions in Social Life: Critical Themes and Contemporary Issues*. London: Routledge.

Benjamin, Jessica (1988) *The Bonds of Love: Psychoanalysis, Feminism and the Problem of Domination*. New York: Pantheon.

Benjamin, Jessica (1995) *Like Subjects, Love Objects*. New Haven, CT: Yale University Press.

Bordo, Susan (1990) 'Feminism, postmodernism, and gender-sceptism', in Linda Nicholson (ed.), *Feminism/Postmodernism*. London: Routledge.

Bordo, S. and Jaggar, A. (eds) (1989) *Gender/Body/Knowledge: Feminist Reconstructions of Being and Knowing*. New Brunswick, NJ: Rutgers University Press.

Casey, Catherine (1995) *Work, Self and Society: After Industrialism*. London and New York: Routledge.

Chodorow, Nancy (1974) *The Reproduction of Mothering*. Berkeley, CA: University of California Press.

Crossley, N. (1997) 'Corporeality and communicative action: embodying the renewal of critical theory', *Body and Society*, 3 (1): 17–47.

Csordas, Thomas J. (ed.) (1994a) *Embodiment and Experience: The Existential Ground of Culture and Self*. Cambridge: Cambridge University Press.

Csordas, Thomas J. (1994b) *The Sacred Self: a Cultural Phenomenology of Charismatic Healing*. Berkeley, CA: University of California Press.

Eisenstein, Hester (1984) *Contemporary Feminist Thought*. London: Allen & Unwin.

Eyerman, Ron (1990) 'Intellectuals and progress: the origins, decline, and revival of a critical group', in Jeffrey Alexander and Piotre Sztompka (eds), *Rethinking Progress: Movements, Forces and Ideas at the End of the Twentieth Century*. Boston, MA: Unwin Hyman.

Featherstone, M., Hepworth, M. and Turner, B.S. (eds) (1991) *The Body: Social Processes and Cultural Theory*. London: Sage.

Foucault, Michel (1980) *Power/Knowledge: Selected Interviews and Other Writings, 1972–1977* (ed. Colin Gordon). New York: Pantheon Books.

Foucault, Michel (1988) *Technologies of the Self* (eds L. Martin, H. Gutman, P. Hutton). Amherst, MA: University of Massachusetts.

Frank, Arthur (1991) 'For a sociology of the body: an analytical review', in M. Featherstone, M. Hepworth and B.S. Turner (eds) *The Body: Social Processes and Cultural Theory*. London: Sage.

Fraser, Nancy and Nicholson, Linda (1990) 'Social criticism without philosophy: an encounter between feminism and postmodernism', in Linda Nicholson (ed.), *Feminism/Postmodernism*. London: Routledge.

Gergen, Kenneth J. (1994) *Realities and Relationships: Soundings in Social Construction*. Cambridge, MA: Harvard University Press.

Goffman, E. (1959) *The Presentation of Self in Everyday Life*. New York: Doubleday.

Goffman, E. (1967) *Interaction Ritual*. New York: Doubleday.

Gouldner, Alvin (1985) *Against Fragmentation: The Origins of Marxism and the Sociology of Intellectuals*. New York: Oxford University Press.

Greenfield, Susan (1997) *The Human Brain*. London: Weidenfeld & Nicolson.

Griffin, S. (1978) *Women and Nature: The Roaring Inside Her*. New York: Harper & Row.

Harre, R. (ed.) (1986) *The Social Construction of Emotions*. New York: Basil Blackwell.

Harre, R. (1991) *Physical Being: a Theory for a Corporeal Psychology*. Oxford: Blackwell.

Hochschild, Arlie (1983) *The Managed Heart*. Berkeley, CA: University of California Press.

Horkheimer, M. and Adorno, T.W. (1972) *Dialectic of Enlightenment*. NY: Herder and Herder.

Kemper, Theodore D. (ed.) (1990) *Research Agendas in the Sociology of Emotions*. New York: SUNY Press.

Lasch, Christopher (1978) *The Culture of Narcissism*. New York: Warner Books.

Lasch, Christopher (1984) *The Minimal Self*. New York: W.W. Norton.

Martin, E. (1987) *The Body in the Woman*. Milton Keynes: Open University Press.

Mead, George Herbert (1934) *Mind, Self and Society*. Chicago: Chicago University Press.

Mellor, Philip and Shilling, Chris (1997) *Re-forming the Body: Religion, Community and Modernity*. London: Sage.

Melucci, Alberto (1996) *The Playing Self: Person and Meaning in the Planetary Society*. Cambridge: Cambridge University Press.

Merleau-Ponty, Maurice ([1946]/1962) *The Phenomenology of Perception* (trans. Colin Smith). London: Routledge & Kegan Paul.

O'Brien, M. (1981) *The Politics of Reproduction*. London: Routledge & Kegan Paul.

Oswald, S. (1989) *Principles of Cellular, Molecular and Developmental Neuroscience*. New York: Springer-Verlag.

Pinel, J.P.J. (1993) *Biopsyschology*, 2nd edn. Boston: Allyn & Bacon.

Reich, Wilhelm (1972) *Sex-Pol Essays, 1929–1934* (ed. L. Baxandall). New York: Vintage Press.

Scherer, Klaus R. and Ekman, Paul (eds) (1984) *Approaches to Emotion*. Hillsdale, NJ: Lawrence Erlbaum and Associates.

Shilling, Chris (1993) *The Body and Social Theory*. London: Sage.

Synnott, Anthony (1993) *The Body Social: Symbolism, Self and Society*. London and New York: Routledge.

Smart, Barry (1996) 'Facing the body – Goffman, Levinas and the subject of ethics', *Body and Society*, 2 (2): 67–78.

Taylor, Charles (1989) *Sources of the Self: The Making of Modern Identity*. Cambridge, MA: Harvard University Press.

Turner, Bryan S. (1984) *The Body and Society*. Oxford: Blackwell.

Turner, T. (1994) 'Bodies and anti-bodies: flesh and fetish in contemporary social theory', in Thomas J. Csordas (ed.), *Embodiment and Experience: The Existential Ground of Culture and Self*. Cambridge: Cambridge University Press.

Van der Kolk, Bassel (1994) 'The body keeps the score: memory and the evolving psychobiology of post traumatic stress', *Harvard Review of Psychiatry*, 1: 253–65.

Wexler, Philip (1996) 'Alienation, new age sociology and the Jewish way', in Felix Geyer (ed.), *Alienation, Ethnicity and Postmodernism*. London: Greenwood.

Williams, Simon J. and Bendelow, Gillian A. (1996) 'The "emotional" body', *Body and Society*, 2 (3): 125–39.

4   Manufacturing Bodies: Flesh, Organization, Cyborgs

Martin Parker

Not surprisingly, forms of (human) organization are very often conceptualized as (human) bodies.[1] After all, we humans assume that everyone has
knowledge about bodies – their own and others – and it is not a big leap to
suggest that we could use that knowledge to illuminate aspects of what is
usually termed 'the social'. So Hobbes's Leviathan has a head, fists and
heart; Spencer or Durkheim's society has 'organic' characteristics; the
market has a 'hidden hand' and contemporary caring organizations have
senses, souls and voices. These are, as Bryan Turner notes, *persona universalis*, corporate bodies (1996: 80) that have a strangely solid, yet metaphorical, life. In this chapter I want to suggest that the organic is more than
just a metaphor where organization is concerned and that organizations *are*
forms of fleshy control. Again, this theme is not new – Weber's spread of
rationalization, Elias's civilizing process and Foucault's notion of disciplinary society suggest pretty much the same ideas. So, of course, does a
great deal of contemporary literature on social/cultural theory and the
body. However, in order to avoid a fetishism of flesh I want to suggest that
we conceptualize these bodies as cyborg ones, not as self-balancing biological entities. In other words, I am interested in exploring some of the
relations between human and non-human, some of the ways that combinations of materials (including flesh) discipline each other in organized
patterns. I refer to this as cyborganization (original term in Cooper and
Law, 1995 and elaborated in Parker, 1998; Parker and Cooper, 1998). Most
importantly, however, I want to show that including warm bodies as one
part of our social theory can lead to some cold conclusions, that flesh
doesn't entail humanism – but more of that later.

Most of the representations of bodies, machines and institutions that
circulate in contemporary academic work on organizations still rely on a
'common sense' dualism between humans and other things. You won't find
many cyborgs in an organizational behaviour textbook. This is despite the
fact that the cyborg has become an increasingly popular metaphor in many
other academic areas. Approaches vary; some writers engage from cultural
theory and literary theory (Best, 1989; Kuhn, 1990; Poster, 1992), others
from technology studies and social theory (Featherstone and Burrows,
1995; Gray, 1995; Haraway, 1991). This chapter will attempt to use

strategies from both of these literatures. I will begin with the former – making some comments about some science fiction books and films as texts that tell us something about the cyborg – and then move to some rather more abstract thinking around the notion of cyborganization and the body in relation to humanism.

Fetishizing flesh

So, why shouldn't we fetishize flesh? Contemporary social and cultural theory has shown a considerable rise of interest in the body over the past ten years (for example, Shilling, 1993; Synnott, 1993; Turner, 1996; and the journal *Body and Society*). No longer simply a metaphor for social structure, for the skeleton of society, it has become a topic of substantial concern in itself. The body has been manufactured as an object of socio-logical concern. Yet I wish to suggest that we should begin by being a little suspicious here and not accept this invitation without thinking rather hard about what it entails. It seems to me that there is a deceptive materialism implied in much of the interest in the body, as well as some therapeutic and ecocentric implications that need more critical scrutiny (see Barry and Hazen, 1996, for example). It is often implied that we are excavating down to some level, a substrate, from which analysis can 'really' begin (and hence 'really' end). What, after all, could be more material than the body? Once these fleshy foundations are clear then social and cultural analysts can describe and theorize how the body gets written upon, how it gets described, inscribed and organized for various purposes. But, equally importantly, they also now know where they stand and how they stand. In claiming something about bodies they have acknowledged both a 'natural limit' to the corrosive anti-empiricism and epistemological doubt that has defined contemporary social and cultural studies *as well as* defining a ground from which to continue the task of demonstrating (yet again) processes of social and cultural construction. Both claims can take place simultaneously; bodies can be written about and processes of embodiment can be theorized. In addition, of course, a new object of study is 'discovered', one that: 'requires an empirical focus, a research agenda, a commitment to a political perspective on the application of sociology, and an infrastructure of research, such as journals, publication series and international conferences' (Turner, 1996: 2). It seems that, even after we have 'discovered' the body, the industry and organization of social science rolls along unhindered by too many doubts, epistemological or otherwise.

But why shouldn't we regard bodies as a natural limit, as a material slap in the face for those idealists, anti-positivists, phenomenologists, relativists (or whoever) who believe that it is constructionism all the way down? For example, if we describe Fordism as the systematic manipulation of human muscle it could be suggested that this form of description is somehow more fundamental, more foundational, than other ways of telling Fordism. More basic than 'strategy', 'population ecology', 'late capitalism' or whatever other synthetic, 'higher level' term we might wish to attach to the material. What could be more defining of human beings than guts, bone and blood? What could be more fundamental to organizations than bodies synchronizing their movements? After all, Ford's inspiration for the moving conveyer belt was supposedly the moving line of carcasses in Chicago abattoirs (Burrell, 1997: 138). Well, as will hopefully become clear later, I don't really see why any category of thing in particular needs to be treated as foundational here. Human bodies are no more foundational than other material or non-material objects. Bodies can only synchronize their movements in an organizational context if they rely on other materials, so which are we to privilege – the clock, the meat cleaver, the accountant's ledger, the freezer or the butcher?

I am suggesting this largely because, loosely following the actor-network theory, or 'sociology of translation', of Latour, Callon et al. (see, for example, Law, 1994, and Lee and Brown, 1994 for a summary and critique), it seems that all these objects are given meaning *relationally*. In other words, they are nothing, mean nothing in themselves but these various bits of matter become something, do something, when they are combined with other things in systems or networks. Bodies, dead cows, metal hooks, beefburgers, slaughtermen and many other human and non-human actors make up organizations. They all become *actants*, points in a network that result in agency effects. My point is that human bodies are only one of the elements in what Seltzer calls the 'body–machine complex' (1992). Not the most important and not the least important – just one of the elements. In order to investigate the relationship between bodies and organizations in these terms I will, in this chapter, be attempting to treat human bodies as cyborgs – as human machine systems – which are in turn systematically combined into modes of 'cyborganization'. In other words, rather than thinking about bodies and organizations, I wish to suggest that the body (whatever 'body' includes and excludes) is actually just one of the many places from which we could begin thinking about organization – but if we elevate it too much we are likely to see little else.

Body/organization dualism

The problem here I think is mainly that, by identifying one category of things called 'bodies', and another category of things called 'organizations', we actually conceal rather a lot. *Homo separatus* is defined against the *persona universalis*, when they might both be *persona ficta* (Turner, 1996: 79). The dualism allows us to position agency, responsibility, causality and so on in one category rather than another. It allows us to elevate and privilege things in a way that ends up telling a familiar humanist story. By humanism here I mean an account that centres human beings as the measure of all other *things*. An account that only allows humans to possess agency, responsibility, causality and so on. The materials I will be using to argue this in the bulk of the chapter are texts that contain representations of cyborgs, simulants, synthetics, androids and so on. The most obvious (and common) argument made here is that many of these narratives tell us something about our ambivalent relationship to technology – fragile human flesh versus cold machines (see Kuhn, 1990 and Seltzer, 1992 for a literary historical review). From *Frankenstein* onwards, we moderns have told ourselves dark tales about the promises of liberation through the application of science. The liberation is often away from the various bondages of the body – less work, less pain – and towards bodily pleasures – comfort and leisure. Yet someway into the story the creation usually turns on its maker. After all, the dominant contemporary image of the cyborg is of a rampaging killing machine with infra-red eyes and guns for hands, or something with a human surface that conceals its incredible potential for technically assisted violence. In typically poststructuralist terms, the human side of the dualism both needs and is threatened by the non-humans on the other side.

The Czech dramatist Karel Capek introduced the word 'Robot' into English through his 1920 play *R.U.R* – 'Rossum's Universal Robots' – though the word itself was coined by his brother Josef (Scholes and Rabkin, 1977: 29). In the play the robots (from the Czech *robota* meaning drudgery, with connotations of serfdom) overthrow mankind and create a new Eden. Robots themselves are a little out of fashion now. Stupid and shaky versions of people in gleaming metal, like Robbie the robot in *Forbidden Planet* (1956), mad computers like Hal in *2001* (1968) or the patriarchal defence grid in *Colossus: The Forbin Project* (1969) have largely been replaced by rather more confusing combinations of real and artificial flesh, metal, plastic skin and positronic brains. Terminators, unisols, synthetics, robocops, androids and simulants in films like *Bladerunner* (1982), *Robocop* (1987), the *Terminator* films (1984, 1991), *Eve of Destruction* (1990) as well as the *Tetsuo* films (1989, 1991), *Cyborg* (1989), *Universal Soldier* (1993) and many others serve to demonstrate something about the importance of the machine-person as a contemporary cultural icon. These are visions of techno-golems. Entities manufactured through the grafting of hard shiny bits of metal into soft flesh – or even with skin that is really a sophisticated form of plastic and memories that are no more than a computer program.

Another common theme in these representations – one less often remarked – is that of the big corporation that has manufactured the cyborg. As I will show, very often these texts contain background references to some part of the state or the military–industrial complex that has, because of greed, ambition or paranoia, invested huge amounts of time and money in a non-human product. After all, it is important that we know that the first television cyborg cost (in 1973) the princely sum of six million dollars. Steve Austin, the *Six Million Dollar Man*, was a product manufactured for various kinds of dangerous espionage. Other cyborg products are similarly built for stigmatizing or dirty work, sub- or super-human labour in which normal human bodies would not last long. As Sanders suggests, they are 'devoid of feeling and free will, mere contraptions for the carrying-out of functions which are programmed from the outside' (1979: 141). That the cyborg then often rebels in a violent way is hence hardly surprising – this is no more than the romantic revolution of the oppressed against the oppressor. Since the cyborg workers are often programmed, given instructions by their makers that they have no choice but to follow, then the guilt for their actions hence lies with the scientists, generals or managers who wrote their software. The metaphor is fairly stark here. Bodies versus organizations, heroic agency versus shadowy conspiracy. After all, Taylor, Bedeaux, Gantt, Gilbreth and so on were attempting to control bodies – the bodies of their employees – in minute detail (see Seltzer, 1992, who compares this factory discipline to Baden-Powell's control of the bodies of boy scouts). Within the organization, aliens with little English like Schmidt needed to be disciplined, shaped, moulded before they could become useful. Like the workers in *Metropolis* (1926), *À Nous la Liberté* (1932) or Charlie Chaplin in *Modern Times* (1936), these bodies become part of factory or office machines. They are the fleshy parts of organizations – those metal, blood, plastic, skin and brick constructions that are always already cyborganization. Cogs inside a bureaucratic engine, corpses moving along inside a Chicago slaughterhouse, uniformed bodies in coordinated motion. To state the argument rather too boldly, the violence of the cyborg or alien could be seen as the vengeance of both product, worker and citizen. The big organization – the state, the corporation, the military – is the problem and a violent form of resistance is articulated as the answer. This new body, made possible by the organization – and made possible by a dualism I will now try to undo – becomes its nemesis.

But, as I have already suggested, we are all already cyborgs. Our bodies are only ever given realization through their connection with non-human materials. The hand becomes a hand when it holds a tool. The eye becomes an eye when it sees an icon. Human agency is hence an effect achieved through the attachment of bodies to various materials in systemic ways. Cyborgs aren't just found in fiction because the relation between flesh and metal doesn't have to be permanent or even proximal. Bionic people write with computers and watch televisions, eat food, drive cars, live in houses (le Corbusier's 'machines for living in') and, of course, have the usual array of prostheses – from spectacles and high heeled shoes to engineered hearts. This approach to the everyday relations between humans and technology emphasizes the role of 'external' things in supposedly 'internal' processes – though inside and outside are terms with little meaning here. The solid world outside and the private spaces inside then become intimately connected and mutually defining – thought as system, system as thought made manifest (Bohm, 1994). Or, as Heidegger suggested, 'the essence of technology is by no means anything technological' – it is, rather, a kind of practice which frames the world in certain ways, and connects humans and nature in particular relationships (1993a: 311). Indeed, if we follow Heidegger's anti-dualist philosophy through to contemporary actor-network poststructuralism, we might decide that there can be no workable distinction between many of these terms – only permeable divisions that we treat as solid. The term 'cyborganization' which I will use below (Cooper and Law, 1995; Parker, 1998; Parker and Cooper, 1998) describes the general process by which human beings always use other forms of being to become human. In this way we can refer to 'cyborganic' spaces populated by 'cyborganisms' – not as science fiction but as common fact. So, how are these cyborgs narrated in contemporary fiction?

The humanist cyborg

The most common reading of cyborg stories is that they represent a combination of technophobia, or at least technoscepticism, combined with a very violent form of body horror (see some of the essays in Kuhn, 1990 for example). I will deal with each of these themes in turn. Central to most of the texts that I mentioned above is a Frankenstein's monster narrative of scientific arrogance. As Amis (1969) and Tudor (1989) note, mad science is a very dominant theme in science fiction and horror films. In other words, the threat is most often not a war from another world or a supernatural intervention but is secular and dependent on something that human beings did in the first place. Prometheus was punished by Zeus for stealing fire and using it to breath life into his clay images – the Modern Prometheus is punished by his own creation. It might be added to this that the embodiment of science in science fiction films has often been the mad computer, robot or cyborg. This tragic monster lives because it was created to fulfil an instrumental purpose but, at some time during the story, we discover the unintended despair and/or anger that this 'object' now feels. The neutrality of science, or the scientist, and their rhetoric about efficiency or progress is revealed as dangerous arrogance as the creature turns out to be both victim and nemesis.

These themes of retribution are common enough in science fiction and horror but in some contemporary cyborg films they are given added impact through a visceral focus on bodily destruction or re-assembly. Though this was again one of the elements in early Frankenstein films – brains in jars, technicolour blood and so on – the new technologies of film allow the exploration and explosion of bodies to be entirely different in its impact. The two Shinya Tsukamoto films *Tetsuo: The Iron Man* (1989) and *Tetsuo II: Body Hammer* (1991) illustrate these themes in graphic detail. Through car crashes, sex, medicine, experimentation and violence the textures of meat and metal, nervous systems and machine systems, are continually combined in brutal ways (see also Ballard, 1973). Nerves become wires, oil is saliva, limbs are tubes, the penis a drill. Respectable and bespectacled Japanese 'salarymen' push metal into their bodies and mutate into violent rusty cyborgs that groan and sigh orgasmically as they batter each other into submission. These two are extreme examples, but in all of these films flesh is penetrated, sliced, crushed, dissolved as the bodies of cyborgs and humans are subjected to a cleansing ultraviolence. It seems fairly convincing then to suggest that cyborg films show us something about our fears of science's colonization of our bodies (see, for example, Shaviro, 1993: ch. 4). To be more specific, they usually show us something about male fears and desires -- there are few female cyborgs and most of the male ones have hard (not leaky) bodies (see Featherstone and Burrows, 1995). If the cyborg is female, as in *Cherry 2000* (1988) or *Metropolis*, they are often sexy but brainless bimbos. Yet, for cyborgs of both genders, we may enjoy their capacity for physical violence or their flawless bodies but, as with Frankenstein's monster, we are surely supposed to feel both horror and pity towards these mutant creations of science.

Now I don't want to suggest that this dual understanding of cyborg films is wrong – science and bodies are clearly relevant here – but I do want to add something to it. I want to do this by looking in more detail at where the science comes from because it seems to me that, in these films and others, the real enemy of the body is no longer science in the abstract, or the single Dr Frankenstein, but the big corporation or state that sponsors them. The demonology of big organizations in science fiction is a topic that, to my knowledge, has not received a great deal of attention (though see Byers, 1990 and some comments in Shaviro, 1993 and Corbett, 1995). However, it is a theme that has been central to much recent fantastic fiction. Spy dramas, such as the Bond films and the Man from UNCLE had the organizations SPECTRE and THRUSH respectively as their most enduring enemies. These were outside enemies, thinly disguised versions of the communist other. However, latterly it seems that many of the plots in programmes like *The X Files*, *Babylon 5*, *Deep Space 9*, *Wild Palms* and the majority of cyberpunk novels (for example Gibson, 1986; Stephenson, 1992) are premised on conspiracy theories about the actions of the internal corporate elite or the military–industrial complex. The us/them dualism becomes problematized as it is harder to work out who 'us' and 'them' are and we begin to suspect that the 'other' might be lurking at the heart of the state. Along these lines, films such as *THX 1138* (1970), *Soylent Green* (1973), *Demon Seed* (1977), *Outland* (1981), David Cronenberg's *Videodrome* (1982) and *The Fly* (1986), as well as *The Running Man* (1987), *Total Recall* (1990) and *Freejack* (1992) contain very clear references to the corporate interests that structure their worlds. In *Rollerball* (1975), for example, the hero 'Jonathan' is lectured by a senior corporate executive when he refuses to be retired from an exceptionally violent gladiatorial game. As with many such sequences, the representative of the organization argues that something has to be the case because this is the corporate interest. In response, the hero asserts his individualism and stresses the immorality of whatever particular action is being undertaken. Jonathan's bruised and bleeding body is continually counterposed to the distant gaze of the suited executives who watch from behind glass. In classic humanist mode, the heroic individual wins through in the end.

A particularly good illustration of the positioning of this moral dualism comes from the four *Alien* films which pit the highly individualistic Ripley against her employer, the Weyland–Yutani Corp. The company (which is 'Building Better Worlds') wants an alien back on earth because, as Carter Burke, the company's representative in the second film – *Aliens* (1986) – tells us, it would be 'worth millions to the bio-weapons division'. The company will sacrifice anyone and employ any means to achieve its goal. *Aliens* contains a boardroom meeting at which Ripley is disciplined for not being aware of the 'dollar value' of the alien-infested spaceship she left to crash. The phrase is repeated later in the film as a justification for not blowing up the L426 installation which is now populated by aliens. Ripley's righteous anger at Burke's attempt to get her and a small girl impregnated by the aliens later in the film leads her to condemn his corporate morality: 'You know Burke – I don't know which species is worse. You don't see them fucking each other over for a goddam percentage.' The cold, twisted organization people who work for Weyland–Yutani seem the real monsters in these films. It is telling that the ship in the first film is called *Nostromo*, an allusion to Joseph Conrad's novel in which '*nostro homo*' – our man – is betrayed by corporate interests. The alien merely follows its nature as it tears flesh whilst 'our men' precipitate its killing through their unthinking loyalty to Weyland–Yutani's instructions.

Though the *Alien* trilogy has cyborg characters, its material monsters were not constructed by the corporation. In the *Robocop* films, however, the cyborg is struggling between asserting a humanist individuality – as Murphy, the policeman whose body was used to make the cyborg – and his status as a product of 'Omni Consumer Products' (OCP). Like the McCandless Corporation's skyscraper in *Freejack*, Omnicorp's corporate office towers 95 storeys over the crime-ridden streets of Detroit. This is a city almost owned by OCP and, like Huxley's *Brave New World* (1932/1994), is shaped by the imprint of its previous corporate dynasty. The Henry Ford Memorial Hospital and Lee Iacocca Elementary School are given passing mentions whilst a showdown takes place at the now aban-doned River Rouge plant – Ford's showpiece factory in the 1920s. The narrative takes us into the heart of this vision of a commercial world in which executives manipulate their bodies to climb the career ladder, observe the dress codes, the washroom status hierarchy and talk a corporate newspeak to conceal the basic immorality of what they are doing. Yet, despite the best efforts of OCP, in the films Murphy/Robocop manages to overcome his product status and stand up for individual judgement against corporate utilitarianism. He never forgets who he really is, just as his police colleagues would rather strike than buy into the corporate line. His singu-larity and sense of duty stand out against the collective corporate culture and he resists violence, psychological manipulation and even disassembly. He refuses to be an 'unit', a 'product' and insists on being Murphy. Again the dualism is clear – the division between bodies and organizations allows for responsibility to be distributed too. The guilty here are those organization people who have sold their conscience for a dollar, who refuse to take responsibility for their actions, who have tortured his body, who try to convince him to believe that he is 'a machine . . . nothing more.' Like the conformist salaryman in the *Tetsuo* films, the obedient military scientists in *Universal Soldier* or Weyland–Yutani employees in the *Alien* films, the condemnation is aimed at the employee who follows or sets the company line. The cyborgs themselves cannot really be blamed because, as the drug dealer in *Robocop 2* tells Murphy – 'I don't blame you. They program you and you do it . . . I forgive you.'

Robocop and the Universal Soldier remember that they are really human, but the T101 in *Terminator 2* becomes socialized into humanity through contact with 'real' humans. He is clearly a machine but his 'learning circuits' allow him to become more. Importantly, like Ripley, he ends up sacrificing himself in order that 'Cyberdyne Systems' will not be able to produce the technology that causes the machines to wage war on the humans. Yet again, the corporation is the cause of the threat and it takes a humanized robot to ensure that Cyberdyne does not make huge profits by accidentally destroying humanity. 'I know now why you cry', he says, before lowering himself into a vat of molten metal. Jane Connor, the woman both threatened and saved by Terminators, sums up the paradoxical humanism of the film: 'if machines can learn the value of human life, then maybe we can too'.

Perhaps the most extreme example of a film that plays with this moral binarism can be found in *Bladerunner*. The cyborgs here are 'replicants', engineered by the Tyrell Corporation to do hard and dirty work on other planets. Unfortunately for the corporation, these manufactured proletarians are rebelling and some have escaped to earth. The Nexus-6 replicants are top of the line models (perfect 'skin jobs'), with implanted memories that can only be detected through 'empathy tests'. They are, apart from their capacity for ultraviolence, all but human. Deckard, who may be a replicant himself but thinks he is human, is employed to hunt these cyborgs down and kill them but suffers something of a crisis after falling in love with one of them, who also believes that she is a human being. The factual and ethical confusion that the film relies on allows us to blur the boundaries between 'humans' and 'machines' in a way that privileges neither. After all, if these androids do dream of electric sheep (the title of the original Philip Dick story from which the plot is developed) then perhaps they are no longer machines? However, the clearest moral position in the film is that taken by Roy, the leader of the replicants, when he visits the Chief Executive of the Tyrell Corporation to demand an explanation for their existence. As in *Robocop*, the product then kills the corporate executive. Again, however, our sympathies are surely with the replicants. They did not ask to be made as they are – self-conscious but with a four-year life span. Their agony and anger was inflicted by the managers in a big organization. Their violence is a revolutionary revenge, not merely an act of random brutality.

In classical mythology the story of Pygmalion suggests a rather different outcome. The King of Cyprus makes an ivory statue of his ideal woman and, after praying for divine intervention, the god Aphrodite brings her to life for him. On seeing King Pygmalion the statue falls in love with him and they marry. By the beginning of the nineteenth century Pygmalion had become Dr Frankenstein. However, at the end of the twentieth century the threat is even more specific – not simply science but the fact that the scientists and their laboratories are owned and controlled by large companies or state bureaucracies. In spatial terms science fiction tells us of shiny buildings and rusting heaps of industrial waste, guarded corporate enclaves and decaying inner cities. The immoralities and amoralities of the big corporation have spawned both the techno-monsters and the urban nightmares. Cyborgs are designed to deal with a corporate problem – programmed to work, to fight, to police, to spy on the company's behalf. These are perfect employees, mobile versions of the production robots that employers already use to replace mere flesh. No doubt Frederick Taylor would rather have worked with a cyborg to refine scientific management than have to continually cajole some recent migrants who could barely speak English. However, this employee/product turns out to be savagely ungrateful. Sometimes this is because its own 'humanity', its memories, its conscience, its individuality motivate it to turn against its makers. In other cases, the Model 406 Gunslinger in *Westworld* (1973) for example, the product simply does what it is programmed to do, without hatred or passion. Either way, the cyborg has no reason to be grateful for being created because its creators have shallow or callous motives.

So, in these texts the villain, the evil creator, seems to be the organization and the romantic response is a violent form of rebellion by a humanist body. In a reversal of H.G. Wells's utopian technological future in *Things to Come* (1936) (which he based on his 1933 *The Shape of Things to Come*), 'the technocrats are now the bad guys and the good guys are the reactionaries' (Franklin, 1990: 25). The body becomes the site of agency against the structural determinism of the corporation, the big body. One of the organs turns against the organization and the future looks brighter already.

Anti-humanist cyborganization

Whilst I think the analysis put forward in the previous section is a reasonable reading of some contemporary conspiracy themes I can see some other ways in which it is rather deficient. On the one hand we have the strangely humanoid and humanist cyborgs – Robocop, T101, Roy and Bishop (the synthetic with behavioural inhibitors from *Aliens*). These characters begin to know themselves, make jokes – 'I may be synthetic but I'm not stupid' –

and gain our trust and understanding. On the other hand, we have these big corporations – Tyrell, Omnicorp, Cyberdyne Systems, Weyland–Yutani and so on. These are organizations populated by utilitarian capitalists, power hungry careerists or selfish research scientists. In a sense, there is no humanity here, merely economic imperatives and the language of strategy, accounting and marketing. In similar ways *Brave New World* was set in the World State's Western European Zone. Huxley named his 'Fordship' the Controller Mustapha Mond, after Sir Alfred Mond, the first Chairman of Imperial Chemical Industries. The key problem for this dystopia, as in Yevgeny Zamyatin's 'OneState' of *We* (1924/1993) or Orwell's *Nineteen Eighty-four* (1949/1954), is how the individual, the person manufactured in a vat, can resist becoming 'just a cell in the social body' (Huxley, [1932]/1994: 81). Yet again, the individual must stand out against the corporate, against the anti-human bureaucracy that wishes to practise 'Human Element Management'. The divide between people and things is firmly in place here. The representations are of heroic bodies and reified organizations *as if these things were somehow different.* So, can the idea of cyborganization help to dissolve some of these boundaries, and what consequences follow if it can?

Organizing involves making patterns that endure in some way. When we organize something we give it a shape, a direction, a meaning. This is not to say that this pattern necessarily lasts, that the 'pool of order' coheres for very long (see Law, 1994), but is to point to the importance of looking at organizing as a process, not as a finished outcome (Cooper and Law, 1995). However, as I suggested above, when these patterns are made they use human and non-human bits and pieces – a bricolage of bodies, words and things. An organization is therefore a network of wetware, software and hardware that makes some kind of sense to a number of people. The things (the non-human things) may be fairly simple – uniforms, company logos, desks, paper – or complicated – computer systems, 95-storey office blocks, cyborg police officers and so on. Taken together, they make a network, a moving mobile, a temporary state of affairs that we can call an organization. Now this surely means that meat and metal are not that radically different. Bodies are no more special than other things. We couldn't *do* 'manager', 'worker', 'academic' or some other element of divided labour if it weren't for all the various props and accessories that allow us to perform such activities. It also suggests that things become things when they are organized by us. For as long as we have been using tools we have been 'posthumans' (Terranova, 1996), which might be to say that we had better understand 'human' better before we start making pronouncements about its overcoming.

Cyborganization should not be conceived of as a thing, or even a collection of things, but as a continually shifting set of relationships. Another way of putting all this is to say that organization is the systematic distribution and redistribution of 'organs', both human body parts and (in an earlier meaning of the word) manufactured tools. For my purposes both senses of organ are conceptually the same thing, since they both embody some notion of being given meaning through connection. This is a physical or conceptual relationship between the organs of a system. The organs of the cyborg and the organs of the corporate body are not that dissimilar in terms of a relationship between parts of a 'system', in the loosest sense of that word. There is a clear relation between such a view and Henry Ford's fantasy of disassembled bodies.

> The production of the Model T Ford required 7882 distinct work operations, but Ford noted, only 12% of these tasks – only 949 operations – required 'strong, able bodied, and practically physically perfect men.' Of the remainder . . . 'we found that 670 could be filled by legless men, 2,637 by one-legged men, two by armless men, 715 by one-armed men and ten by blind men.' (Seltzer, 1992: 157)

This way of thinking about technology and organization clearly moves us away from either a calculative view of systems in which humans are irrelevant or one in which human intentions are sovereign. This is neither humanism nor anti-humanism but rather an attempt to try to see humans as elements in machinic systems – perhaps Deleuze and Guattari's 'desiring machines' composed (partly) of 'eating machines', 'anal machines', 'talking machines', 'breathing machines' and all connected to other machines in endless circuits (1984). The distributions and delegations of cyborganization are hence merely different ways of connecting patterns of repetition and difference, of being like and being unlike. The organization of flesh and other things that constitute the social must therefore be predicated on these shifting divisions and unities, speeds and intensities.

But the warmth of responsibility and the heat of judgement seem to have dissipated now. It is hard to distinguish Robocop from OCP anymore, Mustapha Mond from the World State or (any) body from organization. If bodies are another part of organization, no more or less important than a paper clip, then a particular focus on humans is hardly justified. If we are all cyborgs then why worry about bodies anymore? The angry crowds are gathering, insisting that some-body be held accountable, in order that the dream of social engineering, the Hegelian emancipation of the human spirit, can proceed (see, for a particularly intemperate example, Bookchin, 1995). Given such emotion, it is difficult not to feel like an assassin, standing over the body as it grows cold.

In/human

So, cyborganization is the moving pattern of human and non-human parts. (Human) bodies fit in here, not as starting points or fleshy prime movers, but as elements in the drifting network. Of course these bodies could be doing very different things and we might try to describe them. They could be buttoned up in suits and ashamed to spill food on their chins or they could be oily, sweating and half naked. They could be attached only to a bag of letters or they could be plastered with electrodes, a head-up target display and a jet fighter. They could bring with them gender, ethnicity, baldness and an outrageous taste in earrings and sexual partners. But, more than this, what can we say? Should we try just to let them drift through us, to attempt to reach Deleuze and Guattari's Body-without-Organs, bodies without organization (1984: 9; 1988: 149)? We continue to become all the machine-assemblages that exist around us and through us, but (since we too are machine assemblages) we cannot judge them, or abstract some parts and deem them to be more important: 'The BwO is what remains when you take everything away' (1988: 151). This seems rather a cold ending; surely there must be some warmer alternatives? Well, I can think of two.

I suppose we could none the less take up Bryan Turner's challenge to manufacture a sociology of bodies – perhaps the challenge that motivates the publication of a book like this. It effectively means that we carry on saying that bodies are socially constructed through human interpretive practices and try to get people to pay us for saying it. As I've already suggested, this is not particularly interesting once you have heard it once and anyway doesn't explain how the division between human bodies and other materials is made and sustained. This is not to deny that (human) bodies are important, but also to insist that they are not more important than lots of other things. To restate the assertion that guides this chapter, human being means living as a cyborg in cyborganized worlds.

A rather different alternative might be to suggest, in performative mode, that humanism, ethics, judgement – even Human Resource Management – could learn from embodiment, from the fleshy warmth of the other. Following Bauman's (1993) use of Levinas's ideas about the face and unsolicited obligation, I and others would certainly like to believe that this was the case (see Tester, 1997 for example). Yet, as I suggested at the start, including warm bodies in our social theory doesn't *necessarily* help us humanize organizations, or any other aspects of the supposedly unique 'human condition'. That all depends on how we think of those bodies in the first place. In fact, it could just as well be argued that, in the way that I have presented it here, thinking about bodies might actually de-humanize flesh. I think this is in large part because much actor-network theory and poststructuralism refuses to privilege any one particular connection or material over others. As Lee and Brown suggest, this is because it is 'so liberal and so democratic that it has no Other' (1994: 774). Why should we listen to one account rather than another? Unfortunately, the same problem seems to hold for cyberfeminist arguments about the body (Haraway, 1991). New forms of prosthetic a-humanism may be better than techno-phobia, but they may not, and who is to judge? Neither optimism nor pessimism are suggested and so we are back to Deleuze and Guattari's judgement about judgement – the impossible call to be a Body-without-Organs.

The humanist stories from the popular and academic texts I have referenced that present these cyborg heroes fighting the corporate bad guys assume a hierarchy, a place to see and condemn. A 'god trick' that achieves a tidy ordering of things – bad people, good people and not-people. But the order is assumed, it cannot be proved because all the actants clearly do not agree on it in some consensual and negotiated way. Instead, it could be said that many of the bits and pieces that make up organization are different from each other, but this does not mean that they are hierarchically ordered with humans at the top, or human bodies at the bottom. In order to counter any assumptions of 'naturalness' to these arrangements I want to suggest that organization is the never-ending process of assembling these differences into some kind of pattern. That we usually only ever see it from within our bodies, our organs, and believe that these assemblages of things make sense beyond us is the understandable humanist hubris.

I happen not to like these inhuman (or anti-humanist, see Tester, 1995) conclusions at all, because I too would like to know the warm heart beating at the centre of all human activity (Parker, 1995, 1998). I want to have my finger on its pulse, its hand in mine and our eyes meeting. Unfortunately, to me, the sudden (almost frantic) interest in the body sounds like another attempt to make that romance happen after various forms of relativism have eaten away at the certainties that many hold dear. Though I would like to find some other ways to defend some shorn down form of humanism I can't find any enthusiasm for this 'gap' in 'knowledge', in an attempt to put the 'body' in 'organization' as if this would heal a wound. Ultimately, it seems to me an old attempt to bring human beings back to the centre of things but, following the inhuman logic of cyborganization, only succeeds in spreading them everywhere, including the margins.

Even Heidegger, when distancing himself from humanism, feels the need to comment: 'But this opposition does not mean that such thinking aligns itself against the humane and advocates the inhuman, that it promotes the inhumane and deprecates the dignity of man' (1993b: 233). Well of course. By this essay I do not mean to argue that we should no longer care about other humans, though I do wonder about the 'dignity of man'. It is merely intended to sponsor a little hard thinking about the role that bodies might play in arguments about human beings and organizations. As I have tried to show, it is easy to slip into seeing the human body as a final site of agency, and hence to suggest that other materials are ultimately ruled from the throne of flesh. The call for a romantic rebellion against organization, against structure, which often follows is hence only possible because so much non-human material is left out. If instead we take the relational ontology of cyborganization, or the sociology of translation, as a starting point then a particular interest in bodies becomes less obvious because responsibility and agency are distributed through a drifting network. Ironically, such attempts to excavate down to foundations, or finger point, may say more about our bodily relations and acts of judgement than we often think. After all, in material (and bodily) terms 'when you point the finger, three fingers point back at you'.[2]

Notes

1 Grateful thanks to the audience at the Keele 'Body and Organization' conference, the Popular Culture Research Group at Keele University, and the editors for their comments on earlier versions of this chapter.
2 Remark attributed to John Roberts.

References

Amis, K. (1969) *New Maps of Hell*. London: New English Library.
Ballard, J.G. (1973) *Crash*. Harmondsworth: Penguin.
Barry, D. and Hazen, M. (1996) 'Do you take your body to work?', in D. Boje, R. Gephart Jr and T. Thatchenkery (eds), *Postmodern Management and Organization Theory*. Thousand Oaks, CA: Sage.
Bauman, Z. (1993) *Postmodern Ethics*. Oxford: Blackwell.
Best, S. (1989) 'Robocop: the recuperation of the subject', *Canadian Journal of Political and Social Theory*, 8: 44–55.
Bohm, D. (1994) *Thought as a System*. London: Routledge.
Bookchin, M. (1995) *Re-Enchanting Humanity*. London: Cassell.
Burrell, G. (1997) *Pandemonium: Towards a Retro-Organization Theory*. London: Sage.
Byers, T. (1990) 'Commodity futures', in A. Kuhn (ed.), *Alien Zone: Cultural Theory and Contemporary Science Fiction Cinema*. London: Verso. pp. 39–49.
Cooper, R. and Law, J. (1995) 'Organization: distal and proximal views', *Research in the Sociology of Organizations*, 13: 237–74.
Corbett, J.M. (1995) 'Celluloid projections: images of technology and organizational futures in contemporary science fiction film', *Organization*, 2: 467–88.
Deleuze, G. and Guattari, F. (1984) *Anti-Oedipus: Capitalism and Schizophrenia*. London: Athlone.
Deleuze, G. and Guattari, F. (1988) *A Thousand Plateaus: Capitalism and Schizophrenia*. London: Athlone.
Featherstone, M. and Burrows, R. (eds) (1995) *Cyberspace, Cyberbodies, Cyberpunk*. London: Sage.
Franklin, H.B. (1990) 'Visions of the future in science fiction films from 1970 to 1982', in A. Kuhn (ed.), *Alien Zone: Cultural Theory and Contemporary Science Fiction Cinema*. London: Verso. pp. 19–31.
Gibson, W. (1986) *Neuromancer*. London: Grafton.
Gray, C.H. (ed.) (1995) *The Cyborg Handbook*. London: Routledge.
Haraway, D. (1991) *Simians, Cyborgs and Women: The Re-invention of Nature*. London: Free Association Books.
Heidegger, M. (1993a) 'The question concerning technology', in D. Farrell Krell (ed.), *Basic Writings*. London: Routledge. pp. 311–41.
Heidegger, M. (1993b) 'Letter on humanism', in D. Farrell Krell (ed.), *Basic Writings*. London: Routledge. pp. 217–65.
Huxley, A. (1932/1994) *Brave New World*. London: HarperCollins.
Kuhn, A. (ed.) (1990) *Alien Zone: Cultural Theory and Contemporary Science Fiction Cinema*. London: Verso.
Law, J. (1994) *Organizing Modernity*. Oxford: Blackwell.
Lee, N. and Brown, S. (1994) 'Otherness and the actor network', *American Behavioural Scientist*, 37 (6): 772–90.
Orwell, G. (1949/1954) *Nineteen Eighty-four*. Harmondsworth: Penguin.
Parker, M. (1995) 'Critique in the name of what? Postmodernism and critical approaches to organization', *Organization Studies*, 16 (4): 553–64.

Parker, M. (1998) 'Judgement day: cyborganization, humanism and postmodern ethics', *Organization*, 5 (4): 503–18.

Parker, M. and Cooper, R. (1998) 'Cyborganization: cinema as nervous system', in J. Hassard and R. Holliday (eds), *Organization/Representation*. London: Sage. pp. 201–28.

Poster, M. (1992) 'Robocop', in J. Crary and S. Kwinter (eds), *Incorporations*. Cambridge, MA: MIT Press. pp. 436–40.

Sanders, S. (1979) 'The disappearance of character', in P. Parrinder (ed.), *Science Fiction: A Critical Guide*. London: Longman. pp. 131–47.

Scholes, R. and Rabkin, E. (1977) *Science Fiction: History, Science, Vision*. New York: Oxford University Press.

Seltzer, M. (1992) *Bodies and Machines*. New York: Routledge.

Shaviro, S. (1993) *The Cinematic Body*. Minneapolis: University of Minnesota Press.

Shilling, C. (1993) *The Body and Social Theory*. London: Sage.

Stephenson, N. (1992) *Snow Crash*. London: Roc/Penguin.

Synnott, A. (1993) *The Body Social*. London: Routledge.

Terranova, T. (1996) 'Posthuman unbounded', in G. Robertson, M. Mash, L. Tickner, J. Bird, B. Curtis and T. Putnam (eds), *FutureNatural*. London: Routledge.

Tester, K. (1995) *The Inhuman Condition*. London: Routledge.

Tester, K. (1997) *Moral Culture*. London: Sage.

Tudor, A. (1989) *Monsters and Mad Scientists: A Cultural History of the Horror Movie*. Oxford: Blackwell.

Turner, B. (1996) *The Body and Society*. London: Sage.

Zamyatin, Y. (1924/1993) *We*. New York: Penguin.

5 Situating Complexity: the Body (Nude)

Hugo Letiche

In a postmodern reflection, this chapter explores why the 'body' may be the last stable category still available for analysis. Loyal to the theme of 'local truth(s)', the reflections are grounded in a series of conceptual but also personal meditations on the representations of the body (drawings) found in the author's direct surroundings. The artist of these drawings of the female nude offers in this chapter her commentary. The author explores the limits of **connectionism** or radical complexity theory as a way of looking at the 'nudes', and assert the merit of unstable paradoxical logics of perception. Drawing is conceived of as emblematic of a dynamic logic of (non-)self.

Primacy of the body/disappearance of the body/the 'becoming' (of the) body

> . . . the scandal of disincarnation has interested me more than incarnation, the evanescence of the body. Does the body exist, what can one disentangle in it of subjectivity or objectivity? Can one play with the body as a sort of game of the subject or rather, is there something which definitively resists subjectivity, which is irreducible. I think so . . . (Baudrillard, 1996: 117)

Baudrillard portrays **consciousness** as individual and particular, that is, 'truth' is subjective; and he portrays **physical (non-) existence** as universal and ontic. Disappearance (death) makes continuity, order, linear progress impossible; that is, everything which is individual (self, I, 'me') is relative, partial and limited. Baudrillard is trying to reverse the terms of the mind/ body debate by prioritizing the principle of disincarnation above that of incarnation, and by focusing on the 'object' that animates the 'subject'. Modernism, of course, saw the 'subject' as the source of creativity, life and action. Modernism identified the 'object' with permanence order and 'truth'. Its *artistic rebellion* was 'situationalist'. It demanded more power for the 'subject' and decried how reification – via rigidified social structures and sedimentation in rules, laws and technologies – had encapsulated the 'subject' in the 'object's' lifelessness. Mainstream modernism embraced technology, and identified the advancing technologization of production and organization, not with the death-of-the-subject, but with 'progress'.

The modernist rationalization of society, by means of technology and via new techniques of production such as IT or biotechnology, as well as by means of social engineering (for instance realized in Business Process Reengineering and strategic management) has, of late, come in for a battering. It stands accused of destroying the earth's eco system, of making social harmony impossible and of impoverishing much of human existence.

The key symbols of modernism are under attack. Medicine and the scientific attitude are being criticized; industrial and mass production are being questioned. Resistance to the 'culture of dissection' seems to be on the increase (Sawday, 1995: xi). The 'slaughter' of the natural form has been interpreted to be the basis of modernist thought and production. As Ackroyd and Crowdy have stressed, what else is an assembly line than a slaughterhouse running in reverse – instead of cutting off the pieces of beef, one simply adds on pieces of machinery (1990). In a parallel fashion, the dominating rationality first divides problems into their smallest possible components – transgressing their natural form, in order to reassemble them in 'causal' analysis. In the study of organization it is 'functionalism' which theoretically re-assembles what it first analytically sunders. Dale and Burrell (1995) assert that (in modernism) the 'mirror' and 'scalpel' have overwhelmed the 'body' and 'nature'. Thus the 'slash' inflicted by the surgeon's knife, the divisions created by hierarchy and masculine/feminine dualism, have metaphorically overwhelmed 'organic' integrity. Since the fifteenth and sixteenth century, when anatomists started to dissect human bodies, the problem of the 'transgression' of the human form has become ever more pronounced. Dissection has transformed the 'living human form'. The body has become inert, mere material substance. The emergence of the 'body-as-machine' (the assembly line) has accompanied the disappearance of the irreducible human form (Baudrillard, 1996). Dale and Burrell (1995) want to reverse this process. They are demanding a re-conceptualization of organization wherein identity is not produced by anatomical taxonomy and its conceptual violence, but is 'organic'.

The question is: *Should form – human, organic, organizational – be dismembered and penetrated?* The stripping of (natural) *form* of its mystery and the 'mastering' of nature are being questioned. Baudrillard asserts that the defence of (natural) 'form' originates in an end-of-the-century (or millennium) reaction to the passing of the cultural period most commonly called 'modernism'. 'Modernism' has analysed and assembled, conquered and rearranged, had success and innovated. Its activist self-confidence, key beliefs and will-to-power seem to have run their course. The universe now in place, of consumerist simulacrum and uncertainty, has provoked in some observers a desperate need to try to (re-)find some 'sense of direction' or 'point of reference'. When the 'centre fell out' of modernist belief, the 'body' remained as a potential, last 'certainty' (Berman, 1983). As William James (1962) pointed out, consciousness as we know it depends on the 'security', that phenomenological embodiment can be considered to be stable – that is, when we go to bed we are 'sure' that we will awaken 'in the same body'. If all other certainties are irresolute, at least this one, apparently, remains experientially valid. The culture of postmodernist flux leads fairly logically to an attempt to re-anchor identity in the 'certainty of the body'. In effect, it is an effort to reverse time and to go back to the 'natural telos', which preceded the medical model and the supremacy of the 'scalpel'. A parallel way of thinking can be applied to the notion of 'identity', that is, to the psychology of the 'self'. In modernism the 'me' has dominated progressively more and more over the 'I'. The 'mirror image' of the 'self', that is who we are *supposed to be* and what we *ought to do*, has overwhelmed the 'self' and subjugated spontaneous behaviour. The modern 'civilizing process' has produced a population of self-surveillance. The 'self' has learned to control itself on the basis of the ruling social norms. These norms form the 'mirror' image of the 'self'; the internalized image of how the 'self' ought to be seen. The 'self' has become the 'self-in-the-mirror'. The 'I' is experienced as seen-by-others. Existence is lived and filtered through social norms. 'Rule bound behaviour' predominates over 'impulse'. Conscious action takes precedence over unconscious drives. Is this process reversible? Can the 'mirror' and 'scalpel' really be replaced by the primacy of the 'body'?

An alternative to the examined and analysed body is fairly obvious. The body could simply disappear into 'virtuality'. **Virtual reality** is grounded in a technology and sociology able to surpass the 'body'. Identity is replaced by multiple identity. Rational goal-directed organization is supplanted by competitive advantage gained from networking and flexibility. The body is superseded by avatars. 'Reality' is overwhelmed by consumerist 'hyper-reality'. Interaction is pursued on the Net. In 'virtuality', the fixed form of the body is surpassed in electronic fantasy and *jouissance*. An idea(l) of existence prevails – in 'virtuality' there is invention, creativity and freedom from the constraints of (modernist) identity (Haraway, 1991). Thus, liberation from modernist rationalism is possible via two polar opposites: by means of (i) renewed respect for the 'form of the body' and, through (ii) total disrespect for bodily form.

Neither of the two extremes, I believe, is really tenable. If one **prioritizes form**, one reifies the 'body' and endangers all dynamism. 'Form' becomes an ideal not to be transgressed, changed or interfered with; that is, 'Existence is as it is and is not (no longer) to be meddled with'. If natural form is sacrilized, no place remains outside of the 'real' to launch change, to alter reality or to begin innovation. But by trying to **transcend form** and to experiment in identity, one merely reasserts the traditional Christian mind/body dualism wherein spirit (idea, plan, Utopia) is identified with 'truth'. Such logic severs the link between the 'person' and 'world', 'self' and 'other', nature and technology, perception and physical existence. It strangles the 'self' in an ideal of 'identity' and impoverishes interaction, and thereby imperils originality. 'Self' is reified in an idea of what ought to be. The only dynamic solution is to retain the tension between 'form' and 'non-form', 'incarnation' and 'disincarnation'; that is, to hold on to a lived possibility of a

Postmodern irreducibles	Processes of the postmodern	Postmodern concepts lead to
Body Natural form	(Dis-)Incarnation *Différence* Body-in-the-world	Connectionism Holism
COMPLEXITY		
Destruction of form Technological determinism 'Mirror' and 'Scalpel'	Confusion Alienation Disappearance	Virtuality Fragmentation
Critique of modernism:	Negative modernist processes:	Hyper-modernism leads to:

FIGURE 5.1

dynamic between 'self' and 'non-self'. I opt for such a logic of the 'included middle' between 'self'/'form' and 'non-self'/'form-transgressed'. I realize that this is, in effect, an unstable conceptualization. Polarities are much clearer. The sharp juxtaposition of choices is more riveting. But the instability of categories that imply one another, and of logics that permanently remain unstable, generates dynamic 'life-like' thought. I wish neither to reify the 'body' in a concept of 'form', nor in an idea(l) of 'virtuality'. Thus, I attempt to place the 'body' in a continuous process of 'becoming', such as 'complexity theory' would demand. Figure 5.1 puts this schematically.

Disincarnating 'local truths'

The implicit acceptance of mind/body dualism stretches far enough that we (almost) never see anything of the *surroundings*, in which the textual personae confronting us in intellectual work are created. What artefacts surround the writer? In what circumstance and context has the text been generated? The author's ideological frame of mind, past intellectual positions and theoretical development, are often thought to be relevant; but the author's embodied situation is (almost) always ignored.

To speak of myself, in the winter I work indoors, like almost everyone else who writes in cold, inhospitable Northern Europe. The house wherein I work is chock-full of my wife's drawings of the female body. In the summer I am in France; again often indoors – now because of the glare of the Languedoc sun, which overwhelms my computer screen, and because of the heat that is often overbearing. This time, I am surrounded by my wife's drawings and paintings in all sorts of stages of (non-)completion. Up to now, all these female bodies have never surfaced in anything I have written.

My wife's (Maria's) drawings are 'represented' in this article via the reflection below, and her observations on the reflection are found in her Commentary. Several reproductions of drawings are included for the reader. Since Maria's drawings form (at least one of) the most striking facet(s) to my surroundings, I wish to address their presence/absence in my writing. Not to do so is to sustain the mentalism of subject/object dualism that champions disembodied (dare I say 'virtual'?) consciousness. Such consciousness seems to exist unto itself (in Cyberspace?), as if embodiment was more an impediment to existence than its basis. As cited above in the Baudrillard quote, **disincarnation** (dis-embodiment) is the crucial antipode to the 'subject'. In the concept of disincarnation, Baudrillard wishes to stress the limits of the 'subject'. While modernist **situationalist** rebellion stressed the subject's central position and made sense in its cultural setting, an opposite form of rebellion is appropriate to our times.

The need, now, is to stress the 'object's' force on the 'subject'. Contemporary thought tends to prioritize the positive (the living, existing, occurring); as if *life* was some sort of absolute. But 'reality' opposes; nothing really prevails – 'symbolic death' (as well as 'real' death) overtakes everything. However hard humanity may want to expunge death, it is impossible. Ours is a drama of appearance and disappearance. Everything is reversible – all attempts to live are reversed. Life cannot be perpetuated. It is the *presence of absence* – the realization, within the positive, of the negative, that distinguishes the dynamic paradox of existence. Art is about appearance and disappearance, background and foreground, affirmation and negation. Pure linear, *positive thinking* reflects the effort to erase the principle of the negative. Life, answering to such a logic, would not be 'life' as we know it, but would manifest an unlimited principle of continuity. The crucial quality to life as we know it, is its inability to accept 'the absolute positivization of matters' (Baudrillard, 1996: 122).

Art demonstrates a continual process of 'making appear' and 'making disappear'. It is a ceaseless act of inventing something 'other'. Art portrays disappearance – the seen exists thanks to the not-seen; the artist's style is based on not accepting the way of doing things of others. Constantly making disappear, partakes of the energy of making appear. Temporality is the principle of appearance and disappearance. The reversal of 'temporality' creates an *ex-termine*; a world without the temporal movement of action and cessation. In such a world, there would only be 'extermination' – the repression of dynamism. Art in our world, is based on statements by omission – it lets see by erasing, shows by leaving out. Art is created by highlighting some aspect(s) of presence via acts of absence. By leaving almost everything out, something is allowed to remain.

Baudrillard is convinced that this play of appearance and disappearance is enacted between a prioritized object and an experiencing subject. The ideology of total positivization, which tries to destroy all negative(s), attacks the principle of life itself. Life is *negative*; it is appearance leading to disappearance, moving ever onwards to endless repetitions of the cycle. The *negative* principle to life leads to permanent destabilization. The not-subject is the motor to the dynamic and is the interactive principle of existence. The object's ability to *seduce* the subject, that is, to attract its attention, demands a response and generates interaction. It is the basis to the lived world. The object alone – encapsulated in 'nature' and its principles – is insufficient. The power of negation, in interaction with the subject, leads to consciousness and experience. Thus, paradoxically, I explore a positive principle of negativity.

Connectionism

The terrain between the modernist logic of 'self' and the postmodern logic of *différence* is unstable and indefinable. This terrain is a force field wherein links, however unstable, are continually being forged between opposites. Modernism preserves the opposites and forces the self to choose between them. Postmodernism, paradoxically, preserves and links the opposites. It centres on a play between opposites that are, at once, opposed and complementary. Postmodern connectionism is a way of thinking that sees opposites interlinked in logics of foreground/background, part/whole, local/global. Modernism prioritizes 'spirit', 'consciousness', 'idea'. But modernism's one-sided 'essentialism/mentalism' seems to be more and more difficult to sustain; the countervailing argument for connectionism appears to be growing in significance. Kevin Kelly poses the problem as: 'What alchemical transformation occurs when you connect everything to everything?' (Kelly, 1994: 297).

Connectionist thinking follows an *order-emerging-out-of-massive-connections* approach, wherein a radically bottom-up interpretation of action is explored. Might not 'intelligent' action be the result of myriads of small rather unintelligent, microscopic actions? Maria's drawings can be thought of as the product of thousands of lines, smudges and scratches. Myriad's of nervous, twitching, hand movements were executed with pens and paint brushes and (gradually) created an emergent order that we are accustomed to call 'the drawing'.

Sadie Plant has been developing a connectionist perspective on 'culture' that points to one possible way of examining the drawings (Plant, 1996). What is the organizing principle of the drawings – what is the nature of the 'intelligence' that orders colour, perspective, line and composition? Plant defines such *intelligence* as 'an exploratory process, which learns and learns to learn for itself' (Plant, 1996: 204). 'Intelligence' is not identified with a modernist external, transcendent, superior force; but is a postmodern emergent process that is generated bottom-up. Learning is a process of (mental) self-organization and (material) modification. The brain mutates as it learns, growing and exploring its own potentiality. It is not a serial (step by step) processor (like the early computers) but a parallel processor (continually making multiple interconnections). There is no central guiding

hub -- no single crux to everything, or unique spirit or consciousness. Everything is, at once, in process. This complexity goes beyond what we can grasp. We cannot take it all in while it is happening (Eisner, 1994). We must accept the priority of *event and process*, above *plan and consciousness*. A drawing is an act of self-organizing wherein:

> the extent of the interconnectedness of such systems also means that subtle shifts in activity in one area can have great implications for others, again without reference to some central site. In effect, such systems are continually engineering themselves, growing, emerging and taking shape as a consequence of their own distributed activities. They are self-organizing. (Plant, 1996: 205)

A 'drawing' is not the unique product of 'mind' or 'spirit', that is, of an 'idea' or guiding 'concept'. It is the product of many connected, virtually concurrent, motions. Drawings evolve in a vast web of visual clues, which are linked together and woven into (some sort of) order. Each 'mark' on paper is a visual 'given' in an emerging pattern. The connectionist process resembles the 'Wheeler':

> nasty variant of the well-known society game of guessing the name of an object: what if, unbeknown to the questioner, the participants agree not to pick out an object in advance, so that when a participant is to answer 'Yes' or 'No' to a question ('Is it alive?', 'Does it have four legs?', 'Does it fly?', etc.) he should only pay attention to the consistency of his answer – the object he has in mind be such that his answer is consistent with all previous answers of all the other participants. Thus, the questioner unknowingly participates in the determination of the object; the direction of his questioning narrows the choice down. (Zizek, 1996: 281)

The artist reacts to the visual givens that s/he produces. Each visual clue generates a series of others. Each line, smudge or bit of colour rearranges (however slightly) the order of all the elements in the 'drawing', producing an on-going, complex play, of visual elements. The connectionist logic *refuses* to see man (in the Hegelian tradition) as 'nature sick unto death', that is, as out-of-joint with nature and lacking (in contrast to the animals) a proper 'niche' in harmony with its environment. In the connectionist scenario, the self-organizing potential of material existence generates the possibility of 'intelligence', 'complexity' and 'change'. Small, unto themselves 'minimally intelligent' actions, accumulate into complex patterns. These patterns can break through the threshold of the inanimate to become animate. They transcend the level of the 'spiritless' to create 'meaning'. The 'subject' is the product of 'natural form' – nature dictates iterative complex interaction(s) leading to meaningful *Gestalts*. Man is not (following Heidegger) *thrown* into an indifferent world. Quite the opposite, the 'world' possesses momentum leading to *complexity* and making 'meaning' possible. Art in the connectionist logic is not the imposition of human 'will' or 'being' on matter; but rather reflects a logic of action that closely mirrors the *complexity* of existence.

Thus, the connectionist perspective emphasizes the **process of drawing** and sees in it a generative logic. **Meaning** – significance, identity and intention – emerges from how the chain(s) of signifiers (or 'texts'), unto themselves, inter-connect.

Materials before artist: Lacan, or what's before the 'subject'

In the process of drawing, the drawing materials seduce the artist, that is, the artist is drawn into a game with his/her materials. Colours, pencils, paper etc. are the 'potential of signs'. All sorts of gestures – a choreography of appearances, the symbolic exchange of feeling(s), the challenge of statements – are possible. The artist loses him/herself in his/her art. In art the appearance and disappearance of the subject takes place. Contemporary art is not a place for stating values or realizing social (science) truths, but a place of interaction wherein the artist embraces his/her materials in order to explore: the play of visualization, the enactment of (aesthetic) form, the kneading of artistic possibilities.

'Drawing', seen in this Lacanian manner, is a play of elements ('texts') – rich in connotations, laden with potential meanings not 'under control'. The (artistic) 'texts' imply one another, but defy fixed meanings. They engender the play of person and context, 'meaning' and 'indefiniteness'; they form a signifying field for human action. The Lacanian concept of the subject emphasizes that the 'self' is a retrospective symbolic construct. Only retro-actively, via 'text', can the 'subject' make sense of action (Zizek, 1994). 'Drawing' defies the (Sartrian) dualistic logic that divides the world into an 'in-itself' (the 'material') and 'for-itself' (the 'artist'). A drawing is none of these; or all of them, at once. The drawing possesses 'material' existence (pigment, paper, ink etc.) and 'subjectivity' (feeling, emotion, purposiveness). The amalgam of 'spirit' and 'material' can be interpreted in a 'New Age' perspective. The 'pre-scientific interpretative-mantic procedure(s)' supposedly realize 'a return to the pre-modern universe of wisdom and its sexo-cosmology, i.e. the "drawing" is said to inhabit a universe of harmonious correspondence between the human microcosm and the macrocosm' (Zizek, 1996: 270). Such (New Wave/Jungian) 'holism' assumes that the drawing exists in a universe where everything is in-its-place and has meaning. The Lacanian alternative posits that the subject ('artist' as well as 'spectator') is deprived of any privileged access to 'meaning'. The artist makes choices when s/he 'paints', but s/he also has to accept the impossibility of (any definitive) 'know-how'. If the artist really 'knew how to paint', the exploratory process of juxtaposing elements, trying out combinations and playing with form and colour, would stop. 'Painting' would be mere technique and we know how it should be done. The 'artist' would then produce the 'painting' just like mechanical reproduction does. In one single efficient movement a pre-determined result would be realized. If the 'subject' knows exactly what to do to paint, then s/he cannot act, but is doomed to machine-like activity. Because the 'subject' does not know exactly what s/he is going to do, s/he has to search, experiment and play with possibilities. When the subject knows exactly what to do, 'action' becomes 'routine', 'machine-like' and 'uncreative'. A worker who executes pre-defined tasks, can be judged for his/her expertise and exactitude. But s/he has no responsibility for the 'plan', 'concept' or 'content' of the action. Acts where the subject is truly the author of the event can only be accomplished in relative unawareness of what is to be done and how it is to be done (Elster, 1982). For both the artist and spectator, 'drawing' and 'viewing' is a complex process of small explorative actions, wherein the hand and eye move furtively about the surface of the (in)complete drawing, seeking out connections, structures and tentative senses of order. Via such a connectivist process, elements of perception are drawn together into some sort of (perceived) unity.

One can assert that the process of generative meaning and of emergent structure mirrors 'natural' processes. The artist is, then, not to be thought of as in opposition to nature but as an extension of nature's laws. Art doesn't impose its 'will' on chaos; 'meaning' is not wrested from nothingness. But in the Lacanian reading of the 'subject,' there is no such unity between 'text' (art, language, code) and 'reality' (physical existence). For Lacan, the 'subject' inhabits the gap between the real and the symbolic. The gulf between 'subject' and 'language', 'voice' and 'world' is not breachable. The order of the 'symbolic' and the order of the 'material' can never really merge. In visual art they touch one another, in the sense that the art work is paper, chalk, ink etc. But the 'subject' upsets and destabilizes the physical order by trying to make it 'mean', 'communicate', 'speak'. And the 'subject' upsets the symbolic world by trying to get the 'text' (the drawing, work of art etc.) to re-new itself, to acknowledge the subject's unicity and to abandon well-structured paths for new beginnings and fresh 'ideas'. The 'subject' 'perturbs the smooth engine of symbolization and throws it off balance. The "subject" gives rise to an indelible inconsistency in the symbolic' (Zizek, 1994: 102). The 'subject' only exists after it has upset the pre-existing order – the 'subject' persists as 'interference' (as radio or electrical 'static'), 'disruption', 'disorder'. The 'subject' endures in retrospect, after the text ('drawing') has been made. The 'subject' is after-the-fact and can only be viewed from the symbolic horizon of what has occurred.

Lacan conceptualizes the problem of the 'subject' in relation to topological models of 'curved' space, such as the Mobius strip and Klein bottle. In these constructs cause is (presup)posed by its effects. The 'subject' is a 'break in the chain of signifying causality . . . a hole in the signifying network'; the 'subject's' activity permits the horizon of narrativization–historicization–symbolization to emerge (Zizek, 1994: 102–4). But the 'subject' is not just negativity or empty space, waiting to be filled. The 'subject' is the precondition of the 'real'. The 'subject' makes sense of inert or material existence, which is in-itself senseless. The 'order (or logic) of the drawing' doesn't exist until the artist disrupts existence to create it; the materials (colours, paper, marble, clay etc.) do not 'speak' until they have been used. The 'object' (drawing materials) is both the negative of the 'subject' (something inert and non-human) and the condition of the 'subject' (something to be moulded and kneaded). Thus, in the Lacanian perspective, the 'subject' is a product of its paradoxical relationship to 'object'. The possibility of activity is a precondition to the subject. Drawing, and not what is drawn, is pre-eminent. The possibility of drawing the female nude, is a condition of potential 'subjectivization'. The *process* is more important to the formation of the 'subject' than the result. We need to examine the artist drawing the (human) body, more than the drawings.

First, second and third levels of meaning

Alternatively, semiotics (especially if sociologically tainted) views the drawings as a play of levels of significance. Drawings of the body (nude) possess, on different levels, different 'meanings'. The same 'nude' will 'mean' differently, even opposingly, on different levels. The semiotic **structuralist** interpretation of the image emphasizes how different levels of signification (production–consumption–interpretation) are juxtaposed to one another, in order to produce 'meaning'. Here, the logic focuses on the semiotics of the **art object**. Perception of the 'drawing' is divided into *langue* (the world of the 'object', the shared language known in principle to all), *écriture* (social 'meanings', significances shared in a group/society) and *parole* (personal, experienced response) (Barthes, 1953). The disjunction between the three levels generates a gap between: (i) the art object understood in terms of its materials, composition, visual characteristics; (ii) the social/symbolic/political/economic significance of the art object; and (iii) the viewers' spontaneous visual appreciation. One can try to deconstruct how 'meaning' (or identity) on one level, relates to 'meaning' (and identity) on the others. Different 'degrees' of interpretation nestle in the differences between the levels. For instance, a particular combination of materials (paints, canvas etc.) may signify material desirability (wealth, good taste, privilege) on the second level, and disgust (decadence, narcissism, power-elite) on the third. Thus perception on one level can be contradicted on another. The 'aesthetic' pleasure of first appreciation (strong vibrant colours in a powerful composition) can turn to anger at the repressive 'role model' discovered in second level analysis (the attractive, sexually passive female nude, available for male desire), only to end up a confirmation of the pleasure(s) of 'voyeurism' (the *jouissance* of sexual fantasy) in the third instance. The portrait (painted in the style of German Expressionism) may portray a powerful newspaper owner (status, influence, knowledgeable) and be appreciated as hyper-real (a symbol of German politics in the 20s – without the viewer actually knowing anything about the context; that is to say, it becomes an empty symbol reduced to symbolizing more or less nothing).

Connectionism understands the 'drawing' as over-determined. The drawing can be linked to more than enough 'meanings' – a virtually unending number of 'interpretations' or 'statements' about it are possible. But such 'statements' are not pegged at an initiatory phenomenal level, to be followed by a (more) fundamental level of 'social meaning', that is or is not, caste in doubt by a third 'perspectivist' or 'personal existential' level. The meaning hierarchy of Barthes's triad – that juxtaposes shared rules of communicating (*langue*) with the social connotations conveyed by the work (*écriture*), with experience (*parole*) – draws lines of demarcation between the drawing as 'object', as (social) 'meaning' and as 'meaning relativized'. Maria's drawings,

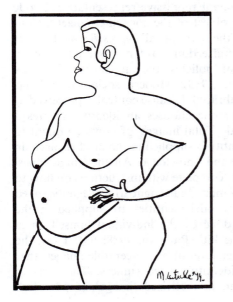 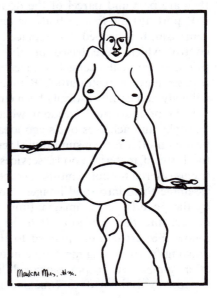

interpreted on this meaning ladder, can be conceived to be 'aestheticized nudes', 'social icons of female roles', and a statement of 'female self-sufficiency'. One can see the drawings as an assertion of 'feminine-ness': they portray women alone, apparently not in need of anyone or anything else, with emphasis on their femine-ness. On the first level, aesthetic values and visual language predominate, but on the second the drawings can be construed to be a tool of 'surveillance technology' trying to dictate norms of appearance and composure while propagating (a form of) social symbolism. On this level, the 'drawings' have become a social strait-jacket, trying to impose role conformity. As indicated, a third level is possible wherein the 'drawings' are not appreciated as an imposed statement of how women 'ought' to be, but are construed (for instance) to offer a message about the unicity of 'identity' (the 'person' is always portrayed alone) and the weakness of 'context' (the drawings are often limited to one, or as few as possible line(s), wherein inside/outside, foreground/background, are at their weakest). Normally we choose one level on which to see the 'drawings'; the simultaneous presence of various levels is unwanted. The question looms, which interpretation really is 'right', that is, possesses 'meaning', 'identity', 'truth'. But I do not want to be forced to attribute a 'meaning' to the drawings. I wish to see them as *connected* to many (possible) meanings without adhering too closely to any one of them. All interpretation is iterative – a moment in the process of interacting with the 'drawings' that can remain unsettled and does not have to be allowed to be reified.

Despite my rejection of the idea of an interpretative hierarchy of meaning, one second level interpretation is so powerful that I think I do need to address it explicitly. It asserts that since the drawings are by an artist who claims they 'are a highly aestheticized rendering of the female body', that they are part and parcel of the dominant repressive representational code that portrays the female body as an object of the consumer society. Consumerism, it is argued, has replaced the 'panoptical' *repressive* methods of control which were based on the unfreedom of the observed (that is, primitive 'surveillance technologies' of 'policing' the subject) with a *seductive* strategy of restraint(s) (Bauman, 1988). Modern social control has willingly and enthusiastically been embraced, because control is perceived as a form of individual freedom where one chooses an identity, creates a 'lifestyle' and achieves one's ego ideal. 'Total images' of how one ought to be are on offer for consumption. Identity is supplied in the market place, in the form of material goods, services and knowledge. All the 'single clues' (items offered for consumption) come 'complete with instructions on how to assemble them into total images. No individual ought to feel handicapped by the poverty of his imagination – model identities are supplied by the market and the only job left to be done by the individual himself, is to follow the instruction attached to the kit' (Bauman, 1988: 63). Thus, the drawings surrounding me can be understood to be 'perceptible images' that offer some sort of pre-packaged 'identity' to consumers. The 'viewer' supposedly is invited to consume an aestheticized 'image' of potential/

idealized 'self'. Symbolic security is for sale; one can 'possess' the 'image' by buying the 'drawing'. By 'mixing and matching' elements from the identity-kit, the consumer can attempt to achieve the social approval that is held out as the reward for possessing the 'right' images. Consumerism, however, plays a double game. It destabilizes self-confidence by constantly thrusting new 'images' on the viewer, while it constantly promises that freedom of choice and safety/security can be realized via the 'images' now on offer. Maria's drawings can be thought of as just another idealized image of the female body, part of a virtually endless procession of consumerist false promises.

Connectedness: but 'this and not that'

I see the drawings as local, partial normative statements, which cannot escape consumerism; but which are not limited to it. I am convinced that the process of visual simplification, that goes into the making of the drawings, is central to their identity. I do not want to split the physical processes of sketching, drawing, erasing and painting from the process of looking at the drawings. I do not want to reduce the drawings to the sociology of consumerism. I am trying to conceive of drawing as para-digmatic of a *learning–creating–growing* process. I am trying to see drawing as a localized piecemeal activity that is emblematic for the sort of non-linear organizing principles whose significance is gaining in import. Drawing is a process that pulls itself up by its own bootstraps. It starts with a few lines or blotches of colour on paper and evolves into a complex visual statement. I am convinced that there is no top-down imposition of 'truth' governing the drawing process. Drawing is an interactive exploration of line and colour, theme and visualization. It cannot be 'true' or 'false', 'natural' or 'artificial'; it is inherently all of these at once. It is this ambivalence, this ontic uncertainty, which Plato feared in the *Republic* and rejected in that text. In a culture which is increasingly fascinated by the *virtual*, the exami-nation of 'drawing' can only gain in significance. 'Understanding' drawing has many points in common with trying to study *virtuality*. In both cases we are faced with a problem of how to interpret the hyper-real space created by drawing and/or virtuality (VR).

The processes of *growth–evolution–development* can be collapsed into one *connected* system. Such a naturalist theory of *complexity* tries to explain the commonalties and differences found in living existence. It tries to under-stand *self-organizing assemblages*, which are neither 'artificial' nor 'natural'. But there is, at present, no terminology that makes such an analysis easy. It is necessary to follow *simultaneous* emergences, discontinuities and bifur-cations, in a logic of anticipation and mutation; though all our normal theoretical discourses are linear causal and reductionist. If we accept that all 'physical, social, and mental reality is non-linear and complex', we will be forced to admit that 'the ideas, inventions and discoveries which

compose . . . human culture are themselves composed of complex interactions, evolving connections and self-organizing behaviour patterns'
(Plant, 1996: 210). If we are going to reintegrate the evolving and learning
characteristic of living processes into our theoretical discourse, we will have
to find a way to admit *complexity* and *connectedness*. Basing our view of
activity on the concept of human (individual) agency just won't do. I
cannot understand Maria's drawings as a mere product of her aesthetic
action, nor as a result of the social (psychology) of which she partakes. As
Plant states:

> There is nothing exclusively human about it: culture emerges from the complex
> interactions of media, organisms, weather patterns, ecosystems, thought patterns,
> cities, discourses, fashions, populations, brains, markets, dance nights and
> bacterial exchanges. There are eco-systems under your finger-nails. You live in
> cultures, and cultures live in you. They are everything *and* the kitchen sink.
> (Plant, 1996: 214)

In this conceptualization of culture, it becomes impossible to know who
speaks and acts, what is cause or effect, where the natural and artificial
begin or end. Is it becoming impossible to 'look' at anything? Is all focus
being lost – is everything being reduced to multiplicity? Plant embraces
Deleuze's solution to these problems:

> 'a system of relays within a larger sphere, within a multiplicity of parts that are
> both theoretical and practical'. What was once the theorist is no longer alone:
> 'Who speaks and acts? It is always a multiplicity, even within the person who
> speaks and acts. All of us are "groupuscules". Representation no longer exists;
> there's only action – theoretical action and practical action which serve as relays
> and form networks.' (Deleuze in Plant, 1996: 215)

But drawing is not a system of 'totalization' that achieves one statement
truth or message. It is a system of 'multiplication' that continually makes
connections between foregrounds and backgrounds, the personal and the
shared, the context and the abstract, the proximal and the distal etc., etc.
For me Plant has arrived at a dead end. It is not a mere coincidence that she
ends her article with a passage from a funeral oration (Deleuze speaking at
Foucault's burial). Connectedness goes berserk when *différence* is collapsed
into mere pulsion and movement, and distinction is overwhelmed. The
'subject' can disappear in an onslaught of raw pulsion(s) – 'there is a sort of
radicalness in the fact of arriving at capturing things before they have any
sense and can be interpreted, before they can be localized' (Baudrillard,
1996: 127). This is a strategy unable to *mean* anything; it has no resonance.
The schizoanalysis of Deleuze and Guattari (1972) propels identity into
the 'imageless organless body' of the desiring-machines; where, to use
Baudrillard's terminology, the logic of disappearance is all-powerful and the
balance with appearance is lost. Total connectedness can lead to a vacuum
(*le vide*) wherein everything disappears into everything else, leaving nothing

behind. 'Drawing' is an activity of connectedness, but it also defines a space wherein 'this' and not 'that' is present, that is, where some sort of identity reigns. Connectedness as pure relativism, and perception as total nominalism, vitiates all interaction. Drawing is then seen as anything and everything. Why draw if what the viewer sees is at random? When connectedness is all-powerful and thus undirected, interaction is overwhelmed. Connectedness does not, then, link the natural and artificial, the visible and the invisible, but it destroys every link. Connectedness is inverted – altered, from an insight into activity and interaction, into an endless process of recursiveness that produces the loss of identity. Plant becomes entangled in a logic of 'knowledge' (*savoir*), 'knowledges' (*connaissances*), 'knows' and 'thinking differently', that is, in reflexivity gone wild!

Différence embodied and embedded

However valuable connectedness may be as a concept to describe the *processes* of making and viewing 'drawing(s)' (processes), I wish to return to the *différence* characteristic of **embodied** and **embedded** existence. The body ensures that we are not *all* in the same place; it keeps us apart and ensures that difference persists (Baudrillard, 1996: 120). Thanks to the *différence* guaranteed by the body, the play of seduction – approach and distancing – is assured. The principle of appearance and disappearance – the presence of absence – is incontestable. The microbiology of the brain and contemporary genetic research are trying to produce another body – a body within virtual reality that is 'essential' and 'universal'. The human genome project and physiological (cognitive) psychology are, in effect, trying to produce an ideological sanctuary from the lived-body. The body as existential form disappears entirely in these hyper-modern projects. The danger is that we are losing the 'body', just as we have already lost the 'soul'. The 'body' may still, now, serve as a referent – a fixed point for a matrix of interpretation where all sorts of other matters can circle and coalesce – but Baudrillard doubts that it will be long able to serve this hermeneutic function. Thus, for as long as it lasts, we can escape the threat of an *autistic logic* of connectedness, which is suited for cocooned monads and psychic nomads, by formulating our thought around the theme of the body.

But total connectedness leads to its opposite, that is, to a state of **no** connectedness, wherein no links are significant and no bonds are prioritized. Likewise, too much emphasis on the *process* of 'drawing' leads one to lose contact with the drawings and their viewers. But it is very hard to know if one really has succeeded in staying in contact with the 'drawings'. At what point is one reflecting on the drawings and at what point have one's fantasies about women and (for instance) their disguises, taken over? The drawings offer the thrill of escaping the limited singular particular body, and entering a universe where the body can be rendered with a single line. It is a world where identity possesses clarity, simplicity and wholeness. The 'drawings' are coherent. They can be seized in a single glance of the eye. Their pleasure is in the aesthetic cogency with which they portray women. But their simplicity is illusionary. Making such drawings demands very complex skills. Real embodiment never involves such fluent and simple lines. The 'drawings' are a fiction. The danger is that viewers will want to retreat into the 'drawings', because actual social meaning and/or individual perception is too complex, conflict-ridden and painful to be sustained. When the possibilities of aesthetic action replace dialogue, interaction and *mitsein*, we are endangered with a retreat from the shared world into a fantasy world. Magical-aesthetic existence, offering a domain of order, refuge and withdrawal, can take over from physical and local actuality. Kevin Robbins has argued that in our world of exploding virtuality – where the existential power of images is ever on the increase – we need to attend to the social quality of the images we choose to live with/in (Robbins, 1995). Our shared experience in the world is increasingly negotiated via the exchange of images. The 'virtual' 'networked' society increasingly functions without us directly meeting others physically. The 'body' is increasingly the 'image of the body' – and it is (often) saturated with fantasy as in advertising, cinema, drawings, on the Net etc. When we eliminate the need to have to respond directly to others, we attack the practice(s) of concern and empathy. Are the drawings distancing the viewer from the female body, or do they bring the viewer ever closer to it? For me, the philosophical error Plant made (despite her critique of Sartre), was to assume that existence (connectedness) precedes meaning (learning, knowing, vision). This assumption leads, irrevocably, to the primacy of process, and puts the 'drawing' (artefact, object, product) on a secondary or derivative level. Plant fails to escape analytical dualism when she makes an anthropomorphic error – identity (meaning) is not man-made or subject-generated. She needed to follow her own logic more radically; significance and identity are in-the-world – they are natural (inherent to existence) *and* artificial (brought to fruition via art, technology, intellectual activity). The key problem is to think identity (the 'drawing', what is to be seen) and absence (the artist's interpretation and 'simplifications') at once. Then there is room for connectedness (the process of 'drawing') and seduction (approach and distance, self and difference). 'Identity' is not a product of human action but an ontic quality. If *identity* and *absence*, *connectedness* and *seduction* are ontic codeterminants of existence, I can preserve the 'drawing' and the 'process of drawing', 'identity' and 'difference', as equi-significant. But identity and absence, as well as connectedness and seduction, create disorder and painful dislocation(s) because they form a logic of non-equilibrium. Exposure to imbalance and reckoning with *différence* is, thus, crucial. Balance and order, linear predictability and uninterrupted continuity, are unnatural; contact, dissonance and contradiction are the basic building blocks of consciousness. A desperate effort is being made in contemporary society to create security and order, to achieve sanitized experience, to neutralize all challenges.

Opposing this attempted deadening repression of *différence*, there is what Richard Sennett calls *the art of exposure* (Sennett, 1973). Do Maria's drawings strengthen your fantasies of withdrawal or do they enhance the logic of 'transitive' (transitional) space? Are they a meeting point where *différence* interacts – a place to pass through on the way to complex experience – or an escape into narcissism and self-enclosure?

Though I think I know in which direction the 'drawings' point, I have to admit to one key reservation. The 'drawings' are recursive; they refer often to known styles (Picasso, Leger, Matisse). In the 'drawings' there are (many) references to the classics of modern art. The drawings have one eye on a receding world, and herein they are nostalgic. That backward glance unsettles me: 'drawing together notions from Benjamin, McLuhan and Baudrillard, I want to suggest that . . . we tend to begin . . . with the rear-vision mirror firmly affixed . . . moving into an indeterminate future with a sort of on-going recursive gaze' (Clark, 1996: 115). The 'drawings' portray bodies as signifying surfaces; through an aesthetization of the self they try, I believe, to make life in an increasingly dehumanized society, bearable. They are, I believe, icons to a life embodied as 'woman', wherein exposure leading to contact and openness, could be a basis for interaction.

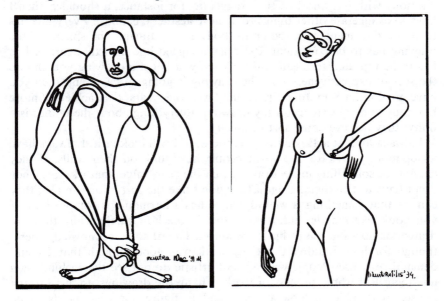

The artist's commentary

I like Picasso, Matisse and Leger; there's a lot of contemporary work I simply don't understand – I don't feel any contact with it. My drawings do not show 'contact'; each time there is just one person portrayed. All the models are depicted unto themselves. They are enclosed in 'lines'. They are in the frame. It's almost as if they were in a cage. Their context isn't alive; it's very flat and one-dimensional. There's no depth to be penetrated. The distinction between foreground and background is not clear – both are, especially in the painted work, the same. None the less, the nudes are never translucent. Their figures are forceful. The nudes even refuse to stay in their frames – their feet, arms and heads, burst the boundaries of the paper and frame. The paper is always too small for them. The model may not want to be noticed or even to be seen; but 'she' is, none the less, eye-catching thanks to the extreme forms I use. The person in the 'drawing' doesn't seek contact; she is just there. But the models do look the viewers directly in the eye; in that sense, they are open. There's no nonsense; the nudes are who they are. They have no pretensions and nothing to hide. For instance, they never have hair before their eyes, or anything blocking their gaze. The face is totally visible; there are no disguises. What I let you see is open, direct – it is there to be seen. But a lot is left out. I am a very dominant force in the drawings; I make drawings that please me.

When I start a drawing by placing a line on paper, a curved or a straight line, within one or two lines the whole drawing is determined. Everything else has to answer to what one has put on the paper. The lines have to be in harmony with one another. If I exaggerate, for instance, a shoulder, then I have to exaggerate other things to achieve aesthetic balance. Every line has to be in agreement with the entire body being drawn. The sphere of the drawing has to be consistent. If I draw a jagged line then that sort of line has to be repeated to create unity. When you begin a drawing you choose the sort of expressiveness that the drawing is going to have; and then you have to continue in that direction. Over the years I've achieved more harmony and consistency in my drawing. Everything about the bodies is a unity; they achieve some sort of *unicity*.

I always look at art. Anything on the wall, I will look at it. I always have an opinion. It irritates me when people have junk on their walls. If they cannot see something in my drawing that they can value, that irks me. They don't have to like them. Even if they don't like the sort of art I make, they can see that something is well drawn or has a harmonious composition. If you don't like female nudes, you can still see how aesthetically they are drawn; or how the use of line is powerful. I want some acknowledgement; though for long I didn't think my work was good enough that I could demand response. People who are not artistic do not see that behind each line there is a whole process of work. I hang the drawings up, here in the house, to be able to look at them and to figure out what needs to be changed. Only a few are, for me, really finished. I can imagine that some people don't know what to say about my drawings. But right now I think I have several really good things hanging here. And people who cannot or will not look at them, hurt me.

You see sadness in my nudes. The models look into the world, but don't really expect a response. They're isolated. The thick lines are defensive; you see the contours but what's really inside is hidden. All the details are erased.

The nudes are me; they all have to do with me. The outside is aestheticized; the inner chaos or mess isn't shown. The drawings are absolute: if the nude sits she really has to *sit*. In my artistic 'language', I'm pretty categorical – things have to be clear. The drawings are just a few lines; they are outwardly simple. There are never 'many words' – the nudes don't speak, they stand there to be looked at. A sphere emanates from the drawings. But the drawings do not open a dialogue. The nudes have a melancholic gaze; they are lonesome. They stand there, looking into the world. The lack of background/foreground in the black and white drawings means that the viewer looks right through the model; but none the less the model is very strongly present. Their honesty, openness, directness are displayed. The aestheticized forms are flowing and flexible – they create an ease of relationship and of interaction. The models dare to look into the world because they are who they are – their honesty is crucial.

My drawings have a right to exist; but I don't really want others to know that I made them. I would constantly like to change my name. I don't want to be asked about my drawings; I don't want to have to react. The drawings are too personal – someone will say 'Are you really so melancholic?' In all the corners of our house there are my women; they just sit (or stand) there. The women are very silent – but under the surface all sorts of things occur. They're asking themselves what they think and feel.

A model plays a role in my drawing in so far as she pleases me. After a while I'm only involved in the drawing; the model disappears. At the start the model gives a sign, a signal. The models are aestheticized in the drawings; but everyone gets (or does not get) aestheticized by their involvement with life. I've drawn hundreds of models, often I can't do anything with the 'beautiful' ones who aren't 'aesthetic'. Many of the very fat models were 'aesthetic'. They've learned to accept their bodies and are making something of their lives. I often exaggerate in the drawings because something that really seems important is worth trying to grasp. Too many lives are mere routine; and are, therefore, not 'aesthetic'. I like having all my women around me. Especially the fat ones – maybe because being fat is forbidden. I often find them very attractive and sympathetic. There is real harmony between their body and person.

I make the best drawings if I'm relaxed and sloppily dressed. If I have to try and be 'pretty', it's disastrous. If I feel in harmony with life, then I have the nerve to set lines powerfully on paper. You have to dare to put strong lines to paper – you venture to do so, if you've been tackling the difficult things in life. You have to brave life – many people are dead; they can't draw. Drawing demands that you choose to let things be seen. For me the danger is that I become so fanatical in my drawing that I lose contact with the people about me. Sometimes, you feel what you want to do and how to go about doing it – but that only lasts for a few drawings and then the wrestling starts all over again.

The studio where I draw is important in so far as I feel I can experiment there. I want to enjoy what I am doing. The process is everything. The surroundings can work as a blockade. Good weather always helps. Summer and light clothes – the feeling you can freely move about – is good for my drawing. People often limit me; you can count on the weather. There's always weather – there's always something happening. I never draw the limiting, restrictive side to things. The more alive the model is, the more different drawings I can make of her. If the model is utterly empty, there's only one solution; go and drink coffee. You notice it on the face. After a quarter of an hour posing, good models start to think. They become reflective. It is really visible – the model expresses her character visually. And that's what I draw. Of course, I can draw what I see, or to make something very different. No one tells me what to do; no one determines the process for me. If the model is too dominant, I go home. A model who lives, is just there, present, visible; and that's what I want. If the model has something to show, then I'm pleased; that excites me. But a lot of people have nothing to offer. In conversations I'm often frustrated, hurt, bored. The other seems to have little to offer and confronts me with the necessity of making life for myself. I want to clamp myself onto the other – to entirely agree with her/him and feel myself fully understood. But I've experienced that things just aren't that way.

Why the body?

What are the reasons for the current interest in writing about the body? Without *agency* and stripped of the primacy of social-political *structure*, unhappy with the dominance of pragmatism and *performativity*, writers are seeking some ground for understanding. Stripped of modernist assumptions, language and issues, intellectuals are so many nudes. Is Maria's affirmation of 'being', concern for reflexivity, attention to openness of gaze and prioritizing of visibility, a valid working agenda? Does she introduce us to a logic of visibility and invisibility, appearance and disappearance, difference and seduction, that makes thinking the present situation (more) possible? Is it our turn, to try drawing?

Bibliography

Ackroyd, S. and Crowdy, P. (1990) 'Can culture be managed? Working with "raw" material', *Personnel Review*, 19 (5): 3–13.
Barthes, R. (1953) *Le degré zero de l'écriture*. Paris: Editions du Seuil.
Baudrillard, J. (1996) 'L'art de la dispararition', *Pretentaine*, no. 5 (May): 117–27.
Bauman, Z. (1988) *Freedom*. Minneapolis: University of Minnesota Press.
Bauman, Z. (1995) *Life in Fragments*. Oxford: Blackwell.
Berman, Marshall (1983) *All That is Solid Melts into Air*. London: Verso.
Bordo, S. (1993) *Unbearable Weight*. Berkeley, CA: University of California Press.
Clark, N. (1996) 'Rear-view mirrorshades: the recursive generation of the cyber-

body', in M. Featherstone and R. Burrows (eds), *Cyberspace, Cyberbodies, Cyberpunk*. London: Sage. pp. 113–34.

Dale, K. and Burrell, G. (1995) 'Under the knife: labour of division in organizational theory', Centre for Social Thought and Technology Workshop, Keele University, UK.

Deleuze, G. (1977) quoted from D. Bouchard (ed.), *Language, Counter-Memory, Practice*. Ithaca, NY: Cornell University Press.

Deleuze, G. and Guattari, F. (1972) *L'Anti-Oedipe*. Paris: Minuit.

Eisner, J.R. (1994) *Attitudes Chaos and the Connectionist Mind*. Oxford: Blackwell.

Elster, J. (1982) *Sour Grapes*. Cambridge: Cambridge University Press.

Featherstone, M. (1991) *Consumer Culture and Postmodernism*. London: Sage.

Featherstone, M. and Burrows, R. (eds) (1995) *Cyberspace, Cyberbodies, Cyberpunk*. London: Sage (also published as *Body and Society*, 1 (3–4): Nov. 1995).

Featherstone, M., Hepworth, M. and Turner, B. (eds) (1991) *The Body: Social Processes and Cultural Theory*. London: Sage.

Gray, C. Hables (1995) *The Cyborg Handbook*. London: Routledge.

Haraway, D. (1991) *Simians, Cyborgs and Women*. London: Free Association Books.

James, W. (1962) *Psychology (Briefer Course)*. New York: Collier Books.

Kelly, K. (1994) *Out of Control*. Reading, MA: Addison–Wesley.

Plant, S. (1996) 'The virtual complexity of culture', in G. Robertson, M. Mash, L. Tickner, J. Bird, B. Curtis and T. Putnam (eds), *FutureNatural*. London: Routledge. pp. 203–17.

Robbins, K. (1995) 'Cyberspace and the world we live in', in M. Featherstone and R. Burrows (eds), *Cyberspace, Cyberbodies, Cyberpunk*. London: Sage. pp. 135–56.

Robertson, G., Mash, M., Tickner, L., Bird, J., Curtis, B. and Putnam, T. (eds) (1996) *FutureNatural*. London: Routledge.

Sawday, J. (1995) *The Body Emblazoned*. London: Routledge.

Sennett, R. (1973) *The Uses of Disorder*. Harmondsworth: Penguin.

Turkle, S. (1995) *Life on the Screen*. New York: Simon & Schuster.

Waldorp, M. (1992) *Complexity: the Emerging Science at the Edge of Order and Chaos*. London: Penguin.

Zizek, S. (1994) 'Supposing the subject', in J. Copjec (ed.), *Supposing the Subject*. London: Verso. pp. 84–105.

Zizek, S. (1996) 'Lacan with quantum physics', in G. Robertson, M. Mash, L. Tickner, J. Bird, B. Curtis and T. Putnam (eds), *FutureNatural*. London: Routledge. pp. 270–89.

PART THREE

PERFORMANCE AND REGULATION

---

6 'The Look of Love': Gender and the Organization of Aesthetics

Philip Hancock and Melissa Tyler

The expansion of organization studies into relatively novel areas of enquiry and method continues to increase in pace and scope. Central to many of the recent theoretical developments within the field has been a concern with the inter-relationship between processes and structures of power and the constitution of subjective identity. This originally emerged in and through the study of the management and control of the 'labour process' under the historically specific conditions of industrial capitalism (see Knights and Willmott, 1989; Thompson, 1983; Willmott, 1990, 1995). While remaining concerned with questions of managerial control and the structure of relations between capital and labour in the workplace, it is to its credit that labour process theory (LPT) has continued to engage with new developments both in the organization of work and with regard to the theoretical tools available to it. In this chapter, we tentatively seek to further this process by combining an LPT-inspired focus on the functioning of managerial control with the recent emergence within organization theory of an interest in the aesthetic dimension of organizational life.

We proceed by way of an exploration of the concept of the aesthetic and its recent emergence as a concern within organization theory. We then consider the significance of the body, and its aesthetic function, in contemporary organizational analysis, focusing in particular on the inter-relationship between corporeality, gender and the aesthetic. Following this, the labour process of a particular occupational segment within the service sector, namely female flight attendants, is presented as a case study of sexually differentiated 'aesthetic labour'. This section of the chapter draws on research carried out on two major international airlines.[1] Central to this section is the assertion that, while on the one hand, the skills of 'status enhancement' (Hochschild, 1983), which female flight attendants are required to deploy, are apparently defined as somehow inherent abilities and so are not recognized, they are, on the other hand, managed in a clearly directive way as integral to their particular labour process. A labour process which is largely concerned with the self management of the 'aesthetic dimension' of their work, both in terms of the beauty of the service provided and the beauty of the service providers themselves. This process is mediated in and through their 'organizational bodies'; that is, through a mode of embodiment which emerges from the manipulation of the body's time, space and movements which must be practised and maintained in order to remain an employee of a particular organization. As such, it focuses upon the ways in which the notion of the aesthetic is clearly central to the labour performed by the female attendants, while at one and the same time, is made to appear marginal to the formal managerial discourse employed and to the formal training and reward system within the organizations.

The penultimate section of the chapter reflects critically upon a range of issues arising from the preceding analysis, focusing not only on the traditional concerns of LPT, but also on the broader philosophical implications of this 'instrumentalization of the aesthetic'; that is, the colonization of the idea of the beautiful as an instrument of corporate managerialism. In the final section we argue that the commodification of the aesthetic dimension within the flight attendant labour process has the dual function of extending managerial control while also reinforcing an essentialized conception of the female aesthetic. Furthermore we note how this process serves to distort the notion of beauty by reducing it to a depthless, and in this particular case, aesthetically valueless symbol of feminine subservience while further extending the domination of a systemic modernist concern with knowledge and control into the sphere of aesthetic experience.

The aesthetic dimension

Originating in Plato's assertion that beauty is itself a 'form', and as such remains timeless, immutable and thus objective, the study of those criteria by which the beautiful may be evaluated and assigned purpose and function has long been associated with the idea and practice of a 'philosophy of aesthetics'. However, attempts to establish such criteria have inevitably been undermined by the ever present objection that the appreciation of the beautiful is inevitably a subjective experience and, as such, immune to the forms of rational assessment that must underpin such objective criteria. Of course, a number of significant and credible attempts have been made to overcome this particular paradox. Kant's (1911) *Critique of Aesthetic Judgement*, for example, postulated that while the appreciation of a beautiful object is in essence a subjective pleasure, its beauty is something which could and should be universally appreciable through the human faculty of judgement. As such, beauty is both a universal and necessary quality of the object in question. Alternatively, Hegel's philosophy of the aesthetic viewed beauty, as expressed through art, as the materialization of the unfolding of the absolute spirit through human consciousness and action. Beautiful art is therefore, for Hegel at least, defined as that which most closely represents the unity of 'nature and spirit' (Weiss, 1974: 318).

While the idea of the 'beautiful' remains central to the concerns of philosophical aesthetics, an etymology of the term suggests a far broader application. Deriving from the Ancient Greek *aisthetikos*, meaning the 'concern of perception' (Vesey and Foulkes, 1990: 4), the term *aesthetics* was originally introduced in 1753 by the German philosopher Baumgarten. His formulation of the aesthetic was in response to the perceived need for a direct philosophical study of human perceptions and sensations which could supplement what was, at the time, a more usual concern with our conceptual models of them. The study of aesthetics was therefore formulated as more than simply the categorization of the beautiful, but rather, as Eagleton (1990: 13) notes, the study of the

> . . . whole of our sensate life together – the business of affections and aversions, of how the world strikes the body on its sensory surfaces, of what takes root in the gaze and the guts and all that arises from our banal, biological insertion into the world.

This formulation of the aesthetic suggests then, far more than simply the appreciation of the qualities of a pleasurable or beautiful object. Rather, it points to an alternative epistemological position; one that credits the sensate as a legitimate mode of knowledge, and which is far more primitive and direct than any rational attempt to order and cognitivize its features and possible implications would allow. It is therefore the unmediated, essentially somatic characteristic of aesthetic knowledge which distinguishes aesthetics from the reception of say symbolic communication. For while the symbolic may well require an aesthetic component for it to be effective, it continues to demand an interpretative and cognitive reception on behalf of the receiver. Symbols must represent or 'signify' something other than themselves, and as such, exist within the domain of rational understanding and articulation. Aesthetic communication, on the other hand, transcends the merely symbolic. It constitutes meaning in its own right as a sensate quality. This is not to suggest of course that aesthetic understanding is somehow essential or ahistorical. Our aesthetic responses are historically conditioned as are our ethical, epistemological or political judgements. Yet they operate beyond the scope of the cognitive, impacting upon the immediate surface of the corporeal and producing an almost ineffable mode of knowing beyond the formal structuring of thought and language.

This understanding of the body as both the immediate site of aesthetic experience and frequently its object has significant implications for any consideration of the status of aesthetic theory. For as Eagleton notes, it was as much in response to this interdependency of the aesthetic and the somatic that the impetus for the recognition of 'aesthetics' as an accepted sub-discipline of philosophy emerged during the eighteenth century Enlightenment as it was to any notion of the disinterested pursuit of knowledge. That is to say, the philosophical appropriation of aesthetics needs to be understood in large part as a response to what was seen as a threat to the Enlightenment belief in the primacy of human reason as the key to all meaningful knowledge and understanding. The philosophical contemplation of the aesthetic, and its concomitant attempt to study and define the nature of the beautiful was, as such, an attempt to colonize the aesthetic in the name of the rational faculties of man [*sic*]. From the eighteenth century at least, the history of the philosophy of aesthetics was therefore about the efforts of Enlightened man to demarcate rational criteria by which sensate 'knowledge' can be classified, appraised and, inevitably, deployed in the service of purposeful action. Within this reading at least, the philosophical attempt to demarcate the beautiful as the criteria for aesthetic judgement can be viewed as little more than an extension of a gendered 'will to truth' and, as such, power, which lies at the heart of the systemic and totalizing tendencies of a corrupted Enlightenment rationality (Adorno and Horkheimer, 1979). Thus, the attempt by the faculty of reason to colonize the aesthetic is by no means something new and is an issue which we return to at a later stage in the chapter.

Despite this historical tendency to either marginalize or colonize the aesthetic, however, the recent decline in confidence in the Enlightenment legacy and its promise of progress through instrumental and technocratic reason[2] has, it would seem, resulted in space emerging for a more open engagement with the implications of the aesthetic. Sensuality, in its broadest sense, is emerging as both an object of analysis and an epistemological disposition worthy of serious consideration within the domain of organization studies. This is not to suggest, of course, that it has shorn free of its appropriation as a tool of rational analysis, quite the contrary. Nevertheless, a growing body of research literature is now starting to emerge that suggests that the value of the aesthetic dimension is starting to be recognized by those wishing to refine their conceptualizations of organizational life. This, in turn, may yet lead to a greater critical understanding of how the aesthetic may itself be embedded within relations of organized domination and control.

With its roots in the 'cultural turn' in the study and design of work and its organization (see, for example, Anthony, 1994; Casey, 1996; Payne, 1991; Phesey, 1993), the increasing significance of organizational aesthetics is to be seen most clearly in what Turner (1990) has described as the 'rise of organizational symbolism'. Self-evidently premised upon the centrality of the sensate in organizational life, this approach to the study of organizational culture has sought to focus on the 'ceremonies, the rhetoric, the moral drama, the *aesthetic* style of organizations' (1990: 86, emphasis added). However, as we noted above, one cannot simply reduce the category of the aesthetic to that of the symbolic, and indeed, more specific attempts to relate the aesthetic, as a mode of understanding, directly to the study of organizations have also appeared recently. Guillén (1997), for example, has systematically charted the impact and influence that Taylorist-inspired organizational practices have had upon the aesthetic qualities of early twentieth century modernism, demonstrating the inherent 'aesthetic' impact managerial strategies may, albeit unwittingly, have on the wider cultural sphere. In a similar vein, Strati (1992, 1996) and Gagliardi (1990, 1996) have both sought to address the importance of studying organizational aesthetics as a means of developing a greater insight into how meanings are structured and promoted within the cultural environment of the work organization. However, while Strati presents a case for the importance of studying previously overlooked examples of organizational facticity, such as the significance of office decor or the location and style of office chairs, as a means of understanding the structuring of social relations within the workplace, Gagliardi appears to provide a more wide-ranging overview of the possible implications for an 'aesthetic' approach to organization studies.

For Gagliardi (1996), the primary focus of such an approach is identified as the organizational 'artifact'. This he defines not only as an externalized product of human agency, but also as something which can fulfil a given aim through its ability, as a physical entity, to be perceived directly by the senses (1996: 565). As such, artifacts are brought into existence as communicative objects which can be deployed to project a desired organizational pathos. The concept of pathos is distinguished here from both the organizational 'logos', the 'specificity of its beliefs', and its 'ethos', the moral component of those beliefs, and is described as a particular way of *perceiving* and *feeling* organizational reality (1996: 568–73) which transcends the cognitive faculties of discrimination and identification. As such, it frees itself of its everyday association with the idea of a pitiful quality and represents what is essentially a non-cognitive way of knowing one's organizational environment (or indeed the organizational environment of another) as it impacts upon the corporeal immediacy of the senses. It is within this context that Gagliardi considers organizational artifacts as able to play a unique role in the structuring of organizational action and the shaping of members' beliefs and cultural values. That is, through managerial strategies of cultural manipulation which more or less rely upon the *aesthetic* qualities of those objects and practices which they deem appropriate as expressing a desired feeling or pathos of collective organizational identity. He goes on to define the process through which such desired aesthetic outcomes are often achieved as that of *landscaping*. This important concept can be interpreted as a process whereby cultural codes, designed to elicit a particular form of aesthetic response, are incorporated into what appear to be 'naturally' existing objects, themselves bearing preordained aesthetic qualities. Through this process, aesthetic communication can take place without the need to establish new objects of sensate appreciation; it can function through that which is already familiar to the aesthetic repertoire of those who come into contact with the organizational environment.

Gagliardi's observations have, we would argue, significant implications not only for an account of the structuring of the organizational lifeworld as favoured by, say, Strati (1992, 1996), but also for a critical reappraisal of the issue of managerial and organizational control. This is based upon the observation alluded to earlier that the unique quality of aesthetic understanding is that it bypasses the rational faculties and as such provides an ideal mechanism for the generation of ideological systems of control. As Gagliardi (1996: 568) notes, these may be seen to 'influence our perception of reality, to the point of subtly shaping beliefs, norms and cultural values'. The implication of this line of thinking is, we would suggest, that current concerns about the role that various strategies of corporate culturalism play in the management and control of the contemporary labour process cannot avoid the question of aestheticization as a project or technology of managerial control.

One of the aims underpinning this chapter, therefore, is a tentative attempt to develop a critical analysis of the construction, deployment and reception of a form of organizational 'artifact' as a mode of managerial intervention, and we do so with specific reference to the flight attendant labour process. The artifacts in question are not, therefore, inanimate objects such as Strati's (1996) chairs. Rather, the subject/objects of our enquiry are the *bodies* of a set of organizational employees who are constituted, we shall argue, due to their gender and occupation, as aesthetic artifacts of a managerially conceived organizational pathos. As such, we aim to re-examine the aesthetic dimension of control within the workplace – the integral relationship between the aesthetic, the corporeal and the gendered nature of work and employment. Furthermore, we seek to address the ongoing attempt to maintain a rational and instrumental dominance of the aesthetic as a central imperative of modern cultural thinking.

However, before commencing an examination of some of the research findings, a brief consideration of the significance of the role of the body as both the focal point of the aesthetic and also as the primary instrument of labour, will be addressed.

The (re)discovery of working bodies

The past ten years or so has witnessed an emergence within sociology of a concern with the body as a site and outcome of social regulation and complex relations of power and discipline (Featherstone et al., 1991; Shilling, 1993; Turner, 1992). Prior to this, even the most radical variants of social theory, often associated with the classical Marxist tradition of critique, had viewed the realm of consciousness and thought to be, above all else, the site of the struggle for emancipation, with the body playing little more than a supporting role as the objectified tool of labour.[3] As such, the body has, like the aesthetic, remained somewhat ironically in a state of persona non grata. Yet the history of the body is integral to the history of human society and no discussion of work and aesthetics would be complete without the figure of the corporeal playing a major role. After all, it operates as both the material expression of the realm of the idea as well as the surface upon which the material environment inscribes its presence. Indeed, one does not need to be concerned with such esoteric concerns as that of the aesthetic to acknowledge the centrality of the body to the tradition and focus of modern(ist) organization studies. For example, the pioneering work of Taylor (1911) is often most poignantly explained in terms of his experimentation on the working body of Schmidt, a man chosen for his brute physical strength and lack of mental vitality. Similarly, Ford's groundbreaking reorganization of the labour process was founded on the spatial control of bodies along a moving assembly line. Developments in human relations thinking, while focusing upon the processes of inter-subjectivity in the workplace, likewise shared the aim of sculpting the human body as an instrument of physical labour. During recent years, studies by Townley (1994), Casey (1995, 1996) and Barry and Hazen (1996) have sought to relate this realization that the body is something that must be regulated and organized by management, with the rise of new regimes of accumulation and modes of work organization, identified with the ideas of post-industrialism and post-Fordism. As Barry and Hazen (1996: 146) note, when it comes to the relationship between work and the body, 'it would seem our bodies have been hopelessly moulded, regimented and made to disappear by managerial and organizational practices, projects that in turn owe their rise to widespread societal and technological movements'.

In addition to this recognition that new modes of organization may require new modes of embodiment amongst employees, recent feminist analyses have focused on the gendered nature of the role and management of the body at work. Cockburn (1991) alerts us to a 'politics of bodies in the workplace'. Similarly, Acker (1990, 1992) has argued that the body is very much a part of a process of control in work organizations. Hearn and Parkin have argued that the management of the dialectical relationship that is 'organization sexuality' is based largely on 'precision in the control of the body' (Hearn and Parkin, 1995: 20). Empirical studies of 'women's work' have identified several examples of occupations in which certain 'properties, qualities and attributes' (De Lauretis, 1989) associated with women's bodies come to be commodified, such as in nursing (James, 1989), clerical work (Davies, 1979) and waitressing and bar work (Adkins, 1995; Hall, 1993). Such studies have focused on the extent to which women's bodies are commodified in the performance of both sexual and emotional labour (Adkins, 1995; Hochschild, 1983). Adkins (1995: 18) for instance, found that the control of women's bodies, in particular the maintenance of a sexually attractive appearance, is central both to 'the gendered organization of work and [to] the forms of control and exploitation to which women workers were subject'.

Yet what has not, we would suggest, been explored explicitly in such studies is the role of the body as an 'aesthetic artifact'. As such, there has been little attempt to consider the significance of the relationship between types of women's work and the management of an embodied and intrinsically 'female' aesthetic. Yet the role and purpose of many women currently in the labour force is, it would seem to us, to perform such an aesthetic function – as embodied artifacts of a managerially conceived, feminine aesthetic. From teleworkers to waitresses, nurses to flight attendants, the presumed inter-relationship between the aesthetic and the feminine is inexorable. Indeed, such a phenomenon can be seen to be deeply embedded within the previously alluded to gendered origins of the eighteenth century idea of the aesthetic. That is, as the feminine 'other' of masculine rationality, the 'sister' of logic, a feminine analogue of reason, 'born as a woman, subordinate to man but with her own humble, necessary tasks to perform' (Eagleton, 1990: 16).

In the following section of the chapter, therefore, we present research findings of a study of women undertaking tasks which reveal not only an emphasis upon their performance as aesthetic artifacts but what appears to be the belief that their ability to achieve this role is based upon an essentialized understanding of their embodied capacity for aesthetic communication as a natural outcome of their feminine gender.

The essentialization of female aesthetics

The research discussed here involved three main phases of fieldwork, each of which explored critically aspects of the labour process of the female flight attendant. The first phase involved two case studies into the recruitment, training and supervision of flight attendants at two airlines which were chosen specifically because, at the time of the fieldwork, they were key players in the highly competitive transatlantic business travel market in the UK. A concurrent analysis of company documentation was undertaken at both airlines. Observational flights were then undertaken in various classes of travel with both organizations – in Economy, Business Class and First Class (ten in total, six with one airline and four with the other). During these flights, particular attention was paid to interaction between flight attendants and between flight attendants and passengers. The second phase involved three series of semi-structured interviews with a variety of airline personnel and with airline passengers: with applicants to airlines (12 in total, 9 women and 3 men); with trainee and experienced flight attendants, including those who were involved in the recruitment, training and supervision of other flight attendants (25 in total, 19 women and 6 men) and with passengers (48 in total, 33 men and 15 women). The third and final phase entailed a content analysis of a wide variety of airline documentation, ranging from company mission statements, recruitment and training literature to advertising and marketing materials depicting female flight attendants obtained from some 48 airlines (out of 64 who were contacted).

The flight attendant labour process

In order to contextualize our analysis, it is important that we first outline briefly what were observed as the primary and recognized features of the labour process undertaken by the attendants we studied. These attendants were employed largely by two airlines providing transatlantic services which were aimed at meeting the demands of a highly segmented and overwhelmingly male-dominated market. As such, they were considered to be the 'elite' of their profession, providing high levels of service to an informed, discerning and culturally powerful clientele. The main functions they were expected to perform were the greeting of passengers onto the aircraft, the explanation and maintenance of safety standards and procedures, the ensuring of passengers' comfort and contentment, the serving of food and drinks, the selling of duty free goods and the administering of basic first aid. They combined processes of manual (serving drinks, clearing up and so on) and non-manual (studying seating plans, organizing the meal services and completing complicated stock-control forms) labour as well as performing aspects of 'emotional labour' (Hochschild, 1983), in that they sought to comfort and reassure passengers throughout the flights while at the same time controlling their own emotions and responses. However, in addition to these we also observed what we considered to be the exercise of forms of 'aesthetic labour', which were manifest yet rendered invisible in terms of the formal recognition of the labour process they undertook. It is to this aesthetic dimension of their labour that we now turn, in our consideration of some of the findings of our fieldwork.

Mapping aesthetic labour

As we have suggested above, early contact with the cabin crew of the airlines in question clearly indicated that the work of female flight attendants requires skills and abilities which they are deemed to possess simply by virtue of being women. These include, for instance, 'caring' physically and emotionally for others through the deployment of 'tacit skills' (Manwaring and Wood, 1985) in anticipating and responding to the needs and expectations of others. As one experienced, female flight attendant put it,

> '. . . this job is more natural for a woman than for a man . . . because females in general are more caring than men . . . women are much more helpful, they are kinder and *more instinctive* . . .' (emphasis added)

Yet, while these 'skills' were clearly understood as necessary to do the job, they were not, it was observed, recognized or remunerated as such by management or, indeed, by passengers or colleagues. However, these 'skills' which female flight attendants were expected to deploy were none the less managed, both by each other and by themselves, through the maintenance of what we would term their *organizational bodies*; that is to say, their bodies were constituted and presented in line with organizational directives both by themselves and through the mutual observation and regulation of their colleagues and, as such, seemed to represent the materialized expression of an organizational cultural ideal to which they all contributed and, as such, mutually regulated.

As the period of fieldwork progressed, what also became clear, however, was that central to this process of 'somatic supervision' was the centrality of the construction, and implicit management, of the aesthetic dimension of their work, both in terms of the service provided and the sensate qualities of the service providers themselves. The presentation and performance of the flight attendant's 'organizational body' acted as a material expression of the airline by which she was employed. As such, it was the body itself that became an organizational 'artifact' through which the employing organization was able to encounter its highly segmented market. To put it in its crudest terms, the feminine beauty embodied in the appearance of the female attendants appeared to embody a sense of organizational beauty which the airline management wished to project. The significance of this aesthetic dimension of the flight attendants was not confined simply to the realm of sight, however. It was an embodied form of aesthetic communication impacting upon all the senses of passengers and fellow cabin crew alike. This is exemplified in one of the training documents produced for the initiation of newly recruited flight attendants. In it the airline outlined its corporate philosophy and brand identity as being intended to fulfil three basic principles. These were:

- to act as a system of *recognition* for staff and customers;
- to establish a tone of *voice* which accurately reflects how the airline conducts its business; and
- to create a flexible *personality* for the airline. (emphasis added)

In other words, through management strategies which are organized primarily around Gagliardi's (1996) notion of 'landscaping', the organizational bodies of these employees were required to embody the desired aesthetic of the company – to speak in an organizational 'tone of voice' and to adopt a flexible organizational 'personality', of which their embodiment becomes the material artifact. Furthermore, this aesthetic performance, which was required of flight attendants in order to maintain the 'look', 'sound' and 'sense' of the airline, was clearly considered to be one of the primary roles of the flight attendants.

Within the airline industry, aesthetic codes on feminine embodiment are implicated in various ways throughout the recruitment, training and supervision of flight attendants. One of the recruitment sessions which we observed was particularly interesting in terms of providing an insight into the significance for the recruitment staff, from day one, of the female body as a 'potential' aesthetic artifact. For example, applicants were rejected from entering the training programme for some of the following reasons:

- they were 'too old';
- their skin was blemished;
- their hair was too short, too messy or too severe;
- their nails were too short or bitten;
- their posture was 'poor';
- they had 'chubby' legs.

Other applicants were rejected on the basis that their weight was not considered to be in proportion to their height, because they were too introverted or because they lacked 'poise and style'. Others were rejected because, as one of the recruitment interviewers noted, they had a 'common accent'. One applicant was rejected by recruitment personnel on the basis that her teeth were too prominent in relation to her other facial features, while others were rejected for being considered slightly 'pear shaped' or out of proportion (Tyler and Abbott, 1998). Applicants to both airlines studied were told constantly that they should be 'well groomed' and particularly that they should 'be polished'; with instructors demonstrating this internalized and shared organizational aesthetic. As one particular recruitment interviewer put it

> '. . . first impression is very important to us. We have to act like a passenger and make an immediate judgment about whether or not we like someone [an applicant] . . . Physically, we look at their make-up, their standard of dress, their hair and especially their hands .. Some people have very old hands or their nails are not well cared for . . . We also look at their posture, their legs and particularly their shoes . . . We would reject an applicant if they were not polished . . . if they looked scruffy, had no grooming . . . or of course, if they had an attitude . . .'
> 'An attitude?'
> '. . . if they lacked sparkle, if they tried to take over, had no personality or if they needed re-modelling.'

The connection between appearance and personality was also an issue that was highlighted constantly. Many of those experienced flight attendants interviewed made connections between the personalities they were asked to project and the 'look' they were expected to maintain. Several of them also suggested that the airline by which they were employed clearly associated profits with the appearance of their flight attendants. To put it simply, images of attractive young women are used to sell airline seats, particularly in the highly profitable sectors of Business and First Class travel. As one female flight attendant, who had recently been promoted from Economy to First Class travel at one of the airlines, put it

> '. . . we are told that we should be sincere and not to look false . . . we should smile but not over-smile . . . that means that we should look friendly but not overdo it . . . We are told that we should have poise . . .'

'What is poise exactly?' . . . 'Well, I suppose it is being enthusiastic but in a calm sort of way . . . being sort of elegant . . . feminine.'

Applicants were thus found to be selected on the basis of their being capable of following stage directions, particularly those on how to project an (organizational) image or 'look': how to have 'poise' and 'grooming', as recruitment interviewers put it. As such, female flight attendants were found to be selected on the criteria of being able to perform an aesthetically appropriate 'organizational body', without making the end result seem like a performance; that is, without revealing any evidence that the performance requires labour. In this respect, the labour process is concealed behind the idea of a naturally organizational 'body idiom' (Goffman, 1959); a natural (and therefore unskilled/unworked) presentation and performance of an organizational body. As one particular recruitment interviewer noted,

'. . . female flight attendants should have poise, they should be elegant . . . they should be . . . well sort of feminine . . . they should have a charm that comes naturally to them . . .'

Those who were successful in gaining admission to the training programmes were reminded constantly to use their 'body language' as much as possible: 'above all, use your hips, hands, arms and your voice'. Yet, they were given no actual training or instruction in this use of 'body language', but were told 'it's just common-sense really'. Three particular uses of body language were considered to be fundamental to the establishment of a 'rapport' with passengers, as training instructors put it and, as such, to the high quality provision expected of them. They were told to

always *walk softly* through the cabin, always *make eye contact* with each and every passenger, and always *smile* at them. This makes for a much more personal service, and is what First Class travel and [we] as a company are all about. It's what we're here for. (emphasis added)

With regard to the formal supervision of flight attendants, they were required to conform to company-specific 'Uniform and Grooming Regulations', which as well as regulations on clothing and shoes, contained stipulations on hair, make-up and height–weight ratios. However, these formal regulations were very much reinforced by more gender-specific and informal peer pressure and self-appraisal. Discipline, as a mode of self-management, as the outcome of peer and self-surveillance, appeared central to the maintenance of the desired organizational aesthetic, with employees constantly under pressure, both external and internal, to ensure the appropriate 'look' and overall image was maintained. Numerous examples of this could be cited here. For instance, one particular trainee flight attendant reported to us that she had been advised to have electrolysis on her upper lip. On another occasion, a very blonde, junior flight attendant was advised by a colleague to dye her hair to make it appear more 'natural' as she had been told that she looked like 'a neon light coming down the aisle towards the passengers'. Similarly, 'weight checks' are conducted as part of routine grooming checks in the airline industry generally and are certainly not unique to either of the airlines into which we undertook case study research. As such, the management of the aesthetic dimension of the female flight attendants' labour process appeared as central to the labour of these women as was the serving of drinks or the demonstration of safety procedures.

Towards a critical reappraisal of aesthetic management

The research findings outlined above suggest that an integral dimension of the work of female flight attendants is their role as bearers, both to their co-workers and their clients, of a distinctive organizational aesthetic. This process of aesthetic communication is, as perhaps one would expect, conveyed through a particular mode of organizational embodiment which is constituted through the landscaping of the female attendants' 'lived bodies' via the inscription of corporately desired aesthetic codes – codes which are identified and manufactured to express the formally established 'organizational beauty' of the airlines in question. The organizational bodies of the attendants thus become artifacts of the organization, much as the corporate logos or the design of the aircraft interiors do, serving to form and communicate a collective organizational identity both amongst its members and to its paying clients. In the penultimate section of this chapter, we intend to engage critically with a number of implications of this process, implications which emerged both in the course of the analysis of the fieldwork findings and through a process of more abstract theoretical reflection.

The aesthetic labour process

As we have alluded to throughout the discussion of the findings derived from the fieldwork, the female flight attendants we studied appeared to carry out labour at two distinct levels. At one level there was the labour that they were formally trained to do and, as such, were financially remunerated for. This comprised largely of seating passengers, ensuring their physical and emotional comfort, preparing and serving meals and generally ensuring that safety standards were maintained during the flight. However, in addition to this we identified a further, somewhat 'invisible' labour process taking place. This was one which was neither remunerated nor particularly acknowledged as labour by management, clients or even by the attendants themselves. This invisible labour process involved the self-landscaping and maintenance of the attendants' lived bodies into aesthetic artifacts; organizational artifacts which materialized an idealized self-image of beautiful service and corporate perfection. The reason that this particular labour process could remain largely invisible was that the aesthetic the airlines clearly wished to project was itself understood as the 'natural' expression of the feminine body. The aesthetic qualities of poise, elegance, slenderness and even gentleness of voice that the airlines wished to associate themselves with were deemed to be natural feminine attributes. Indeed, in aesthetic terms they signified the idea of the 'beautiful' as an essential feminine quality, a feminine quality that would be immediately apparent and appreciated by the predominantly male passengers.[4] Yet, the idea of such natural attributes is itself a mythology. Women in all walks of life have continually to work at reproducing cultural ideals of feminine beauty and this is particularly the case in a job that requires women to work in an environment and role which is generally unconducive to the maintenance of such an aesthetic (Boyd and Bain, 1998). This contradiction can be observed, for example, in the words of a training instructor who, during a training session on First Aid, described lifting sick or injured passengers as being

> '. . . very unglamorous . . . you need to keep your knees together as you bend down . . . your stockings might ladder and your make-up probably runs. You'd fail your grooming check after all that . . . But at least if two of you work together, you can make the passenger comfortable. Then you can sort your hair and make-up out . . .'

These particular employees are, therefore, continually active in producing and reproducing, through constant attention to the maintenance of their organizational bodies, a particular organizational pathos.

Having said all this what, if anything, do these findings contribute to that body of knowledge which has come, over the years, to be commonly referred to as 'labour process theory'? The labour process debate has, in many ways, developed considerably since the appearance of Braverman's (1974) *Labor and Monopoly Capital* and the presentation of its central thesis that the defining characteristic of the labour process under capitalism is the increasing control over the agency of employees by management through progressive 'deskilling' and the separation of conception and execution through the relocation of knowledge of the labour process from worker to manager. Certainly the direct relationship posited by Braverman between deskilling and managerial control has been criticized as a conflation of one particular strategy of control with control itself (Friedman, 1977). Similarly, the contention of the Brighton Labour Process Group that deskilling represents one of the 'immanent laws of the capitalist labour process' (1977: 16) has been brought into doubt by studies such as that by Wilkinson (1983), which observed that policies of deskilling were merely one option amongst a number which could be pursued by employers. Indeed, as Thompson (1990: 100) notes, the evidence now suggests that at 'any given point capital may re-skill, recombine tasks or widen workers' discretion and responsibility'.

While significant elements of deskilling have taken place in the labour process of the flight attendants we observed, for example in the preparation of food due to the introduction of improved technologies of preparation and storage, our findings suggested that in relation to the performance of 'organizational bodies' it was neither a process of deskilling or reskilling we were witnessing, but rather, an instrumentally orientated exploitation of those skills deemed to be possessed 'naturally' by women by virtue of their gender. As such, these skills are not explicitly acknowledged either by management or clients alike. Yet this particular dimension of the attendants' labour process serves, at one and the same time, to reproduce both the conditions of their subjective appropriation as instruments of labour and the social relations which identify women as the bearers of these unique skills and attributes; skills which themselves are a prerequisite for their exploitation as objects of an organizationally imposed feminine aesthetic.

The denigration of the subject

> Comparing man and woman in general one may say: woman would not have the genius for finery if she did not have the instinct for the *secondary* role. (Nietzsche, 1990: 102, emphasis in original)

The process identified above, whereby female flight attendants are subject to an essentialization of their socially defined feminine bodies as encoded artifacts of an *externally* imposed organizational aesthetic, not only represents an appropriation of invisible labour. Rather, it also appears to point to a subjective *internalization* of an essentialized feminine organizational aesthetic; one that serves to reconstitute female subjectivity through a mirror image, or simulacra, of its idealized self. The subject thus emerges, in part, as both a condition and outcome of this 'invisible' labour process of organizational aestheticization. The relative success of this process can be understood as providing the ontological security which the now decentred subject desires in an environment in which the worth of employees is measured by their ability to fulfil the aesthetic standards embedded within the organizational culture they themselves reproduce. The uncertainty of the modern fragmented self, as Willmott (1990: 368) notes, is often satisfied by the individual through 'seeking the occupancy of secure but oppressive positions'. The transformation of the aesthetic dimension of being into a technology of organizational power operates both in and through its ability to draw upon and reaffirm a culturally dominant expectation of women as objects of beauty which at one and the same time reaffirms their subjective sense of self-worth and value. This process affirms Knights and Willmott's (1989: 550) observation broadly derived from the work of Foucault, that 'subjugation occurs where the freedom of a subject is directed narrowly, and in a self-disciplined fashion, towards participation in practices which are known or understood to provide the individual with a sense of security and belonging'.

As such, the subject is willing to sacrifice the anxiety and existential insecurities of subjecthood for the security of the objective carrier of the organizational aesthetic. This is even more effective when, as in this instance, the aesthetic is deemed concurrent with the broader cultural expectations surrounding the notion of an 'ideal self' as articulated through an essentialized conception of female embodiment. For female flight attendants to meet the standards of aesthetic presentation expected by the organization, to be able to embody the organization, is at one and the same time to embody the feminine ideal of the 'beautiful'. However, the Foucauldian-derived understanding that 'forms of power are exercised through subjecting individuals to their own identity of subjectivity' (Knights and Wilmott, 1989: 553) must also be critically receptive to the concomitant process of objectification as derived from Marx (1970). Otherwise, we would contend, the power of a normative critique is inevitably eroded. As such, the process of subjugation we have identified through our case study, in this instance at least, appears to produce an inevitable and parallel denigration of the status of the subject through those processes which also provide the discursive and material resources through which an essentialized feminine subjectivity may be mobilized. That is, that the requirement placed upon them to embody an organizational aesthetic also effectively de-humanizes the employee, who is forced to act in a role of 'ontological subordinate' to the employing organization.

For example, the following extract from the corporate mission statement of one particular airline outlines as part of its corporate philosophy the requirement of its employees to 'embody services that meet or exceed our customers' expectations . . . without which *we have no reason for being*' (emphasis added). What this suggests is an embodied process of organizational anthropomorphism, which simultaneously seeks to subjectify the organization and objectify the employee. The assumption and expression of an embodied organizational aesthetic therefore appears to be a fundamental aspect of the role of the flight attendant as a sexually differentialized labourer. As the aesthetic artifact of the organziation, the embodied identity of the attendant is reduced to the category of object, as the bearer of the aesthetic identity of the now subjectivized organization. Thus, just as the surface of the organizational body of the flight attendant is landscaped and maintained (through diet, exercise, cleansing, make-up, uniformity of dress and so on) so the same techniques of 'somatic supervision' are deployed in order to ensure that inside the organizational body, beneath the 'image of flawless professionalism', as one cabin crew recruitment advertisement described the role of a flight attendant, lives an organizational persona grata.

Is there no truth in beauty?

> Should we worry about the 'uses' of art and beauty in the hands of managers in search of other ends such as short-term profitability or efficiency? (Ottensmeyer, 1996: 189)

In the penultimate section of this chapter, we move beyond the more traditional concerns expressed within the labour process literature and focus upon the broader philosophical issues raised by the incorporation of the aesthetic dimension of human experience into the domain of organizational governance. Throughout the chapter we have argued that strategies of managerial control within this particular form of the labour process have extended their gaze over the sensate dimension of work which, in turn, serves to impact upon the individual sense of identity as a reconstituted aesthetic artifact of the organization. As such, our argument resonates with Eagleton's (1990: 3) observation that:

> The construction of the modern notion of the aesthetic artifact is . . . inseparable from the construction of the dominant ideological forms of modern class-society, and indeed from a whole new form of human subjectivity appropriate to that social order.

The instrumentalization of the aesthetic dimension of the flight attendant labour process can, therefore, be understood as representing an example of the final victory of a systemic modernism. One which, driven inexorably onwards by an instrumental rationality that has already colonized and differentiated both the ethical (Bentham, 1948) and the epistemological (Weber, 1991), now degrades the aesthetic, reducing it to nothing more than another quantifiable and operationalizable variable.

This image of organizational beauty, as embodied in the landscaped materiality of the flight attendant, anchors the aesthetic in a historically specific set of social relations that expresses not the anti-discursive of the sensate, but the discourse of instrumentality premised upon efficiency, calculability and performativity. The beauty of the attendant is reduced to yet another cognitive category, much like the width of the body of the aircraft or the thrust generated from its turbo-fan engines, which is both expected (as an essentialized category of the feminine) and reassuring (in that it confirms the identity of both gazer and those who are gazed upon). As such, it is not only the body of the subject which is both essentialized and yet denied, but the idea of the aesthetic as representing an emancipatory moment.

Critical social theory has long posited the idea of the aesthetic as a form of knowledge, one which offers up a glimpse of the possible state of sensuous being which is transcendent of the material limitations artificially imposed by the performance principle embedded within the imperatives of capitalist modernity. As Marcuse (1979: 69) noted of the aesthetic experience of art:

> Against all fetishism of the productive forces, against the continued enslavement of individuals by the objective conditions (which remain those of domination), art represents the ultimate goal of all revolutions: the freedom and happiness of the individual.

This degradation of the aesthetic is made even more disturbing when one considers that it is not simply the quality of the aesthetic which is corrupted here, but also its attempted appropriation into a system of expression that constitutes a depthless image of feminine subservience as the definitive presentation of the idea of the beautiful. It becomes a medium through which the (mis)recognition of the female subject as an object of male discourse and imagery is operationalized within the everyday working practices of these particular women. As such, the implications of this process extend well beyond the confines of this particular dimension of the flight attendant labour process: 'the Establishment has created and effectively sold beauty in the form of plastic purity and loveliness – an extension of exchange values to the aesthetic-erotic dimension' (Marcuse, 1979: 62).

How far this general mode of critique can be taken depends, of course, on the extent to which one is willing to elevate the category of the aesthetic above the values of instrumental appropriation which have become so central to our modern(ist) sensibilities. As we noted at the start of the chapter, the philosophy of aesthetics has frequently associated the idea of the beautiful with truth and immutability, and as such, as antithetical to the notion of crude utility exemplified in the instrumental aestheticization of the bodies of the organizational employees we have considered above. Yet whether or not we choose to accept such philosophical evocations will, most likely, remain very much a matter of personal disposition on the part of the reader. However, such a critique does, at the very least, point to the possibility of a critical engagement with such developments, allowing them to be understood as representing a further intensification of the labour process above and beyond the usual concerns with skill and the material foundations of ideological control. Such a realization may therefore equally open up the space for competing modes of discourse in which the aesthetic dimension is recognized as both an integral aspect of female labour and, as such, worthy of reward, and as a potential site of resistance to managerial interventions and strategies of control.

Conclusion

The research findings and the arguments elaborated here represent an attempt to develop a critical account of the practice and implications of the managerial colonization of the aesthetic dimension of the female flight attendant labour process. Clearly this attempt has not been without its problems, however. Combining the ideas, concepts and discursive resources of various and often competing modes of thought can often prove to be both treacherous and highly unpopular. Nevertheless, we do believe that in this instance it has proven to be a worthwhile endeavour. By way of a conclusion, we would contend that the following issues have arisen from this undertaking. First, female flight attendants are expected to perform an aesthetic role which is deemed to be intrinsic to their feminine 'nature' and thus, whilst not acknowledged or remunerated as an integral dimenion of their labour process, is nevertheless subject to managerial intervention. Second, to perform this role they must achieve and maintain an aestheticized 'organizational body' which involves being subject not only to organizationally specific prescriptions of the aesthetic, but also to those aesthetic codes which operate in the industry and in society generally and which serve to define the role and identity of the flight attendant. Third, this process of 'instrumental aestheticization' is a component aspect of the subjectivization process which operates more generally within the workplace, particularly as it applies to so-called 'women's work' in that it serves to reinforce a mode of feminine subjectivity which draws upon a range of already dominant cultural codes which are explicitly related to an idealized conception of femininity. Finally, this process is consistent, it seems, with far broader historical developments associated with the modern drive to colonize the aesthetic or sensate dimension of human experience in the name of a systemic rationality. One which, at one and the same time, renders the aesthetic 'knowable' under the terms of a calculable criterion of the beautiful while robbing it of that which provides its unique capacity to reveal dimensions of being that are increasingly hidden from us.

Notes

This chapter is based upon papers presented during 1998 to the British Sociological Association Annual Conference, 'Making Sense of the Body: Theory, Research and Practice' (Edinburgh) and the 16th Annual International Labour Process Conference (Manchester).

1 We are grateful to Blackwell publishers for granting us permission to reproduce empirical data used in a consideration of the relevance of Mauss's theory of 'the gift' to the female flight attendant labour process (Tyler and Taylor, 1998).

2 We refer here, of course, to those developments within philosophy, social theory and other aspects of the social and human sciences which have been variously labelled postmodern, poststructuralist or even post-rationalist (see Cooper and Burrell, 1988, for an early discussion of postmodernism and its significance for organization studies).

3 One significant exception to this can be seen in and through the writings of Friedrich Nietzsche, the most corporeal of the post-Enlightenment philosophers. (For a discussion of this see Hughes, 1996.)

4 Male dominance within this particular segment of the air travel market has become an issue of increasing concern to the airlines themselves, however. For example, as far back as 1990 British Airways commissioned a 'semiotic audit' of their communications strategy in an attempt to encourage (the ever expanding number of) female business travellers to travel with them. The resulting report acknowledged that BA communications did tend to represent women either as 'mother-nanny' figures or as 'sex objects' in their corporate literature. This same semiotic audit was also highly critical of the constant utilization of the 'phallic shape of the plane . . . overcoded with a concentrated use of straight-line (rationality) symbolism' (British Airways Market Research Department, 1990: 4). This report demonstrated clearly that the issue of the symbolic and, implicitly, the aesthetic is something that airline management is being forced to take seriously. However,

despite the report's findings, our own research in this sector does not suggest much progress in dismantling the gendered bias embedded within this field of communication.

References

Acker, J. (1990) 'Hierarchies, jobs, bodies: a theory of gendered organizations', *Gender and Society*, 4: 139–58.

Acker, J. (1992) 'Gendering organizational theory', in A.J. Mills and P. Tancred (eds), *Gendering Organizational Analysis*. London: Sage. pp. 248–60.

Adkins, L. (1995) *Gendered Work: Sexuality, Family and the Labour Market*. Milton Keynes: Open University Press.

Adorno, T. and Horkheimer, T. (1979) *Dialectic of Enlightenment*. London: Verso.

Anthony, P. (1994) *Managing Culture*. Buckingham: Open University Press.

Barry, D. and Hazen, M.A. (1996) 'Do you take your body to work?', in D. Boje, R. Gephart Jr and T. Thatchenkery (eds), *Postmodern Management and Organization Theory*. London: Sage. pp. 140–53.

Bentham, J. (1948) *An Introduction to the Principles of Morals and Legislation*. New York: Hafner Publishing Co.

Boyd, C. and Bain, P. (1998) '"Once I get you up there, where the air is rarified": health, safety and the working conditions of airline cabin crews', *New Technology, Work and Employment*, 13 (1): 16–28.

Braverman, H. (1974) *Labor and Monopoly Capital: The Degradation of Work in the Twentieth Century*. New York: Monthly Review Press.

Brighton Labour Process Group (1977) 'The capitalist labour process', *Capital and Class*, 1 (1).

British Airways Market Research Department (1990) Semiotic Audit of Gender in British Airways Communications: notes to accompany a verbal debrief. Hounslow: British Aiways, unpublished internal publication.

Casey, C. (1995) *Work, Self and Society: After Industrialism*. London: Routledge.

Casey, C. (1996) 'Corporate transformations: designer culture, designer employees and post-occupational solidarity', *Organization*, 3 (3): 317–39.

Cockburn, C. (1991) *In the Way of Women: Men's Resistance to Sex Equality in Organizations*. London: Macmillan.

Cooper, B. and Burrell, G. (1988) 'Modernism, postmodernism and organisational analysis: an introduction', *Organization Studies*, 9 (2): 221–35.

Davies, M. (1979) 'Woman's place is at the typewriter: the feminization of the clerical labour force', in Z.R. Eisenstein (ed.), *Capitalist Patriarchy and the Case for Socialist Feminism*. New York: Monthly Review Press.

De Lauretis, T. (1989) 'The essence of the triangle or, taking the risk of essentialism seriously', *Differences*, 2: 5–6.

Eagleton, T. (1990) *The Ideology of the Aesthetic*. Oxford: Blackwell.

Featherstone, M., Hepworth, M. and Turner, B.S. (eds) (1991) *The Body: Social Processes and Cultural Theory*. London: Sage.

Friedman, A. (1977) *Industry and Labour: Class Struggle at Work and Monopoly Capitalism*. London: Macmillan.

Gagliardi, P. (1990) 'Artifacts as pathways and remains of organizational life', in P. Gagliardi (ed.), *Symbols and Artifacts: Views of the Corporate Landscape*. New York: de Gruyter. pp. 3–38.

Gagliardi, P. (1996) 'Exploring the aesthetic side of organizational life', in S.R. Clegg, C. Hardy and W.R. Nord (eds), *Handbook of Organziation Studies*. London: Sage. pp. 565–80.

Goffman, E. (1959) *The Presentation of Self in Everyday Life*. New York: Doubleday Anchor.

Guillén, F.G. (1997) 'Scientific management's lost aesthetic: architecture, organization, and the Taylorized beauty of the mechanical', *Administrative Science Quarterly*, 42 (4): 682–715.

Hall, E.J. (1993) 'Waitering/waitressing: engendering the work of table servers', *Gender and Society*, 7 (3): 329–46.

Hearn, J. and Parkin, W. (1995) *'Sex at Work': The Power and Paradox of Organization Sexuality*. Brighton: Harvester Wheatsheaf.

Hochschild, A.R. (1983) *The Managed Heart: Commercialization of Human Feeling*. Berkeley, CA: University of California Press.

Hughes, B. (1996) 'Nietzsche: philosophizing with the body', *Body and Society*, 2 (1): 31–44.

James, N. (1989) 'Emotional labour: skill and work in the social regulation of feelings', *Sociological Review*, 37: 15–42.

Kant, I. (1911) *Critque of Aesthetic Judgement* (trans. J.C. Meredith). Oxford: Clarendon Press.

Knights, D. and Willmott, H. (1989) 'Power and subjectivity at work: from degradation to subjugation in social relations', *Sociology*, 23 (4): 535–58.

Manwaring, T. and Wood, S. (1985) 'The ghost in the labour process', in D. Knights, H. Willmott and D.L. Collinson (eds), *Job Redesign: Critical Perspectives on the Labour Process*. Aldershot: Gower. pp. 171–96.

Marcuse, H. (ed.) (1979) *The Aesthetic Dimension: Toward a Critique of Marxist Aesthetics*. London: Macmillan.

Marx, K. (ed.) (1970) *Capital: Volume One*. London: Lawrence & Wishart.

Nietzsche, F. (1974) *The Gay Science* (trans. W. Kaufmann). New York: Vintage Books.

Nietzsche, F. (1990) *Beyond Good and Evil*. London: Penguin.

Ottensmeyer, E.J. (1996) 'Too strong to stop, too sweet to lose: aesthetics as a way to know organizations', *Organization*, 3 (2): 189–94.

Payne, R. (1991) 'Taking stock of corporate culture', *Personnel Management*, July: 26–9.

Phesey, D.C. (1993) *Organizational Cultures: Types and Transformations*. London: Routledge.

Shilling, C. (1993) *The Body and Social Theory*. London: Sage.

Strati, A. (1992) 'Aesthetic understanding of organizational life', *Academy of Management Review*, 17 (3): 568–81.

Strati, A. (1996) 'Organizations viewed through the lens of aesthetics', *Organization*, 3 (2): 209–18.

Taylor, F.W. (1911) *Principles of Scientific Management*. New York: Harper & Row.

Thompson, P. (1983) *The Nature of Work*. Basingstoke: Macmillan.

Thompson, P. (1990) 'Crawling from the wreckage: the labour process and the politics of production', in D. Knights and H. Willmott (eds), *Labour Process Theory*. London: Macmillan. pp. 95–124.

Townley, B. (1994) *Reframing Human Resource Management*. London: Sage.

Turner, B. (1990) 'The rise of organizational symbolism', in J.Hassard and D. Pym (eds), *The Theory and Philosophy of Organizations: Critical Issues and New Perspectives*. London: Routledge. pp. 83–96.

Turner, B. (1992) *Regulating Bodies*. London: Routledge.

Tyler, M. and Abbott, P. (1998) 'Chocs away: weight watching in the contemporary airline industry', *Sociology*, 32 (3): 433–50.

Tyler, M. and Taylor, S. (1998) 'The exchange of aesthetics: women's work and "the gift"', *Gender, Work and Organization*, 5 (3): 165–71.

Vesey, G. and Foulkes, P. (1990) *Collins Dictionary of Philosophy*. London: Collins.

Weber, M. (1991) 'The social psychology of the world religions', in H.H. Gerth and C. Wright Mills (eds), *From Max Weber: Essays in Sociology*. London: Routledge. pp. 267–331.

Weiss, F.G. (ed.) (1974) *Hegel: The Essential Writings*. New York: Harper & Row.

Wilkinson, B. (1983) *The Shopfloor Politics of New Technology*. London: Heinemann.

Willmott, H. (1990) 'Subjectivity and the dialectics of praxis: opening up the core of labour process analysis', in D. Knights and H. Willmott (eds), *Labour Process Theory*. London: Macmillan. pp. 336–78.

Willmott, H. (1995) 'From Bravermania to schizophrenia: the dec(is-)eased condition of subjectivity in labour process theory'. Paper presented at 13th International Labour Process Conference, April, Blackpool.

7   Embodying Management

Ian Lennie

Towards the end of his study of the production of space, Henri Lefebvre makes a sweeping proposition:

> The whole of [social] space proceeds from the body, even though it so meta-morphoses the body that it may forget it altogether – even though it may separate itself so radically from the body as to kill it. The genesis of a far-away order can be accounted for only on the basis of the order that is nearest to us – namely, the order of the body. (Lefebvre, 1991: 405)

This proposition, calling for a radical reassessment of the basis of order, implies an equally radical reassessment of the way that we manage. The space we actually inhabit, Lefebvre asserts, is not the empty space of geometry, but an order. This order is not us, but it comes from our experi-ence of ourselves: it comes from our body. If management is about pro-ducing and maintaining order, then to understand how we manage, we need to understand how management is embodied. In what follows I shall examine a number of accounts of embodiment in management, and the way order both flows from and creates the managing body. This examina-tion leads me to propose a fundamentally different basis for recognizing successful management.

Management without body

The body and the order it produces, Lefebvre suggests, are always in relation: but sometimes that relation is paradoxical, denying its own basis. Order becomes disembodied and so does the body to which it relates. In management this paradoxical relation is so often the norm that it ceases to evoke surprise or even comment. Figure 7.1 offers an example from the cover of an Australian manual, *Just Change: The Cost-Conscious Manager's Toolkit* (Auer et al., 1993). A disembodied head – or, rather, several heads overlapping like the pages of a book – tilts forward from a base, as if hinged. A handle projects from the scalp. Within the head is a stylized eye, and a row of arrows seems to project the eye's gaze outward. As well as the eye, a curious collection of objects floats within the space of the head: a

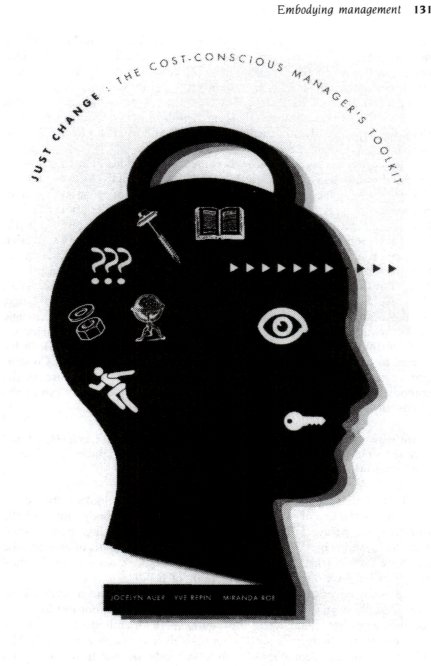

FIGURE 7.1 *(Reprinted with permission of the South Australian Health Commission, South Australian Community Health Association and Commonwealth Department of Health, Housing, Local Government and Community Services)*

screw, a globe, a key, a nut and washer, a running figure, and three question marks. This limbless and trunkless head, as fantastical as a Salvador Dali dream, is the very image of disembodiment. Yet in its place on the cover of a current management text, it can be taken for granted as no more than a skilful illustration of its theme. How does this come to be an acceptable representation of management, evoking identification from managers rather than, say, repulsion, fear or incomprehension? And what sort of order might proceed from a management imagined in this way?

We accept this image, of course, because it is embedded in intellectual and practical traditions going back at least as far as the Renaissance – traditions that themselves give rise to conventional conceptions of management. This particular image is interesting because it lets us decipher in some detail, if only we can get past its taken-for-grantedness, how these traditions work. The image depends on what we shall call for the sake of brevity a Cartesian conception of knowledge. A mind, or subject, conventionally located in the head, is separated from the body of the objective world, and from its own body. But this separation begins from the body, as Descartes himself makes clear. Seeking for models of practice that might establish secure knowledge, he singles out those craftsmen around him who, 'fixing their eyes on a single point, acquire through practice the ability to make perfect distinctions between things, however minute and delicate' (Descartes, 1985: 33). In his appeal to craftsmen, Descartes is not prefiguring William Morris. Concentrating knowledge in the most distancing of senses lets him figure, in the embodied and plural eyes of these craftsmen, the single mind's eye of the philosopher, which alone distinguishes truth:

> We must concentrate our mind's eye totally upon the most insignificant and easiest of matters, and dwell on them long enough to acquire the habit of intuiting the truth distinctly and clearly. (1985: 33)

Like the philosopher, the subject in our illustration looks outward, as indicated by the line of arrows, not from the eyes of the body, but from the single eye of the mind. Through observation, the eye brings back knowledge, as indicated by the book, the globe, and those symbols of enquiry, the three question marks. Through this eye the subject looks out to the 'far-away', in Lefebvre's term, but is not in or of it.[1]

This is the cover of a management manual, however, not a textbook on science or philosophy. A managing subject is interested in not just knowing the far-away, but changing it. But how can a disembodied inward eye intervene in the body of a world from which it has separated itself? The solution to this problem also starts from the body, but not from the eye. Its historical development has been charted by Foucault in his work on medicine (1973), and on forms of discipline in the seventeenth, eighteenth and nineteenth centuries (1991). Foucault reveals, on the one hand, a world scrutinized, watched and surveyed as never before, a world that is studied and documented scientifically; at the same time, however, he charts the parallel development of an array of practical methods for handling, control and regulation. He describes these developments as two 'registers': of Cartesian scrutiny on the one hand, and of techniques of discipline and control on the other. The registers develop separately, yet together:

> The great book of Man-the-Machine was written simultaneously on two registers: the anatomico-metaphysical register, of which Descartes wrote the first pages and which the physicians and philosophers continued, and the technico-political register, which was constituted by a whole set of regulations and by empirical and calculated methods relating to the army, the school and the hospital, for controlling or correcting the operations of the body. These two registers are quite distinct, since it was a question, on the one hand, of submission and use and, on the other, of functioning and explanation: there was a useful body and an intelligible body. (Foucault, 1991: 136)

The intelligible body is known through the mind's eye; the useful body, however, has not so much been observed as moved, assembled, shaped and disciplined. The useful body is one that can be manipulated, handled. It is significant, then, that the word 'manage' first comes into English in the context of handling, in this case of horses:

> The word **manage** seems to have come into English directly from *maneggiare*, It[alian] – to handle and especially to handle or train horses. Its earliest English uses were in this context. The f[orerunner] w[ord] is *mandiare*, v[ulgar] L[atin] – to handle, from r[oot] w[ord] *manus*, L[atin] – hand. **Manage** was quickly extended to operations of war, and from e[arly] C16 to a general sense of taking control, taking charge, directing. (Williams, 1983: 190)

Management first arises not so much from a privileging of sight as of an active touch, of handling. Techniques of handling create the connection that makes the intelligible body conform to the vision of the inner eye. The possibilities implied by the mapping onto each other of Foucault's two 'registers' are succinctly stated by Karl Marx (1958/[1888]: 405) in his eleventh thesis on Feuerbach:

> The philosophers have only *interpreted* the world in various ways: the point, however, is to *change* it.

This thesis has become not only the slogan of revolutionaries, but also of contemporary management, as this manager makes clear:

> 'Certainly I think a lot of my motivation is to change, to make an impact on the system and to see it to some degree be different after I've come in contact with it.'[2]

This ability to systematically change the world is what, for Frederich Engels (1958/[1876]: 89), distinguishes man from the animals: 'the animal merely *uses* external nature', while 'man by his changes makes nature serve his ends, *masters* it'. This mastery is the realization of that desire for power that is only implicit in the gaze of the inward eye, but is completed in techniques of the hand.

For Engels, the visionary eye is itself the product of the hand. Man as animal evolves firstly to *homo faber* and it is *homo faber* who creates *homo sapiens*.[3] For Engels, the key moment in the evolution of humanity was the moment when man first stood upright so that 'the hand became free' (1958/[1876]: 81). This freedom of the hand allowed manipulation of the environment in a way that in turn developed the brain, and this development eventually led to the extension of the hand through the making of tools. Tools multiply the effect of the hand. But through the multiplication of labour made possible by tools, the mind can separate itself from its own labour, and thus from its own hands: '(T)he mind that planned the labour . . . was able to have the labour that had been planned carried out by hands other than its own' (1958/[1876]: 87).

This separation of the mind that directs labour from the hands that carry it out not only multiplies the body, but leads to a further qualitative development, a stage that puts the multiplied body at the disposal of a premeditated vision. As Engels (1958/[1876]: 88) puts it, '(t)he further removed men are from animals, however, the more their effect on nature assumes the character of premeditated, planned action directed towards definite ends known in advance'. Man, he argues, is at this stage in a position to re-create nature, and hence himself. The external world, including humanity itself, has become manageable, at least in theory – a space waiting to be ordered by the vision of a mind that has become separate from it.

The importance and persistence of tool imagery in management should now be apparent. Tools shift the emphasis from knowledge of the objective world to change, manipulation and control. Hence, in our illustration, they mingle – in the form of a screw, a key and a nut – with the symbols of knowledge. This mingling of symbols inside the head suggests, moreover, that knowledge too has become a tool, of value to the mind insofar as it contributes to changing the world. In fact the presentation of the book itself as a 'toolkit' appeals directly to the manager's desire to manipulate rather than just learn. A book is only of interest to management if it is a container for tools.[4]

An order that proceeds from a particular combination of hand and eye is an order that understands the sensual world as manageable, in the sense that it stands waiting to be shaped by the vision of a knowing subject. This standing ready, this becoming what Heidegger refers to as a 'standing-reserve (*Bestand*)' (Heidegger, 1977: 17), moreover, returns to embrace the manager him/herself, whose body is also at the disposal of the preconceived vision, along with the rest of the sensual world. It is particularly apt, then, that our toolkit illustration depicts a complete body only *within* the toolkit/hand. The body depicted, moreover, is not a real body, but a puppet or manikin. It is as if the body, as body, is just another tool of what is now not so much the Cartesian contemplating mind, as the managerial controlling mind. The irony, however, of a manageable order based on disembodiment is that the mind is itself the product of a particular kind of embodiment. Disembodiment, in other words, must itself be embodied somehow and, as such, is also embraced by the order that it creates. The controlling mind is produced within the very process of transformation it has brought about, an irony that is, for Heidegger, a truly vertiginous prospect: '[If] man . . . is nothing but the orderer of the standing-reserve, then he comes to the brink of a precipitous fall; that is, he comes to the point where he himself will have to be taken as standing-reserve' (1977: 18).

This irony is also taken up in our illustration, where the disembodied mind is itself a toolkit standing ready to be picked up by the hand of a manager who is also a toolkit, and so on in a series of receding images, with no final subject-manager to pick up the handle. The manager has him/herself become standing-reserve, on call for further ordering along with the rest of the manageable world. An order that proceeded from the body has forgotten it to the point where disembodiment itself becomes no more than an effect of its own order. What we really have here is an illustration of Lefebvre's contention that the space that proceeds from the body may so metamorphose it as to forget or even kill it.

I should emphasize here that *The Cost-Conscious Manager's Toolkit* is not some contemporary manual of scientific management. In fact, it claims to provide strategies for managing in ways that further social justice in an environment of economic rationalism. So ingrained, however, is the notion that management is the disembodied manipulation of external environments for preconceived ends, however worthy, that the fantasy we have examined is the basis for the visual organization of the entire book.

Losing the feel

This conversion of the disembodied manager into an effect of the process he/she initiated means that all too often the one thing that managers cannot control is management itself. It all too frequently becomes unending, compulsive and exhausting. It empties and disembodies. Managers often understand this, and realize they have somehow to counter the disembodying effects of their practice in order to survive. Here, for example, is one manager talking about how management is encroaching on his sense of himself:

'I certainly take work home and I think a lot about work outside 9 to 5. And I'm told I think too much about it, that I'm too work-focused. I don't mind it, but I notice the long-term effect that it's having. I'm actually quite exhausted at the minute, which is why I'm anxious to get off to Turkey and places with a Mediterranean feel about it. I think it's interesting that people perceive me as working very hard. I perceive that I don't, and yet I know that I stand back and look at that objectively, I do. Eventually you pay the price.'

This manager does not actually experience the effects of management as it happens. He takes work home, thinks a lot about it outside work hours, and is not bothered by this. He is not 'in touch' with what it is doing to him. He has actually to hear from outside himself, from other people, that he is being affected, that he is paying 'the price'. Then, by making himself an object, he can see himself as overworked. He now longs for 'Turkey and places with a Mediterranean *feel*' (emphasis added), because he is ceasing to *feel* himself in management: he is becoming empty, disembodied – 'exhausted' in his words. Restoration is linked to establishing a more embodied self, in this case a feeling self. When asked whether there was a time when he stopped managing he replied, 'In the kitchen or shopping. Because cooking and food is my immediate relaxation. I'm always ripping the gizzards out of a chook or stuffing it with something.' Here he comically emphasizes the aggressiveness and physicality of cooking, in contrast to the growing disembodiment of his management self. In the space of the kitchen he re-establishes a physical self through the dead body of the chicken into which, somewhat aggressively, he stuffs a new sort of life. If he can create a space and time of re-embodiment outside of management, he can go on managing.

Organizing from the body

This manager's experience suggests that when management is disembodying, a place that is not 'managed' is necessary to restore and re-member the forgotten body. But this restoration of the body is also an important factor in his being able to accurately register the effects of management itself – to actually experience his exhaustion. This raises the question of whether a more embodied way of actually managing is possible, and what it might feel like. To answer this requires an artistic digression, because there is not much help to be found in management or organization literature beyond the occasional reminder to keep the body tuned through a regime of physical exercise.[5] The managing body becomes the jogging body. But this instrumental relation to one's body is only another manifestation of disembodiment.

For Merleau-Ponty (1964: 162) the figure of the painter evokes a different relation between the body and the order that it creates:

> The painter 'takes his body with him', says Valéry. Indeed we cannot imagine how a mind could paint. It is by lending his body to the world that the artist changes the world into paintings. To understand these transubstantiations we must go back to the working, actual body – not the body as a chunk of space or a bundle of functions but that body that is an intertwining of vision and movement.

The painter, Merleau-Ponty suggests, does not impose a vision from outside the world. Rather he [*sic*] lends 'his body to the world' and so transforms it. That such transforming is a process of organization, that it creates order, is apparent when T.S. Eliot speaks of the work of the poet:

> the ordinary man's experience is chaotic, irregular, fragmentary. The latter falls in love, or reads Spinoza, and these two experiences have nothing to do with each other, or with the noise of the typewriter or the smell of cooking; in the mind of the poet these experiences are always forming new wholes. (Eliot, 1963: 287)

Ordinary experience tends to be chaotic and fragmented, but poetic experience organizes and connects. It allows us to form 'new wholes'. Eliot speaks of the 'mind' of the poet, but he makes it clear that this is an embodied mind. Thought for a poet, Eliot contends, is 'an experience'. It is as immediate 'as the odour of a rose' (Eliot, 1963: 278). The poet's 'mind' can organize in this way only because all the senses are involved in thought. Embodiment is the way we are implicated in the multifarious possibilities of connection that take us beyond what we already know. Embodiment 'lends' our body to the world by allowing the world to enter into our experience.

To enable disconnected experiences to form 'new wholes' requires that the poet be within those experiences, exhibiting a certain openness of body to let them develop through him/her, because it is the experiences that organize, not the poet who organizes from somewhere outside experience. The critic F.R. Leavis (1963) describes this openness of body when distinguishing the different readings demanded by literary and philosophic texts. Literary texts, Leavis (1963: 213) argues, differ from philosophy in demanding 'a fuller-bodied response', an opening of oneself to all the possibilities of the text. Leavis elaborates this as a different relationship to the 'object' under consideration:

> Philosophy, we say, is 'abstract' . . . and poetry 'concrete'. Words in poetry invite us, not to 'think about and judge' but to 'feel into' or 'become' – to realize a complex experience that is given in the words. They demand, not merely a fuller-bodied response, but a completer responsiveness – a kind of responsiveness that is incompatible with the judicial, one-eye-on-the standard approach suggested by Dr Wellek's phrase: 'your norm with which you measure every poet'. (1963: 212–13)

To 'realize' the text, 'a complex experience that is given in words', is not a matter of measuring or judging it from outside that experience, but experiencing what is there, entering it and letting it enter one's body. Such a process of experiencing is not just a passive absorption into the situation, but also a participation in a process of organization. Realizing the experience, embodying it, claims Leavis, relates it to other experiences that are also embodied, so that 'a certain value is implicit in the realizing' (1963: 213). This sense of relative valuation is an ordering of experience. By comparison, Leavis finds that attempting to summarize his method as a system of rules is, in fact, disorganizing: 'I feel that by my own methods I have attained a relative precision that makes this summarizing seem intolerably clumsy and inadequate' (p. 215).

Leavis is here talking about literary texts, Eliot about poetry and Merleau-Ponty about painting. But the postmodern extension of the notion of textuality to experience in general invites the transfer of these insights beyond the formally containing barriers of the arts. Reading for Barthes (1986: 13), as for Leavis, means being open to a text in a way that lets its organization work in our body: 'to read is to make our body work . . . at the invitation of the text's signs', but that 'text' can be a photograph, a building or a landscape. The issue is a relation between the body and that which is beyond it. Barthes characterizes this embodied reading, like Leavis, as a response to an invitation. Such a response, with its implications of graciousness, courtesy, respect, openness and, perhaps, a certain tentativeness, is a far remove from the dominating self-assurance and detached calculation of the heroes of much management literature.

Open and closed bodies

But how might a manager engage in an embodied reading? Two contrasting accounts follow from managers of community health services in the Australian State of Queensland. Each manager had begun her current job after moving from another State, so that both had to deal with a new environment. Here is the first:

Do you spend a lot of time in the office?

'I like to get around. And then to have a total day in the office. I make a point of whichever areas I'm involved in at least going to a staff meeting at least once a month. If there's something going on, I'll go much more regularly. Sometimes I'll just wander in. They're very welcoming at R–; sometimes I'll just wander in there. People know that I'm available. People are often phoning, calling in. So I have a sense of being very close, and they tell me that I am, that I'm accessible. And that's part of the job.'

Some of this manager's activity could be seen as purely instrumental: gathering information, going to staff meetings where 'there's something going on'. But some of the movement comes across as less directed: 'sometimes I'll just wander in'; 'I like to get around'. Nor can this be put down to random surveillance, keeping people on their toes through its unpredictability. There is a sense of pleasure in moving within the organization: 'They're very welcoming at R–; sometimes I'll just wander in there'. This sense of being close to, and accessible by, the organization is not just arbitrary either. She is convinced that 'that's part of the job'.

While her job is geographically dispersed, she exhibits the same involvement during 'a total day in the office':

> 'I've got a wheel on the door that says whether I'm available or do not disturb or
> out. If somebody wants to make an appointment they would do it with J [her
> secretary]. They don't have to do that. They can wait in the corridor and I'll see
> them, or just come and bang on the door. I walk around the place a lot. The
> admin area's a good place because that's a continual crossing over space. I like to
> get caught up in conversations and stuff. The tea room's another good place.'

The wheel on the door indicates degrees of openness. But staff are not just
engaged by the manager in her own space and in her own way: there are a
range of opportunities for contact, particularly in neutral 'crossing over
space'. Again, there is a sense of pleasure in engagement that is not just
active and controlling. She allows the environment to work on her: 'I like to
get *caught up* in conversations and stuff.' She lends her body to the new
situation, and it in her. She is open to its invitation, and so, while admitting
to still finding Queensland 'something of a culture shock', she seems to have
made a successful transition between the old and the new situations, to the
extent of feeling comfortable and even enjoying her present position.

Now consider the case of a second manager who also came to
Queensland from a southern state, bringing with her what she thought were
'reasonably modern management practices'. It took, she said, 'a fairly
contentious eighteen months' to realize that 'something was going wrong':

> 'It was about coming to Queensland; it's like being in another world, only it
> didn't really hit me at first. I'd just keep running into brick walls and I didn't
> know why. Things are very laid back here. You come to work and go into the
> staff room and start talking about some problem at work and people just look at
> you. They're talking about what's on TV last night or something. They just won't
> talk about work things straight away, and if you do you're made to feel that's
> wrong. I don't watch those shows and I'm not interested in talking about them.
> But you've got to, to some extent. Pretend you're not interested in the job.'

> 'Anything else?'

> 'Well . . . it's not just staff. Like it doesn't seem to matter if someone can do the
> job or not. They just tell you, 'So-and-so's a good bloke.' If he's a 'good bloke,'
> that's what matters most. But I like to see the job done. That's why I'm there. So
> until I worked it out it seemed like everyone was conspiring against me. It's still
> hard. I don't like putting on an act.'

This manager never left her southern identity with its 'reasonably modern
management practices' so that, while coming to Queensland, she was still
embodied 'outside' it, to the extent that it felt like 'running into brick walls'.
Even when she eventually worked out that the organization was not what
she thought it was, she felt she could only bridge the gap in a manipulative

way – 'putting on an act' – which did not make her feel comfortable. She wanted to be in control, and yet separate – thinking about and judging, in Leavis's terminology, rather than feeling into and becoming. Her body was not open to the invitation of her new situation, so only misunderstanding and disruption resulted. She shortly afterwards resigned from that job.

A growing stability of organization

Let us now turn to how making one's body work within the textuality of the workplace leads, in Leavis's phrase, to 'a growing stability of organization'. Here is another manager's account of coming to a decision to dismiss a member of staff. What is interesting about this account is her ability to recount her *experience* of the event. Usually, when you ask managers why they decided to dismiss someone, they give organizational reasons like 'refused reasonable requests', 'stole money', 'forged timesheets', and the like, measuring errant behaviour against an outside standard. What they rarely give is an account of how they came to register this behaviour as disruptive.

Here is how this manager describes her first awareness of a problem:

'There's a gut reaction first off. It's almost a visual concept. This is going to sound quite crazy. It's almost a visual concept of an environment, and you're starting to realize part of the environment is beginning to react negatively to the other parts of the environment. It's that there's an onflowing . . . almost going in a wave-like motion. . .You've sort of got a picture all the time in your head and you become aware of tension going to build because of that.'

There is a bodily registration of a problem – a '*gut*' reaction'. But this body quickly ceases to be an anatomical body. The internal, 'gut' reaction becomes visual and extends out to the environment – 'It's almost a visual concept of an environment.' The disturbed environment becomes a movement in which she participates: 'It's that there's an onflowing . . . almost going into a wave-like motion . . .'. Because the environmental picture is still 'in [her] head' it allows her to experience 'where the tension is going to build'. An environmental disturbance reorganizes her body in an uncomfortable way.

If what she is saying sounds muddled, it is because she is trying to articulate something that our usual geometry of the body and space doesn't allow – how inside and outside are permeable, flow together and sometimes change places. There is movement between them that allows change in the outside to be a bodily experience, not just a conclusion deduced from evidence. Not only inside and outside, but the senses that we separate in thought – vision, feeling – in experience flow into and substitute for one another. A gut feeling is a picture, is a movement, is a tension. This is what Merleau-Ponty (1964: 162) describes as 'the working, actual body – not the body as a chunk of space or a bundle of functions'. Rather, it is 'an intertwining of vision and movement'.

As yet, no particular meaning has emerged beyond a sense of unease, an anticipation of possible future disorder whose traces are present in the world around her. When I ask her to go on, she describes how she begins to explore this unease more actively, moving into the corridor, a space that belongs to no one, but where people overlap in an informal way:

'Well, just walking down the corridor at work you become aware that there's tension in the air, or that things are getting sharper.'

Here she begins to differentiate an outside – 'tension in the air', 'things getting sharper' – that corresponds to an inside – 'a red light going on' in a mental picture.

At this point, for the first time, the other staff member materializes in the account, registered by her body as a touch that is distinctly uncomfortable:

'With him I started to realize it was certainly starting to rub. Some people might come in for a day and be more withdrawn or abrasive to somebody, and that's OK for a day. When it's been a week you ferret around a little and find out why.'

The continued abrasion prompts her to explore the outside more actively, 'to ferret around a little'. It is only at this point that she starts to describe the problem in explicit organizational terms:

'He was the sort of guy who needed a little more supervision than most. If he thought he could get away with something he would. He fiddled his time sheets and things like that. And that was something first brought to my attention by the administrative officer.'

A series of incidents then leads to minuted interviews and the commencement of a formal dismissal process.

In this manager's account, her gut, her sense of touch, vision, waves, the corridor at work, rubbing, the quality of the air, time sheets, the errant staff member – all these enter into an experience of disorder that emerges from a growing sense of connection. This can only happen because, by lending her body to the world, she participates in it and it in her. Through this participation she is implicated in a process of increasing organization of the work space, beginning with an internal unease and progressing to an increasing externalization of the problem to the point where it cannot be managed within that space. She does not begin the process by applying a rule; rather the rule comes as a conclusion to something that has already been experienced. The rule works because an embodied sense of organization has developed towards it, not because it has already prescribed experience in advance. That such an emergent, rather than externally imposed form of organization, is not unusual is suggested by the growing awareness of how order comes about in complex systems:

> The top-down imposition of knowledge becomes redundant, and anything which might be called growth, evolution or development occurs in systems which function without external governors or even centralized controls of their own. They have no pre-ordained designs or goals in sight, but proceed bottom-up, making connections and reinforcing links, in precisely the ways that synapses function in the human brain with which they converge as neural nets. (Plant, 1996: 208)

I would argue that management can happen connectively or synergistically in this way when the manager is embodied within organization – when the body and the space it inhabits are allowed to relate.

To manage in this way is not to pose the body as a new centre of order. We can only organize through being organized; we manage through being managed. We are not outside the space of our own management. I can only create order through embodiment because, in Merleau-Ponty's succinct formulation, 'things have an internal equivalent in me: they arouse in me a carnal formula of their presence' (1964: 164). And the reverse is also true. I have an external equivalent in things: I arouse in them a carnal formula of my presence. This relation between my body and its order means that the results of my management also re-create me. I experience my body through the order it creates, something that suggests a qualification of Lefebvre's assertion that order *proceeds* from the body. We can assent to this as long as it does not imply that the body is the *origin* of order. Order proceeds from, but is not preceded by, the body. The body is not a prior order that is then read onto an outside. In our earlier toolkit illustration, for example, we can argue that a certain disembodied conception of management proceeds from a certain conception of the body – a privileged combination of eye and hand. But that experience of eye and hand is already also an effect of a disembodied order. The issue is one of a relation, not a direction, of causality.

'I walk with a lighter step'

That relation between the body and its order can be very positive, but in a way that should lead us to reassess our notions of managing well. Here is one manager's evocation of the feeling of working successfully:

> 'Oh, I feel light when things are going well, and when things aren't going well I feel heavy. The office feels lighter. The paperwork seems lighter. I probably walk with a lighter step.'

That lightness, that sense that movement is easy, is not just a feeling of her own body, but of the whole environment that it is in as well. Herself, the office and even the paper come together in a lightly moving unity not unlike a dance.[6] Durkheim (1965/[1915]: 422) in fact describes the experience of the sacred in very similar terms, as a 'state of effervescence'. In this state, he goes on to say, 'a man does not recognize himself; he feels transformed and consequently he transforms the environment which surrounds him'. In this transformation the 'outside' and the body are not easily distinguishable. Each arouses in the other a carnal equivalent of itself.

A movement towards the world outside is a more 'obvious' movement of management, and indeed, any current textbook would claim that this is what management is about: change, results, achieving objectives. But this is to neglect the embodied basis on which this ordering of the outside world is made. Suppressing that bodily connection makes the focus on results and objectives in management deceptively obvious. But embodied management does not *end* in a result – in producing an order – because that result flows back to re-embody us within it. The manager we just quoted becomes a part of the lightness she creates. In a real sense, then, management never reaches its end – not in that fashionably workaholic sense of unending innovation and challenge – but, because it is an ongoing relation between the body and its order. Thus our next manager, describing how he uses a planning process to get his organization moving, reverses what are taken to be the usual priorities of management:

> 'In many ways it doesn't actually matter what are the concrete things we're wanting to move on. I did a strategic planning process with the Health Centre that identified four new priorities. Now these priorities could have been any four.'

On the face of it this seems a pretty alarming thing for a manager to be saying: that it does not really matter what the organization is doing. On reflection there are implied limits. The organizational context, a health centre, imposes a certain limitation on possible ends. It cannot become a butcher's shop, for example. Even within these implied limits, it is not suggested that any end is equivalent to any other, otherwise there would be nothing to argue about. But these priorities, he is implying, are only of value if they create a sense of movement in the participants, if they embody a sense of organization and movement and aliveness rather than conformity to ends that are outside the producers of those ends. He makes this clear when he describes the planning process as a relation between himself and the order he wants to produce:

> 'to be able to, I suppose, pull together divergent strands or thoughts or concepts or groups, and be able to feed back to them what they are saying, but in a cohesive fashion. That they go "Ah!" and there's a sense of moving forward, and those sorts of things. So its about process to me, but process that leads to movement, to an organization actually picking itself up and moving along.'

He understands order as a movement, or, rather, a connection of movements – movements that flow between his body and the outside. He first talks of a movement toward himself, a 'pulling together'. This list of what he draws in is truly divergent: 'strands', 'thoughts', 'concepts', 'groups'. Here, as with the manager involved in the dismissal of a staff member, thought, people and material are not different categories of being, but are all elements that go to make up a cohesive whole in relation to him. In an implicit metaphor of cooking, the separate ingredients are brought together by himself to embody a new whole in a process that can then 'feed back' outwards to the other staff. This process of nourishment is an organizing that creates wonder. People go 'Ah!' experiencing the organization anew. They come alive, and 'there's a sense of moving forward'. This process of taking in disparate elements and forming new wholes is that ordering ability assigned by Eliot to poets, but here directed to the organization of work.

The initial movement in which this manager took in diverse strands from outside and embodied them as a new whole is, through the planning process, taken up by others. He now expresses the organization as doing what he seemed to be doing only as an individual at first, so that what results is a life beyond his life: a larger order of which he is now only a part:

> 'And enough people in an organization actually start doing that. So rather than it just being me, enough people are doing that so I can sit back and watch and see an organization get a sense of buzz and a sense of excitement about the work that it's doing, and to be able to argue with itself in a critical and progressive way on how it's working and where it's moving.'

Successful management creates a space of life and movement, 'a sense of buzz and a sense of excitement' that embodies the order it has produced. That buzz, lightness and effervescence is an overflowing of a body that is open to the possibilities of organizing beyond itself. If this embodied sense of aliveness does not come about, then only a sterile order results, regardless of the number of targets achieved and goals fulfilled. This enhanced sense of life flows from a body that does not kill or forget itself through its order, but experiences itself and comes alive through an ongoing process of organization.

Notes

1 I am not arguing here for some sort of physiological determinism. Vision does not have to be experienced in this disembodied way. Merleau-Ponty (1964: 164), for example, offers a quite different relation between the body and vision: 'Since things and my body are made of the same stuff, vision must somehow take place in them; their manifest visibility must be repeated in the body by a secret visibility. "Nature is on the inside", says Cézanne. Quality, light, color, depth, which are there before us, are there only because they awaken an echo in our body and because the body welcomes them.'

2 Quotations from managers in this chapter come from interviews conducted in the course of research on the relationship between professional management and managing in everyday life that made up the author's doctoral dissertation. The

interviews were conducted with managers of community-based health services in Australia and New Zealand.

3 For an account of the modern revival of Engels's *homo faber*, see Metcalfe, 1995: 107ff.

4 I would not wish to imply that this instrumental relation to the world is immanent in tools themselves. A quite different relationship is suggested, for example, in Simmel's essay 'The handle' (1959: 269) when he claims that 'just as the hand is a tool of the soul, so too the tool is a hand of the soul'.

5 Here is a case in point from *The Cost-Conscious Manager's Toolkit* (Auer et al., 1993: 48–9). Under Section 4.1, with its Socratic injunction 'Know Yourself', appears the following warning: 'Initiating and managing a change process is a relentlessly lengthy, tiring and stressful business. Managers we interviewed, although showing signs of strain, demonstrated the stamina to see the process through.' Then follows 'Manager's Checklist No. 8, Fitness and Health', which asks the question 'How's your physical condition?' If the answer is, 'Could be better' it advises: 'Build some form of health or fitness activity into your schedule now, and give it a priority over everything else.'

6 I am reminded here of the title of Rosabeth Kanter's 'new management' text, *When Giants Learn to Dance* (1989). The new global economy, Kanter argues: 'requires more agile, limber management that pursues opportunity without being bogged down by the cumbersome structures or weighty procedures that impede action. Corporate elephants, in short, must learn how to dance' (p. 20). Unfortunately this rather whimsical prospect soon gets swept up in another project of mastery as Kanter assures US management that 'we can once again be masters, not victims of change'. Dancing then becomes no more than a limbering up for the global 'corporate Olympics' (p. 19).

References

Auer, J., Repin, Y. and Roe, M. (1993) *Just Change: The Cost-Conscious Manager's Toolkit*. Wollongong: National Reference Centre for Primary Health Care.

Barthes, R. (1986) *The Rustle of Language* (trans. R. Howard). Oxford: Blackwell.

Descartes, R. (1985) *Rules for the Direction of the Mind* (trans. J. Cottingham, R. Stoothoff, D. Murdoch). Cambridge: Cambridge University Press.

Durkheim, E. (1965/[1915]) *The Elementary Forms of Religious Life* (trans. J. Swain). New York: The Free Press.

Eliot, T.S. (1963) 'The Metaphysical Poets' (1921), in *Selected Essays*. London: Faber & Faber.

Engels, F. (1958/[1876]) 'The part played by labour in the transition from ape to man', in K. Marx and F. Engels, *Selected Works, Volume II* (trans. Institute of Marxism–Leninism). Moscow: Foreign Languages Publishing House.

Foucault, M. (1973) *The Birth of the Clinic* (trans. A.M. Sheridan Smith). London: Tavistock Publications.

Foucault, M. (1991) *Discipline and Punish* (trans. A. Sheridan). Harmondsworth: Penguin Books.

Heidegger, M. (1977) *The Question Concerning Technology and other Essays* (trans. W. Lovitt). New York and London: Garland Publishing Inc.

Kanter, R.M. (1989) *When Giants Learn to Dance*. London: Simon & Schuster.

Leavis, F.R. (1963) 'Literary criticism and philosophy', in *The Common Pursuit*. Harmondsworth: Penguin Books.

Lefebvre, H. (1991) *The Production of Space* (trans. D. Nicholson-Smith). Oxford, UK and Cambridge, MA: Blackwell.

Marx, K. (1958/[1888]) 'Theses on Feuerbach', in K. Marx and F. Engels, *Selected*

Works, Volume II (trans. Institute of Marxism–Leninism). Moscow: Foreign Languages Publishing House.

Merleau-Ponty, M. (1964) *The Primacy of Perception* (ed. J.M. Edie). Evanston, IT: Northwestern University Press.

Metcalfe, A.W. (1995) 'The hands of *Homo faber*', *Body and Society*, 1 (2): 105–26.

Plant, S. (1996) 'The virtual complexity of culture', in G. Robertson, M. Mash, L. Tickner, J. Bird, B. Curtis and T. Putnam (eds), *FutureNatural*. London and New York: Routledge.

Simmel, G. (1959) 'The handle', in K.H. Wolff (ed.), *Essays on Sociology, Philosophy and Aesthetics by Georg Simmel et al.* New York: Harper Torchbooks.

Williams, R. (1983) *Keywords*. London: Flamingo.

8 The Body Topographies of Education Management

Craig Prichard

The intensified *performance* of work can be seen as the key defining feature of contemporary corporate life (Collinson and Collinson, 1997; Harrison, 1994; Wright and Smye, 1997). In both the public and private sectors performance indicators, performance targets, performance management techniques are among the many devices that attempt to intensively codify, measure, judge and discipline the productivity of our body's efforts against those of individualized others. Alongside these techniques are other devices – ways of seeing and ways of doing – which 'help' us to judge and work on our bodies so that their presentation aligns with corporate ideals. Presenting a body that signifies as active, hardworking and under control is an important characteristic in corporate life, particularly for senior corporate post-holders.

> His austere and ferociously hard-working way of life marks him out too from the majority of his well-lunched contemporaries in other boardrooms . . . he is whippet-thin, thanks to tennis and riding, and his neatly trimmed beard might almost be an affectation to distinguish him from the rest of the City. (*Guardian*, 9 February 1996: 2)

Here the performance, action-orientation and a seeming independence of Lord Hollick, Labour peer and chief executive of the conglomerate MAI, from what the *Guardian* takes to be the stereotypical 'fat-cat' life styles of City financiers, is read off from certain physical features, e.g. 'whippet-thin'.[1]

Work performance and body presentation is clearly but one small part of a potentially much wider discussion concerning the embodiment of work. What analytical frameworks might be employed to address this is a key question. The quote above, concerned with Lord Hollick's 'whippet-thin' body, highlights one half of what Crossley terms the 'two poles' of description and the inherent reversibility of the corporeal: it acts and is acted upon or towards (1995: 60). In the quote, Hollick's body is understood as active and acting on its surroundings. Alternatively, we could argue that at the same time Hollick's body can be said to be acted upon by the surroundings and practices of other bodies.

While academic researchers might agree on the symmetry of this duality (Grosz, 1994), they seldom give equal weighting to either the 'active body' or the 'inscribed body'. Particular authors, for example Halford et al. (1997), Connell (1995), Feldman (1991) and Hetrick and Boje (1992), who have sought to engage a politics of the body in their discussion of organizational life, align themselves more closely with one or other of these 'poles' – the body as active (lived practice) or the body as acted upon (inscribed). It is worth emphasizing that such framings (while inherently produced by the syntax of the English language, which requires subject, object and verb) can also be said to denote highly politicized representation work which often forms the backdrop upon which asymmetric power relations and patterns of organizational orderings are worked out – for example, core (permanent, full-time managers) and periphery (part-time, temporary, managed contract staff). The commonplace ascription of managers with active bodies, and the managed with bodies whose action is the target of power (Crossley, 1995: 60), then needs to be inflected with a sensitivity to the symbolic political work involved in such ascriptions.

Substantively, this chapter is part of a continued exploration of the development of a managerial mode of organizing and the formation of the manager in further and higher education (Prichard, 1996a, 1996b; Prichard and Willmott, 1997). The key question which underpins this particular piece is the extent to which the understanding of such developments can be usefully elaborated by bringing the 'body in', or by incorporating the corporeal. The chapter also seeks to contribuite to debate, of which this book is a part, over ways of understanding the 'body'. As a means of marshalling resources provided by other authors and contributing to discussion, I want to develop the analytic of *body topography*. Given that our bodies are irrevocably our 'placement' in the world, a topography, derived from the Greek word topos meaning place, would be concerned with mapping the character of this placement. However, 'topography' might suggest a somewhat static and spatial understanding. I want to suggest a more organic understanding. Just as land topography is a dynamic interaction between soils, vegetation and water, so a body topography is a dynamic interaction between desire (body energy), practices and signification together with the spatial, physical and verbal 'surfaces' of our materiality.

Particularly, I want to suggest two analytical dimensions of embodiment. First, body topography refers to a study of body 'surfaces'. Here I draw on Halford et al.'s (1997) typology of the spatial, verbal and, of course, physical dimensions of bodies. Secondly, body topography refers to the study of the active stratifying of body depth. Drawing on the work of Connell (1995) and then Deleuze and Guattari (1984, 1988), body depth refers to the flows that make us 'up' as sensual, emotional and desiring bodies. The key reason for making this distinction revolves around the 'problem' of the body's surface. Crossley, in his discussion of Merleau-Ponty's phenomenology of the body, highlights the body's reversibility. It sees and can be seen, hears and can be heard, and touches and can be touched. However, there is a limit to this reversibility. Our embodiment is sensuous and emotive, but we cannot experience the sensuality/ emotionality/desire of other bodies directly. There is, in other words, an affective depth to our embodiment which cannot be easily collapsed into a 'body as surface' which relies on the senses.

This is not to suggest that these dimensions of 'depth' or 'surface' actually exist. Limited reversibility is itself a knowledge practice which makes sense of the body in a particular way. 'Surface' and 'depth', as analytical dimensions, are tied into this knowledge practice, but should not be taken as ontological verities. They are analytical devices to make sense of empirical material or to 'read' the body or to read other 'readings' of the body. Ontologically the chapter assumes the existence of body energy, or desire, and spatial, physical and verbal knowledge practices which order and organize human and non-human materials.

The chapter is divided into several sections. The first outlines the body as 'surface' approach, the second deals with 'depth' and the third summarizes these approaches. In the remaining sections the analytic of the changing body topographies is used to illuminate the shift to a more managed UK post-compulsory education sector. Space limitations have prevented the discussion of a number of crucially related issues. Particularly this includes reviews of the organization studies and post-compulsory education management literature in relation to the 'body' and embodiment.

Body topography: surface

Many recent accounts of the body in social theory begin with a discussion of how embodiment has been conspicuously absent in much writing and theorizing. One of the key reasons offered is its underpinning phallocentricism. Arthur Frank asserts (1991) there is a generalized masculinized character to social theory which is underpinned by an assumed unproblematic male body. Feminist theorizing has highlighted the differential conditions of embodiment (1991: 42), and problematized the body as a taken-for-granted presence in debate about social, political and economic issues. At the same time poststructural analysis derived from Neitzsche's work has challenged the dominance of knowledges and explanatory frameworks that rely for their plausibility on the assumption of a substance called 'the mind'. Of course, a reliance on 'mind' links to discussions of attitudes, opinions, rationality, the brain, personality etc. and away from discussions of body difference, reproduction, desire, sexuality, food, fluids and flesh. The body is, as a result, quite literally matter out of place in many fields. In organization and management studies a number of feminism-inspired authors are drawing attention to the body in the field. The book by Halford et al. (1997) is among a number of recent works that address the body by way of the gendered and sexualized character of organizations (also see, for instance, Cockburn, 1991; Hearn and Parkin, 1995). Halford et al. understand the neglect of a specific focus on embodiment as a result of the dominance of a male body as the norm in work organizations. Drawing on the work of Acker (1990), they argue that most work organizations tend to privilege a particular construction of a disciplined male body as the standard body at work. This 'standard body' is assumed to be physically able, disengaged from reproduction, emotionally under control, lacking desire, isolated in its own performance and disassociated from itself. Against this 'standard body' other bodies, particularly female bodies, tend to be judged and identified as problematic for organizations. Halford et al. argue that it is the difference of female bodies from this 'standard body' that forms a key axis around which organizing and managing operates. This difference either disqualifies or qualifies women for particular organizational positions. Halford et al.'s research, in banking, local authorities and health services, shows that the reproductive, menstruating, menopausal female body is a problem for work organizations, while the sexualized female body qualifies it for particular kinds of work or particular stationings in organizations, for example as receptionists/secretaries/nurses. As part of their discussion of the gendered embodiment of life in these work environments, Halford et al. seek to operationalize the notion of the 'lived body'. Their discussion of the politics of this 'lived body' (Cockburn, 1991) has three dimensions – the spatial, verbal and physical.

A spatial dimension refers to the actual and symbolic location of men and women's bodies in the same or different sites within work organizations, particularly the spatial aspects of interaction. This can include, for instance, unwanted touching or close proximity between bodies. For the nurses in the study this included occasions when male doctors would slip their arms round female nurses' waists or shoulders, or stand close behind them (Halford et al., 1997). It also includes how the bodies of male nurses and male medical staff interrelate. In the Halford et al. study the authors note how the physical politics of relations between female nurses and male medical staff often took on traditional heterosexual patterns of dominance and subordination. For male nurses, however, this was quite different. A male nurse told the authors that while a particular male doctor treats female nurses badly, he felt less secure with the male nurse. 'He's smaller than me, so I use that. I stand over him and look down on him' (Halford et al., 1997: 241).

This spatial dimension obviously includes physical sexual harassment, as graphically described by, for instance, Collinson and Collinson in their study of women in non-traditional management jobs (1996). This spatial dimension also includes the way managers mix men's and women's bodies in offices and other work sites as a way of controlling the potential for disruptive behaviour in single-sex groups. While this was broadly understood in the study as a successful tactic in moderating what was seen as the unruly and less desirable aspects of single sex work sites, the more intimate mixing of men's and women's bodies was also often tightly controlled.

Bodies which actually engaged in affairs at work were often segregated later, particularly in banking, where the liaison was seen as potentially a security risk.

The verbal dimension of this politics of the body surface refers to the 'calling up' or the 'speaking about' embodiment at work and how this is used to constitute relations. This dimension includes the way women's bodies, or the eroticized parts of women's bodies, or women's clothing, are often drawn into discussion which, for instance, might form part of general heterosexual banter, or, alternatively, as a means of positioning women as subordinate to men. Halford et al. noted how, as a way of attempting to discipline nurses deemed to be too assertive and challenging of medical knowledge, male medical personnel would make verbal reference to nurses' bodies.

The verbal dimension of a politics of the body also includes how the body is evoked to encourage pleasurable and playful experiences. Work sites are often permeated with heterosexualized banter between men and women, women and women and men and men (Pringle, 1989). This evokes a body that is the site of pleasure and desire. Of course there are often indefinite 'lines' between pleasurable talk and that which is understood as potentially abusive.

The physical dimension of this politics of the lived body refers to the presentation of the body; how it is dressed, how it moves and what this signifies (Halford et al., 1997: 259). This includes, of course, the overt use of physical features of men's bodies to harass women. One horrendous example of this can be drawn from the Collinson and Collinson study (1996). On one occasion, Dick (his actual first name) was in a lift together with other male managers, when he 'took his penis out to show Sheila [the junior sales manager], adding that "if she was lucky she would get some of it"' (1996: 36).

The physical dimension also refers to the use of clothing in the politics of the lived body. The Halford et al. study highlights how differing dress codes heighten the awareness of woman managers as being 'strangers' in a male world. The study also points out how women managers often engaged in conscious efforts to exploit or conceal this difference in clothing. For instance, one woman manager, one of just five in a 'sea of suits' at a banking event, said:

> We are going to stand out aren't we? But you see I try to take advantage of that so I wore a red suit on the basis that all the men would be in grey and dark. So I did stand out and, yes the speaker did come out and speak to me at the end . . . that is part of playing the game isn't it? (1997: 251)

What this framework details are three core elements around which the politics of the body surface are played out. By exploring how the body is organized spatially, physically and called up verbally/discursively it is possible, as Halford et al. have done, to highlight some of the recursive practices that order social life in work organizations. The discussion in this study highlights how managing and organizing work is built around and through the sometimes problematic politics of body surfaces.

However, there are limits to the extent to which a politics of body surface might provide a means for discussing embodiment. What is missing is an engagement with depth; with the dynamic processes by which the social subject becomes the body-subject (Crossley, 1995), or in conventional dualistic terms, the 'owner' and responsible for 'its' body. What is missing from 'body as surface' is a more direct engagement with the flows and codes of perception, emotionality, sensuality and desire through which bodies come to know themselves. This next section discusses the basis of such a framework of body as depth in the work of Connell (1995) and Deleuze and Guattari (1988).

Body topography: depth

Foucault's work on the body (1981, 1991) has helped to broaden and extend social scientific interest in embodiment (Burrell, 1996). As critical attention is given to Foucault's texts, his approach has been widely contested. Yol Jung (1996), for instance, notes that no one more than Foucault has challenged the pretensions of the 'Enlightenment age' by 'unearthing the clinical and incarcerated body' (1996: 6). However, '[Foucault] never came to grips with the body as flesh, the body as subject' (1996: 6). Thus there has been a swing back to recover a phenomenology of the body concerned to show the body as active in its construction of the social world. Yet there is an inherent danger in this move, in that slippage will re-introduce a kind of soft-dualism of social self and body. Shilling's review of 'the body' in sociology demonstrates this adequately (1993). While he chastises Foucault, claiming the body 'vanishes as a biological entity and becomes instead a socially constructed product which is infinitely malleable and highly unstable' (1993: 74), and repeats Turner's point (1984) of the lack of a phenomenology of the body in Foucault's work, there is in his text the danger of losing the analytical purchase provided by Foucault's inscribed body, and reasserting the primacy of the 'individual' as analytically distinct from bodies.

> Furthermore, the emphasis that modern individuals place on the body as constitutive of the self can be seen in many respects as a *retreat* from the world-building activity. (Shilling, 1993: 182, emphasis in original)

While Shilling's political point is well made, there is a need to re-think a body politics that doesn't rely on a return to the dualism of 'modern' individuals *and* 'their' bodies. Shilling turns to Connell (among others) for support in his argument. However, I want to argue that Connell's work on embodiment, which surrounds his texts on masculinities, sex and power, can be read as an attempt to produce an interdependence between a phenomenology of the body, and its inscription. In Connell's 1995 book *Masculinities* he makes a concerted effort to centre his exploration of men and masculinities on what he calls 'body reflexive practice'. As a way of grounding this conceptualization he notes that 'bodies went missing a long time ago in social theory . . . theories of discourse have not overcome this split. They have made bodies the object of symbolic practice and power but not the participants' (1995: 59–60).

As a counter-point to this discursive imperialism, he asserts that bodies both limit and act to challenge social relations. He notes for instance how in some cases men's bodies are 'virtually assaulted in the name of masculinity and achievement' (1995: 58). After prolonged 'assault', a crisis point is reached when social relations must change. In regard to the body's challenges to social relations he notes how the sexual arousal of bodies can alter and challenge dominant discourses on 'normalized' sexual relations. He suggests that bodily arousal (particularly sexual contact between bodies) is actively engaged in transforming social processes. Using a number of accounts of early sexual experiences drawn from his research, he suggests that men's experiments with and experience of their bodies significantly shape their social relations. Thus he argues for the concept of 'bodily reflexive practice' in social theory as an antidote to the dominance of a 'social semiotics of gender' (1995: 65).

> The social semiotics of gender, with its emphasis on the endless play of signification, the multiplicity of discourses, and the diversity of subject positions, has been important in escaping the rigidity of biological determinism. But it should not give the impression that gender is an autumn leaf, wafted about by light breezes. Body reflexive practices form – and are formed by – structures which have historical weight and solidity. (1995: 65)

While I have set Connell's discussion in the context of those that share an understanding of the body as lived practice, opposed to an inscription model, Connell's argument, despite his comments on 'endless play', 'multiplicity' and 'diversity', is an attempt to make these 'poles' interdependent. One example of body reflexive practice Connell gives centres on one man's conversion from heterosexual to homosexual practice. It highlights Connell interlacing of the two positions:

> Don's story is of how the excitement of having his female lover's finger inserted into his anus made Don think: 'What I would really like to have is a relationship with a man where I would be inserted into.' (1995: 60)

Connell's discussion of Don's story, however, begins with a discursively conventional phrasing which is slightly at odds with his actual conceptualization. He writes: 'Don experienced his body and its capacities through interaction' (1995: 60). This has a tendency to drift toward a dualism of mind and body where 'mind', or self, are privileged over the body. Just to illustrate this dualism it is useful to re-write this phrasing from a body's 'point of view'. This might read:

> *The body known socially as Don exposed its capacities to 'Don' in interaction with other bodies.*

Yet this is not far from Connell's approach.

> The socialness of the physical performance is not a matter of social framing around a physiological event. It is *a more intimate connection* that operates especially in the dimension of fantasy . . . in the fantasy of a new social relation where 'I would be inserted into'. This fantasy started from the experience of being finger-fucked. It arose in a social interaction, but it was wholly a bodily experience too. The body's response then had a directing influence on Don's sexual conduct. 'Agency' does not seem too strong a word for what Don's sphincter, prostate gland and erectile tissues here managed between them. (1995: 61, emphasis added)

Connell here is suggesting that the 'sphincter, prostate gland and erectile tissues' are agents in the construction of new social relations for the 'body' known as Don. Another way to write Connell's example is as follows:

> *the collaborative efforts/excitement of sphincter, prostate gland and erectile tissues ignited a desire for repetition of these efforts/excitement in the body known as Don. This desire attached itself through fantasy to a knowledge that homosexual lovers could be found and would oblige the body known as Don of this repetition.*

Of course I have stretched 'Don's story' a little and Connell may not accept this rewriting. But the position reached in rewriting this example amounts to a 'body as depth' conceptualization. Connell's approach, I think, is one influenced by an 'inscription' position but one that seeks to redress the lack of engagement in Foucault, particularly, with the actual sensuous physicality of bodies caught in the midst of social formations.

This conceptualization of the body highlights, in one direction, how flows of effort/excitement, produced by and through the body as organism, are centrally involved in the 'taking up', challenging, or perhaps recreating social knowledges and practices. From this perspective a 'self', which might be assumed to control these flows, is a *construct or effect* of such flows. Social processes and formations, such as education or the family or waged work, then are engaged in attempting to make the linkages between the flows of effort and excitement, and particular knowledges, in very intimate ways. This is, of course, close to Foucault's 'materialism' (1980: 58). It is the hyphen in his concept power–knowledge (Foucault, 1980). The hyphen, which might be read as a series of points or events 'seen' from a distance, describes networks or links between the body (flows of effort and excitement) and disciplines of knowledge (whose effect is selves, relations and discursive formations). What Connell's critique of Foucault's 'determinism'

– that bodies are simply servants of discourse – highlights is the need for a less slavish and determined understanding of the links between bodily desire and the forms of knowledge. Connell's discussion of these issues highlights his closeness to a broadly Deleuzian perspective.

Deleuze and Guattari's twinned texts (1984, 1988) offer a conceptualization of the body which borrows heavily from Foucault, but offers the necessary corrections to the problems highlighted by the likes of Connell, Shilling and Turner. Deleuze and Guattari's 'body' is not simply a servant of discourse, but the site of potentially creative and revolutionary alternatives. Their 'body' is highly sensuous and physical. Yet its experience of the sensuousness of life is not a result of some natural biological organization, but is a response to how the body is 'made up' in the interplay and 'battle' between social inscriptions and desire. Desire is understood in a Nietzschean sense as 'a process of production without reference to any exterior agency' (1988: 154). Deleuze and Guattari's 'body' is a 'Body-without-Organs'. They use this term, as Lash notes (1984: 9), to highlight how 'we do not experience our bodies in terms of their biological organization, or more precisely, that we should not so perceive our bodies'. What we do experience are patterns of intensities/sensations. These are real, but have been organ-ized in the interplay between social practices, knowledges and the desiring body. The Body-without-Organs (BwO) is a conception of a body which attempts to combine these features without resorting to a dualism between mind and body. BwO in an original state 'is non-strata-fied, uniformed intensive matter' (1988: 153). It is conceived as a hollow egg-like form whose surface becomes inscribed by patterns or figures: 'We treat the BwO as the full egg before the extension of the organism and the organization of the organs, before the formation of the strata' (1988: 153).

Strata are the sedimented figures that are socially inscribed upon the BwO. They are patterns which provide lines through which sensation/intensities flow. According to Deleuze and Guattari, there are three strata which form figures on the BwO: organism, significance and subjectification. Organism is the social organization of the organs into an organism. It is worth bearing in mind that Deleuze and Guattari are here talking about how the body is organized in socio-cultural, historical relations – not necessarily how physical organs interrelate. Significance, the next strata on the BwO, is the strata of discourse and language. 'Significance clings to the soul just as the organism clings to the body' (1988: 160). Subjectification is that strata or series of folds which produce the effect of self or selves. The social practices of discipline, surveillance and technologies of the self, highlighted in Foucault's work, are those mimetic practices which produce these inscriptions or foldings upon Deleuze and Guattari's BwO. These seek to govern thoughts and practices, and to produce our subjectivity by 'channelling desire into prescribed pathways' (Fox, 1993: 78).

Of course, Deleuze and Guattari's BwO is not just an analytical device, but overtly a political project (Jordan, 1995) which is significantly at odds with that suggested by Shilling (1993) above. To aid this project, Deleuze and Guattari engage a sense of poetry and drama in their texts. In their discussion of strata in *A Thousand Plateaux* they take up an imperative voice as a way of highlighting how the social (particularly the family) controls the BwO.

> You will be organized, you will be organism, you will articulate your body – otherwise you're just depraved. You will be signifier and signified, interpreter and interpreted – otherwise you're just deviant. You will be subject, nailed down as one, a subject of the enunciation recoiled into a subject of the statement – otherwise you're just a tramp. (1988: 159)

A major difference between Connell and Deleuze and Guattari is the latter's rejection of a Lacanian view of the role of the imaginary in the taking up of discourse (Lash, 1984). As noted above, Connell understands the imaginary as a kind of hinge between the body and the social. Deleuze and Guattari, however, are among philosophers who seek to question and dispose of splits between mind and body. Where Deleuze and Guattari oppose Foucault is in his work's seeming closure of desire. Deleuze and Guattari oppose Foucault's collapse of bodily desire into power's tracings and knowledges. They argue that while power seeks to inscribe pathways along which bodily desire can flow – for example, through capitalist stimulation or oedipal family relations – it is possible that desire will challenge these inscriptions and move in other directions. Bodily desire for Deleuze and Guattari is fundamentally creative movement. It moves for instance more like the root system of grass – rhizome-like. 'It is always by rhizome that desire moves and produces' (1988: 14). True to their political aims, Deleuze and Guattari's body also makes 'maps' of its own – de-territorializing that which has been inscribed upon it.

Body topography: summary

In the above I've suggested that a study of body topography would involve two interlocking and interdependent axes. This is in response to assuming, for analytical purposes, a partial reversibility of body experience (the body sees and is seen, touches and can be touched, but feels pain/pleasure/anger/love which can't be felt by others in the same way). Body 'surface' is the mapping of the spatial, verbal and physical materiality of embodiment while body 'depth', drawn from the work of Deleuze and Guattari, understands the body as political matter which is inscribed, folded and reworked through the dynamic interplay of desire (physical energy), signification and practices. The strength of this approach is its insistence that social activities and processes be understood as flows of desire (real bodily material force) invested in signification and forms of reflexivity which channel and pattern this investment. Subjectivity then is understood as the patterned flows of desire. Yet desire, in this framework, does not indelibly pattern these strata. Desire is mobile and capable of creating new patterns, new topographies of the body. Re-mappings may be creative and also enforced re-inscriptions. To take an example, being sacked from one's job often leads to strong emotions and grief as well as abrupt changes to health and fitness. By relying on a conventional self–body dualism we might say that a sacking challenges and threatens a particular self. From a Deleuzian, or body depth perspective, the loss of a job severs many of the routinized mappings, or patternings, or assemblages over which desire flows. All kinds of mappings are severed. One of the key mappings for men is how work organizations overlay familial patternings of desire. For instance a manager's desire might be invested (projected) positively in trusting his/her boss/manager/company. This overlays mapping of boss/manager/company as father/family. To be sacked by the boss or not to have one's contract renewed, is to cut up and sever these inscriptions which tap deeper mappings of rejection by father and family. Just to demonstrate the inter-relatedness of the body as surface perspective, the severing of these markings or foldings (in a sacking) might 'present' as a loss of 'health' and 'fitness', the removal of the body from particular spaces, its re-covering in different fabrics and the calling up or speaking about the body in new ways – as an unemployed body.

How then might this analytic of body topography furnish a way of describing and explaining managing and managerial work?

The approach suggests that the 'manager' and 'managing' be understood as the spatial, verbal and physical ordering of bodies as surface, and the investment of bodily desire. Bodily desire is invested in forms of discourse, in other bodies, in sets of reflexive practices, but is also unstable and multiple in its directionality. It is worth pointing out here, following Law (1994) and others, that organizations in this conceptualization are not solid, overarching constructions of reliability and domination. They are made up, and the effect of multiple micro-organizings which are constantly under 'attack'. Changes in the flux of desire on the part of the bodies engaged in these organizings may challenge or reconstruct existing foldings in the strata of the body as depth (BwO). The manager is positioned in particular discourses as responsible for reducing these fluxes, even if the manager him/herself is also the site of these fluctuations and counter-investments. The manager's work ostensibly is concerned with narrating and enforcing particular discourses and practices whose aim is to maintain the particular repetitions of movements of desire across the inscriptions on the BwO. Yet given the instability of desire (bodily energy) and its potential to invest itself in other forms of discourse, other bodies, in other forms of reflexivity, resistance to particular dominant ordering is ubiquitous. Small organizing, counter-investments of desire are constantly starting up afresh, constantly under way and potentially always likely to challenge attempts to produce particular repetitions of practices and events.

The changing body topography of post-compulsory education management

The shift to a more managed UK post-compulsory sector (Miller, 1995; Parker and Jary, 1995; Willmott, 1995) can be read as a changing body topography (both senses). It is not just about changed funding mechanisms, new measurement techniques, new languages. It involves changing spatial, verbal, physical embodiment *and* changing investments of desire (bodily energy). I want to illustrate this with material drawn from a post-1992 university. It deals with the broad shift to a more managed university at senior post-holder level.

Example: charisma to managerialism via an 'execution'

In the late 1980s, the high-profile director of a polytechnic in the north of England was forced to resign following what was described by the trade press as a 'colonel's revolt' against him. Broadly, the event can be read in two directions using interview material from those involved. First, it can be understood as a response by senior staff to what they saw as the director's erratic, vindictive and over-bearing 'style' of management. Secondly, it can be read as the ascendancy of a corporate/bureaucratic mode of managing (see McNay, 1995).

In relation to the first reading, one of the former director's early supporters had this to say:

> 'We felt at the time [of his appointment, circa 1980], that what this polytechnic lacked was a public figure. We needed someone who was going to project us into the sector. We were still the smallest and youngest of the new polytechnics. [The director] was someone who could do it.' (Head of department)

The director was said to have 'flair', be 'charismatic', 'a brilliant speaker' and a 'bit of a cowboy'. This era is remembered as exciting and entrepreneurial. Alongside the director a so-called 'rat pack' of senior staff was said to 'virtually run the institution' outside of formal committee structures. The 'rat pack' had nicknames and their own particular language. One was called for instance 'the fat controller'. Entry to the 'rat pack' was through 'initiation'. One dean who joined the former polytechnic at the end of the 1980s, and who became known to the 'rat pack' as 'Huey', told me that he gained his credibility through his 'hard-man antics' at a three-day senior staff conference in France (which latterly came to represent the excesses of the former director's era). The 'rat pack' represents a group of senior staff whose ethos broadly supported and was supported by the former director himself. Yet membership of this 'elect' inner circle created tensions. Towards the end of his tenure, the director was said to have 'got rid of all the people he didn't like' and started to turn on 'those that were good'. One or two maintained that he was 'mentally ill'. All of these issues created what one senior manager called a 'seething mass' of tensions and conflict.

'What caused this seething mass?'

'I actually think it was the director, it was the old director. I don't know? We were changing so rapidly. Certainly the old director had a great deal of involvement in it because we all started . . .'

At this point in the interview he abruptly paused, and gave an interesting description of how the practices developing among people in the institution spilled over into his home life.

'There was this occasion when my wife said to me, "Don't bring any of those practices back from [the former polytechnic] into this house. If you want to play like that when you are at work, you play like that, but don't bring it back into this house." I thought "what is happening to me", now it wasn't just me it was a whole host of people who felt like that.'

Not long afterwards, as this particular story goes, the 'charismatic/vindictive' director was toppled by an alliance of executives and deans. They met secretly at the conference centre one morning and then presented the director and the polytechnic governors with a vote of no confidence. There was an 'independent' inquiry by the governors followed by the director's resignation. A pay-off of some kind was made, which included an agreement that the departing director would not discuss the events in any public forum.

The alternative reading/story of the director's removal concerns the ascendancy of a corporate-bureaucratic mode of managing which was strong on accountability and responsibility, much in the mould set out in the National Advisory Body for Public Sector Higher Education's publication *Management for a Purpose* (1987) (the polytechnic equivalent of the Committee of Vice-Chancellors and Principals (1985) 'Jarrett Report').

The incoming director, in contrast to the 'charismatic' predecessor, was known as a 'safe pair of hands'. There was respect for his financial conservatism and attention to detail, even if, as one head of department said, this meant 'pathetic arguments in management team [meetings] about names: "we can't have that person called a manager or that person called a head". It was conformity down almost to boredom.' A head of department had this to say:

'[the new director] is a managerialist, everything is in its place, it upsets or threatens his sense of law and order if a group forms and it's not in his organizational chart.'

Other things changed. While the former director was known to frequently walk about the campus, the new director was distant and out of touch with the day-to-day rhythms of the institution. He was seen by many as 'hidden' away in 'mahogany row' with his organizational charts, funding spreadsheets and the institution's growing 'library' of policies. Behind the closed doors people were being intimidated and bullied by the new 'managerialists'. One head of department said:

> 'I think there is less mediation of instructions the further up you go. The deans get told in a fairly bloody-minded way to do this [or] do that by Tuesday. They mellow a bit as they tell us, or ask us, and so on down. The sort of brutalist approach gets more obvious at the top. What is very obvious is [that this is] a very *man-managed* institution.'

> 'What do you mean by *man-managed*?'

> 'Well, I mean whatever the pretence and actually whether we talk about men or women, it is very much a traditional image of tough males running the place.' (emphasis added)

And another head (a member of the so-called 'rat pack') said:

> The [Director] is very rigid in his approach and extremely inflexible. The [Deputy Director] is a very difficult character to deal with. He will not allow conversation and unfortunately I don't even think he is aware of it. He makes very pejorative remarks and statements like "You are all academic heads so I'll explain this to you twice." You know, is that supposed to be funny?'

Many academic staff particularly resented the secrecy and control that this corporate 'style' produced. A staff newspaper sprang up, saying in its first editorial that it was 'a response to the information and consultation gap. . . . It takes as its premise the idea that a polytechnic is primarily about people and ideas, not management and products.' Even new heads of departments, whose appointments were either made or closely vetted by the director, were critical of the centralizing, controlling practices.

> 'It's amazing in a small institution that it is so much more centralized. I had more responsibility for staff as a course leader in Birmingham [Polytechnic, now University of Central England], than I do now as a head of department. It makes us feel dis-empowered. Far too much is being churned out by the directorate in terms of policy – but its down to the paper work on your desk, you wonder if they are trying to *tie you to your desk* . . . it maybe looks as if we're puppets on a string.' (Head of department)

In opposition to the ban on any mention of the former director, people started to talk about this period in relation to the current regime. One dean recalled the discussion at the three-day senior staff conference two years after his resignation:

'People felt that they were able to talk about [the former director] and mention his name. People were saying things like, "I haven't been able to mention his name since he went", and "he was a right bastard, but he was good and we miss him now", people were saying "yeah, well we probably are managed better but we miss that vision".'

Discussion

A body topography of the above would address how the competing stories of the changes at this polytechnic are not simply the work of discourses (languages and practices), but the variable processes of investment of desire in different modes of practice, discourses and bodies themselves. These can be mapped through the changing spatial, verbal and physical presence of bodies.

During the former director's tenure, bodies invested in the practices, discourses and body of the charismatic. For the 'elect' these were passionate, exciting, 'playful' times. There were 'crusades' in the discourses of non-traditional student access, student-centred learning and cross-disciplinarity. There was the bending and breaking of rules, the doing of deals. Doors were open, bodies moved about and made their own groupings which enlivened some and ostracized others. One highly symbolic aspect was the fact that the former director did not have a desk in his office. 'What do I need one of those for? I pay you to do the writing', he is remembered as saying. Instead of a desk he simply had a 'old wobbly chair he had brought from his former college', said one of his acolytes. The desk, such a symbol of the due process of bureaucracy, was rejected by the charismatic. Alongside this was the 'due process' of groups like the 'rat pack' and contempt for bureaucratic due process. Yet at the same time there was favouritism, vindictiveness and a 'seething mass' of disputes and conflicts among the 'followers' and with the former director. For bodies whose investment was in bureaucratic due process, order and control, the 'party' of the mid-1980s had to stop! The symbolic 'execution' of the former director, carried out with weighted symbolism in secret behind closed doors by the polytechnic's board, marks the shift to an investment in order and security. Bodies invested in the 'safe pair of hands' and *his* tools of order: policies, budgets, targets, appraisals. Slowly, and as a counterweight to the entrepreneurial culture of the past, there was a shift toward the notion of being a 'manager' not freewheeling and dealing 'academic heads'.

One of the prices of order was the increased confinement of bodies to desks (like 'puppets on a string'), behind closed doors huddled together in vertically integrated 'teams' (faculty management team, university management team, executive team) of other similarly clothed and practising bodies in the controlled spaces of small rooms and executive offices. Here control could be more easily exercised, instructions given and accountabilities more closely monitored than in the large committees and boards or the loose informal mate-like grouping of the 'rat pack'. Yet this requires the increased codification of bodies, the giving of precise titles located in charts, assigned to budgets and verified in audit 'trails'. Another price paid with the investment in security was secrecy, double-talk and masculine authoritarianism. A positive assessment of this would be that people became more responsible and accountable for resources, and the institution was 'better managed'.

Yet the shift to a bodily investment in the corporate order, signalled by the term 'better managed', is itself an unstable process. Body topographies are always partial. The new topography of corporate order, in spite of a ban on official discussion of the past surrounding the former director, was challenged by a remembering of the investment in the exciting entrepreneurial order the former director embodied. Comments such as 'I haven't been able to say his name', represent both the official ban, and the bracketing of turbulent practices and emotionality associated with the 'charismatic order' and the 'execution'. The recovery of the investment in the charismatic order/leader from what many remember as the 'seething mass' of emotionality and conflict, represents a challenge to the investment in the practices, discourses and symbolic bodies of the corporate order.

Of course what I have left out of the account above is a discussion of the changes to funding mechanisms, legal positions and local/national state relationships which occurred with the incorporation of the former polytechnics in 1989 (Pratt, 1997). This is deliberate. Such changes are clearly important but their importance can be overstated, especially in relation to the actual reconstruction of organizational life in particular sites. I would argue that the legal, regulatory and institutional re-inscriptions that incorporation delivered should be seen more as supportive of particular trends in this case, rather than as their author. Many of those who have benefited from or were instrumental in the reconstruction are, however, prone to claim that it was the government's initiatives and programmes for the sector that authored these processes.

Summary and concluding comments

The above is an attempt to draw together materials from a range of sources which address the embodiment of organizational work. A body topography analytic is used to marshal resources for such an analysis. Body topography relies heavily on the work of the poststructuralists Deleuze and Guattari. However, body topography uses the twin analytical axes of body surface – spatial, verbal and physical 'surfaces' of work – *and* body 'depth' – investments of desire (body energy) in discourses and practices – to discuss embodiment. I then used this framework to address the changing character of post-compulsory education management and to narrate the shift from a charismatic to a corporate managerial order in one former polytechnic. Four key issues seem to have been highlighted during this analysis.

First, the analysis suggests that addressing the changing body topographies of organizations offers a way of addressing the interdependence of the emotionality of work, its physical enactment, changing spatial practices and the changing character of broader structuring orders, in this case, the shift to a more managed post-compulsory education sector (Miller, 1995; Parker and Jary, 1995; Willmott, 1995) as part of the reconstruction of the UK's public sector (Clarke and Newman, 1997).

Secondly, by bringing bodies into the analysis of change and understanding embodiment as an ongoing inscription of layered political material, a more convincing and critical account of the tensions that surround the problematics of restructuring organizational life might be advanced.

Thirdly, addressing embodiment reminds one of the precarious, heterogeneous character of what some would call 'organization' and others now prefer to re-word in a verbal form – organizings (Law, 1994).

And lastly, ignored and subordinated perhaps by hegemonic analytical traditions in organization and management studies, the embodiment of organizational life potentially provides a platform upon which to reconsider some of those traditions.

Note

1 The sketch was part of the newspaper's coverage of the merger of MAI with Express Newspapers earlier this year. Why try to make Hollick's body signify this way? One possible reading would be that as counsel to Labour leader Tony Blair on City matters, Hollick, and his now close relationship with Tory-supporting Express Newspapers (through the merger of MAI), is potentially a problem for the Labour leadership which some would argue has already gone too far in alignment with corporate interests. As a way of engaging politically with these issues, Hollick's body is described in a particular way. Rather than being used to signify conformity, greed, indulgence and short termism, which is how the *Guardian* tended to understand the City during this particular period, Hollick's active difference, demonstrated in allusions to work discipline, non-conformity ('an affectation') and abstinence, is used to deal with the thorny problem of supporting Labour's links with Hollick and Labour peers, while at the same time continuing the tradition of criticism of the City.

References

Acker, J. (1990) 'Hierarchies, jobs, bodies: a theory of gendered organizations', *Gender and Society*, 4 (2): 139–58.

Burrell, G. (1996) 'Normal science, paradigms, metaphors, discourses and genealogies of analysis', in S. Clegg, C. Hardy and W. Nord (eds), *Handbook of Organization Studies*. London: Sage. pp. 642–58.

Clarke, J. and Newman, J. (1997) *The Managerial State*. London: Sage.

Cockburn, C. (1991) *In the Way of Women: Men's Resistance to Sex Equality in Organizations*. Basingstoke: Macmillan.

Collinson, M. and Collinson, D. (1996) 'It's only Dick: the sexual harassment of women managers in insurance sales', *Work, Employment and Society*, 10 (1): 29–56.

Collinson, M. and Collinson, D. (1997) '"Delayering manager": time–space surveillance and its gendered effects', *Organization*, 4 (3): 375–407.

Collinson, D. and Hearn, J. (eds) (1996) *Men as Managers, Managers as Men*. London: Sage.

Committee of Vice-Chancellors and Principals (1985) *Report of the Steering Committee of Efficiency Studies in Universities* ('Jarrett Report'). London: CVCP.

Connell, R.W. (1995) *Masculinities*. Cambridge: Polity Press.

Crossley, N. (1995) 'Merleau-Ponty, the elusive body and carnal sociology', *Body and Society*, 1 (1): 43–63.

Crossley, N. (1996) 'Body–subject/body power: agency, inscription and control in Foucault and Merleau-Ponty', *Body and Society*, 2 (2): 99–116.

Deleuze, G. and Guattari, F. (1984) *Anti-Oedipus: Capitalism and Schizophrenia*. London: Athlone.

Deleuze, G. and Guattari, F. (1988) *A Thousand Plateaux*. London: Athlone.

Featherstone, M. and Turner, B.S. (1995) 'Body and society: an introduction', *Body and Society*, 1 (1): 1–12.

Featherstone, M., Hepworth, M. and Turner, B.S. (eds) (1991) *The Body: Social Process and Cultural Theory*. London: Sage.

Feldman, A. (1991) *Formations of Violence*. Chicago: Chicago University Press.

Foucault, M. (1980) *Power/Knowledge: Selected Interviews and Other Writings by Michel Foucault, 1972–77* (ed. C. Gordon). Brighton: Harvester.

Foucault, M. (1981) *The History of Sexuality, Volume 1: An Introduction*. London: Penguin.

Foucault, M. (1982) 'The subject and power', in H. Dreyfus and P. Rabinow (eds), *Michel Foucault: Beyond Structuralism and Hermenuetics*. Brighton: Harvester. pp. 208–26.

Foucault, M. (1991) *Discipline and Punish: The Birth of the Prison*. London: Penguin.

Fox, N.J. (1993) *Postmodernism, Sociology and Health*. Buckingham: Open University Press.

Frank, A.W. (1991) 'For a sociology of the body: an analytical review', in M. Featherstone, M. Hepworth and B.S. Turner (eds), *The Body: Social Process and Cultural Theory*. London: Sage.

Grosz, E. (1994) *Volatile Bodies. Towards a Corporeal Feminism*. Bloomington, IN: Indiana University Press.

Halford, S., Savage, M. and Witz, A. (1997) *Gender, Careers and Organisation*. London: Macmillan.

Harrison, B. (1994) *Lean and Mean: The Changing Landscape of Corporate Power in the Age of Flexibility*. New York: Basic Books.

Hearn, J. and Parkin, W. (1995) *'Sex at Work': The Power and Paradox of Organizational Sexuality*, 2nd edn. Hemel Hempstead: Harvester.

Hetrick, W. and Boje, D. (1992) 'Organization and the body: post-Fordist dimensions', *Journal of Organizational Change Management*, 5 (1): 18–27.

Jordan, T. (1995) 'Collective bodies: raving and the politics of Gilles Deleuze and Felix Guattari', *Body and Society*, 1 (1): 125–44.

Jung, Y.H. (1996) 'Phenomenology and body politics', *Body and Society*, 2 (2): 1–22.

Lash, S. (1984) 'Geneology and the body: Foucault/Deleuze/Nietzsche', *Theory, Culture and Society*, 2 (2): 1–17.

Law, J. (1994) *Organizing Modernity*. London: Blackwell.

McNay, I. (1995) 'From the collegial academy to corporate enterprise: the changing culture of universities', in T. Schuller (ed.), *The Changing University?* Buckingham: Society for Research in Higher Education/Open University Press.

Miller, H. (1995) *Management of Change in Universities: Universities, State and Economy in Australia, Canada and the United Kingdom*. Buckingham: Open University Press and the Society for Research into Higher Education.

National Advisory Board for Public Sector Higher Education (1987) *Management for a Purpose*. London: NAB.

Parker, M. and Jary, D. (1995) 'The McUniversity: organisations, management and academic subjectivity', *Organization*, 2 (2): 319–38.

Pratt, J. (1997) *The Polytechnic Experiment, 1965–1992*. Buckingham: Society for Research in Higher Education/Open University Press.

Prichard, C. (1996a) 'Making managers accountable or making managers? The case of a code for management in a higher education institution', *Education Management and Administration*, 24 (1): 79–91.

Prichard, C. (1996b) 'University management: is it men's work', in D. Collinson and J. Hearn (eds), *Men as Managers, Managers as Men: Critical Perspectives on Men, Masculinities and Managements*. London: Sage. pp. 227–38.

Prichard, C. and Willmott, H. (1997) 'Just how managed is the McUniversity?', *Organization Studies*, 18 (2): 287–316.

Pringle, R. (1989) 'Bureaucracy, rationality and sexuality: the case of secretaries', in J. Hearn, D.L. Sheppard, P. Tancred-Sheriff and G. Burrell (eds), *The Sexuality of Organizations*. London: Sage. pp. 158–77.

Shilling, C. (1993) *The Body and Social Theory*. London: Sage.

Turner, B.S. (1984) *The Body and Society*. Oxford: Blackwell.

Willmott, H. (1995) 'Managing the academics: commodification and control in the development of university education in the UK', *Human Relations*, 48 (9): 993–1027.

Wright, L. and Smye, M. (1997) *Corporate Abuse: How 'Lean and Mean' Robs People and Profits*. London: Simon & Schuster.

9   Bodies in a Landscape: On Office Design and Organization

Johanna Hofbauer

> Small wonder, then, that a mentality which deemed it necessary to make faith 'clearer' by an appeal to reason and to make reason 'clearer' by an appeal to imagination, also felt bound to make imagination 'clearer' by an appeal to the senses.
>
> (Panofsky, 1976: 38)

> . . . virtually everything that man is and does is associated with the experience of space.
>
> (Hall, 1990: 181)

A main issue in the field of research on 'organizing the body' is spatial design. The close interplay of space and body clearly operates in more than a metaphorical sense. In organization, one tends to find 'heads of department' located on the upper floors of office buildings, whereas manual labour is associated with the basement – the term 'shop-floor' hints at this.[1] It is as though a particular location were characteristic for particular types of activity and as though architecture would reproduce this anatomical metaphor with conception (brain) on top and execution (body, belly, heart or hands[2] etc.) on lower levels. However, it requires a closer look to depict a more complex relationship between spatial design and organizing the body.

A vital element of the semiotics of office layout is the experience of space as bodily experience. Office layout, size, furnishing, lighting, equipment, colour or noise, appeal to the senses of their inhabitants or users. Particular configurations of these devices of design and style symbolize particular modes of organization and concepts of work control. There are many ways of translating management principles into features of spatial organization and interior design, some of which are pointed out in greater detail below. Design may, for example, achieve a sense of flattened hierarchies and team spirit; it may stress a system of single combatants or represent an open-door policy and enforce corporate culture as a means of symbolic integration. Space is not just a physical framework and setting for other means and techniques of managerial control. It is a control device in its own right and should be exposed to critical analysis just as much as any other control technique. In the following, I want to ask, on the one hand, how different modes of organization are expressed in office design and, on the other hand, how concepts of office design are consumed and incorporated into organization.

For a socio-semiotic view on office space

Hence, I shall argue for a socio-semiotic view on this field of research which has primarily been the domain of ergonomists and architects. Ergonomics seeks to design the workplace to take account of human needs, but it generally takes little or no account of social structures and economic forces that give rise to the demand to adapt man to machine, equipment and environment. Even considering the efforts that have been made to reverse the formula and adapt the workplace to physiological or psychological needs, ergonomics generally lacks critical reflection of the relations of power and domination in society which underlie the generation of knowledge on risk or safety, or which render certain health issues legitimate (cf. Sundstrom, 1986). A sociological view also contributes to architecture's idea of space. Of course, architectural literature encompasses critical and highly reflective accounts of causes and effects of spatial constructs. Yet practitioners are normally and necessarily preoccupied with issues of function. I would like to raise the question of what political impact the organization of space has on social organization, or what 'politics' spatial design has (cf. Winner, 1980).

These critical preliminary remarks with respect to ergonomics and archi-tecture, however, are not intended to question their overall research effort nor neglect their expertise. A sociology of space devoted to the issue of office design will need to draw on the knowledge of experts. There is actually much to be learnt from architecture, its techniques as well as the imagination of designers. Ergonomic expertise, after all, is indispensable for a humanitarian argument in organization studies. Nevertheless, with a sociological approach I aim to contribute to a more encompassing perspective on office design and to foster a critical view on various modes of spatial design apt to establish and reproduce social order in the workplace. I shall focus on three ideal types of design which, in my view, support or even impose different types of labour control: open-plan office, corridor office and open-design office or office landscape (*Bürolandschaft*). I take these models from Francis Duffy's book *The Changing Workplace* (1992), consisting of a collection of articles which have been an important source for this chapter. His comments, however informative, do not relate to issues of power. That is why I shall mostly use them as working material, that is, subject them to questioning in the course of the argument rather than taking them as self-evident statements of fact.

Understanding plans as texts

I take it as a matter of fact that spatial organization is political organiza-tion, and not only a matter of utility or aesthetics. The organization of space shapes action and interaction. I therefore believe it is also worthwhile studying office design from an industrial sociology point of view on issues of labour control. It is of equal interest for organization studies, particularly with respect to the issue of 'body and organization', and the related question of how bodies are organized into space.

To speak of bodies (rather than individuals, subjects, workers etc.) stresses the material, in the sense of *corpo-real* aspect of organizational life. It draws attention to such simple facts as, for example, how communication and cooperation are a consequence of physical proximity in the office space. On the other hand, spatial distance hampers communication, and may render cooperation difficult, no matter what personal inclinations the potential interlocutors may otherwise have. Virtually every environmental feature can be important and stimulate perception, arouse feelings and shape dispositions. Organization, obviously, is much more than a technical matter of goal achievement through cooperative effort. Organization also means organizing people in space, which exposes them to a complex ensemble of visional impression, acoustic and olfactory experience. Their specific combination influences the awareness of oneself and others. Hence the reason for relating the study of organization to the study of culture in a proxemic sense, focusing on 'people's use of their sensory apparatus in different emotional states during different activities, in different relationships, and in different settings and contexts' (Hall, 1990: 181).

Proxemics opens up a wide field of research which would have to be explored through case studies. For the purpose of this chapter's argument I shall confine myself to the discourse on design and consider concepts of space articulated in plans, that is schemes of space. I cannot give an account of actual spatial experience in these types of offices. Yet, just as organization charts allow us to reconstruct distinct modes of cooperation, division of labour, supervision, spans of control, etc., so this material indicates prototypes of (formal) organization and control. Figure 9.1, for example, is very eloquent even without our knowing anything about this office in reality, and not having spoken to people who would actually inhabit it. In fact, a plan deploys a whole narrative, telling of territories of groups and individuals or of 'socio-fugal spaces'[3] like pathways, about crowded areas or loosely coupled workplaces and intersections. Plans are a sort of dense description of proxemic concepts, telling of material and symbolic technologies, 'dispositives of power' (Michel Foucault) which aim to order space.

Designers of space seek to transform social reality, which includes *the shaping and reshaping of corpo-reality*. The scripts they produce, with drawings and figures, carry an encoded message of conduct and movement. Though the formal language of architecture is highly abstract – note, for example, the absence of representation of human beings – the literate reader will be capable of decoding this message and imagining an animated scenery: there is a line symbolizing a door to be opened or closed by a person. There are figures representing either the desk of a managerial workplace, or groups of desks on which teams will work together. The plan

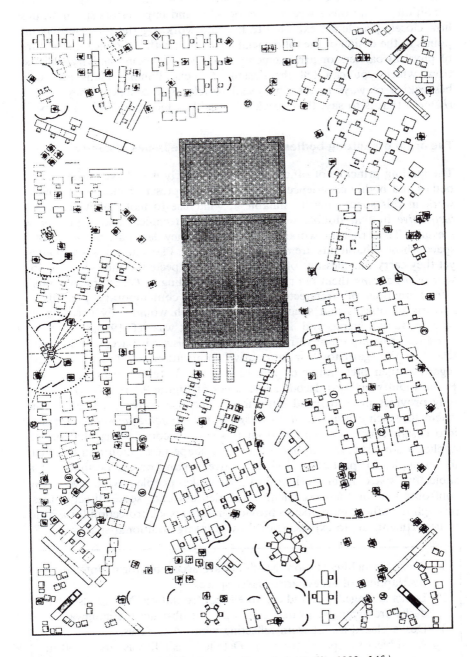

FIGURE 9.1 Bürolandschaft *specimen: floor plan (Duffy, 1992: 14f.)*

consists of a formula for what is going to happen in this space, what conditions of life this space renders possible and imposes: its size indicates how closely people are expected to live and work together, its total layout points to the design of the total social figuration, with a significant structure of physical barriers or arrangements of objects crowding activity (that is, from which you can tell the design of social bonds). Plans are texts bespeaking of ways to inscribe social structures into space. They have a *rhetoric*, that is to say, they speak of a reality which they seek to shape.

The art of organizing bodies into space – some issues of control

The guiding principle of office architecture clearly is to have an impact on bodies and bodily experience. Design models represent concepts of how to work in this space, how to inhabit it, what use to make of it. They are *instructive* in that double sense of holding a technical and a pragmatic message. Their rhetoric works in the way that they designate the shape of a space whose inhabitants are not yet represented. Plans do not show bodies, yet they carry this message of how bodies are expected to move in space by way of *organizing* them *in* or *into* space. According to Christophe Camus's (1996) analysis of architectural discourse in contemporary journals, a rhetoric of objects and space dominates, which would only occasionally refer to human beings and, if so, in an abstract way (cf. 1996: 87).[4]

Hence, it is important to re-read plans and discursive accounts in architecture with regard to their 'normative' implications, that is to say, with regard to their prescriptive or control features. Take, for example, the key Francis Duffy gives to decode some issues of Figure 9.1 (see Box). He not only provides more detailed information but also conveys a sense of the extent to which *psychological, sociological and physiological knowledge* goes into design concepts. I gather from this sort of commentary that design applies a sophisticated *calculus* on how to shape perception and conduct: for example, to 'protect' a desk from overlooking or the occupant of a subjective space from 'feeling lost'; to make people 'avoid eye-to-eye confrontation' or to make them avoid detours and 'sense direct routes' through the office landscape; to provide greater visual protection for a head of department, or 'to express status' by granting additional space.

---

1 A card punching station. Machines are accessible for maintenance; overlapping of access areas saves space.
2 Desks arranged to avoid eye-to-eye confrontation. Notice also that desks are arranged so that chairs do not obstruct the gangway.
3 Desks placed aslant from reflecting window surfaces.
4 A 'subjective space' (ringed). Detailed visibility is about 30 ft; everything beyond is background. Together with screens and plants, this arrangement prevents the individual from feeling lost in the great open space.

5 A plant protects a desk facing a primary route.
6 A primary route, designed to be 'sensed' as a direct route.
7 A grouping of desks, designed to emphasize entity.
8 Desks arranged to avoid overlooking.
9 Space occasionally needed for filing is shared by gangways.
10 Desks near windows, desks have been oriented so that no shadows will be cast over papers being worked on.
11 Greater visual protection for the head of a section is provided by the use, and careful arrangement, of screens, filing cabinets, plants and notice boards.
12 Status expressed by additional space, which also reduces the risk of confidential conversations being overheard.
13 A reserve of space.
14 A rest area near a window. (Duffy, 1992: 14 and 15)

The design of space was a control device before any of such sophisticated landscapes were created. If one recalls the purpose of the very early factory buildings, on the one hand they were supposed to facilitate the organization of the labour process based upon mechanization yet, on the other hand, they were built in order to cope with the notorious problems such as time discipline which occurred in homeworking and subcontracting. N.S.B. Gras argues that factories were even built 'purely for purposes of discipline, so that the workers could be effectively controlled under the supervision of foremen. Under one roof, or within a narrow compass, they could be started to work at sunrise and kept going till sunset . . .' (cited in Pollard, 1965: 11). Besides, the design of tools and equipment has ever since imposed kinesthetic patterns. The assembly line is construed in such a way as to force workers into a certain performance level, the Taylorist desk in the office is supposed to teach clerks the norm of 'keeping order' and a *comme-il-faut* way of efficient practice.[5]

The fact that discipline at the modern, *post-Taylorist* workplace, too, is produced by forces acting upon bodies, through the design of equipment and space, is less obvious. Sophisticated design concepts suggest that workplaces can be adapted to human needs. The overall goal of modern management, according to current slogans in contemporary literature, is to meet the expectations of workers and thereby arouse their intellectual, emotional and social skills for new tasks. Modern office design accordingly attempts to mirror informal relationships or emphasize social bonds among team members, and to create workplaces that attract employees to the extent that an attachment to the workplace as 'second home' is generated.[6] Furthermore, Berg and Kreiner's (1990) study demonstrates how physical settings can be turned into symbolic resources of organizations. They state that physical cues invoke 'emotional memories' (Stanislavsky, in Berg and Kreiner, 1990: 47) and 'help people to adapt to model behaviour which has been learnt, trained, or merely experienced in other situations' (p. 47). An interesting case which illustrates what design can do to perception and how it shapes conduct is Arlie Hochschild's (1983) research on flight attendants, who are expected to practise a 'management of hearts': they are 'trained mentally to imagine the cabin as their own home, whereby feelings are aroused which enable them spontaneously to act out the role of hostesses' (Berg and Kreiner, 1990: 46).

Ideological reading, or the myth of naturalization

The impact of design on office organization is, in fact, increasingly acknowledged by practitioners. The emergence of 'corporate architecture' concepts points to this: 'A basic proposition of corporate architecture is that the architectural, interior and environmental design of corporate buildings and settings has a profound impact on human behaviour in general (in terms of interaction patterns, communication styles, service mindedness etc.) and on human performance in particular (productivity, efficiency, creativity etc.)' (Berg and Kreiner, 1990: 46). Sophisticated office design is becoming more important, particularly in advanced service industries like banks and insurance companies.

However, Gagliardi (1990) sees a lack of research, above all a lack of interdisciplinary research. While researchers dealing with office design are hardly ever interested in culture, those dealing with cultural issues are hardly ever interested in architecture and artifacts (the latter are, according to Pasquale Gagliardi, at best 'paying lip-service to artifacts while neglecting them in substance' (1990: 9)). Additionally, Kleeman (1991) notes that much of design literature is about designers and their work, though design concepts 'tell far more about the societies that build them than about their designers' (1991: 12). Irrespective of the fact that designers work in a socio-cultural context, which shapes their views on form and meaning, their work appears to owe much to truly individual ingenuity and effort. Rather, designers have to be conceived as authors, their *text* and *textual production* being based on and influenced by a socio-cultural subtext.[7] This notion is also suggested by theorists and critics of architecture. Kleeman (1991), for example, stresses that architects articulate what is rendered imaginable and sayable by the underlying social discourse, the prevailing forms of thought, the conceptual tools within architecture. Furthermore, Francis Duffy (1992: 155) states that architects 'struggle to find a vocabulary', which is to say, that they seek to communicate by way of applying an elaborate 'language of things' bound to a system of prevailing symbols and meaning (Gagliardi, 1990: 7).

At this point I should like to address yet another problem that renders it difficult to contextualize the work of architects and which amounts to the fact that cultural and symbolic features of the designers' work tend to remain concealed. Functional buildings appear to be entirely and mainly *useful*. From a common sense point of view their *purpose* is a much more evident feature than their cultural and symbolic significance. According to Roland Barthes, this limitation of perception is generally owing to an ideological conversion of culture into nature, which happens in the process of talking about any objects. It is not only that we are used to speaking in terms of means and ends, but our linguistic systems, too, make us create 'transitive objects'. In this situation, we are supposed to believe we live in a world of practical purposes and functionality, whereas in reality the objects we speak of, equally signify or indicate 'a world of meaning, of rational arguments and alibis' (cf. Barthes, 1985: 260).[8] A further, semiotic, argument claims that function appears to be an evident, 'natural', property of objects because we have come to learn to favour a code *denoting* the sign of 'functional building' as definite and distinct as such. We tend to neglect alternative codes which would *connote* ambiguity and point to other extra – or other functional – ends at the same time, for example, taking office buildings as cultural monuments.[9] Umberto Eco (1988) argues that cultures and societies establish conventional understanding in order to cope with the fundamental ambiguity and polysemics of signs. According to Bourdieu and Passeron (1973), conventions are arbitrary in a radical semiotic, and also sociological sense. They say that any definition of meaning is 'culturally arbitrary', and explain the establishment of conventional, legitimate definitions by the fact that dominant social fractions, such as experts, engage in social combat over legitimate definitions, seeking to render the definition efficacious, which best serves their interests.

In sum, to understand offices or office buildings merely as *containers* of activity, serving a functional purpose, conceals their cultural significance and encourages the 'myth of naturalization' (Barthes, 1985: 249 ff.). Instead, they should be perceived as artifacts, that is to say as objects that have been manufactured or whose shape evolves within a cultural context. The sophisticated design of our era makes it obvious that, in many cases, offices serve an explicit need to represent; but traditional buildings, which seem to lack all symbolic significance, also in fact carry a symbolic message, indicating the historically and socio-culturally shaped mode of organized service labour, expressing the institution of wage labour, of a culture of office hours, of the distinction between home and work, life-world and work-life. The fact of a proper 'functional building' tells a long story about industrial society's mode of production. Besides, the size of the building demonstrates economic power; masses of people assembled under one roof gives a sense of the size and complexity of the organization; the number of floors, their structure, the whole network of numbered rooms is also an eloquent feature.

Organizations may intentionally manage the impression that the building or interior design makes on inhabitants or clients. Or they may make no such attempts, yet negligence, austerity and lack of ornament give a (perhaps unintended) hint of the rational, efficacious conduct expected. Today, we find *ostensive symbolism*, as is the case with insurance companies and bank entrances, where 'the entrance is the organization's face to the world' (Duffy, 1992: 110). On the other hand, there is *ostensive askesis*, 'remarkable for what is omitted at the level of sensory values' (Hemmati-Wagner, 1993: 103). Whether it is ostensive symbolism or lack of ornament, architecture according to advanced design principles or design *avant la lettre*, any building carries symbols representing the mode of organization, and transmits visual messages to those who inhabit the building or to the eye of any other beholder. Spatial organization, in whatever shape, represents and symbolizes social structures and relations of power.

I will now turn to examples of functional discourse in architecture dealing with various forms of *interior* organization, and will ask what concepts of social organization and control are efficacious, or in other words, what types of spatial *dispositives* are at work that support concepts of social order on life and work in the office. Among the wide range of concepts of office design, each of which subjects bodies, organizes individuals into social, symbolic and functional structures in a distinct way, I should like to distinguish, for the purpose of simplification, only the concepts of open-plan office, single office and office landscape.[10] While the main feature of the open-plan office is to line up individuals and expose them to supervision, the 'panoptical gaze' (Foucault, 1974) and 'technical control' (Edwards, 1979), the model of *cellular*, single office pursues the idea of organizing individuals in enclosed workplaces, in 'cells of activity', and incites the micro-politics of 'social distinction' (Bourdieu, 1979). Corridor offices make sense in individualistic concepts of work, where the need to accomplish tasks by cooperation is low and organizational performance is based on individual efforts. Open design in an 'office landscape', in contrast, stresses the cooperative effort ('emphasis is on "communications" rather than on work flow': Duffy, 1992: 82). Open design is said to lead to 'greater teamwork, interpersonal familiarity and spontaneous interaction among those who are mutually accessible' (Steele in Hatch, 1990: 131). The underlying assumption of this design type is that affective bonds rather than management hold organization together (cf. Duffy, 1992: 82). On the other hand, it implies concepts of peer review and self-discipline.

Like a fish in a fishbowl: the case of the open-plan office

The floor-plan of an *open-plan office* renders its 'factory like' features visible (Figure 9.2). In fact, it is regarded as appropriate for work to be organized according to Taylorist principles of management, with standardized tasks, division of labour, and little or no discretion for workers. The design principle at work is apparently to take full advantage of the space available by lining up individuals in ordered rows of desks. Clear space to move, accordingly, is to be confined to a minimum. The classroom-like arrangement, furthermore, makes the 'panoptical gaze' possible, an efficient control device according to Foucault (1974). The panopticon replaces time- and

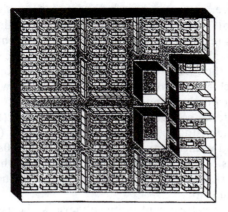

FIGURE 9.2   *Open-plan office (Duffy, 1992: 9)*

personnel-costly personal supervision. It creates a transparent space whose inhabitants are constantly exposed to the gaze of a supervisor, which finally makes them interiorize this gaze. Kleeman (1991) recalls the prototype of this mode of design, Frank Lloyd Wright's famous Larkin building in New York: 'the Larkin building is one large space proclaiming the unity of organization with everyone under the eagle eye of the office supervisor' (1991: 6 f.).

The advantages of open-plan offices are as follows:

- space is saved, there are no wasted corners and corridors are cut to a minimum;
- good work flow;
- ease of communication;
- excellent supervision;
- repetitive tasks can be skilfully organized;
- changes can be made in the layout without difficulty.

But there are disadvantages:

- ordered rows of desks give a classroom effect which is disliked and considered unfriendly by staff below supervisor level;
- there are many distractions, e.g. the appearance of a tea trolley, or the sight of a pretty girl walking down the office;
- outward signs of status are almost non-existent – there is virtually no indication of staff levels other than between the high executive in his office and the rest;
- the individual cannot control his surroundings. (Duffy, 1992: 9)

Duffy, furthermore, gives 'good work flow' and 'ease of communication' as major functional features. Open-plan offices actually resemble the assembly line in this respect. The individual is attached to his/her desk, and, by way of the general arrangement of desks, put in line with his or her fellow workers and their activity. Close interconnection of workplace and occupant can be achieved through technical means, as was the case, for example, in the Larkin building offices, 'Clerks sat on fixed seats that pivoted from their desks, so rigid was the space planning' (Kleeman, 1991). In relation to motion studies expertise, Pélegrin-Genel (1995: 59) gives another example of the ingenuity of designers in the 1930s in coping with kinesthetic problems. They designed the 'rolling chair', which moved on a rail allowing the clerk to switch between the calculator and the typewriter with no need to stand up.

Beyond these rather extravagant technical devices, the assembly line type of arrangement of desks can, on its own, produce a similar effect, as it simply eliminates the need for any superfluous movement. In historical settings, errand boys would operate as couriers, transmitting documents from one desk to the other. Consequentially, there was no longer any formal reason or pretext for leaving the desk or for talking to others (Fritz, 1982: 101). The general layout of open-plan offices mirrors functional organization. It imposes social order through 'mechanical integration' (Durkheim, 1984) and establishes spatial transparency through symmetrical arrangement of desks.

While it is true that open-plan offices in their ideal-typical form render formal communication easy, it is also true that they hamper informal contact. Fellow workers, who are isolated from one another though working together in great numbers, are supposed to stay at their desks and stick to their proper tasks. The circle of colleagues who can be addressed is reduced to one's immediate desk neighbours. Yet, despite proximity between desk neighbours, visual space is confined by a classroom-type arrangement. As the individual worker has no one opposite to make eye contact with, his or her gaze is directed back to their work. No wonder then that colleagues are perceived as a source of noise rather than as company, and that one of the disadvantages attributed to this concept is the problem of distraction. Mutual awareness without the opportunity of talking to one another leads to a feeling of social anonymity, which in turn arouses attitudes of 'indifference' towards fellow workers (cf. Fritz, 1982: 112).

Open-plan offices are supposed to suggest transparency and unity of organization. According to Marberry, the 'lack of colour' was a characteristic feature of open-plan offices in the 1950s and contributed to a standardized look, making further 'industrial references to efficiency and organization . . . potent symbols for the new commercial age' (1994: 4).[11] The effect of unification, furthermore, is achieved through restriction and standardization of equipment to an extent that workers are denied *personalization*, that is, the possibility of deliberately adorning, decorating, modifying, or rearranging their working environment (cf. Sommer in Sundstrom, 1986: 218). The following comment highlights the feeling of alienation that emerges under conditions of over-standardization:

> I'm a fish in a glass container, and there's no way I can make this fishbowl mine. The authorities request that every desk be cleared. Everyone must use the same sort of filing cabinets, the same waste-paper baskets. No posters are allowed. No photographs. Plants have to be a certain height. (Coombs, 1986: 220)

Given the fact of a highly rationalistic atmosphere, designers acknowledge that open-plan offices convey a sense of being nothing but a number and convey a feeling of humiliation (Duffy, 1992: 9). Yet, at the same time, the advantage of the ease of making changes in the layout is noted, which correlates with a 'technically' easily replaceable workforce.

In view of these functional features of open-plan design, social causes and symbolic effects become equally striking. On the one hand, the features of *International Style* architecture, 'open interiors, right angles, parallel lines, machine-like and unornamented precision, technical materials, and glass walls' (cf. Marberry, 1994: 4) represent rationality and efficiency, which also make up the principles of the organization of workflow and use of space. On the other hand, the rigid organization of individuals in the office area and the distribution of bodies in a classroom-type of space, unfolds the symbolic significance of an 'authoritarian'[12] disciplinary regime. According to H.J. Fritz's (1982) socio-historical account of the office, open-plan designs, in general, are meant to create order by disentangling informal networks and relationships. Given the need to utilize space better, on the one hand, and the technical means available to design bigger offices for a greater number of people, on the other, it is possible to *homogenize* the field of vision (*Homogenisierung des Sehraums*; Fritz, 1982: 98). Fritz argues that now management has acquired knowledge on how to use vision as a means of power, space has been turned into a decisive device of office organization. Hence, the open-plan office means a reaction against former spatial complexes with badly arranged rooms, of areas that are difficult to survey, and blind or hidden corners. It is a disposition that creates social order by way of obstructing all non-directed diversity of movement as well as any form of crowding, where one body may screen another.

Additionally, Fritz notes *acoustic* and *olfactory homogenization*. E.T. Hall (1990), too, refers to this phenomenon, pointing out that 'air-conditioning, fluorescent lighting, and soundproofing make it possible to design houses and offices without regard to traditional patterns of windows and doors. The new inventions sometimes result in great barnlike rooms where the "territory" of scores of employees in a "bull pen" is ambiguous' (1990: 107). This problem has also been addressed by Georg Simmel, who points to the fact that visual, acoustic and olfactory homogenization create abstract social unities.

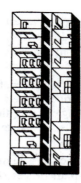

FIGURE 9.3   *Corridor offices (Duffy, 1992: 8)*

Only here, where one saw the innumerable crowd without hearing them, did that high level of abstraction of all that they have in common take place, the development of which is often inhibited by the individual, the specific and the variable that the ear conveys to us . . . The immediate production of highly abstract, non-specific social structure is thus best fostered, as far as it concerns the senses, through visual proximity without being within speaking distance. (Fritz, 1982: 112, my translation)

The cellular model: the case of the corridor office

From the point of view of efficient use of space, theorists of architecture may criticize waste caused by 'bleak corridors with walls whose only purpose seemed to be to provide a framework for dozens of numbered, name-plated doors' (Duffy, 1992: 8). Yet, the *cellular, single office* (see Figure 9.3) is generally appreciated by workers as it allows for the individualization of working space that is missing in open-plan offices (cf. Hatch, 1990: 129). The ability to close the door means a chance to control self-presentation *vis-à-vis* peers, superiors, or clients. A room of one's own, even though it is merely an office, shapes the politics of identity, or, to put it in Erving Goffman's terms, it supports the individual's management of social façade (1959). Accordingly, E.T. Hall (1990) points to the 'significance of architectural features which provide screens behind which to retire. The strain of keeping up a façade can be great. Architecture can and does take over this burden for people' (1990: 104).

Corridor offices *do have* advantages, of course:

- single rooms are easily provided;
- privacy is available: partitions prevent overlooking and can prevent overhearing;
- the time-honoured ways of controlling the environment – light switches, windows that can be opened for ventilation and closed to prevent draughts; blinds to stop sunlight streaming in – these things are understood by all;

- different sorts of office, furnishings, and floor coverings provide a simple guide to status.

On the other hand,

- not everyone – not even everyone who *needs* one – will get their own office, so people will have to share, but small shared offices provide the poorest conditions for mental concentration;
- supervision is difficult;
- communications can be bad, internal telephone calls will disturb everyone from opening to closing time, internal memos will be sent from office to office, and yet much that should be communicated will fail to get through;
- space is wasted in the connecting corridors, behind doors, in corners;
- partitions are expensive to move and may inhibit future changes, often, despite growing inconvenience, the original arrangements are considered sacrosanct;
- the shape of the building makes it difficult to get more than a small number of people together in one place, either as a work group or for conferences. (Duffy, 1992: 8)

At this point, Hall also refers to Phillipe Ariès's (1996) study, *Centuries of Childhood*. Ariès shows that the emergence of specialized rooms (bedrooms, living room, dining room) and especially the separation of rooms for family members, shaped the concept of childhood and contributed to the evolution of the nuclear family. Single offices, though they are neither 'private' nor 'property', equally allow individualization through symbolic appropriation of space. Furthermore, their holders are more likely to enjoy the right to personalize and to apply territory markers. These messages of identity often mirror organizational or professional culture. But even though they are 'individual' only in a weak sense, they nevertheless communicate more or less discrete social demarcation lines which are easily understood by others. Finally, single offices mean the chance of controlling one's environment, which also amounts to the social acceptance of this spatial setting in an individualized working culture, compared to that of the *homogenized* open-plan office.

Enclosed workplaces, indeed, appear to be a privilege for their occupants in general. As Hatch remarks: 'In regard to status, several studies have identified privacy as a central issue. Louis Harris and Associates (1978) found that survey respondents listed style of furnishings, privacy, and floor space as the three most prevalent signs of rank in their organizations' (Hatch, 1990: 131). However, further research points to the need to differentiate: 'low-status individuals found their move from conventional to open offices to increase the perceived favourability of their environment (operationalized as work space adequacy, privacy, and positive interpersonal relationships) while high status individuals experienced a decrease in the perceived favourability of their environment' (Hatch, 1990: 132). These findings stress the importance of contextualizing. Single offices are not desirable or socially significant *per se*. They may, for example, obstruct communication and informal contact and therefore appear disadvantageous. Besides, a comparison between open and cellular office design has to take into account the concrete features of either of the two (in terms of aesthetic and technical features). Finally, it is to be noted that, in order to turn a potential device of status into an actual device of social distinction, one needs to have regard to its *relative* symbolic features, that is, comparative size, location, equipment or material in use:

> While the amount of space allotted to an office worker is perhaps most symbolic of rank and status, the position of the workplace in relation to others is also important; in some organizations, closer to the boss is better. Spaces closest to the areas of highest activity are desirable. Windows are prized by many for access to natural light, as are corner offices. In offices occupying more than one floor, the higher the floor, the more status it usually indicates. Another symbol of prestige is access control, for privacy, or the number of barriers between the worker and interruption or distraction. How many secretaries guard the entrance to the boss's office? Even the presence or the absence of a door may be an indicator. (Kleeman, 1991: 17)

I gather from this idea that status differentiation implies individualization (or, put more precisely, individualization appears to be a pre-condition of status differentiation). The ability to differentiate and create socially significant demarcation lines, then, may turn these functional features into devices of symbolic and social control. The distribution of symbolic resources is a matter not only of individual accumulation but of social favour. Management may make use of this fact and communicate, by way of spatial distribution and allocation, the system of hierarchy, which may otherwise be rendered insidious or neglected. Granting space and equipment is a subtle means of 'managed stratification'. Especially when the desire for additional or more appropriate space comes up against scarce resources, the concession of some additional square metres or of a different location (be it a higher floor or the re-location of an important trespass) may come into conflict.

Figure 9.4 illustrates the situation of social signification in a corridor office setting. I take it as a caricature expressing the fact that the concept of the single office induces a clever management of space. It renders obvious that, as opposed to the open-plan design, where 'excellent supervision' and 'panoptical gaze' serve as significant control devices, the single-office features distribution of spatial assets in the game of social ranking. Or, in other words: *social normalization* is not achieved through homogenization, but *through diversification*, that is, by way of granting or neglecting spatial status markers.[13]

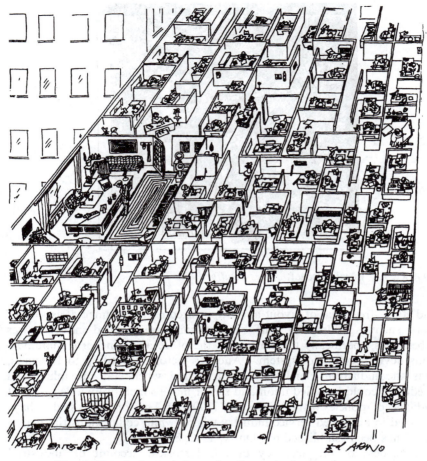

"I'm afraid a raise is out of the question, Benton, but in view of your
sixteen years of service we are advancing you two spaces."

FIGURE 9.4 *Management of space and stratification (drawing by Ed Arno*
in The New Yorker, *18 April 1977, in Sundstrom, 1986: 238)*

Bodies in a landscape: liberalization and regulation of space in an open-design office

The concept of office landscape, or *Bürolandschaft*, emerged in Germany in
the late 1950s. It was a time when both a more humanitarian discourse ethic
had entered management theory and when architects were 'eager to try
anything that would enable them to design a better world' (Hannay, in
Duffy, 1992: 1). Kleeman mentions various factors shaping the development
of office design: the concept sprang from Scientific Management principles
and was influenced by human relations thinking, 'which promoted a relaxed

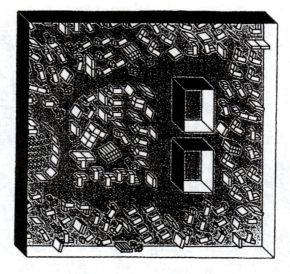

FIGURE 9.5 Bürolandschaft *offices (Duffy, 1992: 11)*

and status-free form of layout and emphasized non-instrumental aspects of work such as addressing staff by first names. The third influence was cybernetics, specifically the concept of the office as a kind of communications device or control system.' 'Another factor', according to Kleeman, 'was the industrial climate during a period when staff discipline and obedience could be relied upon and senior management were able to adopt "advanced" policies without question' (1991: 9). The concept is said to have survived in advanced service industry where 'white collar industrial democracy' has been established (cf. Duffy, 1992: 82).

Regardless of the accuracy of this historical account of 'industrial democracy' and 'staff discipline', it is clear that management discourse at the time was changing.[14] According to Hannay, the slogan of the day went: 'If you want to retain the knowledge you have to respect those who create it' (in Duffy, 1992: 120). Architects who learned this lesson claimed accordingly: 'Although the primary object is to make the office work as efficiently as possible, it is important to remember that staff must be made to feel at ease: if they do not, productivity will suffer' (p. 12). Designers of office landscapes are supposed to have a new stereotype of worker in mind: not the clerk accomplishing routine tasks but the 'competitive yuppie of the new services industries' (Hannay, in Duffy, 1992: 120).

Together with a 'new concept of the worker' (cf. Flecker and Hofbauer, 1997), a new type of work organization emerged. Team-work required a different design of the work space. The group, not the individual, was to make up the basic unit of organization – and, consequentially, of office design too. Cellular offices would set limits to cooperation. The individualistic concept, with lack of space for meetings and a design that hampers communication, was regarded as forcing individuals to communicate through memos, which encouraged bureaucratization, and was no longer regarded as efficient. Hatch reports, from Zalesny and Farace's study, that a move to open offices in fact meant better access to information and was thus appreciated by professionals and managers ('significant decreases in information requests were reported by professionals and managers after a move to open offices' [Zalesny and Farace, in Hatch, 1990: 131]). Duffy (1992) equally notes this advantage of open design: 'If physical barriers come down, and desks are arranged loosely according to need not status in the manner of office landscaping, true cooperation towards a common goal is likely to be engendered' (Duffy, 1992: 82).

With office landscaping a new paradigm entered the scene, making it possible 'to achieve an *organic freedom* both in organizational and building form' (Kleeman, 1991: 7, emphasis added). The term 'organic', according to an exhibition catalogue on modern design, is used to mean a setting in which the parts are linked together in one overriding whole so that they interact and complement one another. Formally speaking, this is empha-sized by means of fluid transitions, smoothed edges, things blending in with each other, and a design that stresses rounded forms in order to show that, as with a plant or an animal, the functional *raison d'être* of an organ does not have to do with itself, but with its becoming part of the whole organism. Indeed, with regard to Figure 9.5 (and, moreover Figure 9.1), the striking lack of straight lines should be noted. The layout of office landscapes looks much more sophisticated than that of open-plan or corridor offices. Diagonal lines and circles suggest the notion of more openness, which would allow for dynamic organization. Design, in fact, seems to follow actual, complex work structures rather than to impose a concept of order. Accordingly, the symbols may be interpreted as making up a structure which evolved in practice, rather than the strict symmetry of a classroom. The immediate association is not the pre-planned city district, built from scratch, but rather a village developed over years and generations, with social territories, recreation zones, pathways and gangways leading to and fro. One might also imagine attractive plants producing a friendlier atmosphere.

Still, even though office landscapes appear to provide a more 'natural' work environment, they are no less artificially constructed, that is, shaped by organizational culture and design concepts. Just as with other landscape concepts, office landscape, too, is cultivated or 'domesticated' nature, contrary to that suggested by the rhetorics of 'organic freedom' (Kleeman, 1991: 7) and the like. A euphemistic reading of open design would also claim to picture *informal* structures rather than to impose a formal pattern of communication. However, it should be clear that by 'picturing' and further-more 'depicting' informal relationships by way of translating them into spatial features, a 'formal' structure is actually re-established, re-constructed out of the 'informal' – which is the way organization emerged, implying discipline and normalization (cf. Cooper and Burrell, 1988: 109).

Office landscaping, according to Duffy (1992: 82), 'expresses in a particularly didactic form arguments for a participative management style'; but, as hierarchical distinctions remain, privileged space which can be discretely separated and protected from overseeing and overhearing has to be created. The claim to privacy and individualization is apparently still valid. Beyond functional reasons (managers having to engage in confidential encounters etc.), this symbolics communicates a stratified social system, where space and the ability to hide from public view remains a major device of status differentiation. However, not even these privileged 'subjective spaces' (1992: 14) should appear to be enclosed. They have to be designed in such a way as to suggest accessibility. Design of work stations and the grouping of desks emphasizes proximity, entity and ease of communication. Standard space per person should be respected, but the arrangement of desks has to render groups easily recognizable. Hence the management of proximity and distance are a significant device in control and status at work. While being together on shared social territory exposes each occupant of it to peer review, spatial distance in a visually and acoustically protected area is the architectural feature that removes this 'burden' from high status executives (cf. Hall, 1990: 104). Under conditions of permanent self-exposure to others, individuals need to keep their social façades under control (cf. also the notion of '*Affektkontrolle*'; Elias, 1976) and to manage the impression they make in order to gain social standing. Research and literature on team-work, indeed, stress the significance of social control.

To be put under scrutiny of fellow workers may incite self-stylization, which in itself demands discipline (cf. Singer, 1993: 75). Furthermore, design concepts up to the standards of modern ergonomics, which acknowledge the need to personalize work space, may very well make use of this need. By providing the means of personalization or by setting standards of good/bad taste, they may in fact impose *corporate* identity concepts on the individual. The group can be a useful agent for the imposition of aesthetic categories on its members. According to the office landscape concept, the territory of a work group should be marked, in order to make the structural outline of the organization clear to everyone. For me, it was interesting to see that, in our case study of an Austrian Bank,[15] the groups reinforced these markers with group symbols. They established a code of status markers, rules of *comme-il-faut* dressing, and conduct according to a certain etiquette additional to the formal texture. The head of department is well aware of these idiosyncrasies and approves of them – 'as long as they don't obstruct performance'. But, surely, they hardly ever obstruct performance. On the contrary, they rather turn out like 'games of making out' (Burawoy, 1979). The attention of the group members is drawn to the distinction of *us* and *them* and to the ongoing game of status competition, over which they easily forget the fact that those battles are taking place on organizational grounds, with organizational means, according to rules conforming with organizational rules.[16]

In conclusion, I want to stress that impression management, which presupposes emotional management and self-stylization, appears to have become a must with open design. Workers are likely to compete with one another and to engage in social distinction struggles, which also shows in ways of using and claiming space. With office landscaping, design returns to the major control device of visual control, that is, monitoring. In contrast to open-plan design, peer review and self-monitoring become important, rather than panoptical surveillance and personal supervision or direct control. Unlike the open-plan office, the use of space appears to be 'freer' according to requirements of mobility and the need to cooperate and communicate. In contrast to single office design which organizes the individual into his or her cell of activity, office landscapes open up space. They are generally regarded as a means to clear away the notorious disadvantages of single space, for example, the confinement of informal communication to personal initiative in spare time. Open design is supposed to overcome the distinction between the formal and informal. Furthermore, it is meant to communicate notions of social hierarchies more discretely. Kleeman reports a case of open design where 'hierarchical power is no longer tied to physical space in an egalitarian scheme that particularly improves the lot of lower-level employees' (1991: 9).

Office landscapes may bring about many ergonomic advantages and overcome flaws of open-plan and corridor settings. However, by stressing ergonomic progress other concepts, such as the issue of control, tend to be concealed. Modern organizations praise their politics of devolutionism, that is, granting the right of discretion and performance control to teams. However, it should be noted that neither devolutionism nor a more pleasant working environment automatically lead to better performance, but are enforced by new forms of control. It is now the peers who are in charge of self-organizing tasks, and who, through the simple fact of being permanently exposed to one another, enforce standards and norms of behaviour at the same time.

The shape of equipment or the arrangement of screens imposes pathways and conduct in space. They may help to make work more efficient and the workplace more attractive, but at the same time they shape conduct and support symbolic integration. Additional to the design of equipment, the design of colours plays an important role in modern office architecture. After all, research on the effects of colour upon office workers (cf. Marberry, 1994: 115 ff.) shows that knowledge about workers 'feeling better' is linked to workers 'performing better'.[17] Ergonomic knowledge has always been closely tied to management problems, either because ergonomics has posed the question of how to accomplish 'comfort and productivity payoff' (Kleeman, 1991) or because management has incorporated new socio-psychological knowledge into its expertise. From kinesthetic problems in the days of the Gilbreth studies, to the notion of 'therapeutic qualities of colour' in contemporary design literature (Marberry, 1994: 119), the underlying concept, now as ever, has been to improve performance. In the course of changing management and design paradigms euphemistic notions have contributed to legitimizing modes of control. Nowadays, the concept of 'organic' design is linked, for example, to the 'health' issue. The following quote refers to 'organizational health' and the 'holistic approach', a rhetoric which also evokes associations of workers' well-being:

> In experimenting with new forms of office furniture and design, Steelcase has identified the new breed of worker as the 'knowledge' worker – a person who in the daily performance of their job has as their primary function to analyse, create, decide, collaborate, and act on information as their fundamental raw material. Noting that 'successful companies base their business on an awareness of the critical forces that affect them – political, economic, demographic, social, and technological forces', Steelcase has also devised a formula for 'organizational health'. This holististic approach factors in all the elements that will affect the performance and strength of a department or company, including people, technology, work process, and architectural place. (quoted in Marberry, 1994: 117)

Résumé

In my argument I have aimed to show that open-design concepts are based on proxemic expertise, rational calculi of group dynamics, or other perception control devices. The overall idea may be to better adjust the work space to human needs. Yet, these needs are as much construed in the process of adjustment as one seeks to meet them. Ergonomic concepts do not simply cope with existing problems, they are equally prescriptive and normalizing as they aim to arouse certain feelings, attitudes and emotions by way of making deliberate appeals to the senses.

Yet, even though ever-more sophisticated design concepts emerge and are welcomed by 'practitioners', they may be contested in social practice which makes idiosyncratic sense of new devices of design. Office landscape, therefore, does not provide a 'one-best-way'. Francis Duffy, for example, reports on workers' initiatives that contested open design solutions and re-negotiated individual spaces. They changed open-design offices into cellular ones in order to escape both the social pressure put on them as well as the 'homogenization' tendencies (Fritz, 1982: 112) which have also been experienced by inhabitants of office landscapes:

> Even today, the increasing impact of participation or, more fundamentally, the shift of power from management to staff, is making office landscaping an untenable concept in Northern Europe. A form of planning of which the openness and completeness reflect powerful centralized management thinking cannot be reconciled with the new ability of staff to negotiate about the physical conditions they would like to appropriate for themselves, such as partitions, access to windows, and privacy. Current anti-office landscaping and highly cellular projects in Scandinavia are the direct consequence of new participative labour laws. (Duffy, 1992: 141)

Sundstrom (1986) accordingly argues that the role of design should not be overrated, because people adapt to environmental changes. His summary and discussion of psychological research on the impact of environment on behaviour shows how little we know about long-term effects of changes in design. Yet, it is equally misleading to claim that the individual gradually 'absorbs' any change. The flaw in this argument is that it is based on a 'simple reading' of items without taking into account their significance in a wider symbolic context. In other words: the question is not how many square metres your new office has compared to the old one. In the long run, people may in fact get used to a smaller scale or a different colour scheme, or any other specific change. The question is, however: what do such changes in scale and colour etc. indicate in a certain context? How does each of these devices relate to other changes, for example to changes in fellow workers' offices, changes to the whole building or site, or changes in organizational structure and management concepts?

In practice, change may not take place all of a sudden, nor should history be ruled out. Just as organizations memorize and 'think' in historical terms (Douglas, 1986), so the individual's interpretation and understanding of new symbols is linked to his/her experience. Accordingly, they read new design devices with 'experienced eyes'. Still, changes in equipment, spatial layout, or colours can be suggestive. They may represent a new vocabulary, a new concept of office design and organization, which in fact introduces or at least supports the emergence of new patterns of perception and conduct.

Office design reflects organization, organizational change and changing organizational paradigms. Last, but not least, the fact that the designers' work is measured by the impact their work has in practice provides a hint of this. Designers live from their art and skill in shaping reality, materially and symbolically – and so do organizations.

Notes

Part of this chapter was presented at the 'Body and Organization' workshop at Keele University, 12 and 13 September 1996, under the title 'Rhetorics of Self-Making: Techniques of Self-Governance in Modern Organization'. I would like to thank everyone who commented on it on that occasion.

1 Mats Alvesson (1988) researched the case of an organization based on 'managerialist' principles, where this architectonic organization was strategically reversed. Top management occupied the ground-floor offices in order to demonstrate how open, ready to communicate and team-oriented the company management was.

2 Today the metaphors are occasionally becoming somewhat mixed, since the modern management discourse of 'devolution' etc. raises workers to the level of 'minds': cf. Paul Thompson and Chris Warhurst (1997). In this work the authors oppose Charles Handy's thesis according to which there would no longer be any 'hands', but only hearts and minds. I take the metaphor of the 'belly of the organization' as a literal translation from the German title of Charles Handy's (1992) *Inside Organization (Im Bauch der Organisation*, 1993).

3 'Socio-fugal space' keeps people apart from one another as it suggests not to stay or gather there (cf. Humphrey Osmond, in Hall, 1990: 108ff.).

4 Christophe Camus (1996) reports that the argument of architectural studies mostly concerns spatial, rather than temporal entities. He argues that this is why human experience of time, the notion of event, history in general, is lacking – be it the history of a building or project, or history in terms of the life-stories supposed to happen in the space construed: 'Et, bien que les discours descriptifs d'objets spatiaux et architecturaux s'alimentent incontestablement d'une culture spécifiquement visuelle, il semble qu'ils s'élaborent, malgré tout, *dans* et *pour* cette expérience fondamentale, la culture visuelle et la spécificité de l'objet architectural venant expliquer que, dans la majorité des cas, il n'est pas question de rendre compte, de manière traditionnelle, du processus temporel qui produit un projet ou un bâtiment.

Ainsi, le plus souvent, il ne s'agit que de décrire cet objet ou cet espace, en faisant occasionellement appel aux sujets humains qu'il implique ou en les convoquant d'une façon souvent abstraite' (1996: 87).

5 Which still seems 'reasonable' (in Taylorist categories), if we trust in a study quoted by Pélegrin-Genel (1995: 126), according to which everybody spends at least 40 minutes per day looking for or arranging documents.

6 According to Marberry (1994: XVI), an American company pushed their employees to work 60-hour weeks by designing offices as 'second homes'.

7 Camus (1996) argues in a similar way in his *Lecture sociologique de l'architecture décrite*: 'Il s'agit alors d'interroger comment certains discours empruntent *quelque chose* (qui est à déterminer) au monde et à ses objets, pour en produire une forme ou une représentation originale qui est, elle-même, susceptible d'engendrer un monde ou un objet nouveau' (1996: 10). Instead of speaking of author, text and subtext, it is of course equally possible to refer here to Pierre Bourdieu's sociology and his notion of a social field of academia, art or literature which produces creative actants, academics, artist or writers. Bourdieu has worked on and written about all of these fields, but I only refer to his work on academics (1984) and the field of literary production here (1991).

8 'Le sens est toujours un fait de culture, un produit de la culture; or, dans notre société, ce fait de culture est sans cesse naturalisé, reconverti en nature par la parole, qui nous fait croire à une situation purement transitive de l'objet. Nous croyons être dans un monde pratique d'usages, de fonctions, de domestication totale de l'objet, et en réalité nous sommes aussi, par les objets, dans un monde du sens, des raisons, des alibis: la fonction donne naissance au signe, mais ce signe est reconverti dans le spectacle d'une fonction. Je crois que c'est précisément cette *conversion de la culture en pseudo-nature* qui peut définir l'idéologie de notre société' (Barthes, 1985: 259, emphasis added).

9 For a thorough debate of these semiotic issues, see e.g. Eco (1988) and Barthes (1965).

10 This selection is, of course, not representative of the modern workplace, or the workplace 'of the future', with virtual offices or homework-places. The questions that would have to be raised regarding these new modes of work organization are, however, too specific to be treated within the compass of this chapter.

11 Yet this was not just a matter of style and concept, but also a matter of available material: 'prior to 1950, most offices were furnished with rows of green metal desks, with grey equipment, partitions, and filing cabinets. Undoubtedly, many of the materials available today were hard to get or non-existent back then' (Marberry, 1994: XV).

12 Authoritarian, as opposed to the Foucauldian notion of 'normalization' through drill or incitement (Foucault, 1974, 1976).

13 Richard Edwards's (1979) findings on the management of difference in payment and symbolic gratification within the paradigm of bureaucratic control spring to mind at this point. In general, one could argue that open-plan and corridor

office very much translate Edwards's two modes of control, technical and bureaucratic, into spatial terms.

14 Francis Duffy rightly points out: 'What is interesting about these arguments is not so much whether they are true or not but that they were made at all. They represent a conscious process of translating fashionable managerial ideas into what is considered appropriate physical form. This is exactly the same step as was taken when motion study ideas were introduced into office design at the beginning of the century' (Duffy, 1992: 82ff.).

15 This case study was part of an interdisciplinary project on 'Intercultural management and multi-methodological research' at the Vienna University of Economics. For further information see Hofbauer et al. (1997).

16 According to Norbert Elias's sociological account on life at Louis XIV's court at Versailles, the King managed to control the complex social scenery by promoting social tension among ambitious peers ('la jalousie de l'un sert de frein à l'ambition des autres'; Elias, 1990: 198, French in the original), while at the same time seeking to render social structures transparent. Indeed, in order to explain how social order is established on the comparatively liberal ground of office landscapes we need only recall this study on space and visible representation of social figuration. Elias reconstructs Louis XIV's concept of social assemblage on the common ground of a basic spatial structure, for example, with rooms dedicated to certain activity and time, where certain courtly rituals were supposed to take place. According to Elias, Louis XIV reinforced social disciplining by the very fact that 'his' noble men and women were gathered under one roof and constantly exposed to the observation of their peers. It is also within this particular historical setting that self-monitoring was no longer practised for the sake of becoming dear to God, but turned into self-monitoring for the sake of disciplining in social-societal encounters (Elias, 1990: 159). One of the main points in Elias's argument is that the King did not have to invest in supervisors who would enforce the strict courtly etiquette. Instead of supervisors, discipline rather evolved due to the fact that proximity among peers mutually encouraged them to control and manage one another.

17 Marberry reports from a study based on evaluations of subjects doing clerical work in one of three enclosed offices of different colours. The research goals of this study leave no doubt about the 'will to know' (Foucault, 1976) associated with this project:

'1 evaluate worker productivity and mood in an office that simulates the interior colour and lighting of a NASA space module ("NASA white");
2 compare workers' reactions to an office painted in NASA white with offices of other scientifically measured and designed colour schemes;
3 gather data on perceived spaciousness and colour preference;
4 recommend colours and lighting for space modules; and
5 establish a colour database for designers and manufacturers to utilize in selecting appropriate materials and finishes for products and design schemes for interior environments'. (Marberry, 1994: 114)

References

Alvesson, Mats (1988) 'Management, corporate culture and labour process in a professional service company'. Paper presented at the 6th Labour Process Conference at Aston, UK.

Ariès, Phillipe (1996) *Centuries of Childhood*. London: Random House.

Barthes, Roland (1965) *Le degré zéro de l'écriture*. Paris: Gonthier.

Barthes, Roland (1985) *L'aventure sémiologique*. Paris: Seuil.

Berg, Per Olof and Kreiner, Kristian (1990) 'Corporate architecture: turning physical settings into symbolic resources', in Pasquale Gagliardi, *Symbols and Artifacts: Views of the Corporate Landscape*. Berlin and New York: de Gruyter. pp. 41–67.

Bourdieu, Pierre (1979) *La distinction: critique sociale du jugement*. Paris: Minuit.

Bourdieu, Pierre (1984) *Homo Academicus*. Paris: Editions de Minuit.

Bourdieu, Pierre (1991) 'Le champ littéraire', *Actes de la recherche en sciences sociales*, 89: 3–46.

Bourdieu, Pierre and Passeron, Jean-Claude (1973) *Grundlagen einer Theorie der symbolischen Gewalt*. Frankfurt-am-Main: Suhrkamp.

Burawoy, Michael (1979) *Manufacturing Consent: Changes in the Labor Process Under Monopoly Capitalism*. Chicago: University of Chicago Press.

Camus, Christophe (1996) *Lecture sociologique de l'architecture décrite. Comment bâtir avec des mots?* Paris: L'Harmattan.

Coombs, O. (1977) *True Tales of the New York Workplace*. New York.

Cooper, Robert and Burrell, Gibson (1988) 'Modernism, postmodernism and organizational analysis: an introduction', *Organization Studies*, 9 (1): 91–112.

Douglas, Mary (1986) *How Institutions Think*. New York: Syracuse University Press.

Duffy, Francis (1992) *The Changing Workplace*. London: Phaidon.

Durkheim, Emile (1984) *The Division of Labor in Society*. Glencoe, IL: Free Press.

Eco, Umberto (1988) *Semiotik*. Frankfurt-am-Main: Suhrkamp.

Edwards, Richard (1979) *Contested Terrain*. New York: Basic Books.

Elias, Norbert (1976) *Über den Prozeß der Zivilisation: Soziogenetische Untersuchungen*. Frankfurt-am-Main: Suhrkamp.

Elias, Norbert (1990) *Die höfische Gesellschaft*. Frankfurt-am-Main: Suhrkamp.

Flecker, Jörg and Hofbauer, Johanna (1997) 'Capitalizing on subjectivity: the "new model worker" and the importance of being useful', in Paul Thompson and Chris Warhurst (eds), *Workplaces of the Future*. London: Macmillan. pp. 104–24.

Foucault, Michel (1974) *Surveiller et punir*. Paris: Gallimard.

Foucault, Michel (1976) *La volonté de savoir*. Paris: Gallimard.

Fritz, Hans-Joachim (1982) *Menschen in Büroarbeitsrdumen*. Munich: Heinz Moos Verlag.

Gagliardi, Pasquale (1990) 'Artifacts as pathways and remains of organizational life', in Pasquale Gagliardi, *Symbols and Artifacts: Views of the Corporate Landscape*. Berlin and New York: de Gruyter. pp. 3–32.

Goffman, Erving (1959) *The Presentation of Self in Everyday Life*. New York: Doubleday Anchor Books.

Hall, Edward T. (1990) *The Hidden Dimension*. New York: Doubleday Anchor Books.

Handy, Charles (1992) *Inside Organization: 21 Ideas for Managers*. London: Random House.

Hatch, Mary Joe (1990) 'The symbolics of office design: an empirical exploration', in Pasquale Gagliardi, *Symbols and Artifacts: Views of the Corporate Landscape*. Berlin and New York: de Gruyter. pp. 129–35.

Hemmati-Wagner, Minu (1993) 'Die Sozialisation von Menschen und Dingen, zum Beispiel im Büro', *Zeitschrift für Personalwirtschaft*, 1: 96–114.

Hochschild, Arlie Russell (1983) *The Managed Heart: Commercialization of Human Feeling*. Berkeley, CA: University of California Press.

Hofbauer, Johanna, Holzmüller, Hartmut H., Kindl, Monika, Lueger, Manfred, Mattl, Christine, Mayrhofer, Wolfgang and Novy, Andreas (1997) *Arbeitsgruppen im Devisenhandel. Eine qualitative Fallstudie zur Kooperation in einer österreichischen Bank*. Dresden: Dresdner Beiträge zur Betriebswirtschaftslehre, vol. 7/97.

Kleeman, Walter B. (1991) *Interior Design of the Electronic Office: The Comfort and Productivity Payoff.* New York: Van Nostrand Reinhold.

Louis Harris and Associates, Inc. (1978) *The Steelcase National Study of Office Environments: Do They Work?* Grand Rapids, MI: Steelcase.

Marberry, Sara O. (1994) *Color in the Office. Design Trends from 1950–1990 and Beyond.* New York: Van Nostrand Reinhold.

Panofsky, Erwin (1976) *Gothic Architecture and Scholasticism: An Inquiry Into the Analogy of the Arts, Philosophy, and Religion in the Middle Ages.* Ontario: New American Library.

Pélegrin-Genel, Elisabeth (1995) *L'art de vivre au bureau.* Paris: Flammarion.

Pollard, Sidney (1965) *The Genesis of Modern Management. A Study of the Industrial Revolution in Great Britain.* London: Gregg Rivals.

Singer, Linda (1993) *Erotic Welfare: Sexual Theory and Politics in the Age of Epidemic.* New York and London: Routledge.

Sundstrom, Eric (1986) *Work Places: The Psychology of the Physical Environment in Offices and Factories.* Cambridge: Cambridge University Press.

Thompson, Paul and Warhurst, Chris (1997) 'Hands, hearts and minds: changing work and workers at the end of the century', in Paul Thompson and Chris Warhurst (eds), *Workplaces of the Future.* London: Macmillan. pp. 1–24.

Winner, Langdon (1980) 'Do artifacts have politics?', *Daedalus*, 109: 121–36.

PART FOUR

SELF AND IDENTITY

---

10 Exploring Embodiment: Women, Biology and Work

Joanna Brewis and John Sinclair

The analysis in this chapter is, in the first instance, informed by the understanding that social order in the modern West has its roots in Enlightenment philosophy which sees reason as the capacity that distinguishes humans from animals and enables us to make our own decisions about how we should live our lives (Bauman, 1983, 1987; Berman, 1990; Cooper and Burrell, 1988; Elias, 1978; Habermas, 1972, 1987; Hebdige, 1989; Jameson, 1991). Despite the ostensible neutrality of this emphasis on reason, however, Enlightenment philosophy can also be identified as gendered, given that certain of its proponents saw reason to be something that men possessed in greater amounts than women. Kant (1974, 1990), for example, considered women to be naturally less capable of developing their capacity for reason than men (Tong, 1989).

If we accept that Enlightenment thinking about the human capacity for reason has informed our modern social order, then it follows, first, that we moderns believe in the ability of human beings to autonomously manage their own lives (Bauman, 1987). Furthermore, the specific way in which we currently view ourselves arguably derives, as Clegg (1990) suggests, from an appropriation of Enlightenment philosophy by thinkers like Saint-Simon and Comte which can be labelled scientific modernism (Brewis, 1996, following Geuss, cited in Reed, 1985: 80–1). For scientific modernism, human beings, possessing the innate ability to reason, can only use that reason to its capacity if they also suppress their bodily passions and instincts; it is characterized by 'the fear that the unrepressed human body will turn out to be a wild animal rutting and snarling in the squalor of its own excrement' (Watts, 1975: 168; also see Bauman, 1983: 36; Elias, 1978; Turner, 1991).

An important instance of the power effects of scientific modernism, in the Foucauldian sense, was the division of Western society into public and private spheres, which began to take hold during the eighteenth century. The public sphere was (supposedly) to be dedicated to rational decision-making in government, production, education and so on, so as to ensure that the nation state flourished. The private sphere, on the other hand, became the sphere of leisure, intimacy and sex, where individuals were nourished and reproduced to meet the demands of the public sphere (Martin, 1989: 16), and where bodily impulses were legitimately expressed (Shilling, 1993: 172).

Further, Weber (1970: 204), writing at the onset of the twentieth century, suggests that the purest form of bureaucracy is to be found in 'the modern European states' and 'all [modern] public corporations'. According to Weber, then, the public sphere housed the closest approximation of his ideal type bureaucracy. This bureaucratization of the public sphere was, it appears, intended to ensure that its operations were entirely rational, safe from the taint of irrationality, instinct and passion. As Weber (1970: 215) points out, the strengths of the bureaucracy are in its objectivity, its 'discharge of business' on the basis of rational rules and procedures. So for Weber the bureaucracy is the modern form of organization *par excellence* (also see Clegg, 1990: 176).

Although the thesis that the modern organization is essentially bureaucratic, premised on reason and logical decision-making above all else, is controversial, it does highlight another important point concerning the way in which Enlightenment thought informs modern social order. It has been noted repeatedly in studies of the modern organization that its structure is such that bodies, and their instincts and passions, play little part in its operations – that this organization operates in such a way as to (attempt to) foreclose the possibility that 'lower order' bodily behaviours might 'impinge' on the 'cool rationality' (McDowell and Court, 1994: 729) demanded in the modern workplace (Adorno and Horkheimer, 1979; Burrell, 1984, 1992; Gramsci, 1971: 297; Marcuse, 1969). Shilling (1993) claims that the body has therefore been ignored in modern organizational design, such that how much work needs to be done and when is calculated regardless of bodily needs (also see Engels, 1973; Synnott, 1993: 252). Furthermore, this apparent 'disavowal' of the body in the modern workplace has been identified by feminist theorists as especially problematic for women, given influential Enlightenment arguments concerning the difference between men's and women's natures, as described above and explained by Martin as follows:

> women are [seen to be] intrinsically closely involved with the family where so many 'natural', 'bodily' (and therefore lower) functions occur, whereas men are [seen to be] intrinsically involved with the world of work where . . . 'cultural', 'mental', and therefore higher functions occur. (1989: 17)

Consequently, it has been suggested that the modern organization is premised on a refusal of what historically has been seen to be female – in short, the body.

Given the above, this chapter aims, using interview data, to explore the accounts given by pseudonymous female respondents of their relationships with their bodies in general, and in the working environment specifically. Given the size of the sample, the use of a mixture of convenience and self-selection sampling to identify the respondents and the deployment of semi-structured interviews to gather the data, no attempt is made here to generalize from the experiences of the respondents to those of working women more generally; rather, the analysis is undertaken in order to provide some insight into *these* women's relationships with their own bodies and what *their* embodiment seems to mean in their working lives. The discussion therefore focuses on how these women 'are', 'live' and 'use' their bodies (Synnott, 1993: 263); on 'what it is to have or to be a [female] body' (Turner, 1991: 22) at and outside of work. In important ways, the discussion is aimed at teasing out the dual status of the body as not only a source of human commonality, but also a source of difference, and therefore inequality (Shilling, 1993: 22–3; Synnott, 1993: 242–4). As Brewis et al. (1997: 1282–3) point out, dichotomies such as gender, which discursively at least is commonly assumed to proceed from biological sex, automatically engender privilege such that one half of the binary divide is elevated above the other. In this case, man is privileged over woman (Butler, 1993: 35; Cixous, 1988; Derrida and McDonald, 1988: esp. 175).

Importantly, these women talked at length of the ways in which their self-identities as embodied beings have developed through exposure to various texts in their social worlds; most significantly the reactions of others. They also referred to the consequences this has for their thoughts, feelings and behaviour relating to their bodies. The data therefore seem to point to an 'outside-in' process of identity development, an engagement with social texts/discourse(s) such that these women have learnt to be, live and use their bodies through being embedded in the wider social. These women, then, reported a sense in which they have come to know what their bodies are, and how they should be used, primarily through the ways in which others experience these bodies, the ways in which men in particular gaze on their bodies and the subsequent internalization of this masculine gaze.

More specifically, the chapter focuses on the following issues:

- The ways in which these women relate to their bodies in gendered ways: their almost universal sense that somehow their bodies are 'lacking' when measured against existing socio-cultural definitions of female beauty; their fluctuating efforts to maintain their bodies in line with this cultural *diktat*, given pressures of work and childcare, which reflects the complexity of their self-identities as women, workers and mothers; and, finally, resistance to these prevailing definitions of beauty on the part of one respondent in particular, and its implications.
- The women's reports of their bodies as problematic signifiers in the working environment – for example, their suggestion that the association of work, and more especially management, with men and men's

bodies means that they have to work to manage the signifying effects of their biological bodies in work organizations.

- Conversely, the women's reports of their bodies as positive signifiers in the working environment – for example, the ways in which they are able to use their bodies to persuade others to cooperate, or the sense they have that women's bodies are less threatening to customers than men's.
- The experience of female biology at work as reported by these respondents – in particular living through premenstrual symptoms, menstruation, pregnancy and motherhood in this environment, as arguably mediated by the ways in which these women engage with or resist discursive constructions of these female bodily processes.

Gender, identity and the body

As suggested above, it appears from the data that the women respondents' relationships with their bodies form an important part of the way that they relate to themselves, and in particular the way that they relate to themselves as female. This reflects Shilling's argument (1993: 125; also see Featherstone, 1991: 190) that the body is now a very significant component of self-identity because of the emphasis that we place on how we look and what we do with our bodies. An issue to which all of the respondents made reference which illustrates this point was weight – all suggested that they either were, or had been, unhappy with the size of their bodies. Those who commented that they currently felt overweight were in the majority; for example, Rachel, who commented that she thoroughly dislikes her body and feels 'governed by her size'. Rachel also suggested that her feelings about her body stem from the age of seven, when her mother first began worrying about her daugher's weight. Her account positions the source of her body image as social – she has learnt who and what she is through the reactions of others.

Helen, who had just finished a fairly strict diet at the time of the interviews, commented: 'well, if I think about my body now, it's overweight. It's overweight in terms of how I see myself, it's probably about a stone overweight, so that's, that's number one, um, negative.' This feeling about herself is, Helen suggests, the result of her having an enduring image of the 'prime physiological state' as youthfulness, without any 'excess fat'. Helen is in her late forties and admits that her feelings about her body size are perhaps unrealistic for 'a woman my age'; that there is an 'inevitability' about ageing about which one just has to be 'stoical'. However, Helen's feelings about her body are clearly influenced by her history – by the fact that she was slimmer when she was younger. This suggests that her body image has been produced not least by the 'long look back', where she compares how she currently looks and feels about herself to how she looked and felt in previous times (Gamman and Makinen, 1994: 157).

Brenda was also somewhat dissatisfied with her body image, suggesting that she worries about her 'backside', which she describes as 'flabby'. For her, this image of herself derives from her comparisons of her body to her mother's, whom she describes as having a 'wonderful figure' and 'no bum at all'. Here, then, we see another source of body image – the comparison with other bodies around us. Interestingly, Brenda also describes herself as having fat ankles, which she suggests derives from her parents commenting on this when she was younger – here she echoes Rachel in her suggestion that her body image derives at least in part from others' behaviour in relation to her body.

Even Olivia, who describes herself as being 'large' and a generous 'size 16–18', but also says she is 'not particularly uncomfortable' with her body, did comment that she has worried in the past about having gained weight. For Olivia, like Brenda and Rachel, her image of herself as fat derives from others' comments on her size:

'. . . I mean like my mum saying "Oh, when are you going to do something about your size?" and "You are never going to meet anyone else", you know, "[You] need to try and do something about yourself" . . .'

Harriet and Hilary, on the other hand, were unique amongst the respondents for feeling that they were perhaps too thin. Harriet suggested that:

'. . . it's *preferable* to be *thinner* rather than *fatter* . . . but . . . I feel that I'm on the end of that range and in some sense it sort of turns back on itself that, you know, you're not supposed to look as though you've just walked out of Belsen [*laughs*] . . .' (emphasis Harriet's own)

Here, Harriet, like other respondents, sees that there are social pressures working on us to maintain a particular body shape.

The respondents, then, all suggest that their feelings about their bodies are socially produced; that they have learnt how culturally (in)appropriate their bodies are through reference to the texts around them (Grafton Small, 1993), whether these texts are other people's bodies, their own bodies at earlier stages in their development or, more commonly, other people's reactions to their bodies. As Butler (1993: 10) says, it is therefore unhelpful to think of the body as an *a priori* on which cultural norms are imposed, because it is impossible to think about, relate to or use the body outside of discourse.

Moreover, the respondents tend to see their bodies as more or less *lacking* when measured against cultural models of female beauty. This is unsurprising when we consider Shilling's suggestion that, as capitalism has taken hold in Western economies: 'the means for managing the self have become increasingly tied up with consumer goods, and the achievement of social and economic success hinges crucially on the presentation of an acceptable self-image' (1993: 92).

Shilling (1993: 148) also returns to Bourdieu on this issue, suggesting that the body has become an important 'bearer of value' in 'cultural and social markets'. Featherstone agrees: 'Within consumer culture, the inner and outer body become conjoined: the prime purpose of the maintenance of the inner body becomes the enhancement of the appearance of the outer body' (1991: 171).

Here then, as in Marx's analysis of the commodity, the exchange value of the body is emphasized over its use value – indeed, to take a line associated with Baudrillard (1993), the symbolic value of the body could also be seen to be increasing. This means that our bodily appearance is crucial both to our feelings of self-worth, and to the ways in which other people judge us. Moreover, Gamman and Makinen (1994: 10–11) claim that women are under particular pressure to consume as 'specific targets of capitalist consumerism', that 'consumer fetishism' has lent to food especially messages of the good life, of wealth and happiness – but that women are also 'objects of consumer fetishism' and thus are expected to be 'impossibly thin'. In a similar vein, Shilling (1993: 65), paraphrasing Chernin, suggests that, unlike men, women are socialized to worry about their bodies and often 'become obsessed with the quest for reduction'. Bartky (1988: 81) points to the consequent amount of effort to which women may go to successfully 'pass' to themselves and others as feminine, talking of the woman who: 'feeling fat, monitors everything she eats' (also see Moore, 1994: 5).

The respondents' sense that they do not 'measure up' in a bodily sense, and their belief that they are, in the main, too fat, is clear from the data already analysed, and reflects the arguments presented above. None the less, as we have seen both Harriet and Hilary feel that they are, if anything, too thin. Hilary noted that, following a weight gain:

> 'I quite liked being rounded 'cause it looked more womanly . . . I think I looked a bit stick-like [previously] . . . it was nice to actually look a little bit more rounded and actually have a bit more shape, and I suppose you think that you look a bit more attractive in that respect.'

For her, then, the cultural image of 'womanliness' is more curvaceous than it is slender. It is certainly true that, as many of the respondents (and Gamman and Makinen, Shilling, Bartky and Moore) point out, the cultural preference in the contemporary West is for us to be 'slim' as opposed to 'fat'; but it is also arguable that the pressure placed on us to 'get our bodies right' (a late twentieth century discipline, to use a Foucauldian term) means that we are likely to continually monitor, and experience anxiety about, our bodily appearance, however closely it appears to match up to social imperatives. Foucault suggests, for example, that there may now be fewer explicit restrictions on what we do with our bodies – for example, it is now acceptable to wear reasonably revealing clothes in public – but that if we do 'undress' in this fashion, we need to measure up precisely to cultural preferences around body size, shape and appearance (Foucault, 1980: 57).

However, it is noticeable that, *contra* the above arguments about the intense cultural pressure to maintain an 'acceptable' body, and the ways in which modern individuals (and women in particular) are constituted to see work on their bodies as a means of shoring up their sense of who they are, many of the respondents suggested that their 'body work' (Shilling, 1993: 118) fluctuates. Melissa suggested that she has 'got out of the habit' of exercising, due at least partly to the demands of her job and her part-time college course, and that she regrets this. Holly remarked that:

> 'I jogged for a while then stopped doing that, then I went to aerobics for a while and stopped doing that. [It] goes in fads, I do something for about three months then give up for three months [*laughs*] . . .'

This she attributes to lack of time and lack of motivation, especially since she started the same course as Melissa. Helen made much the same kind of point and, finally, Olivia said that she also lacks motivation to diet or exercise, and that it is particularly difficult finding time for these activities given that she has her son to care for as well as having a full-time job.

One could argue that this relative bodily neglect may create problems for these women. Freund claims that general well-being demands a close link between mind and body, that it is necessary to be 'in touch' with your physical self in terms of attending to its needs and demands (Freund, cited in Shilling, 1993: 115). Synnott also suggests, somewhat dramatically, that 'no one lasts long by ignoring their bodies' (Synnott, 1993: 2) – which the respondents, given their general concern about these issues, seem to accept. Indeed, Harriet noted that she has had two periods where stress has necessitated her taking time off from work, and that on these occasions 'I've just been stopped in my tracks . . .'. However, there is another issue here. It appears that these women do not take as much care of themselves as they would like because there are other issues in their lives – work and, for the mothers, childcare – to which they feel they have to attend before they spend time on body work. This may suggest that, for these women, their understandings of self are equally dependent on their success at work (and, for some, their success as mothers), perhaps over and above their success in maintaining their bodies – which reflects Knights and Vurdubakis's point that 'Self-identity can . . . be realized only as a constant struggle against the experience of tension, fragmentation and discord. Subject positions are made available in a number of competing discourses . . . Identity is thus of necessity always a project rather than an achievement' (1994: 185; also see Linstead, 1996; Stone, 1995; Walkerdine, 1984).

Following from this discussion of how hard (or not) these women work in their daily lives to perform accepted definitions of bodily femininity, it is interesting to pay detailed attention to the account of one respondent in particular. Tracey, like some of the other respondents, talked of how she has grown to like and accept her body, non-conformist though it has always been to prevailing cultural models. Significantly for Tracey, who describes a dysfunctional relationship with her mother as having left her with concerns that she was too tall and broad to be 'little and feminine', Butler argues that those who are not 'properly' gendered, who do not live up to the cultural imperative of gender difference, become 'abjects'. These individuals 'haunt' the boundaries between masculinity and femininity (Butler, 1993: 8). It is the threat of becoming an ambiguous, disregarded abject that compels us to strive to live up to masculinity or femininity, as implied above (Butler, 1993: 15; also see Brewis, 1996; Brewis et al., 1997). However, Tracey's more recent pride in her body means that she now feels comfortable about breaking, as she puts it, many of the 'rules' about how women 'ought' to look. Her resistance to the internalized norms of her childhood bears testimony to Butler's (1993: 12) argument that the continual performance of gender norms consolidates the norms themselves but also generates opportunities for resistance. As Tracey's experience suggests, our responses to discursive imperatives around our gendered bodies may not so much be compliance as a form of mobilization, an enabling or production of our individual agency, which simultaneously allows us to resist what we are told is true about what our bodies are or should be. Discourse delimits and orchestrates 'thinkable' material possibilities – but being produced as subject also means being enabled to resist the norms which make us subject (Butler, 1993: 13, 15). Tracey, consequently, is subject/ed to gender discourse concerning what her female body ought to look like but, having been constituted as such, she also has the capacity to resist these norms. In this Foucauldian analysis, resistance is immanent within and produced by the power effects of discourse (Foucault, 1980: 142; Knights and Vurdubakis, 1994). Thus Tracey's body presents a challenge to prevalent motifs of gender difference and can be seen as 'assisting a radical resignification of the symbolic domain, deviating the citational chain toward a more possible future to expand the very meaning of what counts as a valued and valuable body in this world' (Butler, 1993: 22).

Indeed, the putative effects of bodies like Tracey's are visible in her own comment that society at the end of the twentieth century not only tolerates but also provides a wider range of femininities, which encompass women like her more easily.

The remainder of the chapter focuses more specifically on the intersection of the body and work; how and why these respondents are, live and use their bodies in the working environment. Here these women's gender to some extent seems simultaneously to precede and produce them – pointing again to an 'outside-in' process of identity development as well as belying any argument that understanding gender as social means that it becomes an easy imperative to 'shrug off' (Brewis et al., 1997: 1291–4).

Perceptions of female bodies at work: problems and challenges

Many of the respondents talked of the ways in which the female body acts as a signifier in the working environment, given the association of work, and management in particular, with men and men's bodies. Melissa reported an instance where she and a female colleague had joked that they couldn't apply for a senior job which had become vacant in their organization:

> '. . . 'cause we haven't got a todger . . . it was a technical, plant maintenance job, you know, very much todger oriented. So we wrote "Todger" on the advert, you see, "Todger required" . . .'

She also suggests that her housing clients (Melissa works in local government) often refuse to believe that she is a manager because she is female, describing their likely response to her as follows: '"I don't want to see a whippersnapper like you! I don't want to see a girl so give me the manager!" . . .'. Other respondents also talked of the ways in which women are judged on the basis of their bodies at work, and their own efforts to minimize these perceptual connections. Brenda, for example, described her efforts to 'blend in' in a previous management role in banking:

> '. . . I was a manager amongst many male managers and there were very few women and I don't know whether there was pressure on me but I felt more comfortable if I dressed in a similar way to the men.'

Brenda chose in this environment to wear more 'masculine' clothes (she refers to wearing a suit jacket), which gave her more confidence and, she feels, generated more respect for her amongst her colleagues. It appears that she made a conscious effort to downplay her biological femaleness, to detract attention from her female body (Brewis et al., 1997: 1287–8; see also Lurie, 1992: ix–xi; Williamson, 1980). Brenda's wearing a jacket could be read as a transformation of her outward appearance, the intention being to signify a masculine – that is to say rational, objective, efficient, precise, disciplined, competitive and assertive – approach to working life. McDowell and Court (1994: 745) refer to this kind of behaviour as a 'workplace performance that constructs [women] as honorary men'.

Also on the theme of dress as a way of playing down femininity, Brenda, who was seven months pregnant at the time of the interviews, pointed out that she had deliberately selected 'dresses that I thought . . . would be smart' to wear to work during her pregnancy. She implied that being pregnant exacerbates the signifying effects of her female body at work (a university), in terms of signalling 'that you have another life, that you have other interests and aspirations other than being a professional or an academic'.

Similarly, Holly spoke of having to manage her body because of the way it speaks of her female sexuality. She says she would never wear a short skirt to work because it would attract comments from both her Probation Service clients (who are mainly male) and the male supervisors of these individuals.

Whilst not referring to dress *per se*, Rachel, who works in social services, suggested that she has to labour to appear 'managerial' because of certain perceptions amongst her client group:

'. . . [in case conferences] families actually accept negative decisions as they see it . . . more readily from, from men that run the conferences . . . I don't think it's a difference in the style of managing the conferences . . . I just think that most people, most families that come through conferences *respect* . . . men's status more than women. I kind of have to work harder at it.' (emphasis Rachel's own)

Belinda, in the NHS, also picks up this issue, suggesting that when she attends meetings dominated by men she almost 'suppresses' her 'femininity', becoming 'very professional' and 'almost asexual' – necessarily, she feels, so that she is taken seriously.

Many of the women managers interviewed by Sheppard (1989: 146) also suggested that the prevailing perception on the part of their male peers or clients is that of a dualism between 'feminine' and 'business-like' (that is, masculine). These women, like the respondents here, often had to work to appear more masculine, because otherwise their female bodies put them at risk of 'not being taken seriously, not being heard, and not receiving necessary information' (Sheppard, 1989: 145). Here we can see the powerfulness of the body as a signifier of gender, and the strategies that women may have to adopt to undermine the meaning-laden properties of their biologically sexed bodies.

Interestingly, to return to the respondents here, Tracey's less-than-traditionally feminine demeanour and body shape works in her favour – she says that, due to her cultivation of a more masculine bodily appearance, her male colleagues in local government see her as 'competent but . . . plain'.[1] Similarly, Rachel suggested that, while she perceives herself to be overweight, she also feels that her size has certain advantages:

'. . . if I'm overweight I can be almost genderless really which is quite useful in a working situation . . . as a *manager* it's easier to be genderless I suppose – I mean not more of a man, or less of a woman, but almost genderless . . .' (emphasis Rachel's own)

Rachel told of how she had been the target of sexual harassment from both colleagues and clients when she was slimmer. We can identify echoes of her story in Orbach's *Fat is a Feminist Issue* (1989). Orbach's central tenet – that women become overweight because they wish to escape conflicting demands placed on them by the cultural model of femininity – is undoubtedly problematic, because it insinuates that fat is essentially undesirable. However, Orbach also claims that women may allow themselves to gain weight as a means of resistance to being categorized as a sexual object, in order to be taken seriously in the working environment (also see Shilling, 1993: 64). For Rachel this is apparently another strategy to mediate the ways in which others react to her female body at work.

Another issue that was raised by the respondents in their discussions of perceptions of women's bodies at work was the kind of connections that may be made between the cultural model of female beauty, discussed earlier, and judgements as to whether women are suited to, or good at, their jobs. Rachel had the following to say:

> '. . . certainly in my 20s, being somebody like a receptionist–telephonist, how you looked was actually quite important. So it was always a kind of battle to, to try and stay thin enough that I, I would be able to get jobs basically . . . I mean I think if you're the front line receptionist person then I think that, um, probably even still today people're [*sic*] actually looking at you size-wise as well . . .'

She also suggests that the same stringent requirements do not apply to men, that men are better able to be larger than women and not be punished for it at work (which would certainly seem to reflect Gamman and Makinen's notion that women are expected to be 'impossibly thin', as cited earlier). Rachel suggests here that whether or not women conform to the stereotype of female attractiveness is a major determinant in them finding and keeping employment – especially in 'front line' jobs. Furthermore, she said that, with regard to her current managerial role, her colleagues may question her ability to control circumstances given her apparent inability to control her body. For Rachel, then, her size is an ambiguous factor in the work environment – on the one hand it renders her 'genderless', as we have seen above, but on the other it may cause co-workers to doubt her self-discipline, and therefore her managerial abilities. Likewise, Olivia argued that, although in her local government job her size does have benefits because her clients may perceive her as more 'personable' and more 'human', she also sees the 'downside' of this:

> '. . . higher management I would say possibly think I'm as laxadaisical [*sic*] about my job as I am about my size . . . that I've let myself go to seed or whatever they are saying.'

Olivia suggests here that her size, whilst possibly less threatening to clients, perhaps again signifies to her managers that she is not able to control her body shape, and therefore raises questions about her self-discipline and performance *per se*. She also agrees with Rachel in another respect – that the same would not be true of a man who was overweight. Indeed, the problems faced by women defined as overweight in the working environment are illustrated by a recent UK industrial tribunal case. Applicant Anoushka De La Banque, who weighs sixteen stone, was told by a NatWest bank recruitment officer at interview that her size would make it unlikely that she would be offered a position (Cook, 1997). Ms De La Banque has an IQ of 172 – so, as she herself remarked, her appearance must have been the primary factor counting against her (Aaronovitch, 1997).

Moreover, Gamman and Makinen (1994: 159) suggest that there is a moral dimension to body work which relates back to Judaeo-Christian notions of the flesh as weak, something to be transcended. Featherstone (1991: 184) also points to the 'virtue' associated with dieting. Thus, as Cook

(1997) also points out, failure to maintain an appropriate body size and shape is viewed as almost sinful and certainly as betokening lack of self-discipline. This of course is particularly problematic at work, where control and discipline are important watchwords.

Finally, pregnancy was also discussed by those respondents who were mothers in terms of the problematic ways in which this uniquely female condition signifies to others at work. The way in which a pregnant woman's body becomes publicly accessible was seen as potentially difficult in the working environment. Belinda, for example, was indignant about the way in which her body had been appropriated by others during her pregnancy in terms of them touching her 'bump'. She also suggested that: 'it's almost like that it [*pregnancy*] gives you permission and people are very, um, forthright with their opinions, you know, about "Oh, how can you leave your child when you go to work?"'

Belinda's experience was of colleagues feeling able not only to invade her bodily space, but also to offer their opinions about her future childcare arrangements. This chimes with Jaggar's point that children are often seen as 'products' which must be raised in particular ways (cited in Martin, 1989: 19). Olivia experienced similar treatment during her pregnancy – having met a former colleague in a lift, he remarked to her that he thought she would have had 'more sense' than to get pregnant, and asked her whether she had 'heard of terminations'. She was outraged by this comment, especially since she only knew the man concerned vaguely. Moreover, Brenda noted that, later in her pregnancy, she began to think

'. . . wouldn't it be nice not to be the centre, complete centre of attention every time you walk into a room . . .? . . . sometimes you wish that you could just be kind of normal again and, and just kind of be accepted for who you are . . . you adopt this sort of pregnancy label in a way and you suddenly become Brenda who is pregnant or pregnant Brenda rather than just Brenda [*laughs*] . . .'

Belinda, Olivia and especially Brenda all point to the fact that a pregnant woman may be subsumed by her pregnancy, so that her biological role in reproduction supersedes other aspects of her persona, such as her professional role.

Perceptions of female bodies at work: opportunities and benefits

None the less, respondents also suggested that having a female body at work is not always or necessarily problematic. For example, some saw their attractiveness to men as a useful organizational resource. University worker Marie, made the point that 'I think it helps me to look presentable and reasonably attractive to industry . . . I just think being a *female* in a male's world can't be a bad thing' (emphasis Marie's own).

Other data suggest that, for Marie, her female body precedes her and defines her at work, but it seems from the above that she actually sees her body as a double-edged sword, because it can also prove useful in terms of marking her out as different and therefore interesting in the work environment. In a similar vein, Hilary who is a nurse, talks of flirting with male colleagues to get her own way at work – 'flattering' them and 'fluttering' her eyelashes. She says that this helps to keep activities at work on an even keel as well as reducing stress levels.

At first glance these accounts may seem problematic – the literature around sexual harassment often claims that working women are forced to offer themselves as sexual commodities to enter into or progress within working life: 'Working women are defined, and survive by defining themselves, as sexually accessible and economically exploitable' (Renick, 1980: 660; also see Bremer et al., 1991; Grauerholz, 1989; Martin, 1989; Yount, 1991). This strategy, it is claimed, colludes with and therefore reinforces prevailing definitions of women as less rational and more bodily than men – and results in negative outcomes, such as sexual harassment. However, it is also very clear that this deluded offering of sexual self is not what the respondents here are talking about. Marie said that:

> '. . . it's not been unhelpful to, to, um, hopefully look reasonably, you know, appealing but I, I wouldn't say there's an allurement element to that. I don't think I've ever kind of gone in to *allure* anybody or, um, use it, um, overtly.' (emphasis Marie's own)

Hilary, similarly, says that she knows when to flirt and when not to. Appearing *overly* sexy, then, is unwise, according to these respondents. Their attractiveness as women is to be managed but never exploited – to 'overdo' it would be to risk attracting colleagues' censure instead of their cooperation.

Another dimension of the respondents' comments about the possible benefits of their female bodies at work is the point that Melissa, Rachel and Belinda all made about women's bodies being a useful mechanism for defusing tension and, in some cases, potential violence:

> '. . . a lot of the times when there are violent customers in reception, we'll let them be dealt with by a woman instead of a man, um, because you know, I don't know, historically it's been quite a calming influence, you know, and, and people actually start to talk to a woman rather than, than talk to a guy . . .' (Melissa)

> '. . . men's socialization to some extent . . . sees it [violence] as "that's not what you do to women", still . . . I think my femaleness is much more likely to, to calm people down somehow . . .' (Rachel)

Belinda described an experience from her days as a psychiatric nurse where she had followed a very tall male patient who had absconded from the ward, and said to him 'Please come back . . . There's nothing I can do . . .', given that he was much taller than her. He capitulated to her request. In expanding on her anecdote, Belinda suggested that sending a 'big burly man' into this kind of situation often 'makes people frightened'. Likewise, Lamplugh suggests that men are more likely to be subject to violent behaviour at work, and that:

> this is not because there are more men than women, but simply that a male is more likely to meet aggression with aggression which more often than not leads to confrontation. Women, on the other hand, are very good at defusing, coping with and avoiding aggressive incidents – indeed they are best at some of the most vulnerable jobs . . . (1996: 67)

Here it appears that Belinda's tactics of persuasion *combined with* her small stature worked better than the more physical techniques which her male colleagues had employed with the same patient.

Moreover, and again pointing to the double-edged ways in which the female body may signify at work, Brenda offered a different perspective on her colleagues' interest in the progress of her pregnancy, suggesting 'most of the time it's quite nice 'cause it means, you know, that people are actually concerned and are excited for you and wanting to talk about it and that's basically what they're saying, isn't it?'.

For Brenda, then, it seemed as if her changing body shape during her pregnancy had to some extent allowed her colleagues to express their concern and affection for her, and that this had been a largely positive experience (although 'occasionally wearing', as already noted). Marie, working in the same university, said she had also felt more 'warmth or concern' while she was pregnant. Similarly, Olivia commented that her senior manager's pregnancy had acted as an 'ice-breaker' when she joined the department, because people had felt able to talk to her about it.

These respondents' female bodies, then, seem to signify in complex ways to others, and men especially, in the organizational environment. Their bodies can be something of a burden – others may, for example, read them as insufficiently 'organizational'. However, their bodies also work in more positive ways – in terms of heterosexual attraction 'smoothing the way' at work, for instance, or by appearing non-threatening to clients.

Finally, this chapter turns to consider the ways in which the women respondents experienced their biologies at work.

Female biology and work

The mothers in the respondent group suggested that the physical effects of pregnancy can cause problems at work. Belinda experienced severe nausea during early pregnancy:

> '. . . I mean, I was going to do home visits [to drug-using clients] and having to pull up by the side of the road and *puke*, you know . . .' (emphasis Belinda's own)

Olivia suffered similar symptoms throughout her pregnancy:

'. . . one minute I could be sat there working on the computer, the next minute I was running down the corridor with, you know, my hands cupped and . . . being sick . . .'

Later in their pregnancies, as Helen pointed out, some women may become very tired and find work challenging in this respect. Brenda agreed, saying that her advanced pregnancy meant that she walked up stairs much more slowly, and that colleagues often joked that she needed 'a winch or a crane or [*laughs*] something like that'. Belinda said that she had found the last stages somewhat difficult at work in other respects:

'. . . my back ached and my feet swelled up and I felt distracted all the time and I had a classic, classic maternal amnesia . . . I'd forget to go and do a home visit and forget to go to a meeting [*laughs*] . . .'

These respondents also pointed out that biological motherhood can have ramifications for working women. Marie talked of her exhaustion when she returned to work very soon after the birth of her second child, and Helen and Belinda both described the experience of leaving their children to return to work as a *physical* wrench:

'Oh, oh it's a physical pull, yeah, it is . . . the other time when I've felt that and quite consciously felt "This is a physical thing that I'm feeling here . . .," I mean it's sort of down in the *gut*, I mean it really is extraordinary, was, was when, um, my parents died and in particular my mother . . .' (Helen, emphasis her own)

'. . . it's like having something torn out of you. It's terrible . . . it was like having something physically ripped out of you . . .' (Belinda)

Belinda also told an anecdote about the potential difficulties caused by the intersection of motherhood and work. She had been about to present a paper to an international conference, when her baby had begun to cry in another room:

'. . . before I'd even realized what was happening, my milk came through, which makes your boobs almost like grow an inch, become incredibly pert, and your nipples stand out like traffic lights [*laughs*] . . .'

Belinda says that she had breast pads inside her blouse, otherwise the milk would have leaked through. She said that this made her feel 'momentarily' very disoriented because it was as if her role as a mother had suddenly intruded into her role as a professional woman – she recovered quickly and continued, but says that the experience was 'extraordinary'. This is another interesting reflection on the complexity of identity – that women may experience their mothering as separate from *and conflicting with* their professional identities.

Other comments centred on the potential difficulties caused by menstruation at work. Helen, who works in a university, talked of the ways in which time and space is structured in organizations, and suggests that this can make life difficult for women who are menstruating:

> '. . . I think that periods can be a nuisance and particularly if, if you've got a heavy period and you have to be, you have to be careful about how long you're going to spend in any one particular place at one particular time. Then you sort of have to excuse yourself from a meeting and I think that's a pain . . .'

Here Helen implies that, if a working woman is menstruating, it is difficult for her to manage the effects of this whilst also complying with organizational demands – and so she may have to make excuses to allow her to escape 'backstage'. Marie also acknowledged this problem, saying that she recalls getting up from her seat to leave a meeting, realizing that her period had started and making a quick exit lest it became particularly 'obvious'. Martin (1989: 92) suggests that the way in which women experience their periods in public places is commonly informed by the powerful medical definition of periods as 'failed [re]production', as something unacceptable and dirty. Shilling (1993: 38), furthermore, argues that the aforementioned paucity of consideration for the body in organizational design is particularly difficult for women, who are expected to manage their biological processes in organizations that do not take cognizance of them.

Rachel had actually experienced what Marie and Helen allude to as problematic, where menstrual blood leaks through on to clothes at work. She described having been away on a training day with her organization at a remote location, and said that her period had started 'with a flood'. By the time she realized, her white skirt was 'covered with blood' and she had no way of obtaining tampons. Rachel said that this had been 'dreadful' and that she had felt 'dirty, stupid, unclean, . . . and angry, angry that my body had got in the way . . .'. Rachel's description of this experience implies a potential clash between women's biology and their public lives, in the sense that 'most centrally no one must ever see you dealing with the mechanics of keeping up with the disgusting mess, and you must never fail to keep the disgusting mess from showing on your clothes, furniture, or the floor' (Martin, 1989: 93).

We might argue that the 'disgusting mess' of menstrual blood seems, in these respondents' accounts, to bear testimony to their biological femaleness and so to be something which must never be in evidence at work, revealing as it does their 'unsuitability' for working environments.

Many of the respondents also talked about the symptomatology of menstruation in the work environment. Both Rachel and Meg (who work in the NHS) suggested that this has worsened as they have grown older. Rachel said that she now suffers migraines as well as pain as part of her menstrual cycle, in the form of 'flashing lights'. She also suggests that she cannot organize her working day to suit her physical condition at any particular time – she cannot cancel meetings because she has a migraine, for example, even though she cannot concentrate properly. Hilary described how her periods had been both heavy and painful in the past, and said that she had often had to take time off from work as a result. Hilary had also experienced debilitating *pre*menstrual symptoms, and says in particular that 'the paranoia was really quite frightening . . . really it was the paranoia that got to me'. Belinda also described feeling 'totally neurotic and paranoid and hat[ing] everybody' prior to her period, and Marie reported behaving aggressively as part of her premenstrual symptomatology.

Further, Hilary argues that being a nurse made her symptoms particularly difficult because being pleasant to patients when she was suffering herself was a real challenge. Hilary, like many of the respondents in this interview programme, works in a so-called 'caring profession'. It is a truism to point out that these professions are female-dominated (see Wilson, 1995: 16–17) and that this is primarily due to the prevailing discourse of gender difference which constitutes women as more interpersonally skilled than men (see, for example, Hines, 1992; Archer and Lloyd, cited in Synnott, 1993: 70). However, what is interesting is that Hilary, Belinda and Marie describe symptoms which are produced by their *biological* femaleness, but which hardly sit well with the *discursive* image of women as empathetic. Furthermore, whereas Marie's aggression is 'out of sync' with the feminine stereotype *per se*, tears and paranoia (Hilary and Belinda) are behaviours that conform to *other* aspects of this stereotype. This reveals tensions in the feminine stereotype itself, as well as suggesting an effect on these women's abilities to function in their 'caring' jobs.

Hilary also described painful periods and premenstrual tension as two of the 'worst things that God could ever give you . . . they are miserable and . . . you just lose control completely'. As Martin (1989: 121–2) points out, premenstrual symptoms are often linked with a temporary loss of discipline, already identified as prized in the modern workplace.

Returning to the issue of how organizations are structured, both Harriet, who works in a university, and Belinda were explicit that organizations are not designed to take account of the symptoms associated with premenstrual days – Belinda suggested that this is because men do not suffer from this particular affliction. Synnott (1993: 67) points to Hite's finding that 69 per cent of women thought men were uninformed about women's bodies and desires, which seems to reflect Belinda's point. Martin, in a similar vein, discusses the perception of women's bodies as pathological: 'Women are perceived as malfunctioning and their hormones out of balance rather than the organization of society and work perceived as in need of a transformation to demand less constant discipline and productivity' (1989: 123).

However, despite frequently severe symptoms, these respondents have developed ways of coping when such symptoms threaten their effectiveness at work. Rachel 'lives on pills' to minimize period pain and Hilary talked of trying various remedies, but now preferring to rely on 'mind over matter . . . [I say to myself] "Look, this is real, but it's not real" . . . you know what the cause is, you just have to put a brave face on . . . I've learnt to take a lot of deep breaths.' Marie also implied that a woman's psychological perspective on her menstrual cycle has a significant part to play in dealing with the symptoms:

'. . . I don't like that word ['gives in'] because sometimes you don't have a choice but it's how a woman *copes* and how much she's prepared to absorb some of these problems and still do her job professionally and I think you get differences in women . . . [it's] inner strength I guess or, or ability to cope with an impact on your job . . .' (emphasis Marie's own)

Marie also talked about the improvizational strategies that she uses if her period starts unexpectedly at work – including washing her clothes and using tissue paper if no tampons are available. Further, she argues that women perhaps need to be more open about the problems that their periods cause them in the working environment. She says that she is quite happy to ask her colleagues to excuse her if her premenstrual aggression surfaces at work.

Moreover, Belinda suggested that she tries to organize her team in a way which minimizes such problems. Here she talks about the premenstrual symptoms experienced by a former colleague:

'. . . she couldn't, er, get her words out right and she couldn't write properly. Yeah, it used to really knock her sideways. So you see as her boss, as her manager, we just used to work round that, um, so, you know, she wasn't writing reports two or three days before her period.'

Hilary also argues that, because she has experienced menstrual problems herself, she is more sympathetic to other women in the same position.

The mothers, likewise, tended not to over-emphasize any difficulties that their pregnancies had caused at work; Belinda, for example, saying that she had actually been very reluctant to complain about her nausea, because she did not want to understand her pregnancy as meaning that she was ill, until it became too hard to cope. At this point she consulted her doctor and he ordered her to take time off work.

What might be described as the respondents' micro-level redefinition of female biology points us to two important issues. First, it suggests that there are attitudinal assumptions which underpin women's relationships with their bodily processes. These interact with the biological components of menstruation, pregnancy and menopause to produce the lived experience of these events. Consequently, we see here how 'social representations and classifications of the body both shape, and are shaped by, the organic body' (Shilling, 1993: 104; also see Lewantin et al., cited in Martin, 1989: 12).

Therefore a woman who understands her biology as being something involuntary and outside of her control, will, we might conclude, have a very different experience from a woman like Marie or Hilary who understands their biology as something to be consciously managed. Second, it appears that these redefinitions of what it means to have periods (Marie's refusal to 'give in', for example, or Hilary's 'this is real, but it's not real') or to be pregnant (Belinda's refusal to understand herself as ill when she was pregnant) constitute what Foucault (1980) would describe as resistance. It is in our own lives where we experience the restrictive effects of discourses around biology and gender difference – thus some of the women interviewed here can be understood to be acting to change their own experience by refusing to define themselves as 'victims' or 'carriers' of certain fixed and immutable bodily processes (Martin, 1989: 130–5). Furthermore, the respondents here were often of the more or less explicit opinion that organizations needed to change so as to accommodate/legitimate female biological processes. Harriet and Belinda particularly emphasized this point, as can be seen from earlier discussion.

Interestingly, the mothers were also, on the whole, eloquent on what Martin refers to as the 'phenomenology' of pregnancy: 'what a woman sees and feels or the significance it has in her life' (Martin, 1989: 110), describing in vivid, and positive, detail how it feels to be pregnant. Martin's working class respondents tended to be more emphatic on the phenomenology of female biology – but the respondents here, by virtue of their occupations, could all be understood as middle class (albeit not necessarily in origin). Shilling (1993: 127–35), following Bourdieu, claims that working class individuals, because of their physically demanding lifestyles, tend to see their bodies as instruments, and so are perhaps more aware of these bodies' functionality. Perhaps then one could argue that pregnancy is an opportunity for middle class women to experience the instrumentality of the body at first hand, because they do not engage in manual work and so commonly would be less aware of the phenomenology of physical processes. Martin also claims that working class women may particularly value their ability to carry children and look forward to pregnancy because 'where access to the forces and means of production in the society is severely limited, reproduction can be (or can at least appear to be) a way of acting in the world, changing one's life, producing a "resource" to be shared or cherished' (1989: 104).

She suggests, on the other hand, that middle class women are often concerned that childbearing poses a threat to their careers. Again, the data here diverge from Martin's account. Nearly all of the mothers emphasized their pleasure in being pregnant, and several also commented that it had made them psychologically *withdraw* from their professional roles to a certain degree. Brenda said that her disengagement was:

'. . . not particularly a negative thing 'cause I very much want to be pregnant. Um, it's the right time of my life and it was planned and all the rest of it so it's not as if, you know, I'm kind of walking round feeling ashamed or guilty or particularly worried.'

Marie suggested that she had felt much the same way:

'. . . maybe when you're pregnant work and things recede a little bit in importance because you know you've got another kind of mission in life, you've got something else that's going to be important to you.'

Belinda, likewise, described the disengagement to which both Marie and Brenda referred. Here, then, the data seem to reflect Synnott's (1993: 2) point that 'Self-concepts change, often dramatically, at puberty, pregnancy and menopause. Body changes change the self.'

In conclusion, the data analysed here seem in some respects to reflect, but in other ways to diverge from, the existing theory around the body, and the body at work in particular. Whilst no grand claims about the significance of the data are intended beyond their relevance in understanding the experiences of the female respondents, it might be argued that the differences between the findings of this study and, for example, Martin's findings about pregnancy, or Shilling's, Featherstone's and Gamman and Makinen's emphasis on body work as a never-ending preoccupation for modern subjects, suggest that the body is by no means a constant, nor that it plays a constant role in our understandings of our selves. Echoing this point, we can also point to the women's differences in opinion about and experience of their bodies (for example, Holly's concerns about the way in which her body speaks of her sexuality compared to Marie and Hilary talking of their bodies' sexuality as useful at work), and their frequent allusions to the double-edged status of their bodies (for example, Rachel's ambiguity about her weight at work). Moreover, the differences and similarities in the respondents' accounts, as well as the ways in which they frequently sought to differentiate their bodily lives from those of men, highlight the aforementioned dual status of the body as a source of sameness, but also of difference and inequality (Shilling, 1993: 22–3; Synnott, 1993: 242–4).

The ways in which these women are, live and use their bodies, both in and outside of work, then, implies that their bodies might be understood as complicated sites which powerful discourses inform, affect and construct in various ways. These accounts of the body also point to the way in which we as subjects can resist what discourse tells us is true about ourselves, to the extent that we can work to change our own, and others', experience of being-in-the-world – for example, the discussion of how the women manage their own and others' biologies at work. This is important because it suggests that the respondents are fully aware of themselves as biological females (and acknowledge the consequent limitations), but, at the same time, do not accept that their bodies are so constraining as to disbar them from full and active participation in (and reconstruction of) the world of the organization.

In sum, the data indicate that we may do well to pay attention to Foucault's (1980) insistence that power is (literally) productive, as opposed to constraining or oppressive. That is to say, the ways in which these women variously internalize or resist the discourses which are available to them about their bodies suggest that they are aware of the materiality of biology, but also that this materiality is only comprehensible through prevailing discursive constructions (Butler, 1993). They are, then, fleshly beings, but the way in which they experience that flesh, as limiting or beneficial, is produced by discourse.

Note

1 This does, however, imply that Tracey's male colleagues evaluate her, not only as a manager, but also as a woman.

References

Aaronovitch, D. (1997) 'Llandudno, where the happy people live', *The Independent*, 13 August.

Adorno, M. and Horkheimer, T.W. (1979) *Dialectic of Enlightenment*. London: Verso.

Bartky, S.L. (1988) 'Foucault, femininity and the modernization of patriarchal power', in I. Diamond and L. Quinby (eds), *Feminism and Foucault: Reflections on Resistance*. Boston, MA: Northeastern University Press. pp. 61–86.

Baudrillard, J. (1993) *Symbolic Exchange and Death*. London: Sage.

Bauman, Z. (1983) 'Industrialism, consumerism and power', *Theory, Culture and Society*, 1 (3): 32–43.

Bauman, Z. (1987) *Legislators and Interpreters*. Cambridge: Polity Press.

Berman, M. (1990) *All That Is Solid Melts into Air*. London: Verso.

Bremer, B.A., Moore, C.T. and Bildersee, E.F. (1991) 'Do you have to call it "sexual harassment" to feel harassed?', *College Student Journal*, 25 (3): 258–68.

Brewis, J. (1996) 'Sex, work and sex at work: a Foucauldian analysis'. Unpublished PhD thesis, UMIST.

Brewis, J., Hampton, M.P. and Linstead, S. (1997) 'Unpacking Priscilla: subjectivity and identity in the organization of gendered appearance', *Human Relations*, 50 (10): 1275–304.

Burrell, G. (1984) 'Sex and organizational analysis', *Organization Studies*, 5 (2): 97–118.

Burrell, G. (1992) 'The organization of pleasure', in M. Alvesson and H. Willmott (eds), *Critical Management Studies*. London: Sage. pp. 67–88.

Butler, J. (1993) *Bodies That Matter: On the Discursive Limits of 'Sex'*. New York and London: Routledge.

Cixous, H. (1988) 'Sorties', in D. Lodge (ed.), *Modern Criticism and Theory*. London: Longman. pp. 286–93.

Clegg, S. (1990) *Modern Organizations: Organization Studies in the Postmodern World*. London: Sage.

Cook, E. (1997) 'Fattism: a hard act to swallow', *The Independent on Sunday*, 17 August.

Cooper, R. and Burrell, G. (1988) 'Modernism, postmodernism and organizational analysis', *Organization Studies*, 9 (2): 91–112.

Derrida, J. and McDonald, C. (1988) 'Choreographies', in J. Derrida (ed.), *The Ear of the Other*. Lincoln, NB: University of Nebraska Press. pp. 163–85.

Elias, N. (1978) *The Civilizing Process: The History of Manners*. Oxford: Basil Blackwell.

Engels, F. (1973) *The Condition of the Working-Class in England*. Moscow: Progress Publishers.

Featherstone, M. (1991) 'The body in consumer culture', in M. Featherstone, M. Hepworth and B.S. Turner (eds), *The Body: Social Process and Cultural Theory*. London: Sage. pp. 171–96.

Foucault, M. (1980) *Power/Knowledge: Selected Interviews and Other Writings, 1972–1977* (ed. C. Gordon). Brighton: Harvester Press.

Gamman, L. and Makinen, M. (1994) *Female Fetishism: A New Look*. London: Lawrence & Wishart.

Grafton Small, R. (1993) 'The fragmented self: a symbol of order and trans-formation'. Paper presented at the 11th Standing Conference on Organizational Symbolism, Barcelona.

Gramsci, A. (1971) *Selections from the Prison Notebooks*. London: Lawrence & Wishart.

Grauerholz, E. (1989) 'Sexual harassment of women professors by their students: exploring the dynamics of power, authority and gender in a university setting', *Sex Roles*, 21 (11–12): 789–801.

Habermas, J. (1972) *Knowledge and Human Interests*. London: Heinemann Educational.

Habermas, J. (1987) *The Philosophical Discourse of Modernity*. Oxford: Blackwell.

Hebdige, D. (1989) 'After the masses', *Marxism Today*, January: 48–53.

Hines, R. (1992) 'Accounting: filling the negative space', *Accounting, Organizations and Society*, 17 (3): 314–41.

Jameson, F. (1991) *Postmodernism, or the Cultural Logic of Late Capitalism*. London: Verso.

Kant, I. (1974) *Anthropology from a Pragmatic Point of View*. The Hague: Nijhoff.

Kant, I. (1990) *Foundations of the Metaphysics of Morals, and What is Enlight-enment?* (trans. L.W. Beck). New York: Macmillan/Liberal Arts Press.

Knights, D. and Vurdubakis, T. (1994) 'Foucault, power, resistance and all that', in J.M. Jermier, D. Knights and W.R. Nord (eds), *Resistance and Power in Organizations*. London: Routledge. pp. 167–98.

Lamplugh, D. (1996) 'Gender and personal safety at work', *Occasional Papers in Organizational Analysis*, 5 (special issue), Department of Business and Management, University of Portsmouth Business School. pp. 64–79.

Linstead, S. (1996) 'Virtual ethnography'. Paper presented at the 14th Standing Conference on Organizational Symbolism, Los Angeles.

Lurie, A. (1992) *The Language of Clothes*. London: Bloomsbury.

Marcuse, H. (1969) *Eros and Civilization: A Philosophical Inquiry into Freud*. London: Allen Lane.

Martin, E. (1989) *The Woman in the Body: A Cultural Analysis of Reproduction*. Milton Keynes: Open University Press.

McDowell, L. and Court, G. (1994) 'Performing work: bodily representations in merchant banks', *Environment and Planning D: Society and Space*, 12: 727–50.

Moore, S. (1994) 'Make way for the third sex', *Guardian*, 13 October, p. 5.

Orbach, S. (1989) *Fat is a Feminist Issue . . . How to Lose Weight Permanently – Without Dieting*. London: Arrow.

Reed, M. (1985) *Redirections in Organizational Analysis*. London: Tavistock Publications.

Renick, J.C. (1980) 'Sexual harassment at work: why it happens and what to do about it', *Personnel Journal*, 59 (8): 658–62.

Sheppard, D.L. (1989) 'Organizations, power and sexuality: the image and self-image of women managers', in J. Hearn, D.L. Sheppard, P. Tancred-Sheriff and G. Burrell (eds), *The Sexuality of Organization*. London: Sage. pp. 139–57.

Shilling, C. (1993) *The Body and Social Theory*. London: Sage.

Stone, A.R. (1995) *The War of Desire and Technology at the Close of the Mechanical Age*. Cambridge, MA: MIT Press.

Synnott, A. (1993) *The Body Social: Symbolism, Self and Society*. London: Routledge.

Tong, R. (1989) *Feminist Thought: A Comprehensive Introduction*. London: Unwin Hyman.

Turner, B.S. (1991) 'Recent developments in the theory of the body', in M. Featherstone, M. Hepworth and B.S. Turner (eds), *The Body: Social Process and Cultural Theory*. London: Sage. pp. 1–35.

Walkerdine, V. (1984) 'Some day my prince will come: young girls and the preparation for adolescent sexuality', in A. McRobbie and M. Nava (eds), *Gender and Generation*. London: Macmillan. pp. 162–84.

Watts, A. (1975) *Psychotherapy East and West*. New York: Vintage Books.

Weber, M. (1970) 'Bureaucracy', in H.H. Gerth and C. Wright-Mills (eds), *From Max Weber*. London: Routledge & Kegan Paul. pp. 197–244.

Williamson, J. (1980) *Consuming Passions: The Dynamics of Popular Culture*. London: Marion Boyars.

Wilson, F.M. (1995) *Organizational Behaviour and Gender*. Maidenhead: McGraw Hill.

Yount, K. (1991) 'Ladies, flirts and tomboys: strategies for managing sexual harassment in an underground coal mine', *Journal of Contemporary Ethnography*, 19 (4): 396–422.

11 What Can a Body Do? Sexual Harassment and Legal Procedure

Janice Richardson

The aim of this chapter is to consider possible poststructuralist insights relating to embodiment and to use these to rethink feminist strategy around sexual harassment litigation. In turn this raises questions about the extent to which effectiveness can be predicted by the adoption of a theoretical perspective, and the relationship between theory and practice.

First, it is necessary to understand the background of the term 'sexual harassment'. This is attributed to Lin Farley (1978), who uses the term in her book *Sexual Shakedown*. She details the results of a consciousness-raising group in which she had been involved. Many of this group of women explained how they had been made to feel uncomfortable or had left work as a result of men's sexual behaviour towards them. This was developed by the ground-breaking work of Catherine MacKinnon (1979). Since the late 1970s, poststructuralist criticism has problematized the idea that consciousness-raising represents the ability of women to replace some sort of 'false consciousness' with 'the Truth'. Whilst accepting this critique, I believe that it was an important moment of oppositional strategy which I will discuss within the context of Foucault's work on power.

In the UK the term has not been enacted in legislation but was implied into the Sex Discrimination Act 1975 by the Court of Session in the case of *Strathclyde Regional Council* v *Porcelli*[1] in 1986. In the case, Mr Cole and Mr Reed used lewd, personal and threatening comments to try to bully Mrs Porcelli into transferring her place of work. Previously, courts had only allowed such claims where a link could be shown between the sexual harassment and some other disadvantage relating to the woman's contract. (The most common situation was that the applicant had refused to have sex with her employer and had been dismissed.) In the case of *Porcelli*, the Court decided that she sustained less favourable treatment (contrary to s.1(1)(a) Sex Discrimination Act 1975) and concluded that, *'the weapon used was based upon the sex of the victim'* (emphasis added). Whilst I am not complaining about the decision, nor would I wish to minimize the pain of women who suffer sexual harassment, I think we must ask how it is that male sexuality can be experienced as a weapon, in this way, at this point in time.

As a result of the court's decision to imply a prohibition on sexual harassment into the discrimination legislation, there is no specific definition of sexual harassment under UK law. It simply comes under the heading of 'less favourable treatment' and under the catch-all category of 'subjecting a woman to any other detriment'. (It is now subject to a EU code of practice.) MacKinnon, in the US, proposed the following definition:

Unwanted imposition of sexual requirements in the context of a relationship of unequal power. (MacKinnon, 1979: 1)

Within the US, sexual harassment is divided into two categories: quid pro quo, in which sex is a condition of employment, and hostile work environment, such as the circumstances in *Porcelli*, in which the environment is poisoned by the use of leering, suggestive remarks, touching etc. There is much work on the efficacy of legal definitions.[2] Similarly, much useful work has been carried out detailing the extent of judicial misogyny within rape trials and there are no shortages of examples within the area of sexual harassment. My aim is not to discuss either of these areas but to concentrate upon the question of how it is that male sexuality can be experienced as a weapon.

Denaturalizing sexual harassment

Sharon Marcus (1992) makes an important point with regard to discourse on rape, which I think is relevant to the discourse on sexual harassment. She argues that much of the focus of rape literature assumes 'that rape has already occurred and women are always either already raped or already rapable'. In other words, it is simply assumed that women are somehow vulnerable to rape and sexual harassment because of their bodies. Rethinking 'the body' allows feminists to challenge the naturalization of this process. Marcus attacks the assumption made by Brownmiller (1975), in her classic analysis of rape, that men simply rape because they can. This not only naturalizes rape but also sexual identity. She calls for analysis of how women become not simply objects of violence, but 'subjects of fear'. (In other words, instead of being pre-existing humanist subjects, one way in which we are incited to become subjects is through fear.)

Put like this, she sounds very like MacKinnon. However, she resists MacKinnon's position of assuming that men can define women through sexual violence and emphasizes the possibility of resistance, of subversion of the script.

Masculine power and feminine powerlessness neither simply precede nor cause rape; rather rape is one of culture's many ways of feminizing women . . . To take male violence or female vulnerability as the first and last instances in any explanation of rape is to make the identities of rapist and raped preexist the rape itself. (Marcus, 1992: 391)

She points out that whereas there has been much research on the way in which rape causes fear, the way in which rape succeeds because of women's fears needs analysis. This is not to assume that law should deny women redress if, having been trained in passivity, they do not behave in the same way as men. It focuses upon the attack itself rather than upon legal redress. To analyse how women are positioned with respect to fear and to challenge this by viewing the rape as a 'script', emphasizes women's agency and their capacity for violent retaliation. Its emphasis on discourse prevents this from simply being an individualist response.

Butler's analysis is very similar theoretically when she suggests that,

Sexual crimes against the bodies of sexed subjects (women, lesbians, gay men to name but a few) effectively reduce them to their 'sex' thereby reaffirming and enforcing the reduction of the category itself. Because discourse is not restricted to writing or speaking, but is also social action, even violent social action, we ought also to understand rape, sexual violence, 'queer bashing' as the category of sex in action. (Butler, 1990: 166)

Again, Butler is not simply conceding to men the ability to define women by virtue of sexual harassment. Like Marcus, Butler emphasizes the way in which identity is not stable, opening up the possibility of its subversion. Her focus away from 'the law' resonates with Foucault's argument that freedom cannot be guaranteed by laws, that the only guarantee of freedom is the act of freedom itself (Foucault, 1986). Concentration on laws can involve focusing upon the wrong point in time: seeing women as victims seeking redress rather than being empowered to resist this subject position. It also ignores law's role in reflecting and reinforcing this position. Both Marcus and Butler draw upon a view of subjectivity which owes a debt to Foucault. I will use his work to develop this analysis of sexuality.

Although Foucault has been dismissed as being unconcerned with feminist issues, particularly his problematic call for the decriminalization of rape (for example, Foucault, 1988: 201); as not giving sufficient regard to agency; as being in the position of the colonizer who refuses (Hartsock, 1990); there has been much feminist interest in his work, particularly *The History of Sexuality: Volume One* (Foucault, 1978) (for an early example, see Diamond and Quinby, 1988).

The main points are probably now familiar. He argues against the idea that sex is some natural drive/instinct that has been repressed by the exercise of power operating in a downward manner, as in psychoanalytic models. Instead, he views power as being productive. To illustrate this, he traces a line from the Catholic confessional in the seventeenth century in which one had to detail all sexual desires, acts and thoughts, through 'the scandalous literature of De Sade' to psychoanalysis and the medical-ization of sexuality. He points to the same process: that the power of the priests and doctors was further increased by their ability to get people to talk frequently and in detail about sexuality. Rather than sex being a 'dark hidden secret that tells us something about our true selves if we can only persuade it to talk', he argues that it becomes crystallized, frozen through the way that people are forced to talk about themselves.

It is the person who is silent, hears the confession, interprets and treats it who is empowered.

> The confessional is a ritual of discourse in which the speaking subject is also the subject of the statement; it is also a ritual which unfolds within a power relationship, for one does not confess without the presence (or virtual presence) of a partner who is not simply the interlocutor but the authority who requires the confession, prescribes and appreciates it, and intervenes in order to judge, punish, forgive, console and reconcile. . .a ritual which exonerates, redeems and purifies him. (Foucault, 1978: 61)

In terms of both the mystique and mechanism of the process, this can be compared to the process of going to law.[3] When a client arrives in the solicitor's office she is looking for consolation, for peace of mind. From a solicitor's viewpoint, it is vital to make sure that every detail of the client's complaint is recounted and recorded to avoid being caught out by some unforseen evidence at the hearing. The process takes on average over an hour of painstaking detail. A statement is then dictated and sent to the client for amendment. If the client is still at work she will always be told to take detailed contemporaneous notes[4] of any harassment. These notes are normally copious. As with the confessional, this process is repeated on a number of occasions.

It may appear strange to compare the solicitor–client interview with the confessional, given that the penitent is linked with an association of guilt. However, the whole process can be interpreted as a struggle over meaning. As has been well documented (Smart, 1989), the women's experiences are filtered through the legal system. This process does not necessarily disregard the women's accounts of the detail of the harassment. It is more insidious in focusing upon, and dissecting every word, every event, for their multiple meanings with a view to their possible reinterpretation at trial. This is strikingly similar to Foucault's description of the confessional.[5]

It is the process which is under discussion, not the attitude of the par-ticular solicitor. The solicitors opting to run sexual harassment claims may well be feminist. (As there is no legal aid for the tribunal work, it is either carried out by trade union solicitors or on legal aid up to the hearing. This is hardly work guaranteed to increase your monthly costs figure.) Never-theless, the way in which this is carried out may be counter-productive if it relies upon, freezes/crystallizes a negative interpretation of what it means to be a 'woman'.

Within this Foucaudian framework, it is clear that this confessional takes place, and potentially empowers the employer, within an already exploitative relationship. Foucault is optimistic in conceiving of power as always creating its own resistance:

> Discourses are not once and for all subservient to power or raised up against it, any more than silences are. We must make allowance for the complex and unstable process whereby discourse can be both an instrument and an effect of power, but also a hindrance, a stumbling block, a point of resistance and a starting point of an oppositional strategy. Discourse transmits and produces power; it reinforces it, but also undermines and exposes it, renders it fragile and makes it possible to thwart it. (Foucault, 1978: 101)

The many 'confessionals' that have made up the discourse about sexual harassment include not only those within the workplace, solicitor/client discussions in preparing the case and the hearing itself but also the consciousness-raising groups which gave rise to the term 'sexual harassment'. This involved women comparing and redefining their experiences. It is possible to view the feminist reaction as a 'reverse discourse'. Just as homosexuals once defined as such have used the label to demand its legitimacy, so women defined by sexual abuse fight back as objects of abuse, using the same language.

Within the work of both Foucault and Butler there is potential for repeating and subverting the way in which men's sexuality comes to be viewed as a potential weapon. However, within Butler's work and her reading of Foucault the emphasis is upon the body as constructed by discourse (Benhabib et al., 1995). To approach this another way, it is possible to start with 'the body'.

Deleuze's reading of Spinoza is useful in starting with the body: 'we do not know what a body can do'. This does not simply try to reverse the priority between mind/body. It involves a rethinking of the body and mind as being both attributes of the same substance, as being given equal priority. Deleuze's reading of Spinoza, through Nietzsche, emphasizes the power of the body. It is worth outlining this in some detail in order to highlight an approach which, like that of Foucault/Butler/Marcus, does not view the body or its meaning as fixed. However, it actually starts with, and emphasizes, the materiality of the body and as such stresses the importance of embodied knowledge. It is this concept of embodied knowledge along with the stress on the power of bodies which is of interest in the context of sexual harassment.

Re-evaluating the body

In keeping with Deleuze's attitude to the book, which he views as 'a little non-signifying machine, . . . the only question is: Does it work and how does it work?' (Deleuze, 1990: 7), I am not going to attempt to summarize his work but to draw out one strand: the work that derives from his reading of Spinoza.[6] Both Gatens (1996) and Grosz (1994) have argued that Spinoza may be useful in thinking sexual difference in a terrain other than Cartesian dualism. This is important for feminists because the mind/body dualism has reflected the dualism man/woman, with woman representing the downgraded, passive body. Irigaray (1985a), for example, has illustrated the way in which philosophers since Plato have envisaged the pursuit of reason as masculine, as a leaving behind of matter/the body, which is designated as 'woman'.

As Deleuze puts it,

> Spinoza offers philosophers a new model: the body. He proposes to establish the body as a model: 'We do not know what a body can do . . .' This declaration of ignorance is a provocation. We speak of consciousness and its decrees, of the will and its effects, of the thousand ways of moving the body, of dominating the body and the passions – *but we do not even know what a body can do*. (Deleuze, 1988: 17–18, emphasis in original)

Spinoza denies any domination of the mind over the body. Both are attributes of the same substance, with neither having priority. All beings are modes of being of this infinite single substance. Central to his theory is 'parallelism', that what is an action in the mind is necessarily an action in the body as well, and what is a passion in the body is necessarily a passion in the mind.

> One seeks to acquire a knowledge of powers of the body in order to discover, in a parallel fashion, the powers of the mind that elude consciousness, and thus to be able to compare the power.[7]

This can be demonstrated by considering the old problem of sex/gender. Social construction theory emphasized that sex was biological and given whereas gender was social and therefore subject to change. This is problematized in Butler's work (for example, Butler, 1993), when she questions the way in which the social is envisaged as acting upon the passive natural body. She reverses the position and ends up showing how our understanding of the 'natural' and the dichotomy between nature/culture is itself a cultural product. Gatens (1996) applies the work of Spinoza to produce a different solution to the question of sex/gender: if the mind and body are both attributes of the same substance then there is a sense in which one is an expression of the other. Neither is viewed as the cause of the other. This materialism revalues the body without claiming that it should be prioritized over the mind. It moves us away from the idea that the body is in any way fixed and ahistorical and that any emphasis of the body must result in essentialism or biological determinism.

Deleuze stresses the illusionary nature of consciousness for Spinoza. It is the site which registers effects but does not know their causes. When a body encounters another body or an idea encounters an idea these two sets of relations may combine to form a more powerful whole, a composition, which results in the experience of joy. Alternatively, it may threaten our own coherence, threaten us with decomposition and we experience sadness. A simple example would be that eating food is a joyful encounter but drinking poison is a sad encounter. Death is the ultimate sad encounter occurring because the body's cohesion is completely incompatible with that of the other body.

Unfortunately, whilst we can experience effects we are ignorant of causes, having only 'inadequate ideas' of them. This is obviously a problem because we will have more sad encounters if we leave matters to chance. Instead of assuming that we desire something because it is good, Spinoza argues that we must recognize that we categorize it as good because we want it. This enables us to move towards adequate ideas of cause. Deleuze prefigures his later work when he states,

> We need, then, to arrive at a real definition of desire, one that shows the 'cause' by which consciousness is hollowed out, as it were, in the appetitive process. (Deleuze, 1988: 21)

Deleuze's stress on power provides him with a libertarian argument. In his definition of power he points out that one of the basic points in the *Ethics* is to deny legislative power. Power 'is inseparable from the capacity to be affected, and this capacity for being affected is constantly and necessarily filled by affections that realize it' (Deleuze, 1988: 97). Just as this involves a move away from legislation from above, it questions the ability of theory to dictate to political practice, a point to which I shall return.

Deleuze draws upon Spinoza to define a body in two ways. First, as composed of an infinite number of particles; the *relations* of motion and rest, speeds and slowness between the body define the individuality of the body. Secondly, it is simultaneously defined by its *capacity* to affect and be affected by other bodies. He calls these the kinetic and dynamic definitions. From the kinetic definition he argues that a body is not defined by its global form or organic functions but by,

> a complex relation between differential velocities . . . In the same way, a musical form will depend on a complex relationship between speeds and slowness of sound particles. It is not just a matter of music but of how to live: it is by speed and slowness that one slips in among things, that one connects with something else. One never commences; one never has a *tabula rasa*; one slips in, enters in the middle; one takes up or lays down rhythms.[8]

Secondly, when turning to his discussion of the capacity to affect and be affected, he underlines that Spinoza does not define a body or mind by its functions or as a substance or a subject. He defines the bodies and minds as modes – a complex relation of speeds, in the body and in thought, and a capacity for affecting and being affected. He argues that,

> Concretely, if you define bodies and thoughts as capacities for affecting and being affected many things change. You will define an animal, or a human being not by its organs and its functions, and not as a subject either; you will define it by the affects of which it is capable. (Deleuze, 1988: 124)

The initial quote, 'we do not know what a body can do', can be understood as indicating that only by experimentation can one know the effects of which one is capable.

> You do not know beforehand what good or bad you are capable of; you do not know beforehand what a body or mind can do, in a given encounter, a given arrangement, a given combination. (Deleuze, 1988: 125)

Deleuze and Guattari (1992) take up this call to experiment; to form assemblages. The concepts of the Body-without-Organs, becomings, rhizome, multiplicity, molecularity draw on and develop this fluidity of boundaries between the self and other. The concept of the 'Body-without-Organs' can be used to move away from conceiving of the body as an organized whole, but as a Spinozan substance that is made of dynamic parts in relation to each other, forming assemblages. These are not synthesized wholes, as in a dialectical synthesis, but are completely open to 'becomings'.

This emphasis on the power and capacities of bodies, along with the attack on the idea of the body as simply being passively inscribed and static, are potentially useful in denaturalizing the body of man/woman. In the areas of organizational theory and state theory, the move away from a humanistic image of the human body to the formation of assemblages attacks the conservative image of the organization or state as operating in a manner analogous to an organic whole. Gatens (1996) uses this re-evaluation of the body to emphasize the embodied nature of knowledge. This does not imply that there is no such thing as truth but that the imagination is embodied. Drawing upon Spinoza/Deleuze opens the possibility of conceiving of the imagination and imaginary images of the body without reliance upon a psychoanalytic model. This is useful for feminism because desire is viewed in terms of making positive connections, eschewing psychoanalytic models which conceive of desire as lack.[9]

As Gatens draws upon Spinoza's work to discuss the effects of imaginary bodies, such as that of the penis as a weapon, it is necessary to clarify what is meant by 'imaginary' in this non-psychoanalytic context:

> An imagination is an idea which indicates the present constitution of the human body . . . For example, when we look at the sun, we imagine it to be about 200 feet away from us. In this we are deceived so long as we are ignorant of its true distance; but when the distance is known, the error is removed, not in the

imagination (since the imagination is) not contrary to the true, and do(es) not disappear on its presence. (cited in Gatens, 1996: 146)

Gatens applies Spinoza's emphasis on embodied knowledge to the male judiciary, whose images of women are derived from their embodied relationships, normally with wives/secretaries. There are a number of studies which illustrate this relationship (for example, Pringle, 1989; Tancred-Sheriff, 1989).[10] These roles reinforce the image of women's subordination within the imaginary, not only of the judges but of many of the legal profession dealing with the claims and, at an earlier stage, with management. (This is not to imply that there is anything predetermined about this nor that it is in any way fixed.) Her use of Spinoza allows us to question the efficacy of training male judges to imagine the effects of sexual harassment, although she argues that they are able to reason its effects. (Hence, Rubenstein's (1988) attempts to get round this problem by asking men how they would feel if they were offered promotion in exchange for sex by a gay man. This is obviously problematic because, not only does it position the audience as heterosexual, it draws upon and reinforces homophobia.)

Whilst the stress upon the embodied nature of knowledge is useful, there is a problem in adhering too closely to Spinoza's epistemology. The transition from the imagination to the realm of reason can be read as reflecting individualism and Enlightenment ideals.[11] This can result in optimism about the possibility of judicial reasoning which transcends the imaginary and which also yanks the effect of going to law for protection out of its social and political context.

Similarly, whilst the emphasis on an imaginary based upon Spinoza's work avoids the conservative aspects of psychoanalysis, in this account, it lacks the role of affect that is central within psychoanalysis. To return to Butler's comparison of sexual harassment to 'queer bashing', there are strong emotions at play. Male identity, in this scenario, is stabilized (albeit never completely successfully) through the exclusion of 'woman'. These theories mitigate against an optimistic view that male judges can make the transition from imagination to other forms of knowledge envisaged by Spinoza.

Deleuze's emphasis on the formation of assemblages from parts of animal/human/machine involves a complete breaking down of boundaries between self/other in a manner that may also be problematic for women. Irigaray, for example, argues that,

> I am certainly not seeking to wipe out multiplicity, since women's pleasure does not occur without that. But isn't a multiplicity that does not entail a rearticulation of the difference between the sexes bound to block or take away something of women's pleasure? (Irigaray, 1985b: 140)

Irigaray's concern is that sexual difference has never been thought. By thinking of the body as parts which form varied assemblages (and by also appropriating the term 'woman' in describing this deterritorialization)

Deleuze closes down the space in which real women's subjectivity could come into being.[12]

Bodies/territories

In the context of concerns about litigation relating to sexual harassment, rethinking the body cuts across a number of related issues: consideration of the body as territory; the body in relation to territory; thinking of the implications of the body/territory as images of the corporeal body; the organizational body and the body politic.

Pateman (1988) points out that women, as housewives, have had 'protection' rather than 'freedom' to sell their wage labour as a commodity. This resulted in women's territory not being their own. The 'private sphere' was never private for a woman. It was her traditional place of work and the place where a man had access to her, hence the need for 'a room of her own'. Within the paid workplace Pringle's work with secretaries (Pringle, 1989) challenges the phenomenology of public/private when she reports that a typing pool is perceived to be private compared to the office of a private secretary who is always accessible to her boss.

The relationship between women's bodies and the state is worth exploring for two reasons: first, it illustrates the ease with which appeals to 'the law' within harassment cases are construed as the need of vulnerable women's bodies for protection;[13] secondly, I want to draw out the relationship between the images of the sexed body, the organizational body and the body politic. Recent work (Brown, 1995; Gatens, 1996; Grosz, 1994) has traced the way in which one image of women's bodies, within patriarchy, is that they are fluid, without fixed boundaries. Worse, this extends to an image of women as being unable to defend their boundaries, whether this means being vulnerable to rape or to conquest. This is linked to the image of the penis as a weapon.

Gatens (1996: 49) argues for work to be carried out on the conceptual dimensions of the relationship between women's bodies and the state. An example that she uses is that 'Women's bodies historically have been seen as unfit for citizenship. Women's bodies are often likened to territories whose borders cannot be defended' (Gatens, 1996: 79). These themes are prevalent when one examines myths of origin of the state. Brown (1995) discusses how, in many disparate myths of origins, from Greek tragedians to Freud to modern social contract theorists, the creation of the state entails the subordination of women. The example she draws upon is that of Weber. Her aim is to 'map the connections between the overt masculinism of international state action (the posturing, dominating, conquering motif in such action) and the internal values and structure of state-ruled societies' (Brown, 1995: 187).

Weber has a double account of the origins of the state. In one set, the origins of the organized political institutions lie in 'men's leagues' of nomadic warriors who live off and terrorize the sedentary population. This is 'war making and state making as organized crime; the origins of politics in juvenile delinquency . . . politics as gang rape' (cited in Brown, 1995: 188), which Brown compares to international state activity. In the other set of origins, institutional authority is gained by the formation of households in which the power of the patriarch is derived from his ability to defend women against pillaging warrior leagues.

Weber's myth is interesting when compared with Deleuze and Guattari's valorization of nomadism and Battersby's suggestion that the language of the nomads or packs take the male subject as norm (Battersby, 1998). This is not to suggest that these are competing empirical accounts of the origin of the state, but that myths, like imaginary bodies, have everyday effects. It is also relevant to consider the question posed in *Spinoza: Practical Philosophy*: 'whether Man might be defined as a territory, a set of boundaries, a limit on existence'.[14]

The concept of 'becoming woman' within Deleuze and Guattari's work can also be understood in the context of this image of women's bodies. In using the term 'woman' to signify a process of becoming deterritorialized they fit too easily into a tradition which views women as subject to dissolution and disintegration; unable to defend neither the boundaries of their bodies nor the state. (The aim here is not to suggest that women should want to defend the borders of the state, nor to assume that there is anything monolithic about 'the state', but to analyse the relationship between images of the sexed body and the body politic. The corollary to this is the questioning of the naturalization of rape/sexual harassment.)

Brown's analysis of myths of origin of the state shows that they have in common a basic political deal about women:

> a deal arranged by men and executed by the state, comprising of two parts: one between men and the other between the state and each male citizen. In the first the state guarantees each man exclusive rights to his woman; hence the familiar feminist charge that rape and adultery laws historically represent less a concern for violations of women's personhood than with individual men's property over the bodies of individual women. In the second, the state agrees not to interfere with a man's family (de facto, a woman's life) as long as he is presiding over it (de facto, her). (Brown, 1995: 189)[15]

When focusing upon organizations this reference to women's position within the public/private divide appears dated. Women now have citizenship and work within the organization. There is arguably a tendency towards a break-up of the family within late capitalism. It is her subtle analysis of this contemporary position and her recognition that the state is often 'the man' in a woman's life, whether in regulating welfare benefits or giving other 'protection', that motivates Brown to urge a critique of the state.

This analysis can be used to socially situate and apply the concerns of Foucault, Butler and Marcus discussed above. Brown points out that what can be a revolutionary claim at one moment can later be transposed by the liberal state into the opposite of freedom. In this example, the 'reverse-discourse' of feminists to name and militate against 'sexual harassment' is now a way in which liberal subjects label and individualize their hurt, turning to the state, or employers in a bureaucracy, for protection. This is the protection that, in myths of the state, was offered by the patriarch within the nuclear family. Brown asks,

> Might such protection codify within the law the very powerlessness it aims to redress? Might it discursively collude with the conversion of attribute into identity, of a historical effect of power into a presumed cause of victimization? (Brown, 1995: 21)

It is only when patriarchal images of women appear unchallengeable that the concern for freedom gives way to concern for protection. This is Marcus's assumption in focusing upon the time of injury rather than this double-edged 'protection'.

Interestingly, Brown refers to 'power' in a way which resonates with Deleuze's focus on the body as a set of relations and capacities. In keeping with this re-evaluation of the body is a re-evaluation of practice to theory. Theory does not dictate practice, as in, for example, the work of Althusser. Deleuze illustrates this by pointing to Foucault's involvement with the Prison Information Group. There was a moment when Foucault was unable to theorize further on prisoners without speaking for them. The only way through this wall/blockage was by acting. This image of action being a line between two theoretical positions and conversely theory being the line between two actions illustrates the anti-dialectical nature of Deleuze's thought. There is no coming together of theory and practice but a movement between the two (Deleuze and Foucault, 1977).[16]

This stress on embodied knowledge implies that there cannot be a definite strategy which is dictated by theory. As Foucault put it, 'The guarantee of freedom is freedom' (Foucault, 1986: 245). It must be practised. As Brown, whose view of power has more in common with Deleuze, argues,

> Particularly for those whose identities have been shaped inter alia through dependence, shame, submissiveness, violation, helplessness, or inferiority, breaking those codes can spring loose latent capacities and generate powerful resistance to domination . . . More recent history suggests that legally and politically codifying justice as matters of protection, prosecution and regulation tends to turn us away from 'practising' freedom . . . (Brown, 1995: 21)

> Whether one is dealing with employers, the state, the Mafia, parents, police, pimps or husbands the heavy price of institutionalized protection is always a measure of dependence and agreement to abide by the protector's rules. (Brown, 1995: 169)

This chapter should not be read as a call to abandon such legal rights as women have managed to secure to enforce dignity wherever they work. Nevertheless, it is important to question the law's assumption that women are naturally vulnerable to sexual harassment; its construction of the penis as a weapon. This construction resonates too easily with the images of women's bodies utilized within various myths of the origin of the state. It perpetuates an image of women's bodies as being 'dissolute' in comparison to the 'integrity' of male bodily boundaries. This should be recognized as a cultural phenomenon that is far from fixed. As Spinoza points out, 'we do not know what a body can do'. There needs to be a 'double vision' in which women both fight for short-term legal rights whilst still holding on to more 'utopian' ideals – along with concern when the former undercuts the latter. In this case, the utopian ideal is not simply that women can protect themselves. It keeps open the possibility of a culture in which the term 'sexual harassment', so usefully deployed by consciousness-raising groups, no longer makes sense.

Notes

1 *Strathclyde Regional Council* v *Porcelli* 1986 (IRLR 134).

2 Particularly interesting is that of Drucilla Cornell, who argues for the adoption of: '(a) unilaterally imposed sexual requirements in the context of unequal power, or (b) the creation and perpetuation of a work environment which enforces sexual shame by reducing individuals to projected stereotypes or objectified fantasies of their "sex" so as to undermine the primary good of self respect, or (c) employment-related retaliation against a subordinate employee, or in the case of a university, a student, for a consensually mutually desired sexual relationship.' This avoids the problems of heterosexism and of focusing upon the judgement of the victim, which easily gives way to the male fantasy of good/bad girls (Cornell, 1995: 170).

3 With regard to rape trials (Smart, 1989).

4 Contemporaneous notes are admissible as evidence. They are still classified as 'contemporaneous' if taken shortly after the event.

5 A point made by Smart (1989); I am relying upon my own experience as a trade union solicitor.

6 For a more detailed discussion, see Richardson (1998).

7 *Ethics* III, 2 (and II,13, schol.), cited Deleuze, 1988: 18. Emphasis in original.

8 Deleuze, 1988: 12; he returns to this theme in Deleuze and Guattari, 1992: 253. This prefigures a number of themes in '1730 Becoming-Intense, Becoming-Animal, Becoming-Imperceptible', such as the reference to girls in terms of speeds and slowness (p. 271); becoming music (p. 299) in Deleuze and Guattari, 1992.

9 'We have only said two things against psychoanalysis: that it breaks up all productions of desire and crushes all formations of utterances' (Deleuze and Parnet, 1987: 77); for their attack on psychoanalysis, see Deleuze and Guattari, 1984.

10 Tancred-Sheriff argued that secretaries can be grouped with receptionists, sales women and airline stewardesses as 'adjunct workers'. She points out that in late capitalism there is a greater distance than previously between employers and employees and between producers and consumers, whose behaviour they wish to control. This 'organizational space' is filled by workers who participate in the authority of management (by enforcing the rules and showing people how to behave within the organization) but who do not make up the rules. She argues that this

work becomes sexualized because the management try to use 'sexually attractive women' within the role.

11 My thanks to David Kelly for this point.

12 Irigaray's argument is complex and deserves more space than is available here.

13 Within the context of EU legislation it has been pragmatic to push for sexual harassment legislation as being classified as a health and safety issue. This is because the UK government has used their veto to block employee protection, wherever possible. Only the health and safety legislation could be passed on a majority vote. Whilst this clearly is a health and safety issue in that the stress of harassment affects women's health, this relies upon and reinforces the image of the penis as weapon.

14 Hurley (1988). In the context 'Man' appears to be being used as universal rather than, as would have been appropriate, 'man'.

15 For the seminal analysis of the hidden sexual contract within the work of the social contract theorists, see Pateman, 1988.

16 For a discussion of this in the context of feminist legal theory, see Bottomley and Conaghan, 1993.

References

Battersby, C. (1998) *The Phenomenal Woman: Feminist Metaphysics and the Patterns of Identity*. Cambridge: Polity.

Benhabib, S., Butler, J., Cornell, D. and Fraser, N. (1995) *Feminist Contentions: A Philosophical Exchange*. London: Routledge.

Bottomley, A. and Conaghan, J. (1993) *Feminist Theory and Legal Strategy*. Oxford: Blackwell.

Brown, W. (1995) *States of Injury: Power and Freedom in Late Modernity*. Chichester: Princeton University Press.

Brownmiller, S. (1975) *Against Our Will: Men, Women and Rape*. New York: Simon and Schuster.

Butler, J. (1990) *Gender Trouble: Feminism and the Subversion of Identity*. London: Routledge.

Butler, J. (1993) *Bodies that Matter: The Discursive Limits of 'Sex'*. London: Routledge.

Cornell, D. (1995) *The Imaginary Domain: Abortion, Pornography and Sexual Harassment*. London: Routledge.

Deleuze, G. (1988) *Spinoza: Practical Philosophy*. San Francisco: City Light Books.

Deleuze, G. (1990) *Negotiations*. New York: Columbia University Press.

Deleuze, G. and Foucault, M. (1977) 'Intellectuals and power', in M. Foucault, *Language, Counter-Memory, Practice*. Oxford: Blackwell. pp. 205–17.

Deleuze, G. and Guattari, F. (1984) *Anti-Oedipus: Capitalism and Schizophrenia*. London: Athlone Press.

Deleuze, G. and Guattari, F. (1992) *A Thousand Plateaus: Capitalism and Schizophrenia*. London: Athlone Press.

Deleuze, G. and Parnet, C. (1987) *Dialogues*. London: Athlone Press.

Diamond, I. and Quinby, L. (1988) *Feminism and Foucault*. Boston: Northeastern University Press.

Farley, L. (1978) *Sexual Shakedown*. London: Melbourne House Publishers Ltd.

Foucault, M. (1978) *History of Sexuality: Volume One*. London: Penguin.

Foucault, M. (1986) 'Space, knowledge and power', in P. Rabinow (ed.), *The Foucault Reader*. London: Peregrine. pp. 239–56.

Foucault, M. (1988) 'Confinement, psychiatry, prison', in L.D. Kritzman (ed.), *Michel Foucault – Politics, Philosophy, Culture: Interviews and Other Writings 1977–1984*. London: Routledge. pp. 178–210.

Gatens, M. (1996) *Imaginary Bodies: Ethics, Power and Corporeality*. London: Routledge.

Grosz, E. (1994) *Volatile Bodies: Towards a Corporeal Feminism*. Bloomington and Indianapolis: University of Indiana Press.

Hartsock, N. (1990) 'Foucault on power: a theory for women?', in L. Nicholson (ed.), *Feminism/Postmodernism*. London: Routledge. pp. 157–75.

Hurley, R. (1988) 'Preface', in G. Deleuze, *Spinoza: Practical Philosophy*. San Francisco: City Light Books. pp. i–iii.

Irigaray, L. (1985a) *Speculum of the Other Woman*. Ithaca, NY: Cornell University Press.

Irigaray, L. (1985b) *This Sex Which Is Not One*. Ithaca, NY: Cornell University Press.

MacKinnon, C.A. (1979) *Sexual Harassment of Working Women*. New Haven, CT: Yale University Press.

Marcus, S. (1992) 'Fighting bodies, fighting words: a theory and politics of rape prevention', in J. Butler and J. Scott (eds), *Feminists Theorize the Political*. London: Routledge. pp. 385–403.

Pateman, C. (1988) *The Sexual Contract*. Cambridge: Polity Press.

Pringle, R. (1989) *Secretaries Talk: Sexuality, Power and Work*. London: Verso.

Richardson, J. (1998) 'Jamming the machines: "woman" in the work of Irigaray and Deleuze', *Law and Critique*, IX (1): 89–115.

Rubenstein, M. (1988) *The Dignity of Women at Work*. Luxembourg: Office of the European Community.

Smart, C. (1989) *Feminism and the Power of the Law*. London: Routledge.

Tancred-Sheriff, P. (1989) 'Gender, sexuality and the labour process', in J. Hearn, D. Shepard, P. Tancred-Sheriff and G. Burrell (eds), *The Sexuality of Organizations*. London: Sage.

12 Body Work: Estrangement, Disembodiment and the Organizational 'Other'

Deborah Kerfoot

This chapter focuses on managerial work, men and masculinity and the interconnections between masculinity and 'being a manager'. My concern is to engage with and contribute to a growing literature on masculinity that seeks critically to interrogate the experience not just of 'being a manager', but also of 'being a man' in contemporary organizational life. Academic commentators have oft sought to explore managerial work from a perspective that sets a challenge to the predominant wisdom of management thinking and teaching in Anglo/American contexts over the past few decades. Frequently mechanistic and hierarchical in its view of the management of organizations of all persuasions, they argue, the traditional conception of organization and its practices has conventionally assumed direct correspondence between managerial decisions and events. Rational decision-making and its expression in planning and policy formulation has most often been seen as separate from and unhindered by the dynamics of the organization. One key interest, now a well-established critique amongst organization theorists, has been to overturn the conventional notion that managerial outcomes can easily be 'read-off' as the dictates of managers; has questioned the whole notion of management per se as a rational, purely analytic, process. Likewise, the socially constructed nature of management power and authority has been amply demonstrated, and the possibilities for change and resistance widely developed. As a component of and central to these debates, managers themselves thence become open to a form of analysis that calls into question their whole *raison d'être* as architects of organizations founded upon and sustained by principles of rationality.

With some notable exceptions (see, for example, Collinson and Hearn, 1994, 1996; Kerfoot and Knights, 1993, 1995; Roper, 1994), few such commentators have sought to look at the 'man' in management, leaving unproblematic the issue of gender even amongst studies whose theoretical focus has turned upon questions of subjectivity, self and identity *vis à vis* management and organization. Seldom has it been recognized that managers are most often men, and that the trend for masculinity to retain a hold on positions of seniority in institutions appears unabated (Calas and Smircich,

1993; Collinson and Hearn, 1996; Institute of Management, 1995). Yet in the day-to-day running of organizations, managers are clearly 'living out' particular gender identities – as men, and as masculine – alongside their identity as manager (Roper, 1994; see also Kerfoot and Whitehead, 1998 for elaboration). Accordingly, a concern in this chapter is to focus upon masculinity as a powerful discourse and to highlight some of its effects in organizations, emphasizing the (inter)subjective processes that constitute a sense of identity for managers. The theoretical framework for the chapter draws on feminist and poststructuralist scholarship (for example, Butler, 1990; McNay, 1992; Nicholson and Seidman, 1996). Informed by the work of Foucault (1977, 1988) and his understanding of identity, subjectivity and the discursive production of identity, the chapter discusses embodiment and estrangement in management – the 'feel' of how it is to be a manager.

Why is the body relevant to a discussion of management? The issue of the body in managerial work and the questions that surround its presence, in terms both of the organization and for individuals, is clearly pertinent. For, as described below, the need for managers themselves to be attentive to the body and aware of its perception by others is perhaps as never before, and where the gaze of the 'other' in organizations is intensified by discourses of managerialism. At all times, managers must be concerned with the effort to prove that they, as managerial bodies, are trustworthy and reliable; for, in the accomplishment of managing their own body, managers display the ability to manage others. By first identifying, and thence occupying, privileged bodily designations, the mark of a 'competent' manager is, foremost, their ability to display the body in a manner that is culturally acceptable to their organization's bodily code. Consequently, the oft-quoted phrase in discussions of organizational culture 'the way we do things round here' takes a new turn of emphasis, acquiring a significance beyond a mere colloquial descriptor of organizational values and procedures. Most obviously this might relate to dress and the physical appearance of the body *vis à vis* codes of behaviour. It could equally relate to size, age, ability and disability, colour and, of course, gender.

In contemporary organizations, it has been suggested that conventional management practices are being supplanted by new means of managing (Farnham and Horton, 1996; du Gay and Salaman, 1992; Wilkinson and Willmott, 1995). In brief, the concern for service quality, flexibility, internal markets and perceived increase in profitability and output performance to be had from, for example, team structures has focused management's attention not only on the structure of organizations directly and their staffing, but also on the skills and abilities of management. Whilst there is plainly a well-justified concern in some quarters for the employment conditions and prospects of hierarchically subordinate staffs, not least in terms of their immediate job prospects and conditions of work, there is also interest in the question surrounding management's potential to 'gear up' to the demands now being made upon them.

No longer is it possible for the modern manager to rely on the hierarchical distance of his [*sic*] position in the company to shield him from dissenting staffs or difficult situations in the day-to-day vagaries of his work. The formal erosion of bureaucratic hierarchies and the concomitant 'exposure' of many managers to their staffs has arguably left managements ill-equipped to deal with the demands of running an organization. Insofar as certain aspects of managerial work turn upon, by definition, the ability to control and coordinate others and their labour, this structural shift – most notably from manufacturing to service industries – and the accompanying trend in attempts to rein in the creative potential of labour, has rendered managerial work at once pivotal yet precarious. Pivotal, in that the output from such organizations depends in large part on management's ability, in theory at least, to communicate with, rather than dictate to, subordinates. This in a manner that demands more sophisticated means of control and direction other than through the traditional impersonal hierarchical chain of command. In this respect, the pressure on (most often middle) managers to deliver the required output is arguably greater than before. Precarious, in that the new-found potential of employees lies in precisely the uncertainty, instability and unpredictability of human relations that managements might otherwise seek to suppress. Calls to 'humanize' managers, through company sponsored events designed to reduce status barriers, social skills training packages, or promoting more women into management, point to a perceived need for those in managerial work *to engage with* rather than dictate to, subordinates, in the fullest sense.

The chapter is prompted by questions born of my being 'around' managers, almost always male, as a woman and a non-manager. Over several years' interviewing, observing, teaching, researching and working with managers in the public and private sectors, I have been struck not least by the manner in which many managers attempt to present themselves, in their own and in organizational terms. It seems little more than a self-evident truism that managers should be concerned with the results of their expertise and of the ventures they manage, and with demonstrating their abilities to others. But beyond this, and however defined, one common feature extends beyond mere ability to deal with everyday technical organizational complexity. Rather, the issue has been one of defining success, and of being 'on top of' things; mastering something over and above merely executing it competently. Many managers have been concerned to demonstrate their 'mastery', to appear always in control of situations and interactions, even where circumstances dictate that this could not possibly be the case. Flowing from this, an additional, related, dimension of many managers' understanding of success has revolved around their own autonomy. Managers are often concerned to play down their links with others, and managerial work is characterized by being at once dependent upon others and at the same time distant from them, hierarchically, symbolically and, frequently, physically.

In another context, Roper (1994) alludes to the phenomenon in describing his experience of researching men managers, being struck 'by the confidence they radiated, by their articulacy, and by their ability to fashion a story with the autonomous "I" at its centre' (1994: v). Even off-duty, many managers are often alarmingly purposive and outcome-orientated, to the point of scrutinizing each and every moment, and every social interaction or engagement, for its productive possibilities. Yet in so doing, and without realizing it, this 'mentality of the end result' overlooks the fine grain detail that could produce a far richer understanding. Constantly looking beyond the subtleties or nuances of situations and human interaction in an attempt to find 'the point', such individuals miss out on possibilities that might be generated by seeing a 'whole picture' – possibilities not only in terms of organizational outcomes but as more full life experiences amongst those around them. Seemingly unable or unwilling to connect with others and with the world in non-instrumental fashion, managerial work appears to support, reinforce and normalize a series of distorted relationships.

Yet, although concerned to hone their presentation of themselves as autonomous and successful, the personal narratives of managers often reveal a more complex reality. For in order to maintain their position and identity within the organization, they must constantly be attentive to their language, movements and physical presentation. Working hard to manage the contradiction of their work situation and the tensions so generated, these men juggle multiple identities in their own organizational arena. The following section elaborates further on issues of managerial and masculine identity.

Body, experience and identity

The emphasis on the discursive production of identity has been called into question by those theorists who take issue with what is held to be its concomitant denial of a political base. Poststructuralist theorizing, they argue, denies not only the possibility of a common base from which a collective politics might be mobilized, but also negates the very truth of men's and women's experiences by rendering all aspects of identity as mere by-products of discourse. The logic of poststructuralist theorizing, so the argument goes, is that we can no longer 'trust our own bodies' and our knowledge of who we are as people; our felt experience as sentient beings is reduced to the status of a residual category, and the very corporeality of the body is thus negated. For many feminists in particular, the body and its history both carries a political dimension and is a political statement. It should come as no surprise, therefore, that some of the harshest criticism might emanate from feminist quarters. Yet equally, others have sought to raid poststructuralism of whatever insights it can offer. Elam (1994), for example, argues for a return to poststructuralism by feminists, sketching the profile of a poststructuralist feminism that retains a clear and defined hold on the political. Following Butler (1990), the purpose of critical inquiry must be to deconstruct the very mechanisms of discourse in order to show how gender is produced; how the body, and its association with particular expressions and practices of gender signification, is maintained. Butler, therefore, takes us beyond gender, to sex and to the 'core' of the body. For her, gender identity is an outcome of politics rather than its foundation.

Such questions are no mere sideshow in either empirical or theoretical work, nor for the study of management. They offer a way of addressing, for many men and women in organizations, the very real issue of themselves as embodied subjects and as managers. They enable us to begin to build a knowledge of organizations, management and managerial processes that recognizes the effects, at the level of the body, of contemporary manage-ment practices. Managers themselves are surely seldom so naive as to imagine that organizations are benign entities or that management is merely their rational expression. As has been intimated, many managers now find themselves subjected to, and subjects of, employment regimes that in a previous era would be unthinkable, in private and public sectors alike. Called upon to deliver, often by whatever means, the desired outcomes that flow, for example, from market-orientated discourses of total quality management, corporate culture programmes and human resource manage-ment, managers are daily exposed to discursive regimes that call for con-tinual constitution and reconstitution of the body. Examples of this required fluidity of the body are clearly present in a number of empirical sites; presentations of the (managerial) body include the need to display 'entrepreneurialism', 'risk taking' and 'competitiveness', even in those organizations where this language has been historically alien. In conse-quence, the body becomes a project, to be fashioned and refashioned amid different managerial discourses. In this respect, bodies are the 'raw material' of organization.

Acknowledging the body and its presentation as fluid is, equally, to state a political position. One that provides for an alternative knowledge of management, not as grounded in and radiating from the body, nor as imposed upon bodies from above, but that recognizes the body as a valid category at the level of embodied experience. Clearly, talk of (re)claiming experience has a particular resonance for those who, in other contexts, have argued that the concept of experience is itself problematic:

> For those outside mainstream feminism, 'women's experience' has never ceased to be problematic. The common ground of sisterhood, long held as white feminism's ideal, was always a more utopian than representative slogan. Worse, it was coercive in its unacknowledged universalism, its unrecognized exclusions. (Weed, 1989: xxiv)

Similarly, Elam (1994), whilst retaining the notion of experience, warns of the impasse to be had in its conflation with explanantion. Qualifying the use of the term, she signals experience as an, albeit muted, form of knowledge, suggesting that there is 'a politics to the invocation of experience' (1994: 66). Elsewhere, McNay (1992) draws on Foucault's later works in her exploration of what are referred to as 'practices of self'. Encompassing the experience of the body, the emphasis on discourse and practice forces us to consider discourse as enabling subjects to understand their own reality, McNay, at one and the same time, retains 'a feel' for embodiment. Plainly, discourses – of managerialism and of masculinity – have a material effect, an 'objective actuality' (Ransom, 1993) in the organization and for individuals. Gender is at once 'both an organizing principle and an organizational outcome' (Gherardi, 1995: 185).

Likewise, the subject positions of man and woman carry a political dimension. Both women and men engage with 'the social reality of male privilege' (Clatterbaugh, 1990: 154), albeit in very differing ways: to be a man manager conveys an authority and status most often denied to all but a few women managers. Management clearly privileges certain knowledges over and above others, but these knowledges are not solely related to the means of running an enterprise. Given the gender dynamics in most organizations, discourses of masculinity speak a gendered language, and also privilege certain bodies – usually male. By way of developing this point, the following section elaborates further on masculinity and the relationship of masculinity to the dynamics of organizations.

Masculinity, organization and the body

In 'modern' Western cultures over the past three decades in particular, the concept of masculinity has aroused significant interest in a variety of quarters. From academic investigations of various persuasions to media and populist stereotypes, the discourses surrounding men and masculinity have proliferated to the point of informing common sense talk of 'a crisis in masculinity' in the late 1990s. As an arena for academic investigation, the concern has, in large part, been to explore masculinity as a social rather than a biological construct. The field of investigation has served to render masculinity problematic and has, for example, extended from early studies of men's narrative (Tolson, 1977) to masculinities in organizational life (Collinson and Hearn, 1996). Similarly, others have sought to document the diversity and multiplicity of masculinities as a means of moving away from simplistic categories of 'masculine' and 'feminine' (see, for example, Connell, 1995). Accepting masculinity as social construct has forced consideration of the historical context of gender relations (Kimmel, 1987) and acknowledgement that 'what it means to be a man' will shift according to time, place or space, and within the lifetime of individuals (see Roper and Tosh, 1991). In their concern to escape the impasse of biological determinism, commentators have increasingly come to recognize that attempts to 'fix' masculinity also deny or downplay questions of difference and self-identity amongst men. Moreover, further acknowledging this multiplicity of masculinities (also Brod and Kaufmann, 1994), some writers have been concerned to identify archetypes of masculinity in a variety of social and organizational locales (Fuller, 1996; Mills, 1998); to identify differences between men and between masculinities (Collinson and Hearn, 1994); and to locate the specific practices of masculinity and its discursive constitution in particular sites and across social institutions (Barrett, 1996; Kerfoot and Knights, 1993).

The work of Carrigan, Connell and Lee (1985) has, since its early incarnation as an investigation of the actions and behaviours of men, been used extensively in the theoretical and empirical elaboration of masculinity. What they referred to, in its earliest reference, as 'hegemonic masculinity' has come to inform an escalating number of studies concerned to explore men's behaviour in a variety of settings, frequently in relation to men's sexuality and the preponderance of institutionalized heterosexuality. Likewise, the social phenomenon of men's dominance has increasingly been examined by reference to hegemonic masculinity, both in its empirical and theoretical usages. As by what is now a shorthand for certain (pre)dominant expressions of manliness, hegemonic masculinity has assumed a status as perhaps the single, most widely used concept in the study of men and masculinity. In this regard, the concept of hegemonic masculinity has itself achieved a near-hegemony in investigations of men's behaviour, even beyond the confines of sociological inquiry (Kerfoot and Whitehead, 1998).

Whilst men's behaviours may most obviously exhibit hegemonic characteristics, in that they are elevated and privileged as influential at any one time or place as *the* behaviours governing success in any given environment, the concept of hegemonic masculinity remains problematic. In both public and private sectors, the observation that some women, in addition to many men, can be found in management positions forces reconsideration of the concept of hegemonic masculinity and its explanatory potential. For it is evident that some women, in much the same manner as their male colleagues, act out the behaviours and bodily displays associated with hegemonic masculinity and are equally as competitive, aggressive, instrumental and as 'masculine' in their orientation. In that organizations have themselves been described as masculine enterprises (Connell, 1995), perhaps it should come as no surprise that women are subjected to, and subjects of, this dominant and privileged way of being amid cultures of entrepreneurialism that deny other means of expression.

Attempting to illuminate further the organizational conditions that sustain such cultures and their associated behaviours, whilst simultaneously recognizing that hegemonic masculinity can extend likewise to women and their behaviour, the concept of the masculine subject has been developed elsewhere (Kerfoot and Whitehead, 1998). Masculinity then, in this respect, exists merely as a way of being: the term encapsulating privileged ways of, most often, men expressing their sense of 'what it is to be a man' in a given spatial and temporal location (Kerfoot and Whitehead, 1998). Following from this, masculinity is inevitably precarious and subject to disruption even though its outward displays and bodily presentation may belie the experience of contradiction or uncertainty.

Consequently, masculine subjects exist in ambivalent relationship to the body, wherein the body is at once an enterprise, as much as any corporate entity, to be honed, regulated and 'occupied' as a matter of personal conquest. As such, masculine subjects exist in instrumental, if at times ambivalent, relationship with the body, ever concerned to attune their presentation of themselves in order to appear 'in touch' with the needs and requirements of the organization if not those of their own emotions. Having 'no recourse to a body that has not always already been interpreted by cultural meanings' (Butler, 1990: 8), masculine subjects must be mindful of the need to 'keep one step ahead' in whatever managerial and organizational discourses are the vogue. Ever watchful of shifting demands, masculine subjects must continually move within and between bodily displays at a moment's notice amid the uncontrollable dynamics of organizations, further sustaining the conditions of their own disembodiment.

Privileging rational forms of knowledge and instrumentality as a way of being in the world, masculinity is defined in opposition to the 'other' that is outside of itself, principally to alternative or subordinated ways of being such as are represented by gay men, or by women as 'the feminine'. This point is pursued below.

Masculinity and the other

As Hollway (1996) suggests, the concept of the other has achieved significant status in critical theory of various persuasions, particularly in psychoanalysis. Concerns with the other in psychoanalytic theory refer to the development of self, where the other exists in relation to – and in opposition to – the self of an individual. The work of Lacan (1977) has, most obviously, proved central to the development of studies in the field of self and identity, spawning inumerable avenues of debate concerned with understanding 'woman', 'the feminine' and 'the other' (see, for example, Bracher, 1993: 83–137).

In brief, Lacanian psychoanalysis presupposes the development of human subjectivity to be shaped by structuralist conceptions of language. Lacan's purpose is to assert 'self-consciousness' as occurring at the point at which the human infant recognizes its emerging separation from the other, and where patriarchal rule replaces unity of the child with its mother. Upon entry to the symbolic domain of language, the child learns of the domination of the phallus, where 'woman' is absent (see Fraser, 1992 for discussion). Similarly, in object-relations theory, men are seen to dominate and desire women largely because of the possibilities this offers for a return to this imaginary childhood bond of mother and infant (see, for example, Chodorow, 1978). Broadly, woman and the other is men's fantasy in attempting to revisit the symbolic unity and fulfilment of early life. In this respect, disengagement from the mother in an effort to secure a separate identity leads to difficulty, insofar as it provokes anxiety and sustains defence mechanisms – setting off the 'good' against the 'bad', masculine against feminine – which are themselves counterproductive to the formation of a secure and stable identity. From this perspective, the public and private oppression of women is reducible to a single point in that it is seen to stem from men's need to buttress masculine identity. Leaving aside the reductionism inherent in object-relations theory and the essentialism of Lacanian psychoanalysis in which the phallus appears ontologically prior in the symbolic order (see Kerfoot and Knights, 1994 for elaboration), the concept of the 'other' developed in pychoanalysis remains useful. Developed to good end by feminists, although most often in the limiting context of discussions of patriarchal dominance, it at least allows for the possibility of recognizing the difference between woman, as embodied flesh, and 'woman' as a category produced in discourse; allowing the separation of woman as signifier in language from real women (see Frosh, 1987 for elaboration) for purposes of critical interrogation. Consequently, woman is not only separate from the discursive category that bears her name, but moreover is distinct from and distinguished by her/its relationship to men/masculinity. In sum, despite its methodological and empirical injunction to a categorical conception of masculinity (also Roper, 1994), such theorizing enables the development of a means of studying the 'other', of whatever persuasion, in work institutions, their organization and their management.

For Lacan, 'woman' is the 'other' of masculine desire, for it occupies the place of that which is missing or absent in self. Woman, as a discursive category, cannot be conceptualized other than as that which is always outside of and beyond mere biological flesh. Expressed, and experienced, as a 'lack of', woman and the feminine is thus the missing piece of the identity jigsaw puzzle that might facilitate fulfilment of a whole self. Our discomfort in our identity (who we are as people) and in the project of our identity formation, is thus accounted for by the search for this closure of identity that might be resolved through achieving the unity of self with other. But this is self-evidently problematic since the other can never be fully captured in such a manner as to facilitate a secure identity. Subjects can retain no hold on discourse other than in mere momentary passing. Moreover, what counts as 'real' at any one point differs in alternative physical, spatial and temporal settings. Consequently, the secure identity of a whole self can never be reached. For many men this most obviously translates into denial or suppression of the feminine, in themselves and of others around them in organizational contexts as elsewhere. The masculinity of groups of male shop-floor workers in, for example, Collinson's (1992) study can be read as an example of managing the discontinuity between everyday lived experiences of 'men's work' and its stereotypical ideal in masculine imagery. The men in Collinson's factory achieve a kind of bargain, controlling the unknown, elusive and indefinable other through the negation of women and the feminine. Likewise, the managers in Watson's (1994) investigation of a telecommunications products company are made uneasy by the presence of female managers. In a manner communicable to the women, these man managers reconstitute an image of themselves as protecting and caring for women, whilst at the same time denigrating women's contribution to the management of the company. As Hollway (1996: 29) expresses it:

> depending on their anxieties, defences and statuses, men project parts of them-
> selves on to others of different categories, in order to experience themselves as
> living up to a masculine ideal. In this theoretical context, mastery over self can be
> understood as working, not just through rational processes, but through
> projecting unwelcome parts onto others. In this way, men 'master themselves',
> bringing themselves into line with whatever they regard as acceptable ways of
> being men.

As has been alluded to, women may also exhibit masculine behaviours: for this reason the concept of the masculine subject is useful in allowing an escape from gender essentialism and returning us to 'the very signifying practices that establish, regulate and deregulate identity' (Butler, 1990: 147). None the less, far from disallowing the potential of theorizing on the 'other', the concept of the masculine subject enables discussion of those (masculine) subjects, both male and female, who are preoccupied with a particular mode of being defined here as masculinity. That said, my concern in this chapter is more with the social rather than the psychic dimensions of masculinity, and with the relationship between masculine subjects and the body in a given context, that of managerial work. Elsewhere (Kerfoot and Knights, 1996), I have argued that the specific conditions of managerial work and their association with masculinity aggravate and exacerbate the potential for self-estrangement and disembodiment. The following section develops aspects of this work in relation to the body and delineates some key areas argued to be problematic for the managerial body.

Embodiment and estrangement

Masculine subjects invest themselves predominantly in practices of gender signification that, at any one time, reinforce what it is to be a successful manager, however problematic and anxiety-provoking is its lived experience. Yet the search for a secure gender identity renders masculine subjects self-estranged and disembodied as a result of the preoccupation with their own externally assessed competence and associated definitions of status, success and target-setting (Kerfoot and Knights, 1996). Moreover, in its pursuit of instrumental objectives, most notably towards others and to themselves, their self-estrangement is made all the more so for lack of reflexivity. Constantly concerned with the perceptions of others, such indi-viduals seek to judge and prejudge their actions and those of people around them in terms of how they might be regarded by others. Decisions become instances of how speedily, accurately and effectively one might appear to be 'in tune' with predominant discourse in an organization. Preoccupied by the concern for 'how it's seen', managers often seek to control their personal presentations of themselves, in dress, manner, appearance and language and in their actions and practices. Similarly, in their use of predominant organizational expressions of competence – not least in demonstrating their own self-competence – many managers often willingly but unwittingly reinforce the very discourses that exacerbate their own estrangement. Returning to Watson's study referred to above, he comments:

> I criticized one male manager for hurting the feelings of a woman colleague to whom he had joked, 'Having an early night?' as she left her office at 7.15 pm one evening . . .
> 'Look at me what a big tough guy I am. Look at the long hours I can put in.'
> 'But you do it?'
> 'Pathetic isn't it?' (1994: 201–2)

Although Watson's concern lies outside the academic study of masculinity, his work signals further the unreflective estrangement that leaves his interviewees lacking in the emotional energy needed to question what they are doing other than at a surface level. Many had rationalized the situation both for themselves and for their families, even in their more intimate relations:

> 'The wife knows that if I don't turn up at seven o'clock, I will turn up when I turn up. It doesn't become a major family issue.' (manager, Watson, 1994: 202)

Most obviously, masculine discourses reinforce instrumentality as subjects attempt to control social relations as a way of managing the experience of disembodiment and self-estrangement (Kerfoot and Knights, 1996: 89–92). For, in their efforts to stabilize the unpredictability of human interaction, masculinity and management practice transform all relations into instances of instrumental control. But social relations are neither sufficiently predictable nor stable as to render them commensurate with masculine designs. Hence, the control that is so desired is at once further out of reach, and yet all the more desirable for being so. Plainly, some will 'manage' the experience better than others; some will safeguard their position by denying or downplaying their emotions or their emotional and more intimate links with others (Kerfoot, 1999). Furthermore, the struggle to appear to be competent is made more potent by the need to disguise the fact that it is a struggle for many masculine subjects. Some succeed and others fail where 'success' is experienced, in part at least, as the control of the body and its outward display, and in the control of emotions and of their physical expression.

Flowing from this, an additional point relates to the silence that surrounds masculinity, estrangement and the experience of the body. In a work of fiction, Tom Wolfe's main character describes the phenomenon:

> . . . herein the world was divided into those who had it and those who did not. This quality, this **it**, was never named, however, nor was it talked about in any way. . . There was instead, a seemingly infinite series of tests. A career in [management] was like climbing up one of those ancient Babylonian pyramids made up of a dizzy progression of steps and ledges, a ziggurat, a pyramid extraordinarily high and steep; and the idea was to prove at every foot of the way up that pyramid that you were one of the elected and annointed ones who had **the right stuff** and could move higher and higher and even – ultimately, God willing, one day – that you might be able to join that few at the very top, that elite who had the capacity to bring tears to men's eyes, the very Brotherhood of the Right Stuff itself.
>
> None of this was to be mentioned, and yet it was acted out in a way that a young man could not fail to understand. . . Why, it seemed to be nothing less than **manhood** itself. Naturally, this was never mentioned, either. Yet there it was. **Manliness, manhood, manly courage** . . . (Wolfe, 1973: emphases in original)

Although in his original text, the novelist is speaking of pilots and of flying, the above selection and its narrative is relevant to the discussion of the body, its feel and its presentation to others. For the 'it' that is never named finds resonances in managerial work and for managers who invest time and bodily resources in apeing its central tenets. Constantly reminded of the requirement to be alert to the attentions of others, managers must likewise be aware of the need to conceal such efforts and maintain the silence that surrounds their performance. Experience of stress, of weakness and of failure must at all times be hidden, passed off as something other than the lived experience of discomfort and discontinuity with their organizational surroundings and its demands. Whilst silence can be drawn upon to sustain the outward appearance of competence, as one of a range of bodily and linguistic devices in the managerial armoury, it can equally reflect feelings of anxiety. Speaking of what they refer to as the 'silence and din' of organizations, Harlow et al. (1995) allude to the ambivalence of silence in organizations, where silence is, at times, a corrosive phenomenon; a defensive mechanism; a weapon against marginal groups or outsiders; a put down of others. Standing in opposition to the imagery of the 'lone hero', charismatic leader or maverick in management, this understanding of silence and its relationship to the body forces us to reconsider managerial work and those subjects who occupy its designation as, at best, in positions of precarious collegiality, and at worst, as figures of extreme isolation.

Signalling the ambiguous and ambivalent relationship of the managerial body, not least to itself, leads further to exploring other aspects of the experience of managing. If managerial work, either by definition or design, can provoke and exacerbate disembodiment and estrangement, a question arises as to why those engaged in its practices might collude in maintaining such an obvious instrument of their own anxiety. Momentarily leaving aside self-evident material concerns, employment stability and related career matters, an answer lies in one of the very conditions that makes managerial work uncertain and unstable – yet attractive – to many managers in the first place. For management activity offers the tantalizing possibility of taming the unknown 'other', either through direct relations with hierarchical subordinates or commanding the impersonal dictates of the market by whatever managerial fad or fashion is currently 'sexy' [*sic*]. The 'feel' of managing then, may equally be at once both isolating in its demands, but enlivening in its sexualized possibilities. This sexuality relates not just to the institutionalized heterosexuality that has been referred to in the above discussion of masculinity. It equally relates to the psychic charge and social cachet to be had from 'success' in managerial work. Many managers describe what they commonly refer to as the 'buzz' or the 'kick' to be had from their work and in the feeling of mastery that it, at times, offers. Consequently, the very uncertainty sustaining managerial insecurity can equally be a source of particularized pleasures. In their descriptions of the power they wield, real or imaginary, managerial narratives are frequently suffused with an eroticized expression that belies the reality or mundaneity of the task to hand. The experience of successfully 'managing' and its feel is at one and the same time as sexually charged as it is dangerous, not least because of its status as precarious and fleeting. In this respect, 'woman' as the other is of less significance than the unknown other of one's fellow men. Whilst heterosexuality may be brought into the service of management (Collinson and Hearn, 1996) and incorporated into management practices, 'Work is constitutive of masculinity, and gratification of this sexuality can only come from other men' (Gherardi, 1995: 52). Arguably, managerial work is thus generative of its own, internally fuelled momentum.

Summary and conclusion

This chapter has been concerned to engage with and contribute to the growing area of academic investigation surrounding the interconnections between men, masculinity and managerial work. My particular interest has been critically to interrogate masculinity in relation to the body and organization in the context of management. Masculinity, in whatever form or manifestation, is taken to be an outcome of the interplay between discourses and the intersubjective dynamics of organization rather than a fixed or biological essence of individuals. By way of developing the concept of masculinity, and of furthering its investigation beyond biologically grounded gender dualisms of 'masculine' and 'feminine', masculinity is here theorized in relation to subjectivity and identity. As a discursively constituted mode of being, masculinity is thus always in process; continually shifting as an expression of, most often, 'manliness', competence and what it is that defines success in any one locale. This is to regard masculinity as culturally and socially produced. Plainly, organizations and managerial work in particular are but one expression of, one site of practice for, the production and reproduction of masculinity. Organizations are obviously more than the sum of their 'masculine' features; likewise, masculinity is not exhaustive of the behaviours and characteristics of individuals. Rather, it has been my concern in this chapter to focus on work organizations as one arena for the constitution and reconstitution of a certain form of masculinity. In the organizational setting, this masculinity is defined in relation to its association with expressions and demonstrations of organizational and personal competence; of risk taking; of a form of organizational and personal 'success' where an instrumental orientation toward others and to the world appears axiomatic.

Self-evidently, this power-play of instrumentality has consequences beyond the level of the subjectivity and identity of individuals to the material and economic inequalities seemingly inherent in many 'modern' corporations. Against a background of capitalist work organizations in which competitiveness has been elevated to a defining principle, it is perhaps unsurprising that masculine-type management practices are in the ascendancy (Kerfoot and Knights, 1996). This is to restate a political position; one that recognizes organizational inequality as in part an outcome of masculine-dominated managerial discourses and practices. In turn, organizational inequality – with respect to the 'other' in the form of women, 'lesser' men, gays etc. – sustains masculine-dominated managerial discourse and practice.

Pursuing this investigation of masculinity, and of highlighting the linkages between masculinity and the body, I have drawn on and developed work begun elsewhere on the masculine subject (Kerfoot and Whitehead, 1998) and on embodiment in managerial work (Kerfoot and Knights, 1996). Emphasizing the relationship between masculine subjects and masculinity as their behavioural expression, the chapter has sought to identify links with the body and the experience of the body. Disembodied with respect to their own emotions, masculine subjects strive to gain control of the unknown other as a means of securing a stable identity. In the context of managerial work and in pursuit of this stability, the body becomes a site for the continual production and reproduction of what it is to be competent as a manager, and most often, as a man. To this end, masculine subjects 'occupy' or 'inhabit', rather than fully experience, the body.

Preoccupied with the need constantly to display the body as 'in touch' with the demands of the modern corporation, masculine subjects find little room for expression of emotional or non-instrumental forms of connection with those around them; seeing little beyond the immediate task to hand and its purposive-rational goals, such individuals engage with others in purely instrumental fashion. Unable or unwilling to look beyond 'the point' of relations with others in the organization, masculine subjects find little means of articulating alternative modes of engagement. For, to begin to speak 'from the body' of the experience of instability, uncertainty and disconnection, however momentary, is to admit weakness, where weakness is a source of shame and failure. Masculine subjects are thus at one and the same time caught up with their own behavioural displays and yet remain unreflective as to what they display, to whom and why.

In their attempts to 'achieve', often for unspecified ends or for its own sake, masculine subjects depend, in part for their very existence, on the approbation of others. Requiring continuous confirmation and affirmation of themselves as 'successful', masculine subjects and masculinity as their behavioural expression deny alternative experiences of the body. To this end, it has been my purpose to suggest that estrangement and disembodiment are both conditions and consequences of a masculine orientation to the organizational and social world.

These issues force us to consider the effects of contemporary management practices at the level of the body; how and in what way managerial discourses and practices impact on the body and on managers' experience of the body – of self-estrangement, contradiction and uncertainty. At times discomforted with themselves and frequently disquieted by the demands made upon them in regimes of ever-intensifying modern management practice, managers are none the less 'required' to maintain at least the appearance of power in organizations. I have contended that, most often for many men, the experience of managing 'comes' with an eroticized feel, albeit a psychic charge even more transient than the management regimes in which it is embedded. To this end, at the level of the body, managerial work is clearly double-edged, as anxiety-provoking as it is seductive in the promise of certainty that is offered, but so seldom experienced.

References

Barrett, F.J. (1996) 'The organizational construction of hegemonic masculinity: the case of the US Navy', *Gender, Work and Organization*, 3 (3): 129–42.

Bracher, M. (1993) *Lacan, Discourse and Social Change: A Psychoanalytic Cultural Criticism*. Ithaca, NY: Cornell University Press.

Brod, H. and Kaufmann, M. (eds) (1994) *Theorizing Masculinities*. Thousand Oaks, CA: Sage.

Butler, J. (1990) *Gender Trouble: Feminism and the Subversion of Identity*. London: Routledge.

Calas, M. and Smircich, L. (1993) 'Dangerous liaisons: the feminine in management meets globalization', *Business Horizons*, March–April: 71–81.

Carrigan, T., Connell, R.W. and Lee, J. (eds) (1985) 'Toward a New Sociology of Masculinity', *Theory, Culture and Society*, 4(5): 551–604.

Chodorow, N. (1978) *The Reproduction of Mothering: Psychoanalysis and the Sociology of Gender*. Berkeley, CA: University of California Press.

Clatterbaugh, K. (1990) *Contemporary Perspectives on Masculinity: Men, Women and Politics in Modern Society*. Boulder, CO: Westview Press.

Cockburn, C. (1985) *Machinery of Dominance: Men, Women and Technical Know-how*. London: Pluto.

Collinson, D.L. (1992) *Managing the Shopfloor: Subjectivity, Masculinity and Workplace Culture*. Berlin: de Gruyter.

Collinson, D.L. and Hearn, J. (1994) 'Naming men as men: implications for work, organization and management', *Gender, Work and Organization*, 1 (1): 2–23.

Collinson, D.L. and Hearn, J. (eds) (1996) *Men as Managers, Managers as Men*. London: Sage.

Connell, R.W. (1995) *Masculinities*. Oxford: Polity/Blackwell.

du Gay, P. and Salaman, G. (1992) 'The cult(ure) of the consumer', *Journal of Management Studies*, 29 (5).

Elam, D. (1994) *Feminism and Deconstruction*. London: Routledge.

Farnham, D. and Horton, S. (1996) *Managing People in the Public Services*. London: Macmillan Business.

Ferguson, K. (1984) *The Feminist Case Against Bureaucracy*. Philadelphia, PA: Temple University Press.

Foucault, M. (1977) *Discipline and Punish: The Birth of the Prison* (trans. A. Sheridan). London: Tavistock.

Foucault, M. (1988) 'Power and sex', in C. Gordon (ed.), *Power/Knowledge: Selected Interviews and Other Writings 1972–1977 by Michel Foucault*. London: Harvester Wheatsheaf.

Fraser, N. (1992) 'The uses and abuses of French discourse theories for feminist politics', in M. Featherstone (ed.), *Cultural Theory and Cultural Change*. London: Sage.

Frosh, S. (1987) *The Politics of Psychoanalysis*. London: Macmillan.

Fuller, P. (1996) 'Masculinity, emotion and sexual violence', in L. Morris and E.S. Lyon (eds), *Gender Relations in Public and Private: New Perspectives*. London: Macmillan. pp. 226–44.

Gherardi, S. (1995) *Gender, Symbolism and Organizational Cultures*. London: Sage.

Harlow, E., Hearn, J. and Parkin, W. (1995) 'Gendered noise: organizations and the silence and din of domination', in C. Itzin and J. Newman (eds), *Gender, Culture and Organizational Change*. London: Routledge. pp. 91–107.

Hollway, W. (1996) 'Masters and men in the transition from factory hands to sentimental workers', in D.L. Collinson and J. Hearn (eds), *Men as Managers, Managers as Men*. London: Sage.

Institute of Management (1995) *National Management Salary Review*. Kingston-upon-Thames: Institute of Management.

Keenoy, T. (1990) 'HRM and work values in Britain'. Paper presented to the International Study of Work and Organisational Values, 19–22 August, Prague.

Keenoy, T. (1990) 'HRM: a case of the wolf in sheep's clothing?', *Personnel Review*, 19 (2).

Kerfoot, D. (1999) 'The organisation of intimacy: managerialism, masculinity, and the masculine subject', in S. Whitehead and R. Moodley (eds), *Transforming Managers: Gendering Change in the Public Sector*. London: Taylor and Francis.

Kerfoot, D. and Knights, D. (1993) 'Management, masculinity and manipulation: from paternalism to corporate strategy in financial services in Britain', *Journal of Management Studies*, 30 (4): 659–79.

Kerfoot, D. and Knights, D. (1994) 'Into the realm of the fearful: power, identity and the gender problematic', in L. Radke and H. Stam (eds), *Power and Gender*. London: Sage.

Kerfoot, D. and Knights, D. (1995) 'The organisation(s) of social division: constructing identities in managerial work'. Paper given to the 12th European Group on Organisation Studies (EGOS) Colloquium, 6–8 July, Istanbul.

Kerfoot, D. and Knights, D. (1996) '"The Best is Yet to Come": searching for embodiment in managerial work', in D. Collinson and J. Hearn (eds), *Men as Managers, Managers as Men*. London: Sage.

Kerfoot, D. and Whitehead, S. (1998) '"Boys Own Stuff": masculinity and the management of further education', *Sociological Review*, 46 (3): 436–57.

Kimmel, M. (1987) *Changing Men: New Directions in Research on Men and Masculinity*. Beverly Hills, CA: Sage.

Lacan, J. (1977) *Ecrits: A Selection* (trans. A. Sheridan). London: Tavistock.

McNay, L. (1992) *Foucault and Feminism*. Cambridge: Polity Press.

Mills, A. (1998) 'Cockpits, hangars, boys and galleys: corporate masculinities and the development of British Airways', *Gender, Work and Organization*, 5 (3): 172–89.

Nicholson, L.J. (ed.) (1990) *Feminism/Postmodernism*. New York: Routledge/Chapman & Hall.

Nicholson, L. and Seidman, S. (eds) (1996) *Social Postmodernism: Beyond Identity Politics*. Cambridge: Cambridge University Press.

Ransom, J. (1993) 'Feminism, difference and discourse: the limits of discursive analysis for feminism', in C. Ramazanoglu (ed.), *Up Against Foucault*. London: Routledge.

Roper, M. (1994) *Masculinity and the British Organization Man since 1945*. Oxford: Oxford University Press.

Roper, M. and Tosh, J. (eds) (1991) *Manful Assertions: Masculinities in Britain since 1800*. London: Routledge.

Tolson, A. (1977) *The Limits of Masculinity*. London: Tavistock.

Watson, T.J. (1994) *In Search of Management*. London: Routledge.

Weed, Elizabeth (1989) 'Introduction', *Coming to Terms*. New York/London: Routledge.

Wolfe, T. (1973) *The Right Stuff*. London: Pelican.

Wilkinson, A. and Willmott, H. (eds) (1995) *Making Quality Critical*. London: Routledge.

Index

Page references in italics refer to Figures

weight 195–6, 197, 201, 202–3
Wells, H.G. 80
Westworld 80
Wexler, Philip 62
Wheeler 93
Wilkinson, B. 121
Williams, Linda 34
Williams, R. 133
Willmott, H. 122, 123
Wolfe, Tom 241
Wollstonecraft, Mary 39
women 31
  beauty 121
  biology 205–11, 212
  ejaculation 32, 36–42, 45

identity 194, 195–9, 206–7
masculinity 236
nature 193
as other 237–9
rights 39
sexual feelings 38
sexual harassment 204, 215, 227
subordination 223, 224
work 114–15, 126
see also female body; femininity
work organization *see* organization
work performance 147, 185
Wright, Frank Lloyd 175

Zizek, S. 93, 94–6